THE VISUAL FIELDS
Text and Atlas of Clinical Perimetry

THE VISUAL FIELDS

Text and Atlas of Clinical Perimetry

DAVID O. HARRINGTON, M.D.

Clinical Professor Emeritus of Ophthalmology
University of California, San Francisco
School of Medicine
San Francisco, California

MICHAEL V. DRAKE, M.D., A.B.

Associate Professor of Ophthalmology and Chief
University Eye Clinic
University of California, San Francisco
School of Medicine
San Francisco, California

SIXTH EDITION

*with 318 illustrations
and 3 plates, with 2 in color*

THE C. V. MOSBY COMPANY

St. Louis • Baltimore • Philadelphia • Toronto   1990

 **Mosby**

Editor: Eugenia A. Klein
Assistant Editor: Barbara S. Menczer
Project Manager: Carol Sullivan Wiseman
Production Editor: Pat Joiner
Book Designer: Susan E. Lane
Editing and Production: Top Graphics

SIXTH EDITION

Printed in the United States of America

The C.V. Mosby Company
11830 Westline Industrial Drive, St. Louis, Missouri 63146

Library of Congress Cataloging in Publication Data

Harrington, David O.
    The visual fields: text and atlas of clinical perimetry/David
O. Harrington. Michael V. Drake. -- 6th ed.
      p.   cm.
    Bibliography: p.
    Includes index.
    ISBN 0-8016-2073-2
    1. Perimetry. 2. Visual fields. I. Drake, Michael V.
II. Title.
    [DNLM: 1. Perimetry. 2. Visual fields. WW 145 H299v]
RE79.P4H3   1989
617.7'5--dc20
DNLM/DLC
for Library of Congress

GW/MV/MV 9 8 7 6 5 4 3 2 1

PREFACE TO THE SIXTH EDITION

The prior edition of this book was published in 1981, a time which one might properly consider as the dawn of a new era in perimetry. During the late 1970s and early 1980s computerized automated perimeters came of age. Progress throughout the past few years has been impressive. The incredibly expensive, cumbersome machines of a decade ago have given way to a new generation of cost-efficient, sensitive instruments used routinely in large clinics and research institutes and commonly in small group and solo doctor practices.

With this dramatic explosion in perimetric technology, there has been an equally impressive rebirth of interest in the visual fields and perimetry in general. The relevant literature has numbered hundreds of articles per year throughout the 1980s. Visual field and perimetric symposia are commonplace in the United States, Canada, Japan, Europe, and elsewhere. The International Perimetric Society now counts hundreds of members worldwide, and its biannual scientific meeting is one of the highlights of the ophthalmic calendar. Progress in technology and increased interest in the medical community have spurred perimeter manufacturers to continue to update and improve their products. The only drawback to this plethora of instruments is that the consumer is now faced with a somewhat bewildering choice of more than two dozen visual field machines. Further, as is the nature of highly technical equipment, improvements (or at least modifications) are announced constantly. Today's champion is tomorrow's also-ran.

All the exciting changes in *perimetry* notwithstanding, the essential components of the visual field system have remained the same. Visual field studies are still performed on patients who suffer from the same diseases that patients have suffered from for decades and who have the same anatomy we have all shared for millennia. Further, it remains the physician's responsibility to interpret the results of visual field tests and to use this information to the effective, compassionate benefit of those served. Many of the most sophisticated computerized perimeters have programs that use advanced statistical manipulations to assist the physician in this interpretive task. At their best, these programs help make visual field interpretation faster and more objective. It is essential to remember, however, that these sophisticated techniques must be based on a thorough working knowledge of the anatomy, physiology, and pathology of the visual system, particularly as they pertain to the visual fields.

As has always been the case, the focus of this book is the visual fields, not perimetry. As the perimetric field expands, our need to master the fundamentals intensifies.

Reflecting the substantial changes in the way visual fields are tested and the way visual field charts look, there is much new material in this edition. An entire chapter on automated perimetry has been added, along with a substantial revision and updating of most of the remaining text.

Many of the older illustrations have been deleted, and over 80 new illustrations were added. Older illustrations often appear in somewhat schematic form, having been copied from the original data in each patient's chart.

Although Chapters 2 and 3 are devoted to perimeters of various description, we make no attempt to explain in detail any of the machinery currently available. We describe a few essential characteristics of some of the more popular instruments. Our discussion is purposely not all inclusive. The instruments we describe have been used routinely for at least 5 (and in one case 50!) years. We are actively aware that research in the discipline continues and that what we use today may be obsolete tomorrow. Because we expect the rapid expansion of knowledge in this area to continue, we have done our best to consistently stress fundamentals. This is done in the hope that, as new knowledge becomes available, it will be compatible with and added to the foundation laid out within these pages.

Many members of the Department of Ophthalmology at the University of California, San Francisco (UCSF) contributed meaningfully to this edition; we will mention a few.

Peggy Yamada, Yvonne Alden, Hilda Leavy, and Eric Lindstrom are the ophthalmic technicians who staff our automated perimetry service. In addition to performing their general tasks flawlessly, they alerted us to many interesting cases referred from outside physicians or our general clinic. Several of these cases appear as illustrations.

Michael Narahara and Bruce Morris provided excellent photographic services. Joan Weddell, a veteran of prior editions, is responsible for the new artwork.

Charlie Hufford and Hilda Leavy typed the manuscript. This was a reprise of an early role for Hilda, who performed this same task for the fifth edition of this book and who joined the staff at UCSF as an ophthalmic technician when Dr. Harrington retired from active practice a decade ago. Many of the residents at UCSF contributed cases or otherwise assisted in providing data that was eventually incorporated in this volume. Dr. James Ahn was particularly helpful during his neuroophthalmology fellowship.

Our colleagues on the faculty of the Department of Ophthalmology have been particularly helpful. Doctors Marc Lieberman and Jay Enoch have contributed actively to visual field and perimetric teaching at our institution and have been important catalysts in the continued growth of our visual field service. Our entry into the automated perimetry arena on a practical daily basis followed Dr. Jorge Alvarado's visionary insistence on putting an Octopus perimeter in our general eye clinic in 1979.

Two of the greatest assets of the Department of Ophthalmology at UCSF are the (unrelated) Professors Hoyt. Dr. Creig Hoyt was involved in this project at its inception; his unselfish assistance during that critical period was essential to our task. Dr. William Hoyt's contributions are prominent throughout whole sections of this volume, particularly Chapters 14 through 16. Most of the new illustrations in those chapters were from cases seen and collected by Dr. Hoyt. We sincerely appreciate his assistance. It is noteworthy and comforting that Dr. Hoyt was also acknowledged in the first edition of this book, published 33 years ago.

Finally, a special acknowledgement goes to Dr. Steven G. Kramer, Chairman of the Department of Ophthalmology and Director of the Beckman Vision Center and the Koret Vision Research Laboratory at the University of California, San Francisco. Without his active support and encouragement, this edition may never have come to light.

Michael V. Drake
David O. Harrington
San Francisco, 1988

PREFACE TO THE FIRST EDITION

This book is a clinical guide to the examination and interpretation of the visual fields. It is based upon twenty years' experience in the teaching of perimetry to graduate students of ophthalmology, neurosurgery, and neurology and results from a long-held desire to crystallize this teaching experience for the student and the busy practitioner.

The examination of the visual fields is a subjective test. The interpretation of the results of such a subjective examination is dependent upon many factors, not the least of which is the personality of the patient and the examiner and the rapport between them. It is not possible to evaluate the results of a visual field study performed by a technician as well as if you had performed it yourself. No two perimetrists will conduct their study of the visual fields in exactly the same manner. No perimetrist should use exactly the same technique of examination on every patient. Responses will differ depending on age, speed of comprehension, state of health, rapport with the examiner, and many other factors. It follows, therefore, that the visual field examination must not be conducted according to a rigid routine, and that ingenuity must be exercised to obtain the most information from the test. With this in mind, the section of this book devoted to the techniques of perimetry is couched in general terms as far as the actual conduct of the visual field examination is concerned. At the same time the student is supplied with the tools required to perform the examination and an account of their construction and the general principles underlying their use.

No methods or instruments for visual field examination have been described unless I have used them with personal satisfaction. Whenever possible, techniques have been simplified. It is my sincere conviction that elaborate machinery is unnecessary for adequate perimetry, and that the simpler methods focus attention on the capabilities of the examiner rather than on the instrumentation employed. In short, the man behind the perimeter is more important that the equipment he uses.

No other diagnostic procedure available to the ophthalmologist offers a challenge or opportunity equal to that of perimetry. The examination of the visual field need not be the tedious chore that it is usually considered. There is great personal satisfaction to be derived from the careful quantitative study of a visual field defect, its interpretation and correlation with other signs and symptoms of disease, and its analysis and evaluation in terms of the localization and pathology of the lesion in the visual pathway which produced it.

I have tried, in this book, to communicate my enthusiasm for visual field study to the reader just as I have tried through the years to pass it on to my students. If the book is successful in this it will have served its purpose well.

For my own interest in the study of the visual fields I am largely indebted to three men:

To Dr. Frederick Cordes, who saw the need for a perimetrist and student of neuro-ophthalmology in his Department of Ophthalmology at the University of California School of Medicine, and who encouraged me in every way to pursue the study which would lead to a teaching position on his staff.

To Dr. Howard C. Naffziger, in whose Department of Neurosurgery at the University of California I served for a period, and who has given me continuing help and encouragement through the years by affording me unusual opportunities to examine many of the patients on his service, both clinic and private. He taught me to follow the patient from the perimeter to the operating table and to correlate my visual field studies with the pathological lesions which produced them.

To Dr. H. M. Traquair, on whose service in the Royal Infirmary in Edinburgh I spent most of a year, who taught me the techniques of visual field examination and interpretation which are so obviously reflected in this book. All persons interested in the visual fields will be forever indebted to Dr. Traquair for his work in advancing and popularizing the concept of quantitative perimetry and the importance of the visual field examination in the diagnosis of lesions of the visual pathway.

It has also been my good fortune to have had the highest degree of cooperation and understanding from such other outstanding clinicians in the Departments of Neurosurgery and Neurology as Dr. O. W. Jones, Jr., Dr. Howard A. Brown, Dr. Edwin Boldrey, Dr. John Adams, and Dr. Robert Aird, not to mention the long list of young men on the Resident Staff whose loyalty and cooperation are so essential to a long-term study such as this.

All of the material in this book is drawn from personal experience in the study of the visual fields. It is a compilation of my own clinical experience and, as such, it emphasizes the clinical viewpoint. I have, of course, drawn freely from the literature for the chapters on the anatomy of the visual pathway and its vascular supply. I have long been convinced that the clinical perimetrist must have such a background for the proper understanding of his subject.

Because of my experience with Dr. Traquair I have naturally tended to reflect his terachings and adhere to his broad concept of the quantitative examination of extrofoveal visual acuity, but only in so fart as I was able to apply them in my own experience.

The old cliché that "one picture is worth ten thousand words" is nowhere more applicable than in a book of this type. Illustrative material is essential to the understanding of visual field interpretation. This book was originally conceived as an atlas, and this concept is underscored by the retention of the "Atlas" in the title.

I am proud of the illustrations in this book, which are almost entirely original and have been drawn largely from my own case records. The anatomical drawings are from sketches which are a composite of my own dissections and a study of the classic literature on the subject. I am indebted to Dr. William Hoyt for assistance in the preparation of the sketches for Figs. 36, 37, 38, 40, 45, 49, 50, and 51. Where I have borrowed directly from the literature it has been with the author's permission, as noted in the legends.

I have been most fortunate in securing the services of a notable group of artists whose patience and unusual skill are reflected in their work.

Miss Sylvia Ford, formerly of the University of California Medical Illustration Department, Division of Ophthalmology, is responsible for Plates I to IX. Miss Kay Hyde, Medical Illustrator for the U.S. Veterans Administration Hospital at Fort Miley, San Francisco, has drawn most of the black and white illustrations, both anatomical and visual fields, and has given me the utmost in cooperation and assistance. Mrs. Laura Gilleland, of the University of California Medical Illustration Department, has supplemented Miss Hyde's work on visual field charts and black and white anatomical drawings. Mr. Ralph Sweet, Chairman of the Department of Medical Illustration at the University of California, drew the central panel of Plate VIII and has given much valuable advice and assistance in reviewing many of the drawings as they were completed. A number of the photographs are the expert work of Mr. Henry Rafael at the U.S. Veterans Administration Hospital in San Francisco.

No acknowledgment would be complete without paying tribute to the tedious work and infinite patience of Miss Myrtle Gable and Mrs. Elizabeth Valentine, who read, corrected, and typed the manuscript from its original longhand script.

David O. Harrington

San Francisco, 1988

CONTENTS

THE VISUAL FIELDS
Text and Atlas of Clinical Perimetry

INTRODUCTION

The visual field is that portion of space in which objects are simultaneously visible to the steadily fixating eye. It is somewhat more than one half of a hollow sphere, situated before and around each eye of the observer, within which objects are perceived while the eye is fixating a stationary point on its inner surface. Objects visible on the inner surface of this sphere stimulate portions of the retina and, through the conducting nerve fiber bundles of the visual pathway, the visual cortex in the calcarine areas of the occipital lobes. The intensity of these stimuli depend on their (1) proximity to the visual axis, (2) size (the number of retinal elements covered by their image), (3) brightness (the lumens of light emitted from their surface), and (4) receptor integrity.

Traquair's comparison of the visual field to "an island hill of vision surrounded by a sea of blindness" has firmly established in clinical practice the quantitative method of perimetry as advocated by Bjerrum, Rönne, Sinclair, and Walker. It has focused our attention on measuring the field of vision in terms of visual acuity and is the basis for the profile charting of visual field defects in static perimetry.

When one considers that retinal sensitivity is greatest in the foveal area and decreases in direct proportion to the distance of the rods and cones from the fovea, it is apparent that visual acuity within the visual field does likewise. It follows, then, that small objects are seen distinctly within the visual field only when they are near the visual axis and that larger and brighter stimuli are required if they are to be perceived in the peripheral field.

Visual acuity as measured with the Snellen letters also varies with the proximity of the test letter from fixation. In the normal eye with 20/20 vision at fixation, acuity decreases rapidly in the peripheral field so that at 2 degrees from fixation it is reduced to 20/30. At 3 degrees, visual acuity is approximately 20/40; at 5 degrees, it is 20/70; at 10 degrees, vision measures 20/100; at 20 degrees, vision is 20/200; and at 40 degrees, it is about 20/400.

In terms of visual acuity, the hollow sphere of the visual field becomes the "island hill of vision surrounded by the sea of blindness." Objects nearest the visual axis are seen with greatest clarity, as though they were situated on a peak directly below the observer's eye. As the contour of the hill slopes downward and outward from the peak toward the shoreline, smaller objects become invisible and only stimuli of gradually increasing size or intensity are seen. Because of the relative constancy of visual acuity in different portions of the visual field in normal eyes, the island of vision has a remarkably constant shape and size.

The island is oval, with a regular coastline rising abruptly from the sea in precipitous cliffs. These cliffs are surmounted by a sloping plateau that rises toward an eccentrically placed summit, which in turn slopes steeply upward to a needlelike peak. Beside the summit is a pit or well that extends downward to the level of the sea. This is the *blind spot.*

To the normal eye, viewing this island as from a helicopter poised directly over the peak, the entire panorama of its surface is in view but, as in any panoramic view, the objects nearest the observer are the most distinct. Thus minute objects on or near the summit of the peak are seen with greatest clarity, whereas those situated on the plateau must be larger to be visible. On the coastline at the bottom of the cliffs, only large patches of white are visible.

The limits within which a certain size object can be seen by the normal observer can be surveyed on the hill as a contour line and plotted on a map or chart. These are the *isopters* of the normal field. Normal isopters or contour lines are relatively constant in size and shape, but they show certain characteristic variations and abnormalities when disease affects the visual pathway. The correct interpretation of these variations in visual acuity within the visual field, and hence of the isopters, may make it possible anatomically to localize within the visual pathway the site of the lesion that has produced the variation.

If we know the normal visual acuity for any portion of the visual field, that is, if we know the isopter or contour line within which a stimulus subtending a given visual angle is visible to the normal eye, we can correctly interpret variations from this normal in terms of damage to the visual pathway.

The surface of the retina receives an image of objects in the visual field in much the same manner as a photographic film records a landscape. The nerve fiber bundles of the retina are arranged in a pattern that is repeated in the visual pathway from the optic nerve through the chiasmal decussation and on into the cortical visual center in the occipital lobes. The visual field corresponds to an inverse cross section of the visual pathway at any point from the receptor organ in the retina to the terminal center in the occipital cortex. Thus any defect or abnormality of the visual field may, through correct interpretation, reflect disease or damage to a specific portion of the visual pathway.

The purpose of perimetry is to detect these revealing defects in the visual field, to measure them quantitatively in terms of visual acuity, and to chart them as normal or abnormal contour lines or isopters.

Perimetry, then, is a special type of psychophysical examination. It requires a trained examiner with a knowledge of the available techniques and instruments and their special physical and optical properties.

The clinical applications of perimetry also demand knowledge of the anatomy and physiology of the visual pathway and its contiguous structures and the psychologic factors that may influence the responses of the individual subjected to the test.

THE ART AND SCIENCE OF PERIMETRY

The aim of perimetry is to quantitatively examine visual acuity in all portions of the visual field. This implies careful survey of the island hill of vision and its subsequent contour mapping, or, in the case of static perimetry, its profile in any given meridian or its height at any given point.

All manner of variations in the surface and coastline of the hill should be detectable and later subjected to analysis and interpretation. Because of the complexity of the terrain, no single instrument or method of examination will suffice to survey the entire hill adequately, and the perimetrist must be aware of the limitations of a given method and the point in the examination when one instrument or method should supplant another.

There is an art to the proper examination of the visual field that is being more and more neglected in recent years.

With the increased complexity and sophistication of the instruments of perimetry, there is a tendency to view the visual field examination as a wholly scientific procedure, the result of which is an objective measurement of visual function that is immutable, exact, and repeatable. The fallacy of this view is readily seen when it is realized that the visual field examination is a psychophysical evaluation of an individual's visual and mental status at a given time. No matter how elaborate the instruments, the test is subjective, cannot be considered truly scientific, and, in many ways, is more of an art than a science.

With more demand on the ophthalmologist's time to include an increasing number of complicated procedures in a routine eye examination, less time is allowed for visual field testing. Faced with the need to do tonometric, tonographic, gonioscopic, fluorescein angiographic, ophthalmoscopic, photographic, biomicroscopic examinations, and all objective tests, the harassed clinician understandably delegates such subjective examinations as history taking, vision testing, refraction, and perimetry to paramedical personnel.

These subjective examinations require a degree of psychic evaluation that will often determine the validity of the findings. The visual field examination cannot be isolated from the total evaluation of the patient. The physician must assess these values, and the more important the visual field studies are to establishing a diagnosis, the greater the need for the personal attention of the clinician.

Numerous case reports in this book illustrate the need for great flexibility in the visual field examination. In some instances only minimal threshold stimuli will suffice to detect early, subtle deficits that may be all-important in establishing a diagnosis. In other cases the grossest stimulus, such as a waving white towel, is needed to demonstrate a field defect characteristic of a specific disease process in the visual pathway. Sometimes visual field loss is the only diagnostic finding and may be missed or misinterpreted because of the limits imposed by a rigid examination technique.

The time-consuming routine visual field examination will lose its drudgery when the perimetrist faces the challenge of each patient as a psychobiological problem from whom all possible information is to be extracted. It is rare indeed that some information cannot be obtained about a patient's peripheral visual acuity. Fields of a sort and much information as to brain damage can be obtained from semicomatose patients, from psychotic patients, from small children, and even from animals. Obviously, other than standard techniques must be used in these instances.

I

EXAMINATION OF THE VISUAL FIELDS

The visual field examination should be geared to the patient. The type and number of tests performed, the manner in which the tests are administered, and even the interpretation of test results will vary, depending on factors such as the patient's age and general health and the presumptive diagnosis. The visual field test is often a critically important part of the evaluation, but like any medical test, it is only a part of the picture.

Before the examiner actually settles down to the task of "taking the field," it is important to obtain a complete medical history. Before ordering sophisticated, costly, and time-consuming tests, such as bilateral full-threshold computerized perimetry, a careful physical examination, including at least confrontation perimetry, should be completed.

The following are among the many useful hints or clues that can indicate a significant visual field defect to the informed examiner:

1. When questioned directly, the patient may give a history of a positive scotoma or may even draw out the limits of the defect.

2. A patient's manner of avoiding obstacles in the examining room sometimes indicates a significant field defect, such as a homonymous hemianopsia or an inferior altitudinal defect.

3. The manner in which a patient reads the Snellen test letters may reveal the nature of a visual field loss. For example, the patient may say that the first letter is seen better if fixation is directed at the second one. Patients with chiasmal lesions and bitemporal hemianopsia may start reading the test line backwards. The patient with a tiny central or paracentral scotoma may leave out parts of letters, reading F for E, C for O, or P for R.

4. A history of deficient color vision of recent origin may indicate a relative color scotoma.

5. Patients suffering visual field loss associated with a migraine can commonly give detailed descriptions of the classic picture of a scintillating scotoma followed by a spreading depression.

All of these and many other subjective visual complaints can point the way to a specific field defect and save much time when the visual field is actually tested.

Several studies have shown that most visual field defects could be predicted by the medical history or physical examination. In a more general sense, the physician may simply ask if the patient has diabetes, has suffered a stroke or severe head trauma, or has a history of glaucoma, cataracts, or retinal disease. A persistent headache or signs and symptoms of endocrine imbalance may be the initial sign of significant intracranial problems.

The physical examination should concentrate on the ophthalmic examination and the neurologic examination. Many patients with visual field defects will have defective visual acuity, increased intraocular pressure, ophthalmoscopically visible retinal or optic nerve problems, media opacity, pupillary abnormalities, or cranial nerve or gaze palsies.

The instruments and techniques available to measure the visual field vary from the very simple to the extremely complex. No one method is the best for all patients under all circumstances. The modern perimetrist must have a working knowledge of many methods to choose the most appropriate test for each patient. Although many types of manual perimetry are best performed by physicians, it is impractical for them to perform detailed, computerized automated perimetry on patients. In their current trim, such tests take up to an hour per patient, and the realities of a busy practice rarely allow that degree of physician-patient contact. For this reason, the overwhelming majority of automated fields are performed by technicians. Technician-patient interaction is extremely important in achieving quality field results. The importance of educational programs for technicians must be stressed. Involving technicians actively in managing the visual field service allows them to contribute more effectively as members of the patient care team.

Many of the standards of current practice follow the pioneering work of Professor Hans Goldmann. A partial summary of Goldmann's requirements and fundamentals of exact perimetry follows:

1. To perform exact relative perimetry with white targets, an adaptation equilibrium must be established, the contrast between target and perimeter background must remain constant, and the basic illumination must not show appreciable change.

2. Under such conditions, a quantitative relationship may be found between targets of varying size. A quantitative comparison of the sensitivity of individual points thus becomes possible on the basis of perimetric data gained with different size targets.

3. The function of any retinal point is characterized not only by its different sensitivity but also by its power of summation for different size targets. The summation power of the normal retina is constant over wide

areas of the visual field. Distinct perception decreases summation, whereas dark adaptation seems to increase it.

4. The visual field tested with white stimuli is influenced by the sharpness of the target border. Refractive errors and cloudy media diminish the relative field considerably. The inner isopters in particular should be examined only with corrective lenses, and visual fields of patients with media opacities must be evaluated with caution.

Examination of central or foveal visual function and peripheral vision must always go together. It is generally inaccurate to say that visual acuity is reduced to 20/50, and the visual field is normal. In such circumstances, there must be a general depression of all isopters, such as might occur with media opacities, or there must be a central scotoma that would be detectable with proper perimetric techniques.

Visual field examination is a threshold measurement. It is impractical to examine every point in the entire field of vision, so a limited number of areas are selected for testing. These areas may be selected randomly or purposefully. When testing these points, the goal is to establish the minimum detectable light stimulus. Repeatedly testing the threshold at the same point will not generate a single value, but rather a distribution of values that will vary about a mean. In trained young normal observers, the repeated threshold measurements will vary from 0.1 to 0.3 log units. The threshold values printed by currently available visual field machines represent an approximation or a mean threshold value.

Currently available machines measure the minimum contrast between stimulus and background. Threshold stimulation can take place in total darkness or against a background of measured luminance. In the latter case, one is measuring the minimum contrast between stimulus and background. This threshold is the smallest measurable difference in luminance that the patient can usually detect. For static perimetry, threshold represents the 50% point on the probability of seeing curve. This definition predicts that if a light of "threshold" intensity were shown to a patient 100 times, the patient should be able to detect the light 50 times and would not be able to detect the light 50 times. As the intensity of this stimulus light, or the difference between the intensity of the stimulus light and the background illumination, increases, the patient should have a greater than 50% chance of detecting the stimulus. The converse would also be true. A number of factors determine this difference in threshold measurement: the physical characteristics of the stimulus; preretinal factors such as pupil size, media opacity, and refractive error; receptive and neural factors; psychologic factors; and the patient's general health. All of these factors will be considered in detail in the examination and analysis of specific visual field defects in the pages that follow.

1 PERIMETRY WITHOUT SPECIAL INSTRUMENTS

It is not always possible to perform a visual field examination under ideal conditions. In examining bedridden patients or in places where perimetric instruments are not available, considerable ingenuity may be required to utilize existing facilities as effective substitutes for fully equipped offices. As clinicians, we often encounter situations that mandate visual field testing without special instruments. Fortunately, with a small amount of effort and experience, one can often examine the visual field quickly and effectively under these conditions.

CONFRONTATION TESTING

Among all perimetric methods, the confrontation test is probably the most widely used. It has become a part of the routine physical examination performed by many physicians and by the majority of neurologists and neurosurgeons. It is used frequently by optometrists and ophthalmologists as a rapid screening visual field test. The confrontation test is a relatively crude and purely qualitative method. It is suitable for identifying gross defects in the peripheral field but is less than ideal for finer testing or scotometry. In many situations, however, it is the only practical form of clinical perimetry available. It is certainly the quickest way to assess the overall integrity of the visual field. Despite its limitations, when properly performed, the confrontation test may be of great value.

As a rule, the confrontation test is performed with the examiner and patient facing each other about 0.5 meters apart. The examiner wiggles an index finger in each of the four quadrants of the field and asks the patient whether he or she can see it. When used in this manner, the method is capable of detecting only the most gross defects. Subtle or small defects are commonly missed. If one keeps a few simple points in mind, the sensitivity and reproducibility of confrontation fields can improve significantly.

To begin confrontation testing, the patient is instructed to look directly into the examiner's eyes. When testing the right eye, the examiner should instruct the patient to close or occlude the left eye, and then the examiner should correspondingly close his or her own right eye. Thus the patient's right eye looks directly into the examiner's left eye. The visual field of the patient's right eye will be lined up to correspond closely to the visual field of the examiner's left eye. Using the finger-counting method, the examiner's arms are extended and the hands moved forward until they are roughly halfway between the examiner and the patient (Figure 1-1). The hands are usually placed approximately equidistant from a vertical line separating the right and left hemifield. Beginning with the hands in a fist, one or two fingers are extended from either or both hands, and the patient is asked to relate what he or she sees. The two hands may be placed in corresponding horizontal areas of the field (e.g., the upper temporal and upper nasal quadrants) or noncorresponding areas (e.g., the upper temporal and lower nasal quadrants). The patient's responses are noted on the medical record.

Assuming that the examiner's visual field is normal, the patient should be able to identify and count fingers in the various quadrants with about the same ease as the examiner. Additionally, because the examiner maintains fixation by staring directly at the patient's eye, and vice versa, even minute fixation shifts are detectable.

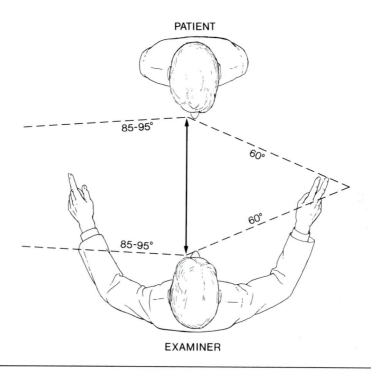

FIGURE 1-1   Confrontation visual field testing. Examiner's hands are placed about halfway between examiner and patient.

The specific manner in which a fixation loss occurs may yield valuable information about the visual field, particularly in unreliable or poorly responding patients. Many patients inadvertently look toward the hand that projects the fingers as soon as the examiner's fingers are extended. No matter what the patient's verbal response, this is good objective evidence that there is visual function in the region being stimulated.

Several important steps can be taken to further standardize confrontation visual field testing. First, the test should be carried out in good lighting, ideally coming from behind the patient, but under all circumstances, uniform throughout the patient's visual field. Second, a relatively plain background allows the patient to detect the stimulus most reliably. Third, it is more suitable to require the patient to count the examiner's fingers than to simply identify which of the examiner's hands is waving. Counting fingers in the visual periphery is a more demanding task. It requires better patient concentration and is a more sensitive test of visual function.

To increase sensitivity further, we often use double simultaneous presentation. Using this method, the examiner has both fists in view at all times but selectively flicks out one or two fingers in either or both hands. Patients who can count fingers in both the right and left hemifields separately will, under some circumstances, only be able to count fingers reliably in one hemifield when double simultaneous presentation is used and there is a relative field defect in the opposite hemifield. When using double simultaneous projection, it is essential that all areas of the visual field are illuminated equally.

The sensitivity of the double simultaneous presentation is illustrated by a recent experience I (MVD) had when examining a bedridden patient. The patient could not answer my questions, but when both fists were placed in the visual field and the fingers of one or the other hand extended, the patient would invariably look toward the extended fingers for a few seconds before staring back at me. When I used the double simultaneous presentation method, the patient consistently looked toward the fingers extended in the right hemifield, indicating a relative left hemianoptic field defect. Radiographic investigation confirmed the presence of a right-sided mass lesion.

The confrontation field method just described can be made even more sensitive if small specialized test objects are used. These can be relatively sophisticated, such as a 5- or 10-mm disc or plastic sphere mounted on the end of a dull black wand about 2 feet in length, or relatively unsophisticated, such as a name tag, a dropper bottle, or the cap for a ball-point pen. Using these small test objects, one can fairly reliably map the blind spot and with a little practice look for scotomas of varying size and intensity. Little practice is required to estimate fairly accurately the number of degrees from fixation at which the object first appears in the field. The object is then moved slowly in toward fixation to uncover any gross scotomas. Pericentral and central scotomas, hemianopsias, and quadrant defects can often be surveyed with considerable accuracy. If a patient demonstrates good visual acuity, a 5-mm test object is probably the stimulus of choice; however, there is no limit to the size of the object that may be used successfully, from a 2-mm white bead to a large sheet of paper or a naked ophthalmoscope light.

If proper care is taken, one can elicit fairly consistent and sensitive information when performing confrontation fields with small test objects. As indicated previously, these methods may be most appropiate for bedridden patients, particularly in nursing homes, where more elaborate visual field testing is either impractical or impossible. Under these circumstances, the confrontation visual field may be the only way to follow up a patient with significant ocular disease. As such, the provider's ability to perform quality confrontation field examinations can be of pivotal importance.

2 MANUAL PERIMETERS: INSTRUMENTS AND USE

The basic specifications for a good perimeter or tangent screen are fairly straightforward. The basic principles of perimetry apply regardless of the type of instrument used. Each of the many perimetric methods available has advantages and disadvantages. Thorough knowledge of these basic specifications and principles, as well as the advantages and disadvantages of various methods, enables the examiner to choose the most appropriate visual field test for each patient.

Over the years a great number of manual perimeters and perimetric techniques have been developed. During the past several decades the field has been dominated by the tangent screen and Goldmann perimeter for clinical work and by the Tübinger perimeter for experimental work. Many other devices (e.g., Harrington-Flocks screener, Lumiwand) have been developed, but these instruments have largely fallen by the wayside with the development of computerized perimeters.

MANUAL VS. AUTOMATED OR COMPUTERIZED PERIMETRY

The coexistence of sophisticated manual perimetry with computerized perimetry has led to some polarization within the user community. There are proponents of manual perimetry, proponents of computerized perimetry, of both, and, we imagine, of neither.

In our clinics the discussion of whether or not to perform manual or computerized perimetry usually focuses on whether or not kinetic or static perimetry is preferred. When performing kinetic perimetry, a stimulus is chosen and moved (kinetic) throughout the visual field to determine the region in which it is visible. The area within which a given target is perceived is known as that target's *isopter*. When performing static perimetry, a test site is chosen and the stimulus intensity or size changed until it is large enough and bright enough for the patient to see it. (One may also start with a large or bright target and make it smaller or dimmer until the patient cannot see it, thus measuring essentially the same end point but from the opposite direction.) Thus the stimulus is stationary, or static.

Although static or kinetic perimetry may be performed using manual methods, most visual field tests using the Goldmann perimeter or a tangent screen rely primarily on kinetic techniques. Conversely, although some computerized perimeters allow kinetic testing, the overwhelming majority of tests on computerized perimeters are static.

There are several reasons why this is the case. One of the main advantages of kinetic perimetry is that relatively large areas of the field can be traversed in fairly short order. Depending on the patient's responses and the presumptive diagnosis, one can move fairly quickly over areas of little interest and spend relatively more time examining critical regions.

An example would be performing a tangent screen field examination on a patient who is suspected of having a pituitary mass and thus is at risk for loss of function in each of the temporal hemifields. If subnormal responses occur in the temporal hemifields, the examiner can move quickly to the vertical line dividing the nasal and temporal fields and test on one side and then the other, back and forth several times to delineate whether the defect in question truly respects the midline. The examiner can adjust not only the size and intensity of the test object, but also the area being tested and the speed with which various areas are traversed. We find that manual perimetry is most useful for patients who may have relatively large geographic visual field defects, such as might be seen with space-occupying intracranial lesions, localized retinal detachments, or tumors.

Furthermore, some patients have defects that appear readily with kinetic perimetry but disappear with static perimetry. This statokinetic dissociation is seen primarily in patients with intracranial pathologic conditions. It is related to the difference in the way the visual system perceives a stationary "on/off" stimulus compared to a moving target.

The ability to adjust target presentation speed, direction, and location is also the main drawback of kinetic perimetry. When performing serial field examinations spanning intervals of many months or years, it is critically important to reproduce prior testing methods precisely. Because manual kinetic perimetry allows great variability in stimulus presentation, it is correspondingly very difficult to reproduce each of these steps exactly. If a subtle change is noted in the latest of a series of examinations, it is sometimes nearly impossible to tell whether the change was due to an actual alteration in the patient's visual field status or simply to a minor alteration in test methodology.

Another significant drawback of manual kinetic perimetry relates to the ability to customize the test as it is being performed. To customize a test effectively, one must interpret the patient's responses during the test and then have a reasonable idea of what these responses mean. This allows the examiner to predict what type of field defect the patient is most likely to have and then

to search specifically for that defect. That the examiner must make decisions and change the test strategy accordingly introduces bias into the examination. If the bias is correct, the examination is more efficient. If the bias is incorrect, the examination may skip over defects that the examiner thinks should not be present or may find nonexistent defects where the examiner thinks they should be. There are countless anecdotal references to technicians who have confused the right for the left eye during a test and dutifully plotted the blind spot on the wrong side of fixation. In some of these instances, the true blind spot has been shown as a scotoma; in other cases, it has been missed entirely.

Because of the difficulties of bias and a potential lack of reproducibility, we prefer careful static perimetry for detecting and following subtle nongeographic defects. The most common use for this methodology is in detecting glaucoma and following up patients with this diagnosis. As previously mentioned, one can perform effective static perimetry with the tangent screen or Goldmann perimeter. The Tübinger perimeter was constructed mainly as a static profile perimeter. Unfortunately, static perimetry by any means is a tedious, cumbersome, and at times boring process. It is difficult for the patient to concentrate fully for the 30 to 90 minutes that one of these tests may take. It is perhaps even more difficult for a technician or examiner to concentrate throughout a whole day or a series of days of visual field examinations. In many ways, then, computers have been the salvation of static perimetry. The computer can present targets according to a random sequence that is undecipherable by the patient. The computer can test the patient using the exact same target presentation methodology over and over for years and years, and the computer does not get bored! The test is still difficult for the patient, however. Human interaction between the examiner and patient is extremely important in helping patients concentrate throughout a visual field test.

Computerized perimeters and static perimetry have something else that ties them together. It is simply much easier to program a computer to perform a static test than it is to program the computer to perform a kinetic test. The same decisions regarding speed and direction of presentation that make it tough for a human examiner to effectively reproduce a kinetic visual field examination make it tough to write a program that will guide the computer smoothly through such a test. A static test, on the other hand, is relatively straightforward. Because the target does not move, the machine only has to choose a site, choose a target intensity, and then record whether the patient responds yes or no.

Thus we tend to choose between manual and computerized visual field services according to the disease process we believe the patient has. One other differential point is that patients who have difficulty concentrating may need the continual human feedback that manual perimetry allows. Some patients just cannot perform adequately with computerized perimetry. Patients who do not perform well with a computerized perimeter often do not perform

very well with the Goldmann perimeter or tangent screen testing. However, a small subgroup does well enough with manual perimetry that useful data can be obtained. For reference, in our practice, fewer than 5% of patients are poor candidates for automated perimetry but good candidates for Goldmann or tangent screen perimetry. If a large number of patients fail with the computerized perimeter and then do well by manual testing, it would probably be wise to review the use of the computerized perimeter with the person performing the field tests and the manufacturer.

PERIMETERS

Theoretically, the ideal manual perimeter would be one half of a hollow sphere with a curvature radius of at least 1 meter, with the patient's eye at the center of the sphere and the examiner outside the sphere but still able to observe the patient for attentiveness, fixation, and reactions. Using an even larger sphere would allow more accurate visual field defect detection and plotting; but a larger sphere is also more cumbersome and may be impractical in the clinical setting. Such an instrument might also include (1) completely free movement of test stimuli in all directions; (2) rapidly interchangeable test object size, brightness, and color; and (3) a pantograph for automatically recording the stimulus position at any given moment.

With minor variation, the foregoing is essentially a brief description of the remarkable instrument designed by Professor Hans Goldmann during the 1940s (Figure 2-1). A more detailed description of this perimeter is found in the manufacturer's brochure written by Professor Goldmann:

> It is a spherical projection perimeter with a recording device. A Nitra lamp illuminates a circumscribed peripheral area above and inside the bowl, which is of 300-mm radius and painted matte white. The lamp is shaded from the rest of the hemisphere by a hood. A portion of the light is sent by a condenser through a hollow lever arm containing the projection system for the perimeter target. By this means slight variations in the brightness of the lamp affect background and target luminosity equally. The movement of the projection arm is produced by a pantograph controlled by a handle which slides on a vertical plate of opal glass illuminated from behind on the back of the perimeter. This plate carries the recording chart. Each position of the handle corresponds exactly with the position of the spot of light on the hemisphere. By slow movement of the handle across the surface of the chart, the visual fields may be examined for 95 degrees on each side of fixation. A telescope through the back of the hemisphere allows for constant observation and control of the patient's eye and in it is a light, variable-sized, fixation point. A slide allows the target to vanish and reappear noiselessly. The projected targets are ellipses of varying sizes from $\frac{1}{16}$ to 64 mm^2 and are easily changed by stops. A series of neutral filters permits geometric reduction in the luminosity of

the targets from 100 to 3.16 millilamberts. The basic luminosity of the target has been fixed at 33 times that of the background and a photometric device is incorporated in the instrument to ensure the constancy of this ratio. If a perimeter does not automatically keep this contrast between background and target luminosity a constant, it is unusable for exact relative perimetry, and previous projection perimeters have not done so. Hitherto, such a constancy has only been found with perimeters using paper targets.

Because of the importance of this constant ratio of background to target luminosity, the photometric adjustment of the perimeter should be effected before each examination, but after the patient is seated before the instrument, since lighter or darker faces and clothes can alter the background luminosity by several percent.

The perimeter may also be equipped with color filters for red, green, and blue.

The combination of flexibility and reproducibility allowed by this ingenious instrument firmly established its position as the reference standard perimeter in the postwar period. The Goldmann perimeter represented a

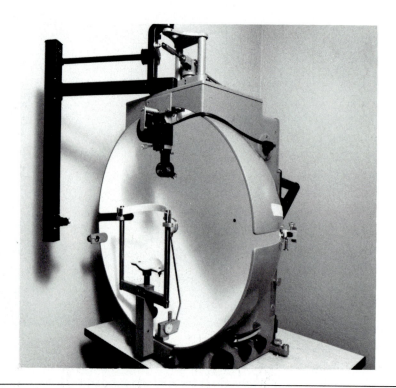

FIGURE 2-1   Goldmann perimeter.

quantum leap forward in our ability to record and analyze data from the visual fields. Much current perimetric research centers on developing new and better software to run the current computerized perimeters. In many ways, however, the hardware portion of computerized perimeters—the actual perimeters themselves—are basically adaptations of the Goldmann perimeter. Even in its fifth decade of production, if used optimally, the Goldmann perimeter is unsurpassed in its ability to detect and describe visual field defects.

Another exquisitely designed manual perimeter appeared during the late 1950s. This was the Tübinger perimeter designed by Professors Harms and Aulhorn (Figure 2-2). The Goldmann perimeter allows both kinetic and static perimetry, with kinetic perimetry being its predominant mode in common usage. The Tübinger instrument emphasizes static perimetry. In many ways the development and popularization of static perimetry on the Tübinger perimeter led directly to the incorporation of static methods in computerized perimeters two decades later.

The Tübinger instrument was used primarily for static perimetry in research settings. Static perimetry allows for great reproducibility and sensitivity

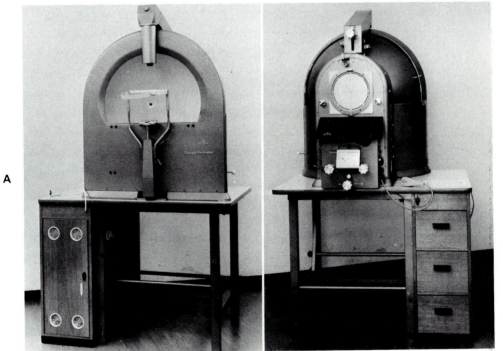

A   B

FIGURE 2-2   Tübinger perimeter. **A,** Front view showing projection system. **B,** Rear view showing controls, pantograph, and charts for both static and kinetic perimetry. *(Courtesy Oculus Optikgerate, Dutenhofen, Germany.)*

for two basic reasons. Its great reproducibility derives from the fact that the only stimulus presentation variables are the test site location and the stimulus size and brightness. Compare this to kinetic perimetry, in which the examiner must choose not only the area to be tested and the target size and brightness, but also how that area will be traversed, the speed at which the target will be moved, where the target will begin, and where the target will end. For example, one can present the target in a radial fashion, beginning in the periphery and moving toward the center of the field or beginning in the center of the field and moving toward the periphery. One could present the target in a circumferential or spiral pattern, beginning at fixation and going out or vice versa. A figure-eight, S-shaped, or any other pattern could be chosen to examine a given area of the field. Furthermore, the target can be moved quickly or slowly; it can begin fast and then slow down, begin slow and speed up. We could go on and on. The additional variable of target movement adds tremendous flexibility to visual field testing procedures, but this flexibility comes at the expense of a great deal of complexity and at the risk of significantly diminishing reproducibility.

The great sensitivity of static perimetry relates to the fact that the reduced number of component variables in the testing procedure allows the examiner the freedom to vary each of those components more precisely. When performing static perimetry, the test site and stimulus size are chosen. The only remaining variable, then, is stimulus intensity. Starting with either a suprathreshold (brighter) or infrathreshold (dimmer) target, the examiner adjusts the target brightness until its detection threshold is established. In practice this threshold is crossed several times during each examination. If we start with a suprathreshold target, one that is bright enough to be seen at the test site chosen, we make it dimmer and dimmer until the patient cannot see it. We note the intensity at which the target disappeared. We then decrease the target luminance even further and begin to increase the luminance until the patient once again detects the target. With a normal patient, these two points should occur at similar luminance levels; in our example, the luminance at which the target disappeared should be just slightly below the luminance at which the target reappeared (Figure 2-3). To increase accuracy and because there is normal physiologic threshold variance, the threshold at a given point can be tested over and over again and the results averaged to provide a highly accurate estimate of the sensitivity at the point tested.

The main drawback to static perimetry, and the reason that manual static perimetry has been performed almost exclusively in research settings, is the amount of time needed to determine threshold at each individual test point. One would have to perform 15,000 threshold determinations to map out the entire visual field at 1-degree intervals, making this method impractical for mapping large areas of the visual field in the clinical setting. Therefore only selected areas of the field are tested. This allows the examiner to determine with great accuracy the sensitivity threshold at the points tested, but means a significant portion of the visual field must be ignored.

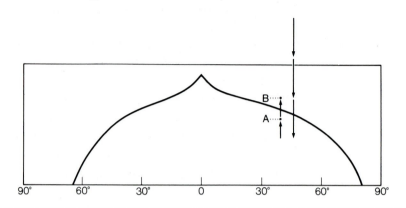

FIGURE 2-3   When performing static perimetry, one first chooses test site and then varies target intensity to determine threshold. In this example, patient did not see initial stimulus, so stimulus intensity was increased *(large arrows)* until the patient could detect light. Stimulus intensity was then decreased until light disappeared. *Threshold* is given as halfway point between dimmest suprathreshold stimulus detected *(A)* and brightest infrathreshold stimulus not detected *(B)*.

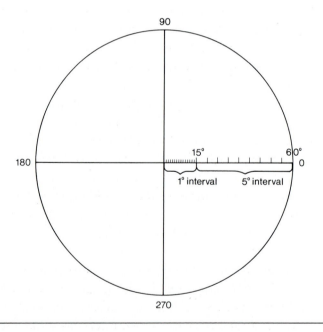

FIGURE 2-4   Typical test site location along 0- to 180-degree meridian for manual static perimetry. Test points are spaced at 1-degree intervals inside 15 degrees and at 5-degree intervals between 15 and 60 degrees.

When using the Tübinger perimeter the sensitivity threshold is accomplished by testing along a few select meridians. If one were to test along the horizontal and vertical meridians (0 to 180 degrees and 90 to 270 degrees), the general practice would be to test at 1-degree intervals from fixation out to 15 degrees away and then at 5-degree intervals from 15 degrees eccentricity to the periphery (Figure 2-4). This requires about 55 test points per meridian. Even with a trained examiner and reliable patient, such an examination may take an hour or more, especially for defects that require repeated testing for increased accuracy. Furthermore, even after testing is completed, vast regions of the visual field remain unexplored. The alternative to meridian testing is a random or symmetric grid pattern; this alternative has been employed most commonly in computerized static perimeters.

Because this is a book about visual fields and not about perimetry per se, this description of perimetry and perimeters is relatively brief. A more in-depth treatment of the processes and pitfalls of examining the visual field, as well as instructions for proper use of various instruments, is available in manufacturer's manuals and a series of excellent textbooks listed in the bibliography. After one has become familiar with the appropriate literature, there is no substitute for hours of hands-on practice under the guidance of an experienced perimetrist.

THE GOLDMANN PERIMETER

When first approaching the Goldmann perimeter and when subsequently reading Goldmann perimetric charts, it is important to understand the symbols used to designate targets of varying size and brightness. In standard Goldmann nomenclature, the target size and intensity are indicated by a Roman numeral (from O to V), an Arabic numeral (from 1 to 4), and a lowercase letter (a through e). Thus a Goldmann target would be designated as I2e or V4e, etc. The various letters represent the size and intensity of the light shown as follows: the initial Roman numeral represents the size of the target in square millimeters. Beginning with 0, indicating a target that is 0.062 mm² the area changes by a factor of 4 with each additional Roman numeral. Thus Roman numeral I = 0.25 mm², Roman numeral II indicates 1 mm², Roman numeral III indicates 4 mm², Roman numeral IV indicates 16 mm², and Roman numeral V indicates 64 mm².

The Arabic numeral following the Roman numeral indicates the relative intensity of the light projected. Beginning with Arabic numeral 1, each additional numeral indicates a light that is 3.15 times brighter than its predecessor—that is, a Goldmann 2 target is 3.15 times brighter than a Goldmann 1 target, or a 2 is 3.15 times dimmer than a Goldmann 3 target. The number 3.15 is used because it is the square root of 10, or 0.5 log units. Stated another way, each Arabic numeral luminance modifier changes the brightness of the target by a factor of 0.5 log unit.

Finally, the small letter following the Roman and Arabic numerals indicates a minor filter. Each minor filter adjusts the luminance by 0.1 log unit. The "a" filter is the darkest, and therefore the stimulus intensity increases by 0.1 log unit for each letter up to "e."

To summarize, the Roman numeral indicates size, the Arabic numeral indicates major light intensity filter, and the lowercase letter indicates the minor filter.

Incremental changes in target size and the relative change in luminance used for these stimuli were chosen carefully. It turns out that the target luminance of a relatively large dim stimulus is the same as an appropriately smaller but brighter stimulus. Goldmann found that increasing the target area by a factor of 4 and decreasing target luminance by 0.5 log unit maintains approximately the same stimulus value. Correspondingly, decreasing the target size by a factor of 4 and increasing the luminancy by 0.5 log unit again maintains the same target luminance. Looking back at the Goldmann-designated numerals and letters, we see that many of the targets are equivalent to others in the system. For example, with a Goldmann target II3e, we can also project a stimulus of approximately equal value by using a I4e (one fourth the area, but 0.5 log unit brighter) or a III2e (four times as big, but 0.5 log unit dimmer).

Now that we have explored the interrelationships between various Goldmann targets, we must begin by calibrating the machine (see instructions given with the instrument) and seating the patient for the actual test. It is important at this point that the patient be comfortable and relaxed. The examiner should spend a few moments discussing the nature of the examination with the patient, explaining what will be seen and how the information will be used. It is important at the beginning of a test to reassure the patient that the targets cannot be seen all of the time. Furthermore, we stress that very dim targets will be used on purpose—in fact, as soon as we determine that a patient can see a given target, we move to a dimmer target until we find one so dim that it is not perceived.

A system of signals should be agreed on, such as a tap on the table when the test object appears. Hand signals are better than verbal responses. In some cases, with particularly responsive patients, we instruct the patient to tap harder and faster when he or she sees a target very well and to tap slower and more lightly when he or she does not perceive the target very well. This is particularly useful in attempting to plot very early scotomas. In these circumstances, the target light often passes from an area where it is perceived clearly, through a zone of uncertainty into a region where it is not perceived, and then finally through another zone of uncertainty until it once again is seen clearly. It is easy for the examiner to record the patient's responses if the firmness and speed of the patient's finger or a pencil tapping on the examination table is noted. The light in the room must be dimmed so that it is less than that of the background luminance of the perimeter bowl. When viewing the patient's eye through the telescope, the bowl luminance will allow enough light for the examiner to monitor fixation, as well as make notations on the perimeter chart.

The size of the test object chosen for the first examination depends on a number of factors: (1) the patient's central visual acuity, (2) the state of the media, and (3) individual characteristics, such as the patient's mental status, speed of reaction, and ability to concentrate. For a relatively normal patient, we tend to start with a I2e or I4e target. We choose this target because its isopter, the region in which it can be seen, generally includes most of the area within 30 degrees of fixation. A target of this size and intensity will therefore allow one to map out the blind spot effectively in patients with good concentration. We like to begin by mapping out the blind spot, because this is a good test of patient reliability, and it also shows the patient what it looks like when the target is seen dimly, such as on the temporal side of the blind spot; more brightly, as it will be in the region closer to fixation; and when the target disappears entirely, as it does in the absolute scotoma, of the blind spot itself. Thus within a few minutes of beginning the test the patient is fairly well oriented to the range of responses that may be required.

If the isopter for the I4e target is diminished and therefore falls inside the 25 degrees of eccentricity usually needed to plot the blind spot, the examiner increases the target luminance and/or size until the blind spot can be mapped effectively. Using this 25- to 30-degree isopter as a reference point, the stimulus value of the target is increased to examine the peripheral field and decreased to examine the central field. One may choose to examine single or multiple isopters, depending on the clinical question to be answered and other factors surrounding the examination.

We have found it helpful to use different colors of ink to indicate different isopters. While testing a patient, we mark where the target appears or disappears using an individual dot or X. After the entire examination is completed, we use the appropriate color of pen to connect the dots and thus form the familiar ovoid patterns that represent the various isopters. Scotomas within the isopters are often colored in entirely to indicate that the corresponding target was not seen anywhere within this particular scotoma. The Goldmann field chart provides a grid on which one can indicate which colors represent a given target size and luminance value.

The appropriate speed to move the test object along the perimeter bowl varies somewhat in velocity with the object size and the patient's reaction time. Generally, a movement rate of 2 to 3 degrees per second seems appropriate. We usually start in the far periphery and move the target toward fixation until it is seen. This marks the peripheral edge of the isopter in question. We may move to a different area of the field and search for the peripheral edge of the isopter along another meridian, or we may continue along the original meridian until we reach fixation, noting any diminution in patient response.

Numerous detailed descriptions of test strategy are found in the literature, such as the Armaly-Drance suggestions for plotting glaucoma fields using a combination of kinetic and static perimetry. It is optimal to use a careful, intelligent approach to examining each field; it is imperative that this approach be standardized for following up patients over time.

TANGENT SCREENS

Of all perimetric techniques, visual field examination with a tangent screen is the most flexible. Although it has its limitations, when performed properly, the tangent screen technique is capable of detecting and mapping visual field defects effectively.

The tangent screen finds its greatest usefulness within 30 degrees of fixation. This is because the patient either has to sit uncomfortably close or the screen has to be unusually large to be able to accommodate the peripheral field. It should be remembered, however, that the useful average area of a normal tangent screen can be increased to about 60 degrees temporally and nasally by simply moving the fixation target from the center to the periphery of the screen and using its entire width to plot half the visual field. Although this technique is useful from time to time, most peripheral defects extend inward to within the 30-degree radius and are detectable with standard fixation target placement.

Tangent screens have been used effectively for decades. During this time many modifications have been suggested and tried, but in general the simplest designs have stood the test of time best. Practice with the tangent screen increases its elasticity and makes it possible to perform comprehensive surveys of the visual field quickly. We often find it useful to conduct tangent screen examinations on patients even though we plan to examine them subsequently with the Goldmann or a computerized perimeter.

Because of the vast number of distances at which the screen may be used, the visual angles subtended by test objects of varying size upon its surface are many. Used at close range with test objects up to 75 cm in diameter, the tangent screen is capable of testing the depth and density of the almost absolute defect, whereas with the 0.5-mm test object at a distance of 2 or even 4 meters, it provides an accurate measure of visual acuity within the central field. For the same reason, a defect that is 1 cm in diameter when examined at 300 mm will be 6 cm in diameter when examined at 2 meters. At 2 meters this larger defect will be of more diagnostic value because its shape, size, uniformity, and density can be studied more accurately.

In general, tangent screens should be designed individually and constructed according to the needs, office space, and desires of the perimetrist. With this in mind, the following list gives the general specifications of a good tangent screen, some permissible variations, and some details of our own preference:

1. Space permitting, the screen should be 2 meters square.

2. It may be fixed to the wall, either stretched on a wooden frame or hung from a curtain roller, so that it can be rolled up out of the way when not in use. If the roller type is used, it should be weighted at the bottom and fastened to the floor when opened up so that it does not sway back and forth while being marked with pins or chalk.

3. The best material is soft-finished cloth such as black felt.

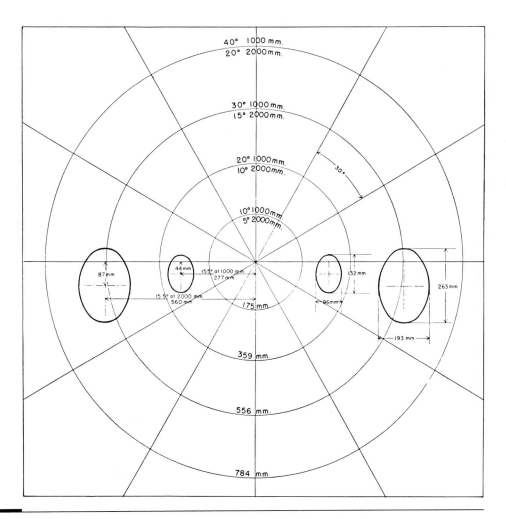

FIGURE 2-5 Dimensions of markings on tangent screen. For screen to be used at both 1 and 2 meters, radial distances in millimeters from fixation are averaged. For example, tangent 15 degrees at 2 meters = 0.26795 × 2000 = 535.9 mm; tangent 30 degrees at 1 meter = 577.3 mm. Average of these two figures = 556.6.

4. If a screen is marked by stitching to indicate the meridians of visual fixation, the stitching should be done in dull, black thread. The radial meridians should be marked at 30-degree intervals, and concentric circles should be marked at 5, 10, 15, and 20 degrees for the 2-meter distance, which will correspond with 10, 20, 30, and 40 degrees at 1 meter. Two blind spots should be indicated on each side of fixation, one for the 2-meter distance and one for the 1-meter distance (Figure 2-5).

5. It should always be possible to examine the field on the tangent screen at varying distances, two of which are multiples of two (500 mm and 1 meter, 1 and 2 meters, etc.). Whether the screen should be fixed and the patient movable or vice versa depends largely on the space availability and the arrangement of the consultation or perimeter room. In general, the patients are more easily moved than the apparatus.

6. A variety of fixation targets are needed. They should vary from 1 mm to 10 cm (Figure 2-6). White tapes may be attached to the two upper corners of the screen so that they can be crossed in the center when testing for large, dense central scotomas. The patient fixates where he or she thinks the tapes will cross even though the actual crossing point cannot be seen. All fixation targets should be readily available and easily interchangeable. When visual acuity is markedly reduced, fixation by proprioceptive sense may be used. The patient is instructed to place the index finger at the center of the chart and then to stare where the finger is. This, of course, shortens the distance to the screen and thereby reduces the size of the field defect, but it ensures accurate fixation, which may not be possible otherwise.

7. Adequate and even illumination of the tangent screen is vitally important. Equal light should come from all four sides. Unfortunately, this may require a cumbersome and expensive installation. Adequate illumination can be achieved by means of simple spotlights directed from above and placed

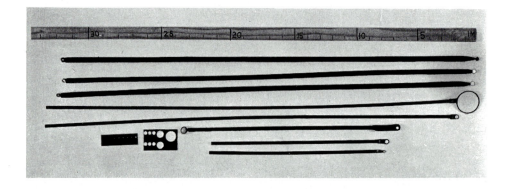

FIGURE 2-6   Test objects and test object carriers. These include spherical, plastic disc, pointed stimuli, and homemade tangent rule.

slightly to one side. It may be necessary to use two spotlights, depending on the distance from light to screen. An ordinary outdoor advertising reflector lamp, which gives a spot of about 6 feet in diameter from a distance of about 6 feet, is generally adequate. If the light is too bright, it can be dimmed by placing paper or plastic discs of various sizes in front of the light source. A rheostat allows the examiner to vary the intensity of the light and thus enhances test sensitivity.

Our preference is to use a 2 square meter black screen on a light wooden frame mounted on the consultation room wall. A chin rest is not necessary. Experience has shown that the patient is usually more comfortable and relaxed when seated naturally in a straight-backed chair. Fixation is adjusted for height either by moving the fixation target up or down or by raising or lowering the patient's chair or stool. Fixation targets, such as matte white print on a dull black cardboard, may be fastened anywhere on the screen.

TANGENT SCREEN EXAMINATION

As with any method, the patient should be seated comfortably. The nature of the examination should be explained. It is generally advisable to start the routine examination at the 1-meter distance. The 1-meter distance provides sufficient magnification of scotomas to enable their detection with relative ease and at the same time encompasses approximately 30 to 35 degrees of field, which is enough to include all but the most peripheral defects. If it becomes necessary to explore small central scotomas in order to outline a defect in great detail, the 2-meter or even the 4-meter distance may be used.

The size of the fixation target used depends on the central visual acuity. The need to use corrective spectacle lenses depends on the nature of the patient's refractive error and the area of the field being explored. An accurate refraction is essential, because the blur induced by an inaccurate refraction can seriously distort a patient's performance. When in doubt, the patient's spectacles can be worn, especially if the patient has an extreme correction or a fair amount of astigmatism. In some cases, the patient may use a trial lens with the spherical equivalent of the correction, which may be held close to the eye during the field examination.

It is often useful to begin by outlining the blind spot with a test object large enough to be seen easily at 30 or 40 degrees of eccentricity. For instance, a 20-mm test object will appear immediately in the patient's peripheral field and will disappear completely in the blind spot. Its disappearance into the blind spot is a dramatic demonstration to the patient of what is meant by the loss or absence of the stimulus. After the blind spot has been located, it should be outlined carefully with a small test object (between 1 and 3 mm). The size of this test object depends upon factors such as the patient's visual acuity and mental alertness. With small stimuli it is possible to detect early nerve fiber bundle loss and/or extensions of the blind spot. When testing with small objects, it is particularly important to remember to move the stimulus at a standard rate (2 to 3 degrees per second) and with a steady hand.

The stimulus can be mounted on a dowel approximately 1 meter long and 1 cm in diameter, which has been covered in black felt. By having the stimulus target mounted on one side of the wand, rather than on the end of the wand, the examiner can rotate the wand 180 degrees and make the target appear or disappear (Figure 2-7). When a sudden rotation of the wand causes the target to disappear, the alert patient will detect this stimulus loss immediately and report it to the examiner. If disappearance of the target is not reported, the patient's attention must be called to the fact. This can be done with larger targets if they are white on one side and black on the other side.

When the examination is resumed, the test object may be brought slowly into view while remaining in the same area of the tangent screen, and the patient should again detect its presence. This maneuver is particularly important in analyzing defects critically for size, shape, and density.

Any point of disappearance or reappearance is marked with a black pin so that increases in the field defect can be seen as the test progresses. It is convenient to start by exploring the oblique meridians, and, if they are normal,

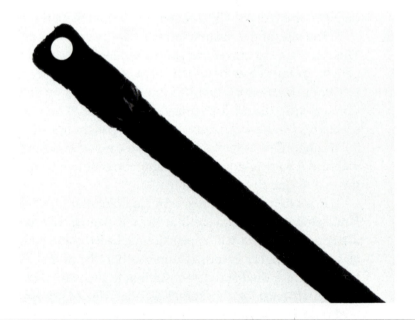

FIGURE 2-7   Stimulus target is mounted on side of wand rather than at very tip so that examiner can rotate wand 180 degrees and make stimulus target appear or disappear.

continue with the vertical and horizontal meridians. If a defect is found in any test area, it should be explored immediately for size, shape, and density. This is usually done best by moving the test object from blind to seeing areas, at right angles to the border of the defect. Having established the size and shape of the area of visual loss for a given test object, one establishes its density, uniformity, and the sharpness of its borders by examining the defect with larger and larger stimuli. Conversely, if the defect was first detected with a large stimulus, its size and shape should be established for smaller objects and/or color. A defect that appeared first to be an isolated scotoma in the upper nasal quadrant when tested with a 6-mm test object, may be found to be only the denser area of a fully developed nerve fiber bundle defect when tested with a 1- or 2-mm target.

When answers are conflicting and confusing, when the test object seems to come and go and the patient is obviously confused as to whether or not the test object or its carrier is being seen, the examiner is probably testing at about the patient's visual threshold. This can be very difficult for the patient and can lead to fatigue. A larger test object will help orient the patient to the examination and should, in fact, allow the examiner to obtain reasonable diagnostic information. If the patient fatigues quickly, it is best to allow a rest period before continuing. If the patient is sluggish, senile, or simply too ill to respond to the average examination, the tempo must be slowed to match the reaction time. In general, usually we can tell within a few minutes whether or not a patient is a good candidate for the tangent screen. If the patient is not a good candidate, special tactics are necessary.

The examiner's approach depends on the patient's needs and the situation at hand. Some patients must be exhorted constantly to maintain position and fixation; others become nervous or even distraught when badgered into compliance with the requirements of a field test. With the tangent screen, as well as with the other instruments, one must not rely too much on the accuracy of the first examination. Many patients perform somewhat better the second time they are tested.

In all instances, the tangent screen examination should be conducted by the physician or under the physician's close supervision. Interpreting field loss can only be done optimally when the examiner has the opportunity to evaluate the patient's attitude and responses and the reproducibility of the findings. The character of the visual field defects (i.e., the size, shape, and density) should be analyzed by the examiner during the examination rather than from the concluded chart, which illustrates the defect graphically. Although it is possible for a technician to detect a field defect, it is the physician's responsibility to analyze and interpret the field defect. With this close supervision the physician can both use the information gained from the quality of the patient's responses and monitor the test for accurate techniques and reproducibility.

The requirements for test objects and test object carriers vary with the uses contemplated for the tangent screen. A few general principles should be applied when purchasing or constructing test objects:

1. They should be capable of being varied in size quickly and easily.

2. They should be replaceable or cleanable so that soiled or faded test objects can be brought up to specifications or discarded. The test object should be fastened to the carrier in such a way that no bright pin or metal rim is visible. When mounted, it should be possible to flip or reverse the test object easily during the examination to cause it to disappear or reappear.

3. Colored test objects are best when they are saturated and thus are probably most safely stored in a drawer.

Considerations for test object carriers are relatively straightforward:

1. They should be rigid enough so that there is a minimum of vibration when the test object is being moved along the face of the tangent screen.

2. They should be approximately 1 meter long.

3. The carrier should either be painted dull matte black, be constructed of a dull matte black finish, or be covered with black felt. Probably the simplest and most practical carrier is the felt-covered wooden or plastic dowel or rod. This is easily made by handstitching a strip of felt around the rod.

CHARTS

Charts for recording the visual field examination are a method of indicating a flat projection of a hemispherical surface and of recording a survey of the hill of vision in terms of contour or isopter lines. Thus the field will be graphed as a series of irregular circles with perhaps some areas where the contour lines are close together, indicating a steep slope to the hill, and other areas where the contour lines are separated widely. There may be depressions and large segments in which the map shows the hill of vision to be eroded away. These may be indicated as erosions of the shoreline, sector defects, or ravine-like depressions extending from the center outward, charted as scotomas.

All of these variations in the visual field must be recorded in graphic form and for this purpose standard printed charts have been developed that show the meridians tested, the distances from fixation and degrees, and the relative position and size of the normal blind spot (Figures 2-8 to 2-11). Perimetrists tend to vary their charts in minor ways for their own purposes, and manufacturers of perimetric instruments print charts suitable for their own devices.

Static perimetry measures the profile or section of sensitivity of the hill of vision and results of these examinations are charted both as the profile of the hill (Figure 2-12) and in terms of its contour lines or isopters. Tübinger perimeters have several special monocular charts that fit in their pantographic device.

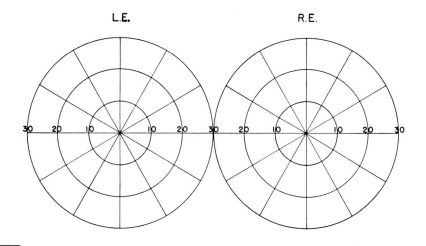

FIGURE 2-8   Chart for recording visual field from tangent screen examination.

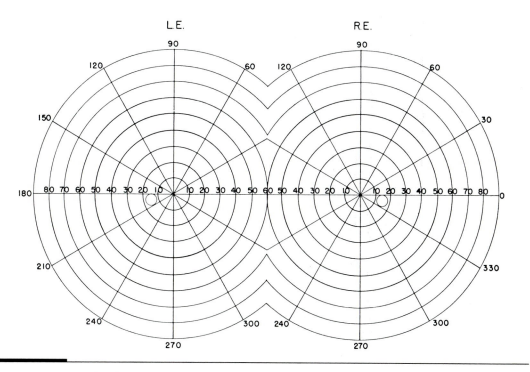

FIGURE 2-9   Simple chart for recording visual field from examination with arc perimeter.

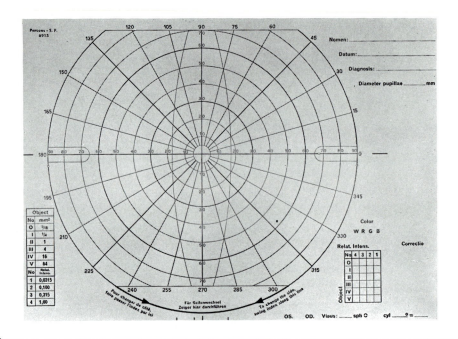

FIGURE 2-10 Chart for Goldmann perimeter.

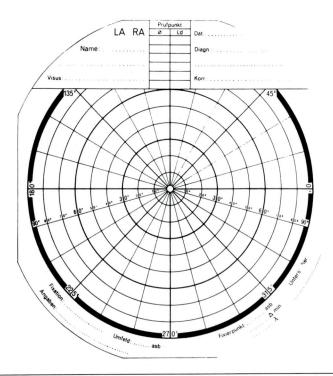

FIGURE 2-11 Recording chart for kinetic perimetry on Tübinger perimeter.

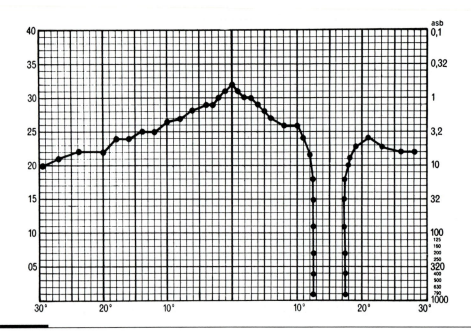

FIGURE 2-12 Recording chart for static or profile perimetry with Tübinger perimeter showing normal section of sensitivity profile for central portion of field.

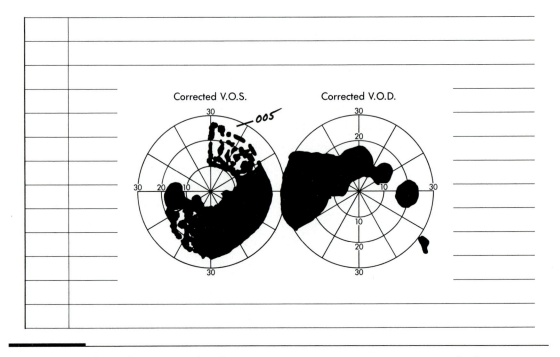

FIGURE 2-13 Charts showing results of tangent screen examination in patient with glaucoma.

In general, the charts supplied with the Goldmann and Tübinger perimeters and similar devices are satisfactory in recording results of field examinations performed on these instruments. Several manufacturers print charts for use with tangent screen perimetry. The ones that we find most useful are relatively small pieces of paper (approximately 3 × 5 inches) that are gummed on one side. The paper is large enough to display the right and left fields side by side. After completing an examination, one simply transfers the information to the gummed field chart and then attaches this directly to the patient's medical record (Figure 2-13). We have found this useful both for following patients serially in our offices and for sending reports back to referring physicians.

Virtually all commercially available charts follow the standard practice of indicating the right and left eye as the patient sees the visual field and not according to the anatomy of the visual pathway. There should be space to indicate the patient's name, date, examiner's name, isopters tested, and corrected visual acuity. It is useful to have the refraction used during the examination for reproducibility on serial follow-up. We make notes as to the patient's reliability and pupil size. Small pupils can significantly depress the isopters both centrally and peripherally. This can be particularly important in patients who are treated with miotics for glaucoma. They may have relatively mild visual field defects before treatment, but when tested after taking miotics, the field defects may appear worse. If it is possible to vary the illumination in the visual field examination space, this must be noted.

Notation of the isopters tested may be made directly on the chart or to one side with arrows indicating the isopter line. Tangent screen isopters should be indicated as a fraction, the numerator indicating the size of the test object in millimeters and the denominator representing the distance of the patient from fixation in millimeters. Thus the fraction 3/2000 indicates that a 3-mm target was used at a distance of 2,000 mm. If colored objects are used, this should be indicated in the numerator of the fraction, for instance, 1 white/ 1000. Goldmann perimetry isopters are designated by a standard code indicating the size and brightness of the target.

With the information listed here, it is possible to duplicate reliably the testing conditions under which a given visual field result was obtained. Serial follow-up can then be approached with a reasonable degree of security.

3 COMPUTERIZED PERIMETERS

Computers have revolutionized perimetry. In many ways the marriage between the computer and the perimeter is natural. Testing the visual field requires precise repetition and meticulous attention to detail. In the optimal circumstance, the patient's response to the stimulus is the only variable. Testing the same patient repeatedly or testing multiple patients in sequence can be tedious, if not downright boring. Under most circumstances, especially when using static perimetry, a binary yes/no (seen/not seen) answer is all that is required of the patient. All of these aspects seem tailor-made for computerization.

Beginning with a machine constructed along the basic lines of a Goldman or Tübinger perimeter, it has been possible to develop sophisticated software programs that direct the machine to perform the visual field test. Targets can be presented at any designated point or series of points within the hemispheric perimeter bowl. They can be of virtually any size or intensity. When a given program is chosen, the machine follows exactly the same pseudorandom sequence of test site presentations. The computer is "happy" to do this over and over for the same patient or for any number of patients in a series. The patient responds by pressing an electronic button when he or she sees the target; the machine records this as a positive response. The machine records the patient's response to each stimulus and then proceeds with the test. Furthermore, on-board microcomputers can store data over many years and can even process data statistically to aid the interpreter in making a clinical judgment. These and other facets of computerized perimetry led to its development during the mid-1970s and to its tremendous popularity today. As has been the case with computerized products in all phases of our lives, active research and development have made the products more practical or "user friendly." In the case of computerized perimeters, each succeeding generation has tended to be more sophisticated and less costly than its predecessor. Our original Octopus perimeter system, for instance, cost more than $100,000 in 1979 (Figure 3-1). Its installation required 2 days and it took up about as much room as two examination lanes in our clinic. The current office model costs

about one sixth as much, requires essentially no installation save plugging it in, is one third the size of the original model and portable, yet still contains most of the capacity of the original. Some other instruments are even less expensive and more flexible.

Perhaps the greatest contribution of automated perimeters is the effect they have had on perimetry in general. The introduction of these machines into clinical practice has caused an explosion of interest in the visual fields and perimetry. A key reason for this increased interest has been the standardization that automated perimetry allows. Each of the great advantages in perimetric technique during this century has had improved standardization as its core. Early work with the tangent screen and later work with the Goldmann and Tübinger perimeters, allowed researchers and clinicians to improve their ability to calibrate their instruments and to record data in a reproducible fashion. No matter how carefully calibrated the instrument and technique were, however, each individual test was performed by a human examiner, and as such the test was subject to technician variability. Under the best of circumstances, this variability was minimal, given the same examiner in similar circumstances over time. Comparing fields generated by different examiners in different centers and perhaps even in different countries was an uncertain art at best. The contrary is the case with computerized perimeters. Commercial units are supplied with a standard array of programs that direct the perimeter to repeat exactly the same test year in and year out. Furthermore, data from

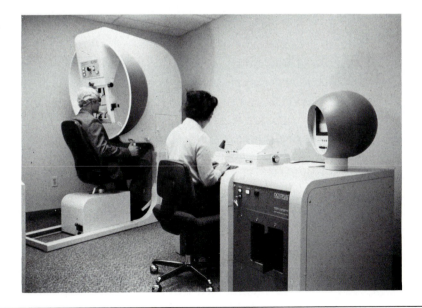

FIGURE 3-1   Octopus perimeter system. Fixation monitored on video screen. *(Courtesy Hitron Corp., East Providence, R.I.)*

separate centers can be compared more easily because for most purposes a Humphrey 30-2 program (for example) performed in San Francisco is the same as one performed in Tokyo or London. Data from multiple centers can be pooled for analysis; investigators and clinicians from all over the world can essentially speak the same language when it comes to visual fields.

The introduction of these new computers has also seen a surge in the number of visual field examinations being performed and in the visual field research appearing in the literature. By the mid-1980s visual field symposia were commonplace and the literature was brimming with articles on perimetry and the visual fields.

The overall quality of visual field examinations performed in the clinical setting has undoubtedly improved. Many proponents of manual perimetry will argue, probably correctly, that the best possible visual field plotting can still be done by the physician examining his or her own patient. The data gained from a perfectly performed visual field examination on the tangent screen or Goldmann perimeter, which includes information about *how* the patient responded, is difficult to improve upon. However, in today's world it is the rare physician who has the time to carefully plot each patient's visual fields. Commonly this task is given to technicians, and no matter how good the technician's skill, another variable is still introduced into the measurement process, and the physician is removed from the patient during the test. Subtle signs of uncertainty and hesitation that might provide useful information to the physician about the quality of the patient's perception are lost. Although outstanding results may be achieved with manual perimetry in the individual case, computerized perimeters can be expected to earn higher marks for sensitivity, specificity, and reproducibility in the patient population as a whole.

BASIC APPROACH

A large and ever-changing population of computerized perimeters is available. The machines and their software programs are evolving so rapidly that an attempt to describe current instruments specifically is fruitless. Specifications, model numbers, etc., change rapidly. However, several basic design features bear further description.

With rare exception, computerized perimeters examine the visual fields using static techniques. A test site is chosen and then the stimulus intensity is varied to determine the patient's visual threshold at the point in question. This is generally done by a "repetitive bracketing" procedure. The machine begins the bracketing sequence by projecting a light of such intensity that a normal patient should see it easily at the chosen test site. If the patient sees the light and responds by pushing the button, indicating "yes," seen, the machine tests other areas of the visual field and then returns to the original site and projects a dimmer light. This process continues until the light is so dim that the patient cannot see it. The threshold has been crossed. As the test continues, the machine increases the stimulus intensity level at the point in question. After just a few sequential increases, the threshold will be crossed again and the patient will once again see the light and press the "yes" button. The machine now has in its memory information concerning the dimmest light that the patient can see (minimum suprathreshold) and the brightest light that the patient cannot detect (maximum infrathreshold). The threshold, then, lies between these two points (Figure 3-2).

In practice the threshold value is estimated. There are two reasons for this. First, for time considerations the machine must move in relatively large steps, generally dimming or brightening the light by 0.2 to 0.4 log unit. Using such a system, threshold determination is only accurate to ±0.1 log unit. Second, repeatedly determining the threshold in the same point does not give a uniform value but rather a distribution of values. Even in normal patients these values can vary by as much as 3 dB over a period of only a few moments. This short-term variation, or *fluctuation,* makes it impractical to try to measure the threshold with ultimate accuracy on a single determination. To get a more reliable estimate of threshold, one must go through the repetitive bracketing sequence several times and then express the threshold in terms of mean and standard deviation. As is the case with manual static perimetry, the increased sensitivity and reproducibility of static perimetry is gained at the expense of a great deal of time. The results of a static threshold test are generally expressed in a decibel scale derived from the reciprocal of the log intensity of the light

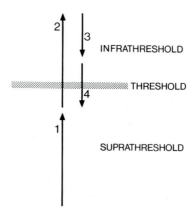

FIGURE 3-2   Repetitive bracketing as it might be performed by typical computerized perimeter. In this example initial target presentation *(1)* is suprathreshold. Second target presentation *(2),* dimmer target, is infrathreshold. Third target presentation *(3)* is slightly brighter than second but is still infrathreshold. Fourth target presentation *(4),* brighter still, is once again suprathreshold. Machine estimates threshold occurs halfway between stimulus intensity *3* and *4.*

projected: 1 dB = 0.1 log unit. Because we are using a reciprocal system, dimmer lights—lights detected in more sensitive areas—are indicated by high numbers. Relatively insensitive areas are indicated by low numbers. Most current machines operate over a dynamic range of 3.5 to 4 log units (35 to 40 dB). Therefore the most sensitive areas of the visual field are represented by numbers in the middle to upper thirties. Increasingly deep scotomas are represented by increasingly low numbers down to zero. In applying these numbers to Traquair's metaphor of the island hill of vision in the sea of darkness, the decibel numbers can be thought of as representing the height above sea level that the island rises to at the point in question.

In addition to performing full thresholding, many computerized perimeters perform suprathreshold or threshold-related screening examinations. When performing a *suprathreshold* test, the machine projects stimuli of the same intensity to each of the chosen test points throughout the field (Figure 3-3). This light is generally bright enough to be seen by a normal patient at all the points in question (hence the name "suprathreshold"). If the light is seen, the patient presses the "yes" button; if the light is not seen, the patient presses the "no" button. The only data obtained by such an examination are yes/no data; no attempt is made to quantify the depth of the defect. This test is much faster than the full threshold test but gives correspondingly less information. A relatively shallow defect will be indicated with the same response as an extremely deep defect. Moreover, the sensitivity of a suprathreshold screening pattern is relatively poor. This relates to the fact that there is a significant slope to the contour of the island hill of vision. Using the same stimulus level to check the entire field means that one either is testing with a stimulus that is too bright to give sensitive information about the central field or too dim to be detected at all in the peripheral field.

To help overcome this problem, threshold-related methodologies were developed. In a *threshold-related screening strategy,* the intensity of the initial

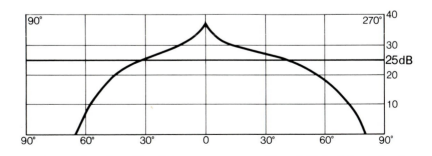

FIGURE 3-3   Suprathreshold static perimetry. In this example fairly dim stimulus (25 dB) is projected to patient. Stimulus is bright enough, however, that it should be detected at virtually all points within about 30 to 40 degrees of fixation.

suprathreshold stimulus varies, depending on the eccentricity of the test site (Figure 3-4). In general, most of these programs test with a stimulus that is approximately 0.5 log units (5 dB) brighter than the patient should see at the point in question. Therefore a much dimmer test light will be used centrally than peripherally. The patient's response and the reporting method are essentially the same as with the suprathreshold test, however. In the case of a positive response, the machine prints a symbol to show that the patient's sensitivity at the point in question is near normal. If the patient fails to respond to the stimulus, a negative mark or black box is printed, but no attempt is made to measure the depth of the visual field defect. The increased sensitivity of the threshold-related method, however, makes it preferable to the simple suprathreshold method in virtually all circumstances.

Several stimulus presentation techniques are available, but they are basically of two types. The first is *projection stimulus presentation,* similar to that used on the Goldmann perimeter. The second is a *light-emitting diode (LED) system* in which the individual stimulus points are determined by placing a large number of light-emitting diodes in the perimeter bowl itself. The projection system is in many ways more flexible, allowing for variable resolution in test site location, as well as permitting kinetic or color perimetry if so desired. The drawbacks of the projection system pertain mainly to the mechanical aspects of presenting and moving the test target. The LED system has the advantages of being totally silent and essentially maintenance free. It has the disadvantages of not allowing kinetic perimetry or variable test site location and not being easily adaptable to color perimetry. In practice, however, several hundred more LEDs are usually implanted in the bowl than can be used in a given examination. The resolution allowed by these machines, in some areas on the order of 1 to 2 degrees, is adequate for all but the most unusual problems.

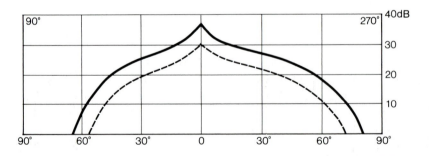

FIGURE 3-4   In threshold-related screening strategy, stimulus intensity is varied, depending on test site location. Brighter stimuli are used peripherally. *Solid line* represents expected normal; *dotted line* indicates consistently suprathreshold test stimulus intensity, which varies with eccentricity.

The microcomputers that are an integral part of automated perimeters have become quite sophisticated. They relate to the hardware portion of the instrument, the patient, and the physician in several important ways.

The most basic of these interactions is the program that directs the test. After the operator chooses which area of the patient's field is to be examined (such as the central field or peripheral field) and the examination strategy (full threshold, threshold-related screening, etc.), the appropriate computer program takes over the test. Based on assumptions in the computer memory about patients of a certain age or a specific sampling of certain areas of the field, the program will choose an appropriate stimulus level to begin the test. The test point sequence and the test stimulus intensity are determined by the patient's responses. Each patient response adds slightly more information to the computer's memory and thus allows the computer—and subsequently the physician—to make an increasingly accurate prediction of the contours and extent of the visual field.

In some of the more sophisticated instruments, the interaction between the patient and the computer during the test is quite complicated. In these instruments the machine begins the test by sampling the threshold at a few carefully chosen points. After gathering these data, the machine essentially predicts what the island of vision will look like based on these few points. It assigns a predicted value to each of the points that it is going to test throughout the remainder of the examination. As the machine proceeds through the test, it uses this predicted value to help determine an appropriate starting point for the actual threshold being processed. For example, if the initial sample indicates that the entire field is depressed, the machine will begin thresholding each point with much brighter stimuli than if the initial indication had been that the field were normal. In some programs this information is continually updated throughout the examination. Thus, as the thresholding process is completed at each additional test site, this new information updates and modifies the computer's prediction of the actual contours of the visual field. This updating continues throughout the examination. The result of such an examination is the machine's best prediction of the contours of the visual field, based on all the points tested during the examination period.

Many machines have the additional ability to store patient data on discs for later use. This allows the computer to make use of data from previous examinations to assist it in choosing appropriate stimuli and to make statistical predictions as to whether the field has stayed the same, gotten worse, or improved. Stored data can also be transferred to a personal computer or mainframe computer for storage, analysis, or other purposes.

After the data have been collected, they can be displayed in a wide variety of formats. There are pros and cons to each of these display formats; we will illustrate some of the most popular.

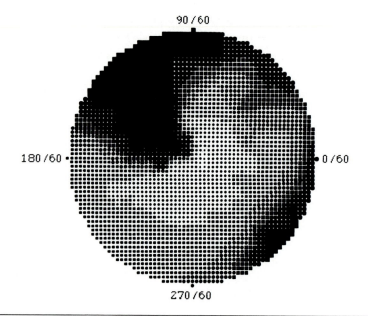

FIGURE 3-5 Gray-scale, or halftone, display from Octopus perimeter system. This field shows severe depression in superior-temporal quadrant. Numbers above, below, left, and right of printout indicate circumferential axis in degrees (numerator) and distance from fixation to edge of printout, also in degrees (denominator).

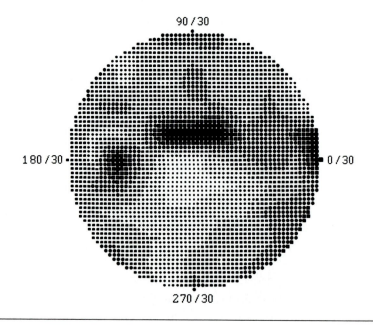

FIGURE 3-6 Octopus system printout of visual field of left eye from patient with large, dense, superior, paracentral visual field defect. Field also shows generalized peripheral depression and nasal step defect.

The gray-scale, or halftone, display is perhaps the most familiar and the most comforting (Figures 3-5 and 3-6). In many ways it resembles a two-dimensional, black-and-white geologist's survey map, as though the island hill of vision were photographed from directly above. Dark areas on the halftone display correspond to areas of depressed sensitivity; bright areas correspond to areas of greater sensitivity. When viewed from afar or slightly out of focus, one can often imagine quite accurately where appropriate isopter contour lines, familiar from kinetic perimetry, would be placed on such a display.

The main drawback of the gray scale is its relative lack of precision in indicating the actual threshold of a given test point. There are two reasons for this. The first is that the gray scale uses representative symbols to indicate a range of values. Typically a given grid pattern represents threshold values over a 5-dB (0.5-log unit) range (Figure 3-7). This is accurate enough to give a reasonable impression of the field's appearance at a given spot, but it is not sufficient for following fields over time. Such a system might use one grid-point density to represent sensitivity thresholds between 16 and 20 dB and another slightly darker grid-point density to represent sensitivities between 11 and 15 dB. If one examined a field serially, a fairly significant drop from 20 to 16 dB would show up as no change on the gray-scale printout. However, an insignificant drop from 16 to 15 dB would show up as a symbol change because these two numbers arbitrarily happen to be represented by different grid patterns. Symbolically, an insignificant drop from 16 to 15 dB would appear the same as a much more important 20 to 11 dB drop. Therefore the gray-scale printout has a somewhat limited usefulness in determining whether or not subtle change has occurred over time.

Additionally, it is important to keep in mind that only a few of the points represented on the gray scale were actually test points during the examination. Typically only 70 to 75 points are tested when a full threshold strategy is chosen for the central 30 degress. A gray-scale printout of this region, however, uses approximately 2,000 individual symbolic representations. The additional symbols represent the computer's attempt to fill in the spaces between the

Symbol	⠿	⠿	⠿	⠿	▦	▦	▦	▦	■
dB	51–36	35–31	30–26	25–21	20–16	15–11	10–6	5–1	0
asb	0.0008–0.25	0.31–0.8	1–2.5	3.1–8	10–25	31–80	100–250	315–800	1000

1 asb = 0.318 cd/m²

FIGURE 3-7   Symbolic grid legend from Octopus perimeter. Each symbol grouping represents range of sensitivity as indicated by relative (dB) scale or absolute (apostilb, abbreviated asb) scale.

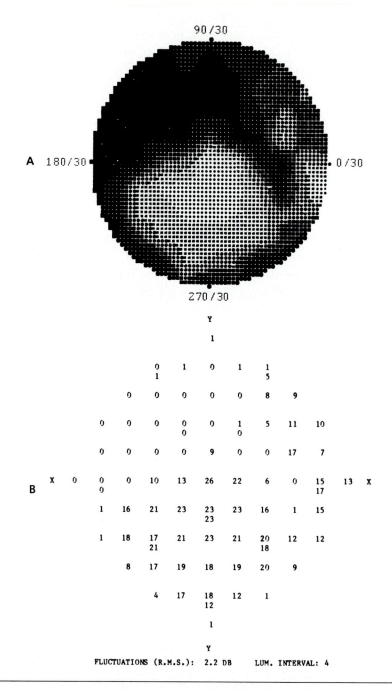

FIGURE 3-8 **A,** Recording gray-scale chart of Octopus visual field defects in patient with advanced glaucoma with nerve fiber bundle defect. **B,** Numerical printout from Octopus perimeter of defect seen in **A.** Numbers represent reciprocal of log intensity of light detected at each point in question. Thus higher numbers on printout represent dimmer stimuli, which indicate more sensitive area within visual system.

actual test points. This gives a more pleasing and easier to read representation, but the computer's predictions, particularly in steep-walled defects, can be misleading.

Perhaps the most accurate representation is given by the numerical print-out of the actual determined threshold values (Figure 3-8). As just mentioned, these numbers represent the reciprocal of the log intensity of the minimum detectable stimulus at the point in question. Stated more simply, higher decibel values indicate greater sensitivity; lower decibel values indicate less sensitivity. Obviously, full-threshold values can only be generated if a full-threshold test strategy is chosen. The full-threshold test strategy is the most time consuming but it also produces the most accurate and reproducible data. Most of the advances in sensitivity, specificity, and reproducibility that we ascribe to au-

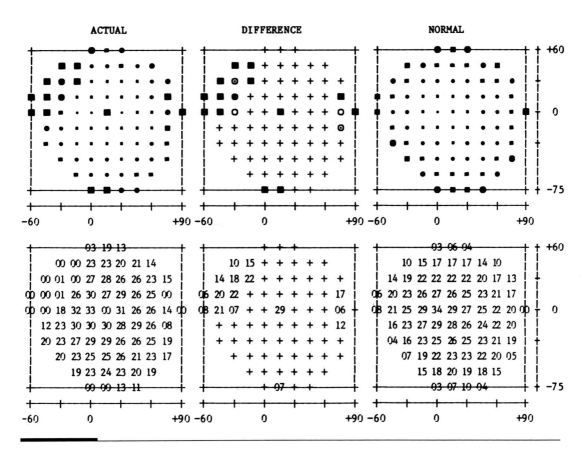

FIGURE 3-9 Octopus subtraction table. Patient's actual test results are subtracted from presumed normal and difference is printed in decibels. On substraction table higher numbers indicate deeper depressions. In this example, displays along top row contain symbolic representations of values printed along bottom row.

tomated perimetry derive from using full-threshold strategies. We find screening strategies useful under limited circumstances.

The main drawback to the numerical display is that such printouts are extremely complicated and bewildering at first glance. Considerable experience is necessary before these printouts can be used confidently. However, we strongly urge anyone who is using automated perimetry regularly to invest the time it takes to learn to read the numerical printouts comfortably. Only by doing this can one take full advantage of the tremendous potential offered by computerized perimetry.

To assist practitioners in interpreting fields, a third type of display, a subtraction table, is available (Figure 3-9). In many ways this display method is a combination of the other two. In most subtraction tables the patient's actual field is compared to age-matched or predicted normal fields. If the patient's own threshold values fall within a certain acceptable range of normal—typically 4 to 5 dB—then a symbol indicating normality or near normality is printed. If, however, the patient's sensitivity values are 0.5 log unit or more below predicted, then a numerical value representing the depth of

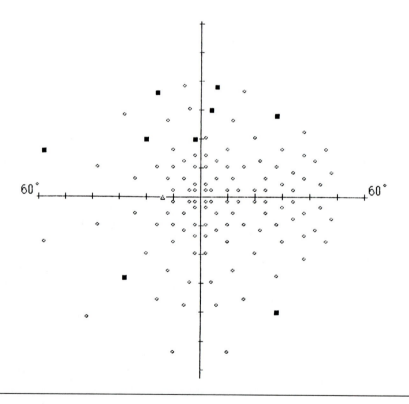

FIGURE 3-10   Two-level screening test from Humphrey Field Analyzer. Open, ovoid circles represent areas where patient's response was normal or near normal. Small black squares represent areas where patient's response was subnormal.

the defect in decibels is printed. For example, if the predicted normal sensitivity at a given point is 30 dB and the patient's actual threshold is 26 dB or more, a simple symbol is printed, indicating a normal response; however, if the patient's threshold is 20 dB, the number 10 is printed, indicating that the patient's response is 10 dB below predicted normal. This subtraction scale is referred to as a depth of defect scale by some manufacturers.

The subtraction table is not as easy to read as a gray scale, nor does it give the precision of the full numerical printout. But because it is more accurate than the gray scale and easier to read than the numerical printout, it is often a satisfactory compromise.

Because screening field examinations do not determine the actual threshold of the point in question, they rely exclusively on symbolic representations of sensitivity. Screening tests are basically divided into two-zone or three-zone examinations. In a *two-zone screen* a stimulus of given intensity is presented to the patient and the patient responds yes or no, seen or not seen. A plus sign or open circle or similar symbol is printed if the response is affirmative, and a black square is printed if the response is negative (Figure 3-10). No

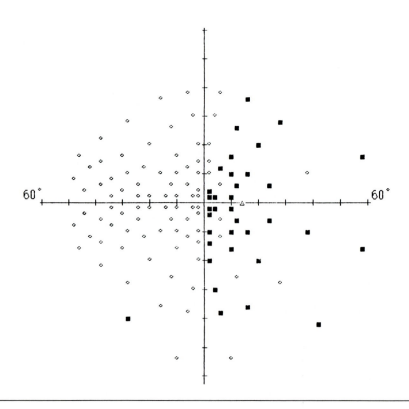

FIGURE 3-11 Two-level screening test from right eye of patient with chiasmal compression syndrome. Disturbed points are concentrated in temporal field, whereas nasal field is essentially normal.

attempt is made to determine whether or not the defect so indicated is very shallow or absolute. The *three-zone test* makes some attempt at quantitation by retesting the site of all initially negative responses with an even brighter target. Depending on visual function, the patient may see the normal target or may miss the normal target but see the brighter target or may miss both the normal and the brighter targets. If the patient misses the normal target but sees the brighter target, an intermediate sensitivity level is indicated and an appropriate intermediate symbol is printed.

The great advantage of screening tests is that they are much faster than full-threshold tests. The disadvantage is that they produce fairly vague information. We use them in selected circumstances, such as when we are searching for an altitudinal or hemianoptic defect, in which the qualitative information given by the screening test may be sufficient for diagnostic purposes (Figure 3-11). We almost always follow a positive screening test with a careful quantitative test using either computerized or manual perimetry.

Some computerized perimeters offer profile printouts similar to those made popular on the Tübinger static perimeter. These have had limited usefulness. When manual static perimetry is done, the test points and the central field are often as close as 1 degree apart. Computerized static perimetry most commonly tests points that are fully 9 degrees apart in the oblique meridians. Profiles generated from such wide spacing can be vague or even misleading.

In general, then, a common fact regarding display choices is that those containing the least amount of data are the easiest to read and vice versa. Unfortunately, as Keltner has said, "There is no free lunch."

TESTING PARAMETERS

One of the most important ways that computerized perimeters enhance reproducibility is by requiring the examiner to specify a series of test parameters before the examination can begin. These vary somewhat from machine to machine but commonly the patient's age, pupil size, and refractive error must be entered before the machine will initiate the test. The printed test results will include these data at a minimum, and the interpreter can make note of it when reading the field chart.

Additionally, reliability measures are often included. In essence, these are the machine's way of indicating such variables as the patient's attentiveness and cooperation during the test. The four reliability measures used most frequently are assessment of fixation quality, false-positive responses, false-negative responses, and short-term fluctuation.

Fixation

Adequate fixation is an absolute requirement of reproducible perimetry. All phases of the perimetric examination, from initial data collection to final

interpretation rely on the assumption that the patient maintained steady central fixation throughout the examination. Computerized perimeters assess fixation in two basic ways.

In some machines, fixation is assessed either by means of eye movement sensors or a closed-circuit video analysis of pupil position. These are augmented by a video image of the eye that is monitored by the examiner. In these systems, a fixation deviation prompts the computer to disregard the patient's prior response. The computer modifies its test sequence to return to the test site later during the examination and retests while fixation is maintained. The benefit of such a system is that it is "real time" and very accurate. It essentially monitors fixation during each and every stimulus presentation throughout the entire examination. If fixation is lost, the machine simply retests the point later, until the entire test is completed.

The drawback of such a system is that the monitoring equipment is often very expensive—sometimes accounting for 25% to 50% or more of the total cost of the perimeter—and may be subject to mechanical malfunction. Furthermore, the most sensitive systems measure inadvertent and unavoidable fixation deviations, such as those that occur with systole and respirations. To be clinically appropriate, these systems must be damped in such a way that they ignore deviations of less than about 2 degrees. If the system is set at too sensitive a level, then it will record a large number of fixation deviations, and the test may be prolonged to the point that the patient cannot maintain concentration.

The other major type of fixation monitoring is so-called blind spot monitoring as developed by Professors Heijl and Krakau. In these systems the position of the blind spot is determined early in the examination. Then at specified intervals throughout the examination stimuli are projected on the blind spot. If fixation has been maintained, these stimuli will not be detected. The negative response is interpreted as fixation is maintained and the test proceeds. If fixation has shifted and the patient can see stimuli that are projected where the blind spot should be, a fixation deviation is noted. With some machines this deviation is simply indicated to the examiner and printed on the final field chart. On other machines all of the data collected since the last satisfactory fixation determination are thrown out, and each of these points is retested. The main drawbacks of the blind spot fixation method are that it only monitors fixation at intervals and that it necessarily prolongs examination time (because fixation is assessed by a separate series of stimulus projections and patient responses). It is possible for significant fixation deviations to occur without registering fixation loss if the loss occurs between fixation checks. Further difficulty in monitoring occurs in fields having large, dense defects that include the blind spot. Patients who have a dense temporal hemianoptic defect will not see stimuli projected anywhere in the entire temporal half-field. Significant fixation deviations can remain undetected. Under such circumstances a blind spot–fixation monitoring system is useless, and fixation

must be assessed by the examiner viewing the patient through a telescope similar to that on the Goldmann perimeter or by the video image displayed on some machines.

The advantages of the blind spot–fixation system are that it does not require much additional expensive or temperamental equipment and that both clinically and experimentally it seems to monitor fixation as effectively as the more complicated methods.

False-Positives

Current generation projection perimeters are fairly noisy. There is often a whirring sound as the projector moves its aiming lens from one position to another in the field. This may be followed by an audible click as the shutter moves to allow stimulus projection. An overeager patient or one who is not cooperating well can use this auditory cue as a signal to depress the stimulus response button. To guard against this, most machines will produce the sounds of stimulus projection without actually presenting a stimulus several times during the examination. If the patient responds to the sound alone, the machine records this as a false-positive response. This is a "yes" response to a nonexistent stimulus. This response is generally indicated to the examiner immediately so that he or she can reinstruct the patient as necessary. Additionally, the final printout chart gives some indication of the number of false-positive responses recorded in relationship to the number of opportunities the patient was given to respond to the click alone.

False-Negatives

False-negative responses are generated by patients failing to respond to a known suprathreshold stimulus. To test for false-negatives, the computer first determines sensitivity at a given point but then comes back to this point later in the test and presents a light that may be 10 to 100 times or more brighter than the stimulus the patient responded to at this same site earlier in the examination. If the patient fails to respond to this second significantly suprathreshold stimulus, a false-negative response is recorded. False-negatives generally indicate inattention. Whereas one or two false-positive responses can occur in a reliable but anxious patient, false-negative answers are uncommon except in patients with tremendously dense defects or in those who have real difficulty cooperating with the examination.

Fluctuations

As we described previously, the numerical value generated by full thresholding strategies is only an approximation of the actual sensitivity of the test point. This is because even in normal circumstances there is measurable sensitivity

variation when testing the same point over and over again. However, this measurable deviation is generally within ± 3 dB of the mean threshold value for the point in question. For a given patient the amount of this scatter, or *short-term fluctuation,* can be measured and the interpreter can assess whether it is normal, questionable, or excessive. Fluctuations are determined by the perimeter measuring the full threshold at some number of points twice during the span of a given examination and then comparing the two values. Fluctuation is usually expressed as a root mean square value indicating the predicted fluctuation per point.

In our experience, completely normal young patients generate fluctuation values in the range of 1 to 1.5 dB. In older patients this may range as high as 2.5 dB or so in the absence of any detectable disease. Fluctuation values above 3 dB are unusual in the normal population.

High fluctuation values may indicate more than a simply unreliable patient. We commonly see high localized fluctuation as a very early sign of visual dysfunction in patients with segmental visual field loss. Furthermore, moderate to severe visual field loss from any cause is associated with relatively high fluctuation values. It is important to keep these points in mind when interpreting visual field results.

CUSTOMIZED PROGRAMS

One of the most attractive features of computerized perimeters is that they allow the examiner to choose from a wide variety of programs and even to customize programs to fit an individual patient's needs. As attractive as it may seem, such flexibility is fraught with danger. Whenever one customizes an examination for a patient, one is basically committed to using the exact same custom program to followup that patient. Perhaps the greatest benefit of computerized perimeters is that they can perform the same test over and over again. Unfortunately, if the examiner changes the instructions frequently, the great asset of long-term comparability is lost.

We rarely use customized tests, perhaps 1% of the time. Whenever we perform a custom test we also perform one of our usual standard tests. That way we can compare the standard tests over time, regardless of whether or not the custom test adds to our data base.

Among the many menu choices available, we use only four or five programs to examine well over 99% of our patients. We have found that a program based on examining the central 30 degrees with a full-threshold strategy has been satisfactory as a standard approach.

VISUAL FIELD INDICES

In describing computerized perimetry we have generally avoided describing specific software packages because they change continually. Our reluctance to describe specific software programs notwithstanding, computerized statistical data manipulation is among the most exciting potential advantages of computerized automated perimetry. The "visual field indices" illustrate some of the ways in which computerized data reduction can be useful clinically.

Our discussion of the visual field indices is largely conceptual, partly because knowledge in this area is evolving rapidly and partly because slight but significant differences between products of various manufacturers make it inappropriate for us to describe any one product in too much detail. It is incumbent upon the user of any one of these products to become thoroughly familiar with the operating manuals available from the manufacturer at the time of purchase.

The basic concept of a visual field index stems from the need to collect a large amount of data and then reduce it to a more manageable number or series of numbers that accurately reflect the condition of the visual field. In many ways a visual field index is similar to a grade point average; a student takes a variety of courses over several years under differing conditions, and, through a complicated but straightforward formula, all of the data are reduced to a single number. Although that single number necessarily excludes nuance or specific information, it can give a fairly accurate indication of overall performance. To take our analogy further, if you were to compare a given student's annual grade point average throughout a college career you could, at a glance, assess whether the performance had improved, declined, or stayed about the same.

Clinically, visual field indices can be used similarly. A glance at an index from an examination can, subtleties aside, determine grossly whether or not the function measured was approximately normal or mildly or severely deviated from the expected normal. When comparing visual fields over time, the same function can be examined to determine whether or not it is stable, deteriorating, or improving. In fact, the software programs available from some manufacturers will automatically examine serial data and calculate whether or not the slope of a line measuring sensitivity throughout a series of examinations indicates a statistically significant change.

We will use a few examples from the automated perimeters with which we have the most experience to describe how these indices are derived and how they may be used. A central concept in the application of visual field indices is that visual field loss occurs in two basic patterns, diffuse or localized, and that segregating and measuring separately the diffuse and localized components of the loss may be useful in diagnosis and follow-up of appropriate patients. The visual field indices help us to examine and quantitate the distribution of loss within the visual field.

When looking at the diffuse or uniform portion of the loss in a given visual field, one starts by determining the mean sensitivity of the points tested. To do this accurately requires careful, accurate threshold determination in the fashion performed currently on many of the more sophisticated static perimeters. For the sake of our example we will assume that the normal island hill of vision is actually a flat surface and that the normal sensitivity at each point throughout the field should be the same. If 50 points within the central visual field were measured, and each point generated a value of 30 dB, then the "total sensitivity" of the visual field would be 1,500. This number divided by the number of points tested (50) would yield a mean sensitivity of 30 dB per point tested. Let us assume that this represents a normal finding. If a patient with moderately significant generalized depression were tested and the total sensitivity for all of the test points were added together and equaled 1,000 dB, the mean sensitivity (1,000 divided by 50) would be 20 dB per test site. If we subtract this mean sensitivity of 20 dB from the normal mean sensitivity of 30 dB, we then generate a mean defect (MD) of 10 dB.* A mean defect of 10 dB per point can be generated in a variety of ways. The extreme examples are that every point in the visual field can be symmetrically depressed exactly 10 dB, or, conversely, one third of the points tested could be depressed to zero and two thirds could be normal. In either case, the total number of decibels derived by measuring the individual sensitivity at each point in the field and adding them together would equal 1,000. Dividing that number by the total number of test points (50) would equal a mean sensitivity of 20 dB.

In practice an MD of 10 dB is relatively large. When looking at MD values that more closely approximate the normal range (generally about ±2 dB), the influence of a mild, generalized depression is correspondingly greater than the influence of a small but severe localized depression. For example, in a patient with mild media opacity the visual field might be diffusely depressed to an average level of 26 dB, generating an MD of 4 dB. Although at a glance the numerical scale or gray-scale printout of this field would not appear to differ much from that of a normal field, an MD of 4 dB would be considered meaningful under most circumstances. If, on the other hand, a patient had a very dense scar that severely affected a small area of three test points, such that their sensitivity were zero, but spared the remaining 47 test points, the MD would be much smaller: 47 test points × 30 dB/point = a total sensitivity of 1,410 dB ÷ 50 total test points = a mean sensitivity of 28.2 dB/point, or an MD of (30 dB − 28.2) = 1.8 dB. Thus a relatively mild generalized depression affects the MD significantly, whereas a very severe but localized depression affects the MD only slightly. The MD value is thus an indicator of the diffuse or uniform component of the visual field loss.

---

*Note that some manufacturers use the term "mean defect," with a positive sign, indicating a depression from normal, and a negative sign, indicating a supranormal response. Other manufacturers use the term "mean difference," with the signs reversed: a negative difference indicates a depression, and a positive difference indicates a supranormal response. Confusion arises because both terms are abbreviated "MD." This again underscores the importance of consulting the appropriate owner's manuals when interpreting information from a specific machine.

To measure the localized or nonuniform component of the loss, a second visual field index is calculated. The Octopus system refers to this index as the loss variance, and the Humphrey system refers to this index as the pattern standard deviation. Nomenclature aside, this index determines whether or not the loss measured in a given visual field varies geographically (e.g., loss variance) or is symmetrical throughout the visual field. The math involved in determining this is extremely complicated and will not be explained here.

An alternative method used to quantitate the nonuniform component of the loss is to measure the standard deviation of the deviation from normal. In simplified terms, if the distribution of loss in all segments of the visual field is equal, then the loss variance will be approximately zero. If the deviation from normal occurs relatively symmetrically throughout the visual field, the standard deviation of this deviation will be very small. However, if one area of the visual field is extremely abnormal compared with other areas of the visual field, the index sensitive to distribution of the visual field loss will reflect this appropriately.

In the examples we used to describe the MD, we showed that a relatively mild degree of loss that occurred uniformly would produce a significantly abnormal MD. However, since this loss occurred symmetrically and equally throughout the field, the loss variance (and the standard deviation of the loss) would be essentially zero. On the other hand, when all of the loss is concentrated in a few severely affected points occurring in an otherwise normal visual field, the MD is not affected much at all, but we expect a meaningful elevation of the index sensitive to nonuniform loss.

In the practical case, one usually finds that some component of both indicators is disturbed. When looking at a single examination result one may evaluate the field as to whether the diffuse or localized indicator is more severely affected. When evaluating examinations serially, one can assess whether the diffuse, localized, or both components remained stable, improved, or deteriorated. In a simplified example, a patient with an arcuate defect due to glaucomatous field loss would be expected to generate a relatively mild abnormality of the diffuse or uniform loss indicator and a more severe abnormality of the localized loss indicator. A patient with a media opacity due to a cataract would be expected to have more loss in the uniform indicator than the localized indicator. If a patient has a pathologic condition that would be expected to produce a more generalized loss (such as media opacity) and an additional condition that would be expected to produce more localized loss (such as a localized inflammatory retinal lesion), and if deterioration were evident during follow-up examinations, the visual field indices may be useful in helping the clinician determine which problem has worsened.

In considering the basic conceptual construction of the two indices described here, a concern is that the short-term fluctuation or measurement error inherent in static threshold determination may tend to affect the index representing the localized component of the loss. Some portion of the index representing the distribution of localized loss may be due to measurement error or fluctuation alone. To help factor this out, currently available software packages determine the short-term fluctuation during each full thresholding examination in which visual field indices are to be calculated. Using a sophisticated statistical equation, the portion of the index indicating localized loss attributable to measurement error is factored out. A more refined index is created, which is intended to indicate the loss variance, or standard deviation of the deviation, *without* regard to the measurement error. Because the data are effectively corrected for measurement error, this index is referred to as the *corrected* loss variance on the Octopus machine or the corrected pattern standard deviation on the Humphrey machine. In practice these corrected values have found greater clinical utility than the uncorrected values.

In addition to these basic indices—the uniform component of the loss, the nonuniform component of the loss, the short-term fluctuation, and the nonuniform portion of the loss corrected for the measurement error—a variety of other calculations, display modes, and data reduction functions are available. Understanding these features requires a bit of study—the instruction manuals are generally dozens of pages in length—but we have found them useful adjuncts to our daily patient management. The task of sifting through years of serial visual field data on an individual patient has been streamlined and made more objective. Although room for improvement always exists, the availability of visual field index–calculating software has been a definite positive step.

4 SPECIAL PERIMETRIC TECHNIQUES

Many special techniques have been advocated in the constant search for a quicker, more objective method of visual field examination. Perimetry in diminished light has become so common that filters for decreasing test object brightness are included as standard equipment in some of the manual projection perimeters described previously.

It is common knowledge that cloudy media will materially alter the visual field, exaggerating the appearance of any defects. Variations in test object luminosity and background luminosity have all added their bit to our increasing knowledge and at times have succeeded in uncovering field defects earlier in their development than would have occurred using standard illumination alone.

EXTINCTION PHENOMENON

Bender's application of double simultaneous stimulation for the purposes of eliciting the extinction phenomenon has been an important contribution to the field of perimetry. As Bender explains:

> Clinically speaking, extinction of sensation is defined as a process in which a sensation disappears or a stimulus becomes imperceptible when another sensation is evoked by simultaneous stimulation elsewhere in the sensory field. But the definition needs modification because there are so many variations in the manifestation and in the conditions under which the phenomenon occurs.

Bender selected the term *extinction* because the first patient in which he studied the phenomenon in detail had a wound of the left parietooccipital region of the brain and described the phenomenon "as if the 'light' in the right field was extinguished by the stimulus introduced in the left field." As soon as the stimulus was removed from the left field, he once again saw the stimulus on the right. Extinction does not occur in every patient with homonymous hemianopsia. It does not always occur on each examination of the patient; it may be elicited in seven or eight out of ten tests. It does not always imply complete loss of sensation but may show only a decrease or obscuration of the sensation, whether visual or painful.

When used as a part of the confrontation test, double simultaneous stimulation adds value and refinement to the examination. We have had numerous experiences in which a rough confrontation examination using double simultaneous stimulation revealed a homonymous hemianopsia that had remained undetected by standard methods with a single stimulus.

In using the double stimulation method the examiner exposes two equal-size test objects simultaneously in opposite halves of the visual field and advances them from the periphery toward fixation at equal speeds. The two stimuli are exposed in opposite quadrants, 180 degrees from each other. The patient is asked to indicate whether one or two objects are seen and also where they are located. Steady central fixation must be maintained. The examiner may present a single object in the right field and then in the left field and then in both right and left fields simultaneously. In each case the patient is asked to say whether one or two objects are seen and to indicate the location. This alternate single and double stimulation should be repeated quickly eight or ten times. In cases of true extinction the patient fails to perceive one of the two simultaneously exposed objects seven or eight out of ten times, and the extinguished test object will always be in the same hemianoptic half or quadrant of the field.

There is as yet no satisfactory explanation as to why extinction occurs. Clinically, however, it is of some use to note that the extinction phenomenon is most often seen in patients with parietal lobe disease.

AMSLER GRID

The Amsler grid has long been used for detecting small central scotomas and metamorphopsia in macular diseases (Figure 4-1). It is a subjective test in which the patient fixes attention on the center dot of a black grid on a white background, or vice-versa, and describes the appearance of the grid lines at or close to fixation. Distortion of the grid lines around fixation indicates the presence of metamorphopsia such as might occur with macular edema. Absence of portions of the central grid indicates a scotoma. The test is useful in explaining impaired visual acuity due to minute macular lesions.

The Amsler grid patterns have been used for dynamic visual field testing in the examining chair or at the patient's bedside. By rotating the grids and using 1 or 2 mm spherical test objects at a distance of about 35 cm, one can plot visual field defects to approximately 45 degrees in all meridians.

As with tangent screen examination, preliminary outlining of the blind spot is necessary to assure that fixation is steady.

The test is economical and time saving and can detect visual field loss in neurologic disease and in glaucoma with a fair degree of accuracy.

AMSLER RECORDING CHART
A replica of Chart No. 1, printed in black
on white for convenience of recording.

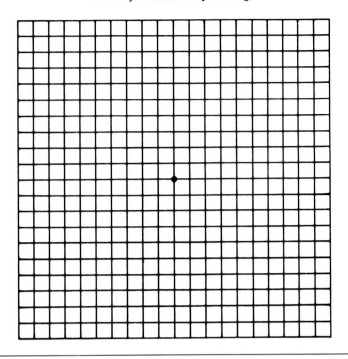

FIGURE 4-1   Amsler grid.

ANGIOSCOTOMETRY

Measurement of the retinal vessels' shadows at the upper and lower poles of the blind spot (angioscotometry) has been studied intensively. It is believed by some that widening of the angioscotomas corresponds closely with fluctuations in intraocular pressure in early cases of glaucoma. In practice, specific examination for angioscotomas is tedious and time consuming and has not been adopted widely. Experimental clinical trials with the Octopus perimeter using a customized 1-degree grid detected angioscotomas easily for a distance of 15 to 20 degrees.

MULTIPLE PATTERN METHOD OF VISUAL FIELD EXAMINATION

In the mid-1950s Harrington and Flocks designed a multiple pattern method of visual field screening that gives static suprathreshold tachistoscopic presentation of multiple stimuli. This instrument is a precursor of the computerized perimeters described in Chapter 3. The Harrington-Flocks screener

(Figure 4-2) was designed to provide a rapid, reasonably accurate screening method that detects visual field defects in a high percentage of the unknown numbers of persons with these defects.

This principle has been applied more recently by Keltner and Johnson, who have performed tens of thousands of tests using a suprathreshold static screening methodology and a computer-assisted perimeter. With the cooperation of the State of California Department of Motor Vehicles, these tests were performed on volunteers in conjunction with their driver's license applications. The Harrington-Flocks screener provides essentially the same data. It is portable and can be obtained at a fraction of the cost of even the least expensive computerized perimeter. It does not, however, allow one to perform quantitative perimetry.

The method uses the principle of tachistoscopic, or flash, presentation of simple abstract patterns of dots and crosses to the fixating eye (Figure 4-3). These dots act as visual stimuli in the various parts of the visual field. The patterns are printed in white fluorescent ink on white cards so that under ordinary illumination only a black central fixation dot is visible. When the card is illuminated by a flash of ultraviolet radiation (black light) of approximately 250 msec duration, the pattern stands out clearly against the background of the card and acts as a stimulus to extrafoveal vision. The ultraviolet light flash duration is sufficiently long to allow the subject to see the pattern but is too short to allow a fixation shift. If a portion of the visual field is

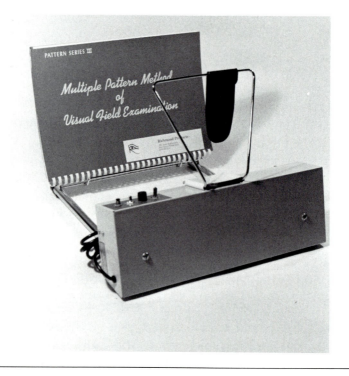

FIGURE 4-2   Harrington-Flocks screener. *(Courtesy Richmond Products, Boca Raton, Fl.)*

defective, patterned stimuli in that area will not be seen and the patient will describe the pattern erroneously. A composite of 33 stimuli covers most of the visual field within the central 25-degree radius. Errors in describing the patterns may be checked off on a chart of the pattern composite as a means of recording the examination (Figures 4-4 and 4-5).

The pattern cards are bound in a book of 20 cards with an Amsler grid on the back cover for macular function testing. The patterns are exposed one at a time in a box containing the black light tube and equipped with a chin rest so that the patient's eye is at a fixed distance of 330 mm from the card.

In the center of each card is a 5-mm black dot for fixation. In a moderately well-lit room, the pattern is completely invisible until activated by the ultraviolet light. In brighter rooms there is less contrast between the pattern stimuli and the background. This increases the sensitivity of the test. If a light meter

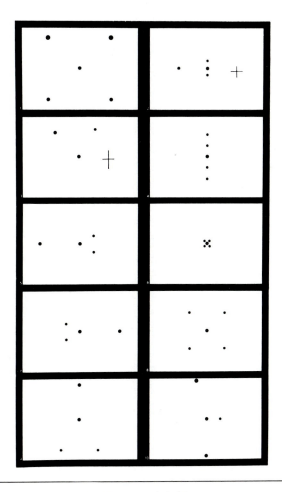

FIGURE 4-3   Patterns of multiple pattern method of visual field examination.

is available, the measure of room light on the card should be approximately 5 footcandles.

With the Harrington-Flocks screener the first ten cards of the series are exposed to the right eye. The second ten cards present the same stimuli in a different sequence to the left eye. All patterns exhibit three or more stimuli in the visual field, some on each side of the vertical meridian.

The ten patterns for each eye are made up of round dots that vary from 1 to 8 mm in diameter. The larger dots are at the peripheral limits of the field, and the smaller dots are closer to fixation.

When using the Harrington-Flocks screener or when using screening programs on computerized perimeters, it is important to remember the limitations of screening methodology. These tests are meant only to detect visual field defects and not to quantify them. If a defect is discovered using a screening method, careful manual or computerized quantitative perimetry is indicated to verify the presence of the defect and to describe it in more detail.

The incidence of undetected or unknown visual field defects in the general population is very low. In the studies by Keltner and Johnson, as well as in other series, this incidence is less than 5%. In practice, if one excludes patients who have a history of cerebrovascular accidents that would be likely to produce hemianoptic field defects and patients who have obvious cataracts, retinal disease, or glaucoma, the incidence of unsuspected visual field defects is probably less than 1%. The sensitivity and specificity of any test used to screen such a population become critical. In this instance, the sensitivity of the test refers to its ability to detect an abnormality when a visual field defect is present. A high percentage of false-negative tests, tests in which there are

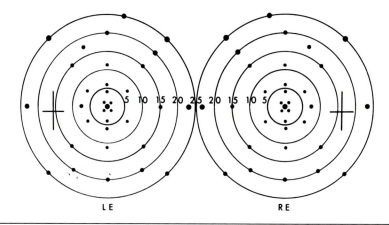

LE   RE

FIGURE 4-4   Composite of ten patterns for each eye of multiple pattern method of visual field examination, demonstrating location of stimuli in central area of visual field. This may be used as recording chart to check off erroneous responses during examination.

no defects found but in which the patient actually has visual field loss, would indicate poor sensitivity. Conversely, a high percentage of false-positive tests, which indicate the presence of a defect in a patient who turns out to have a normal field, would indicate poor specificity.

Under the best circumstances, visual field testing may approach 95% sensitivity and 95% specificity. Values higher than this do not occur reliably. For screening large populations, a figure of 95% sensitivity would be adequate, indicating that one was detecting 95 out of 100 abnormal visual fields and correctly labeling them as abnormal.

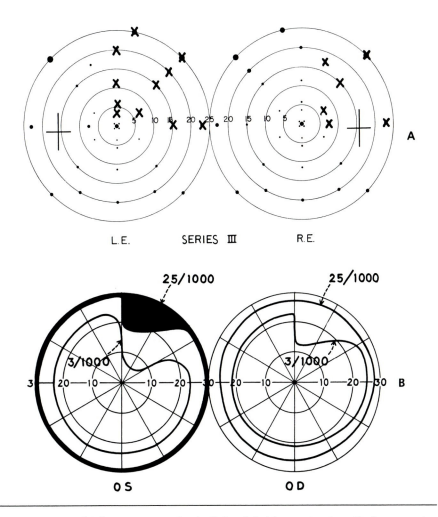

FIGURE 4-5 **A,** Responses to multiple pattern method of visual field examination. **B,** Comparative tangent screen field study of incongruous homonymous hemianopsia resulting from cerebrovascular disease of left temporal lobe.

Under mass screening circumstances, however, a specificity of 95% presents some problems. If we estimate that unsuspected visual field defects occur in only about 1% of the general population, once patients who are likely to have visual field defects based on a history of significant stroke, cataract, glaucoma, or retinal disease are excluded, we would expect only about one person out of every 100 to have an occult visual field defect during mass screening. A specificity of 95% would indicate that five out of every 100 patients would have false-positive results, that is, they would have visual field defects that on further testing would turn out to be nothing more than artifact. Under these circumstances an abnormal result is five times more likely to be a false-positive test than representative of a real defect. One must bear this in mind when contemplating screening large numbers of patients in the office setting. Under most circumstances a reasonable history and physical examination, combined with simple confrontation perimetry, will detect those patients who need further quantitative study.

In general, mass screening is appropriate only in public health circumstances or when the patient will not otherwise be examined by an individual physician.

ARMALY-DRANCE TECHNIQUE

Armaly has developed a method of selective perimetry as a screening device in glaucoma, in which a large number of positions in the central visual field are examined both kinetically and with static stimuli. Seventy-two positions are examined by static perimetry on the 5-, 10-, and 15-degree parallels, and a selected number of nine positions in the nasal periphery and two in the temporal periphery are examined kinetically.

Drance has modified the Armaly technique and devised a method of his own for defects in the temporal field. He feels that these methods are highly accurate but still believes that any defect found by the screening method should have a more accurate visual field analysis.

COLOR PERIMETRY

The use of colored test objects in perimetric tests is controversial. Even the strongest advocates of color perimetry are careful to emphasize the complexities of the method and the difficulty of interpreting the results. It has been difficult to prove that a clinically significant difference in sensitivity or specificity is achieved by performing routine testing with manual or computerized perimeters using colored test objects. Because of a lack of standardization and the complexities of interpretation, we do not use color perimetry routinely except under one circumstance. The one exception is the red desaturation test for patients with suspected subtle hemianoptic, quadrant, or altitudinal defects. One preferred test object is the red bottle top available on any standard mydriatic eyedrop. To perform the test, one approaches the patient as if to perform confrontation perimetry. The patient fixates on the examiner's eye, and the examiner brings the red object into view in a position 5 to 10 degrees away from fixation in the lower temporal quadrant. Maintaining approximately the same degree of eccentricity, the test object is moved slowly from the temporal inferior field to the nasal inferior field and back. The patient is asked to identify any change in the object as it is moving. If a subtle hemianoptic defect is present, the red test object will often appear pale or desaturated in that portion of the field. If the test works well, the patient will respond briskly as soon as the test object crosses the midline. After testing the inferior vertical midline, the superior vertical midline is tested, as well as the temporal and nasal horizontal meridians.

This test is relatively sensitive and very simple. It is particularly useful when a very subtle defect appears with other testing methods and additional diagnostic confirmation is desired.

PEDIATRIC PERIMETRY

Visual field studies are performed uncommonly on children, especially children under 10 years old. This is because it is usually assumed in advance that such examinations are unreliable or even impossible to perform. This assumption seems to be predicated on the belief that examinations of children must be conducted in the same manner and with the same techniques as employed with adult patients. Happily, this assumption is invalid.

Modern imaging techniques have decreased the importance of visual field tests in detecting and localizing intracranial mass lesions. These imaging techniques are sensitive and largely noninvasive. However, imaging equipment is not conveniently available in many areas, and the field examination can add important information in the early stages of evaluating a patient with a suspected pathologic problem. This may be particularly important in pediatric patients. In addition to being expensive and frightening, these "noninvasive" examinations may require a general anesthetic in children. Although a negative visual field test (normal) does not rule out a pathologic problem in a questionable case, a positive visual field test may play a key role in demonstrating the need for further investigation.

When variations in technique are applied with flexibility and imagination, motor responses may be obtained from some patients with visual field defects that make verbal communications between the patient and examiner unnecessary. Using these techniques, perimetric evaluation is possible in seriously hearing impaired patients, in preverbal children, in patients with an insurmountable language barrier, in psychotic patients, in semicomatose patients, and in experimental circumstances, even in dogs in which homonymous hemi-anopsias have been induced by intracranial surgery.

These motor responses to visual stimuli may be seen as (1) a shift in ocular fixation that occurs suddenly and repeatedly when a stimulus is brought from a blind to a seeing area in the visual field, (2) head movements toward the stimulus, (3) pointing motions, sometimes almost involuntary, and (4) changes in facial expression elicited by stimuli in the seeing area as contrasted to the anopic portion of the field.

For example, a left homonymous hemianopsia in an infant 1 year of age was detected by watching his facial expression respond happily to a pleasur-able visual stimulus presented on the right side as contrasted with total in-attention to the same stimulus presented on the left. In this case, moving hands or lights elicited a variable and inconsistent response that was inconclusive on repeated testing. The infant had been declared congenitally blind. Later it was noted that the baby reacted with bright smiles to a game of peakaboo with his older brother. Using the brother as a visual stimulus and playing the peekaboo game without sound first on the left and then on the right side, the baby responded invariably with a pleasurable response to the stimulus pre-sented from the right and inattention when the stimulus was presented from the left. The field defect and the presence of a right-side congenital cerebral aplasia were confirmed several years later with more sophisticated techniques.

The most useful form of visual examination for infants and young children under the age of 6 is the confrontation technique. The short attention span of children in this age group makes a quick, simple test mandatory, and a child's central fixation can be maintained best by a constant patter of talk from the examiner or a parent. It is usually wise to seat the small child on the parent's lap, so the parent may, if necessary, also control the child's head movements. The other parent or a friend or sibling makes a good fixation point over the examiner's head or shoulder.

The peripheral field in four quadrants may be checked in a matter of seconds using a small toy as a stimulus. If the child has brought a favorite doll to the examination, one may use this as the initial test object, switching quickly to a collection of toys in decreasing size, depending upon the response. Such toys are available in almost infinite variety. The larger ones, such as dolls, animals, and toy autos, are simply hand held and are brought into view from the peripheral field until the child turns his or her eyes or head to look at and reach for the object. This confrontation test may be quantitated some-what by decreasing the stimulus size. Miniature toys can be glued to the end of a pencil or a black plastic knitting needle. Deficient responses in one area of the field may be explored with these miniature stimuli and, if cooperation is good, with small bright beads stuck on the point of the knitting needle.

Another effective quantitation method is to reduce the room illumination during the test until just enough light remains to observe the child's responses. If the child is old enough to walk or crawl about, a useful variant is to toss three or four miniature toys or bright beads on the floor on each side of the room and observe the manner and speed with which the child retrieves these objects.

Older children (6 to 10 years of age) can respond accurately to standard tangent screen testing. By making a game of "catching the fireflies" or something similar, in which stimuli are made to wink on and off in different areas of the darkened tangent screen, one can get consistent and accurate responses from small children. By this method a bitemporal hemianopsia was detected in a 4-year-old girl with craniopharyngioma.

It must also be remembered that young children's responses can vary as widely as their intelligence. One may be able to use sophisticated perimetric methods with excellent results. Accurate quantitative visual field studies are often accomplished with just a little patience and friendliness. The Harrington-Flocks screener can be used successfully in some children. We have found the method accurate and, on occasion, it has revealed diagnostic field loss that was unsuspected or had been missed by examination with standard perimetric methods.

In theory a child should be able to count the dots as they appear on the pattern cards. The Harrington-Flocks screener is therefore of the most value with children 6 years of age and over. It has been used successfully, however, with children under 4 years of age who pointed to the targets they had seen even though they could not count them. Figure 4-6 shows the multiple pattern visual field composite chart of a 6-year-old boy with a supracellar chorio-epithelioma with chiasmal pressure from above. The subsequent tangent screen field study, which was conducted without difficulty, revealed an inferior temporal quadrant defect with a sharp vertical border, indicating chiasmal involvement. The perimetrically localized lesion was confirmed later.

If a child is over 6 years of age, it may be possible to undertake definitive and quantitative perimetric studies on tangent screen or Goldmann perimeter. A 0.5-degree central scotoma was successfully demonstrated in a 7-year-old boy with an eclipse burn on the fovea. On another occasion, an 8-year-old child who had been diagnosed as hysterical, was able to outline accurately a typical arcuate nerve fiber bundle defect resulting from a healed and very small area of juxtapapillary choroiditis. The fundus lesion was diagnosed retrospectively after the field defect indicated its presence and position.

We have used computerized perimetry successfully with cooperative children above age 6. A child is seated in front of the perimeter and given the response button. The field test is explained as though it were a video game with a button being used to turn out the little lights as they flash on.

Some children respond well to describing the game in terms of shooting down invaders from space (a scary thought!). When performing such an examination it is generally wisest to begin with a screening strategy that uses relatively few test points. A 40-point central screen will only require a couple of minutes of cooperation, but may reveal significant pathologic conditions. Longer or more involved tests are often associated with diminishing returns.

Special attention must be given to helping the child maintain fixation. Constant monitoring and positive feedback are essential.

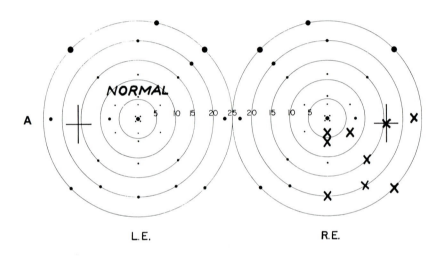

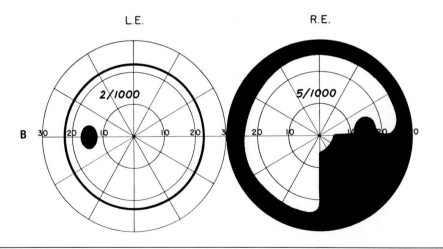

FIGURE 4-6   **A,** Composite of multiple pattern cards showing right inferior temporal quadrant defect in 6-year-old child with suprasellar chorion epithelioma. **B,** Tangent screen field study of same child.

The incidence of hysterical amblyopia of varying degree and severity is relatively high in patients 10 to 15 years of age. In the majority of these patients the visual deficit is reversible; frequently these children are so amenable to suggestion that the elaborate routine of a complete ophthalmic examination is sufficient to cure their amblyopia. No other part of the workup is as important to the diagnosis as the tangent screen visual field.

In a typical case there will be gross concentric contraction, sometimes to within 6 or 8 inches from fixation, with a 5-mm, 10-mm, or even larger stimulus. If the field is examined at 1 meter and again at 2 meters, the contraction will be the same size in inches on the screen for both distances. This is a true tubular field. It cannot be the result of an organic pathologic process, which would produce a cone of vision with the contracted field twice as large at 2 meters as it is at 1 meter. A true tubular contraction is spurious and must be functional in origin.

During repeated examinations, it is often possible, through suggestion, to expand the field gradually so that at the end of the procedure the previously contracted field has become normal. It is best to perform this examination without witnesses. If done in the presence of parents, it causes the child to lose face, and reversal of the defect may become much more difficult. Such therapeutic examinations may be a source of great satisfaction to the examiner and the patient.

In summary, the rewards of perimetric examination of children are considerable. The techniques call for some ingenuity, flexibility, and patience and are a challenge to the examiner. The detection of diagnostic defects in the visual fields of infants is possible. The native intelligence, alertness, and natural curiosity of small children often make it a joy to work with them. Much diagnostic material is available if an effort is made to uncover it. The techniques of pediatric perimetry vary from the crudest forms of confrontation to the most sophisticated and quantitative analysis of complicated defects.

QUANTITATIVE LAYER-BY-LAYER PERIMETRY

In 1981 Enoch and colleagues published a monograph summarizing work on an intriguing process that attempts to use special perimetric techniques to localize pathologic conditions to various layers of the visual system. Simplistically, a rotating or nonrotating static stimulus is used to determine threshold. The stimulus differs from the normal uniform circle of light projected by conventional perimeters, however, in that it resembles a windmill fan with alternating black and white blades. Generally their experiments were performed with targets that contained one to four black veins per disc. The target is projected so that it stimulates a given area of the visual field. If the stimulus is rotated, like a spinning windmill, the corresponding photoreceptors will detect a series of off-and-on transitions related to the speed at which the stimulus is rotated. Enoch and associates found that the best results were obtained when their targets were rotated at a speed that gave six to eight off/ on transitions per second.

By measuring the detection threshold of a nonspinning weathervane pattern, this technique attempts to quantify the visual system's "sustained-like" function. By measuring the detection threshold of the spinning weathervane pattern, this technique attempts to measure the visual system's "transient-like" function. In a series of sophisticated experiments Enoch concluded:

> It is apparent that disease processes or anomalies affecting either the inner or outer plexiform layers will alter the sustained-like function and that the transient-like function seems to be altered only in anomalies of the inner plexiform layer.

The complex and controversial nature of these methods has relegated them mainly to the realm of the laboratory or clinical research center. It is beyond us to predict whether these methods will ever find routine clinical use. Of course, similar statements could have been made about computerized perimeters a generation ago or about the Goldmann perimeter a generation before that.

5 ANATOMY OF THE VISUAL PATHWAY

The neuroanatomy and physiology of the visual system are the subject of sophisticated, active research. Although a working knowledge of pertinent anatomy and histology is essential to understanding defects in the visual fields, an exhaustive anatomic description of the visual system is not appropriate here. Instead, we present a clinically oriented overview.

The bibliography devoted to the anatomy of the visual pathway is extensive. Historically, the outstanding names include those of Brouwer, Zeeman, Polyak, Putnam, Holmes, Clark, Hoyt, Hubel, and Weisel. More recently Minckler, Rhoton, and others have contributed greatly. Some of these authors' works are summarized in the second volume of *System of Ophthalmology,* by Duke-Elder and in Walsh and Hoyt's *Clinical Neuro-Ophthalmology,* fourth edition, by Miller. Much of our knowledge of the visual pathway, from the ganglion cell layer of the retina to the lateral geniculate body, derives from the degeneration studies of Brouwer and Zeeman and, more recently, Hoyt. These authors produced minute retinal lesions and then studied degeneration in the retinal nerve fiber layer, the optic nerve, the chiasmal decussation, the optic tract, and the lateral geniculate body. In the early 1930s Polyak reported similar experiments in which he injured minute portions of the area striata of the occipital lobe of monkeys and traced the resulting degeneration in the nerve fibers of the optic radiations. His lifetime work was published posthumously in 1957. Numerous studies have been made of the visual system of both humans and animals, and we now have a fairly complete picture of the visual pathway from the retinal photoreceptors to the calcarine fissure of the occipital lobe.

In primitive animals nervous activity was expressed in simple and immediate reflexes so that afferent sensory impulses were simply transformed into ready responses. With the vertebrates the sense of smell began to govern behavior, and the cerebrum became largely an olfactory center. A salient factor in the evolution of humans was the replacement of smell by vision as the dominant sense. These changes depended on (1) the development of a macula, which made exact vision possible; (2) the decussation of fibers in the chiasm, which allowed physiologically corresponding areas in the two retinas to be associated for the purposes of binocular vision and stereopsis; and (3) improved control of eye movements, making possible conjugate movements and convergence, which allowed humans to bring two images precisely upon corresponding retinal points.

The visual pathway is a sensory tract and corresponds to the general type of afferent tract that carries impulses to the brain (Figure 5-1). The first-order neuron is the photoreceptor (rod or cone).* The photoreceptors synapse with the bipolar cells, the second-order neuron. These neurons synapse with the

---

*Neurobiologists often refer to the ganglion cell and its axon as the first neuron and the fiber of the optic radiation as the second neuron. We chose to refer to the photoreceptor as the first neuron, the bipolar cell as the second neuron, the ganglion cell and its axon as the third neuron, and the optic radiation as the fourth neuron, because this latter nomenclature is used more prominently within the ophthalmic literature.

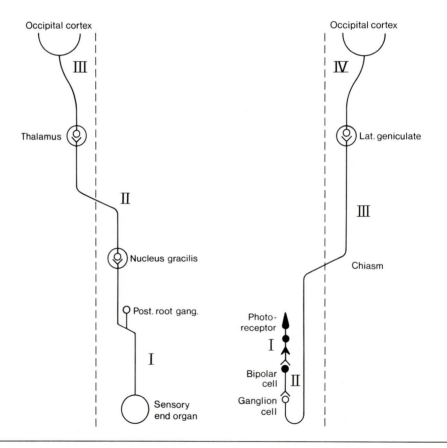

FIGURE 5-1   Comparison of neurons of visual pathway with those of somesthetic sensory tract. *(After Duke-Elder.)*

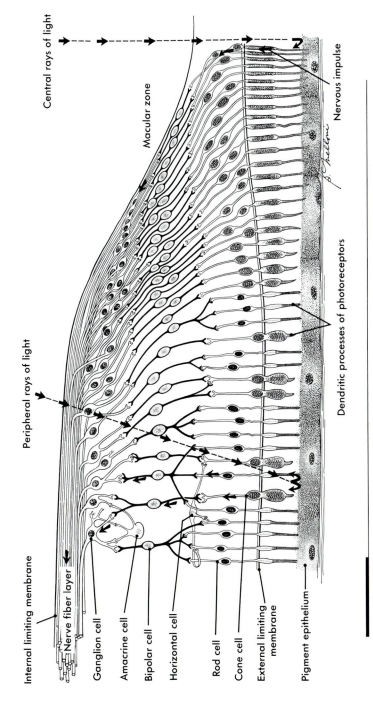

FIGURE 5-2   Microscopic anatomy of retina. *(From Melloni BJ: What's new, Abbott Laboratories, Abbott Park, Ill.)*

third-order neuron, the ganglion cell. Axons from the ganglion cells cross the surface of the retina as the nerve fiber layer and pass through the sclera as the optic nerve (Figure 5-2). The pattern of the retinal nerve fiber layer is consistent and characteristic (Figure 5-3). It has five major parts: (1) the papillomacular bundle, divided into a superior and inferior portion, within which are concentrated approximately 65% of the retinal nerve fibers; (2) the superior arcuate fibers, which arch around the papillomacular bundle from the horizontal raphe to the optic nerve; (3) the inferior arcuate bundle, which arches around the papillomacular bundle from the horizontal raphe into the optic nerve; (4) the superior radiating bundle, which passes through the superior portion of the retina into the optic nerve; and (5) the inferior radiating bundle, which enters the optic nerve from the inferior nasal quadrant of the retina.

This specific and consistent arrangement of the retinal nerve fiber layer forms the basis of analysis of visual field defects resulting from retinal or optic nervehead lesions. Nerve fiber layer analysis sees its greatest practical use in

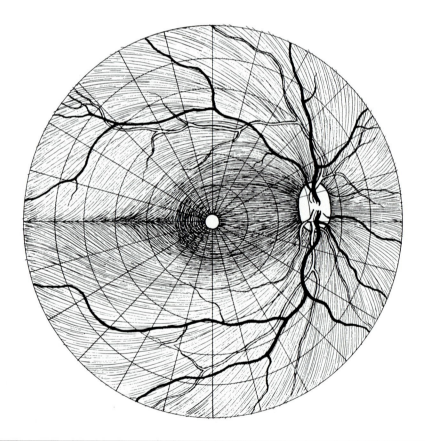

FIGURE 5-3   Nerve fiber pattern of retina in its relationship to retinal vascular tree.

the correlation between visual field defects, optic nervehead morphology, and retinal nerve fiber layer photography in glaucoma patients.

Entering the optic nerve, the fibers from the retinal periphery lie in the deeper external part of the nerve fiber layer and enter the periphery of the nerve. Those fibers from the peripapillary area lie in the internal layer of the nerve fiber layer (nearest the vitreous) and enter the central portion of the nerve.

Hoyt and Tudor showed that retinal nerve fiber layer axons arising in the papillomacular area between the fovea and the optic disc pass directly into the optic nerve on its temporal side adjacent to the central vessels. In the intraorbital optic nerve, the fibers are at first grouped in essentially the same pattern as in the optic disc, with the macular bundle occupying a sector-shaped area in the temporal portion of the nerve. As the chiasm is approached, the macular fibers move centrally into the nerve and lose their bundle arrangement to become more widely and diffusely dispersed within the nerve.

The chiasm is formed by the junction and partial decussation of the optic nerves. The superior temporal fibers from the peripheral retina maintain their position in the upper outer quadrant of the optic nerve and become the superior uncrossed visual fibers of the chiasm. In similar fashion the inferior temporal uncrossed fibers maintain their lower outer quadrant position within the nerve. There is no rotation of these fiber bundles within the optic nerve, and they enter the anterior portion of the chiasm in the same relative positions as they held within the optic nerve.

Traditional teaching has indicated that a retinotopic organization is maintained throughout the visual system. More recent work, such as that by Horton, Greenwood, and Hubel has shown that nerve fibers emanating from adjacent retinal cells become widely scattered in the optic nerve. This indicates that retinotopic order is not uniformly present throughout the visual system.

Midway through the chiasm, the upper uncrossed quadrant fiber bundle begins to extend more medially, whereas the lower quadrant bundle occupies the entire inferior lateral portion of the chiasm.

As these uncrossed fiber bundles pass from the chiasm into the optic tract, the inferior quadrant bundle shifts laterally to occupy the inferior lateral portion of the tract, whereas the superior quadrant fibers move from their dorsal portion to a medial location in the tract (Figure 5-4, *A*).

The crossed fiber bundles from the nasal retina, destined to decussate in the chiasm, also follow a characteristic and constant pattern. Inferior quadrant fibers maintain this position throughout the nerve and into the chiasm, and rotation does not occur. Superior fibers remain superior to the midportion of the chiasm.

At the chiasm the inferior quadrant fibers cros immediately in the lower anterior chiasm. Some fibers loop across and into the contralateral nerve at its junction with the chiasm. As the fibers approach the optic tract and the posterior chiasm, the crossed lower quadrant fiber bundle moves laterally and enters the side of the optic tracts.

Upper nasal quadrant fiber bundles cross in the dorsal and posterior chiasm and enter the medial and inferior half of the contralateral optic tract (Figure 5-4, *B*). The fibers representing the temporal crescent of the visual field (i.e., the peripheral nasal retinal fibers) occupy both dorsal and ventral areas in the chiasm.

As mentioned previously, macular fibers are scattered diffusely in the optic nerve, chiasm, and optic tract, mixing freely with peripheral quadrant bundles except for a short segment of the anterior optic nerve, where they form a small and compact bundle. Compared with the extramacular axons, macular fibers are of small caliber. They occupy a large portion of the optic nerve and chiasm and about two thirds of the optic tracts.

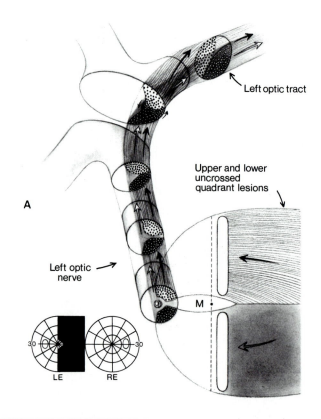

FIGURE 5-4   **A,** Fiber projection from uncrossed retinal quadrants in monkey. Retina is represented below on right. Vertical white bars are photocoagulator lesions. Macula, *M,* has not been destroyed. No rotation of quadrants occurs until optic tract is reached. Corresponding hypothetical visual defects are represented in lower left diagram. *(Courtesy WF Hoyt, MD and O Luis, San Francisco, Calif.)*

As retinal axons pass from one optic nerve through the chiasm to the ipsilateral and contralateral optic tracts, two types of fiber segregation occur. The first type is segregation into crossed and uncrossed retinal axons. The second type is rearrangement in the chiasm of retinal axons according to fiber size. Small-caliber fibers, primarily from the macular region, generally rise from the central part of the optic nerve to the superior areas of the chiasm and optic tracts; larger caliber fibers, from peripheral retinal areas, descend during passage through the chiasm into the inferior portions of the optic tracts.

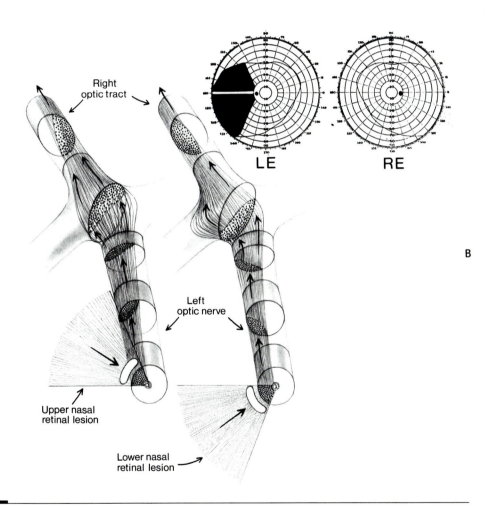

FIGURE 5-4, cont'd. B, Visual fiber projections from upper and lower crossed retinal quadrants of monkey. Hypotheticl visual field defects caused by photocoagulation lesion are shown in upper right corner.

The anterior and posterior-inferior chiasm are the two areas that contain no macular fibers. All other portions of the chiasm contain large numbers of small-caliber axons.

On gross examination the optic chiasm is a transversely oval body averaging approximately 14 × 8 × 4 mm in size. It lies covered by the pia mater in the cisterna basalis of the subarachnoid space, resting behind the tuberculum sellae and the chiasmatic sulcus. It varies somewhat in its relation to the posterior part of the pituitary body; it may lie behind the dorsum sellae or, rarely, far forward in the chiasmatic sulcus. In approximately 80% of cases, the center of the chiasm lies over the posterior two thirds of the sellae. Only 12% of chiasms lie directly over the center of the sellae. Four percent are prefixed with very short optic nerves, and 4% are postfixed, with very long optic nerves and the center of the chiasm lying behind the sellae.

The relationships of the optic chiasm are as follows (Figure 5-5). Above it lies the cavity of the third ventricle. On each side and in close contact is the internal carotid artery just before it divides into the anterior and middle cerebral arteries. In front and in very close relationship are the two anterior cerebral arteries joined by the anterior communicating artery. Posteriorly lies the interpeduncular area with the tuber cinereum and infundibulum. Below the chiasm the pituitary body lies in the fossa of the sella turcica in the sphenoid bone, covered by the diaphragma sellae. Occasionally a sphenoidal sinus may undermine the entire chiasm. Between the chiasm and the diaphragma sellae is the chiasmatic cistern.

The optic tracts begin in the posterior lateral angle of the chiasm and run laterally and backward. Each tract consists of (1) uncrossed temporal fibers from the same side, (2) crossed nasal fibers from the opposite side, (3)

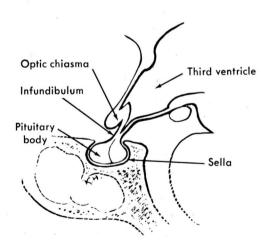

FIGURE 5-5   Sagittal section through chiasm showing its relationship to third ventricle, pituitary body, pituitary stalk, sella turcica, and sphenoidal sinus.

uncrossed macular fibers from the same side, (4) crossed macular fibers from the opposite side, and (5) diffusely scattered macular fibers. As a whole, the tract resembles a rounded band running between the tuber cinereum and the anterior perforated substance and continuing posteriorly as a flattened band of fibers to sweep around the cerebral penduncles in close association with the posterior cerebral artery.

The lateral geniculate body (LGB) is a small oval body appearing on the posterior lateral part of the thalamus. It receives 80% of the fibers from the optic tract. The geniculostriate (visual) fibers terminate in the LGB, whereas the extrageniculostriate fibers pass over or through it to the surface of the pulvinar and then to the superior colliculus. The LGB is the end station for the retinal ganglion cell fibers of the optic tract. It consists of six laminae. Crossed retinal projections terminate in laminae 1, 4, and 6, whereas uncrossed fibers terminate in laminae 2, 3, and 5. Corresponding points in both retinas are represented in the lateral geniculate body in columns of cells from all six laminae. Damage to several laminae will thus give rise to asymmetric defects in the corresponding homonymous visual fields (Figure 5-6).

Retinal ganglion cell fibers terminate at the level of the lateral geniculate and synapse on cells that project to the cortex. Damage to retinal ganglion cell axons at the level of the optic nerve, chiasm, or tract will lead to axon degeneration and a resultant optic atrophy. Damage to the geniculate fibers radiating to the cortex will likewise lead to atrophy of that neuron. In a developed human visual system, however, transsynaptic degeneration is not

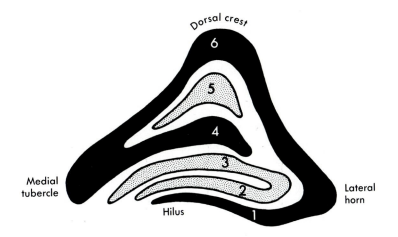

FIGURE 5-6   Schematic representation of laminae in right lateral geniculate body. Crossed retinal projections terminate in laminae 1, 4, and 6. Uncrossed projections terminate in laminae 2, 3, and 5. Selective partial involvement of one or more of these laminae will produce asymmetric homonymous visual field defects, depending on extent of laminar damage.

seen. Thus a homonymous hemianoptic field defect unaccompanied by optic atrophy (after several weeks) would indicate damage to the visual pathway posterior to the LGB.

Hoyt has pointed out that the generalization that upper retinal fibers remain above and lower retinal fibers remain below does not hold for the lateral geniculate body. During the evolution of the mammalian visual pathway, the geniculate body rotated through an angle of approximately 90 degrees. As a result, the upper or dorsal retinal fibers were displaced laterally. This rotation in the arrangement of the visual fibers of the retinal straightens out in the optic radiations. Thus, with the exception of the lateral geniculate body itself, upper retinal fibers remain upper, and lower retinal fibers remain lower throughout the visual pathway.

After leaving the lateral geniculate, the visual fibers travel to the visual (striate) cortex. They run in a broad and widely dispersed band referred to as the optic (geniculocalcarine or geniculocortical) radiation (Figure 5-7). The dorsal fibers of the radiation pass backward in a fairly direct route from the LGB to the visual cortex. The ventral fibers initially travel forward and somewhat downward. They then loop backward around the inferior horn of the lateral ventricle (Meyer's loop) and continue on to the visual cortex. The visual fibers, no longer in a compact band as in the most anterior parts of the pathway, are vulnerable to a wide variety of insults.

The relationship of the afferent visual pathway to the cortex is quite definite, with a well-defined retinotopic organization of the striate cortex (Figures 5-8 and 5-9). Anatomic facts, physiologic experiments, and clinical observations lead to the conclusion that the macula is represented in the posterior portion of the striate cortex. Dobelle and associates have stimulated the human visual cortex and mapped the visual field position of the resulting punctate light sensations, which are called *phosphenes*. Analysis of the phosphene map indicates that successive stimulation of points further from the tip of the occipital pole produces phosphenes progressively more distant from the point of fixation. These results confirm the general view of cortical organization derived from the field defect studies in humans and from anatomic and electrophysiologic studies in monkeys.

The macular segment of the lateral geniculate body, as found by Frönee and by Brouwer and Zeeman, represents a large portion of that nucleus. As with the retinal macular fibers in the optic nerve, the geniculate fibers that subserve macular function constitute a significant portion of the geniculocalcarine radiation. A correspondingly large region of the striate cortex is devoted to macular function.

Historically, anatomic, physiologic, and clinical evidence of macular representation in the cortex was somewhat conflicting. The weight of current evidence supports bilateral representation. The evidence for bilateral representation includes quantitative visual field studies on patients who have had

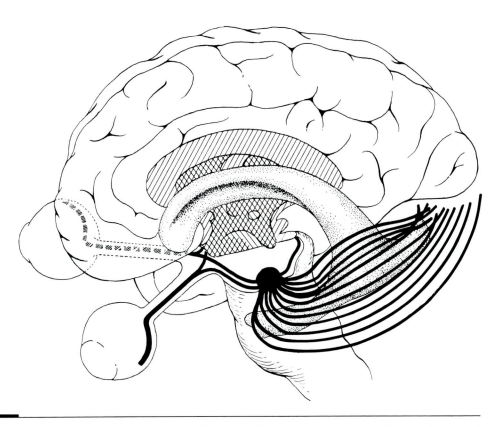

FIGURE 5-7 Schematic representation of visual pathway from retina to calcarine fissure of occipital lobe. Cutaway view from gross dissections shows distribution of visual fibers in optic radiation.

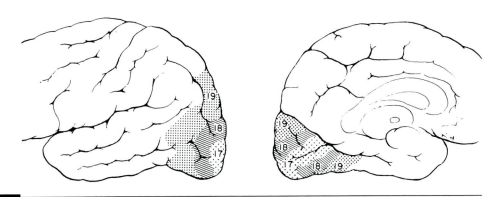

FIGURE 5-8 Visual area or striate cortex in occipital lobe. Lateral and mesial views show Brodmann's area *17* (striate area), *18* (parastriate area), and *19* (peristriate area). Area *17* is sharply delineated cortical termination of visual pathway.

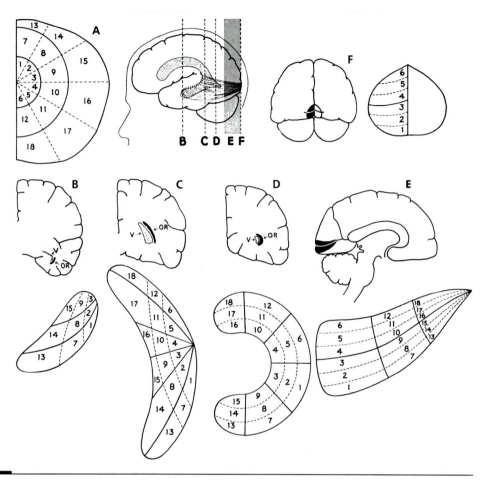

FIGURE 5-9   Schematic representation of architecture of geniculocalcarine pathway with projection of striate cortex and nerve fiber bundles of optic radiation onto visual field. **A,** Right homonymous half-field divided into sectors and concentric zones representing projection of various bundlles of optic radiation in temporal and parietal lobe and striate cortex calcarine fissure of occipital lobe. **B** to **D,** Coronal sections, seen from in front, through temporal, parietal, and parietooccipital lobes of left cerebral hemisphere, showing planes of section, relationship of optic radiation to lateral ventricle, and division of visual fiber bundles within radiation into sectors and concentric zones corresponding to their projection onto visual field. Note in plane of section through temporal loop of Meyer **(B)** only lower half of radiation is represented and in planes **B** and **C,** which section anterior radiation, macular fibers *(1* to *6)* are laminated on lateral surface of radiation (as postulated by Spalding, 1952); in plane **D,** which sections posterior part of radiation, macular fibers are interposed between and completely separate upper and lower peripheral fibers (as postulated by Polyak, 1957). **E,** Medial view of left cerebral hemisphere showing striate cortex of calcarine fissure divided according to its projection on right homonymous half-field. **F,** View from behind striate cortex at posterior tip of left occipital pole, showing projection of macular portion of right homonymous half-field.

surgical resections of one occipital lobe and anatomic (such as the horseradish peroxidase studies of Minckler and associates) and physiologic studies on animals. Furthermore, it appears that either direct connections or callosal intrahemispheric connections account for at least part of macular cortical function.

Implicit in the foregoing discussion of anatomy is the understanding that large portions of the visual pathway are in intimate relationship with various other parts of the central nervous system. With rare exceptions, patients with pathologic lesions affecting the visual pathway will not only have visual complaints but other neurologic disturbances as well. The combination of symptoms and signs from these other areas of the nervous system, along with visual disturbances, is extremely important in localizing lesions within the central nervous system. Thus the perimetrist should be familiar with general neuroanatomy, as well as with specific neuroanatomy of the visual pathway. This knowledge forms the basis of one's ability to interpret visual field defects effectively.

6 VASCULAR SUPPLY OF THE VISUAL PATHWAY

Circulatory disturbances may affect the visual pathway either directly or indirectly. For example, depending on its size and location, a hemorrhage or ischemic infarct in the occipital lobe may produce total homonymous hemianopsia or a tiny hemianoptic scotoma. A tumor in the same area may produce extensive visual field loss by a combination of direct pressure on the nerve fiber bundles and interference with the local blood supply. A major cause of visual field defects found in patients with a brain tumor is vascular interruption rather than direct pressure by the tumor itself (Figure 6-1).

The blood supply (Figure 6-1) may be compromised in several ways. The vessels may be destroyed or damaged by trauma; the vessels may actually compress the visual fibers, as in aneurysms of the circle of Willis; or pressure on normal or arteriosclerotic arteries by visual fibers that have been displaced against the vessels by a remote tumor may impede the blood flow to the visual pathway. Atherosclerotic or stenotic arterial insufficiency may impair the blood flow to visual centers. In general, one can localize vascular lesions accurately by the typical (normal) vascular supply visual defects they produce.

TYPICAL (NORMAL) VASCULAR SUPPLY

The retinal vascular supply has two parts: (1) the choroidal circulation from the ciliary arteries, which supplies the pigment epithelium rods and cones and outer nuclear layers; and (2) the central retinal artery, which supplies the remainder of the inner retina.

The foveal area, peripheral retina, and optic nervehead have a rich network of anastomoses, and there is some anastomosis between the small branches of the central retinal artery and the choroidal circulation near the optic disc.

The four main branches of the central retinal artery follow the general pattern of the retinal nerve fiber layer, with superior and inferior temporal branches arching around the fovea and ending at the horizontal vascular raphe. Anatomic and clinical evidence suggests that the vascular demarcation of the raphe is more exact than in the nerve fiber bundles. The arteries lie in the nerve fiber and ganglion cell layer of the retina (Figure 6-2).

Henkind and Levitsky studied the angioarchitecture of the papilla and the lamina cribrosa. They concluded that the defined network of polygonally arranged vessels in the papilla is largely supplied from the choroid, with possible occasional retinal capillary connections. The lamina cribrosa has a rich capillary network supplied largely by branches of the circle of Zinn-Haller and the choroidal arterioles.

These anatomic studies are further supported by Hayreh's fluorescein angiographic studies of normal and atrophic optic nerveheads. When optic nerve atrophy is secondary to retinal lesions, the choroidal vessels in the disc fill normally, although the disc fluorescence is less than normal. In other forms of optic nerve atrophy, disc fluorescence is generally reduced.

By means of simultaneous artificial elevation of intraocular pressure and fluorescein angiography in normal human eyes, Blumenthal and his co-work-

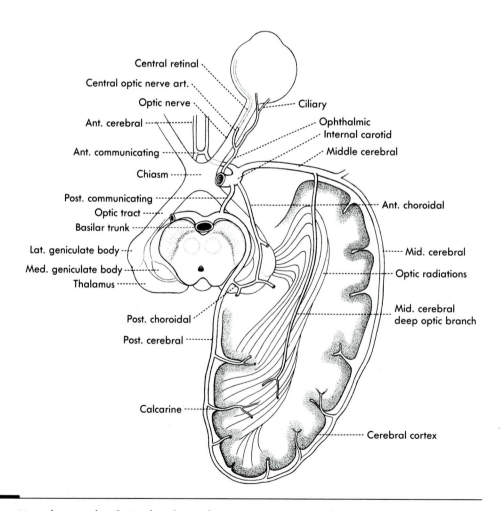

FIGURE 6-1   Vascular supply of visual pathway from retina to occipital cortex.

ers have described controlled studies of intraocular pressure effects on the intraocular vascular bed. They have demonstrated that although the retinal and choroidal vascular systems are both derived from the ophthalmic artery, these systems react quite differently to increased intraocular pressure. Blood flow ceases in the choroidal circulation at intraocular pressures significantly lower than those required to stop flow in the retinal vascular tree.

The ophthalmic artery supplies the optic nerve sheath with a fine and rich network of vessels that anastomose with each other and with the branches of the lacrimal, middle meningeal, and short posterior ciliary arteries in the posterior orbit. These branches from the sheath enter the nerve and supply its superior and lateral periphery.

The pathways of the ophthalmic artery in the orbit and optic nerve vary considerably. Similarly, the origin and course of the posterior ciliary arteries are quite variable. The central retinal artery originates from the ophthalmic artery in only about half the cases. In other cases it comes from a trunk common with the ciliary arteries and penetrates the inferior aspect of the nerve. The surface of the nerve is vascularized by pial branches, and the depth of the nerve is vascularized by intraneural branches. Vascularization of the center of the optic nerve is assured by collateral branches from the trunk of the central retinal artery in most cases. An individual and separate central retinal artery of the optic nerve is rare.

The central retinal artery commonly has a major role in the blood supply of the anterior part of the optic nerve. It contributes to both the peripheral

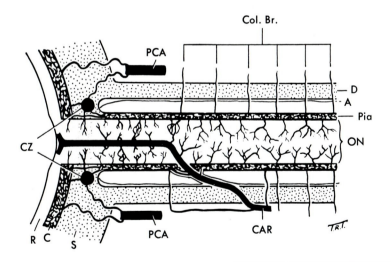

FIGURE 6-2   Arterial supply of optic nerve according to Hayreh. Central retinal artery gives off branches in dural sheath. There is no central artery of optic nerve. *A,* Arachnoid; *C,* choroid; *CAR,* central artery of retina; *Col. Br.,* collateral branch; *CZ,* circle of Zinn-Haller; *D,* dura; *ON,* optic nerve; *PCA,* posterior ciliary artery; *R,* retina; *S,* sclera. *(From Hayreh SS: Br J Ophthalmol 47:651, 1963.)*

and axial systems. Anastomoses are usually established by the pial branches of the central retinal artery with the recurrent pial branches of the circle of Zinn-Haller and choroidal arteries, and with the pial collateral branches from the ophthalmic artery and other orbital arteries. The main branch of the central retinal artery passes to the center of the nerve and runs forward into the optic papilla and onto the retinal surface.

The rather sharp division of the optic nerve blood supply into three areas—superior peripheral, inferior peripheral, and central—helps to explain some of the visual field defects that are so characteristic of optic nerve lesions (e.g., altitudinal field loss). Nerve fiber bundle defects seen in patients with arteriosclerotic optic atrophy, which closely simulates nerve fiber bundle defects seen in glaucoma, are also explainable on the basis of the blood supply.

The chiasm is supplied by a complicated network of anastomotic arterioles. Functional defects therefore cannot be attributed to occlusion of a single artery, but only by a more widespread by intratissue capillary disturbance caused by either degeneration or external compression. Dawson studied the chiasmal circulation thoroughly. Cursory inspection of the vascular networks on the optic chiasm suggests no constant pattern, but more detailed examination shows a well-defined arrangement. Two sets of arterial and anastomotic systems, prechiasmal and circuminfundibular, are defined in the chiasmal region.

In a comprehensive series of autopsy observations on the arterial blood supply of the extracerebral portions of the visual pathway, Bergland and Ray studied the chiasmal circulation in detail. They point out that the optic nerve, chiasm, and optic tracts pass through the circle of Willis (Figure 6-3), coursing below the anterior cerebral and anterior communicating artery and above the posterior cerebral and communicating arteries and the basilar artery. This oblique course from the chiasm through the circle of Willis permits a natural division of its blood supply into a plentiful inferior vascular group from the choroid and posterior vessels of the circle, and a sparse, superior group from the anterior portion of the circle.

The optic tract and lateral geniculate body are supplied by a series of vessels into these structures at various levels in their backward course. In the anterior portion the tract derives its blood supply from the same arteries that supply the posterior chiasm, namely, the internal carotid, the middle cerebral, and the posterior communicating arteries.

The posterior two thirds of the optic tract are supplied by the anterior choroidal artery. This artery arises from the internal carotid and runs backward closely associated with the tract. It gives off branches to the temporal lobe and the lateral ventricle, as well as to the tract, the lateral geniculate, and the beginning of the optic radiations.

The lateral geniculate body also receives branches from the posterior choroidal artery and the posterior cerebral artery.

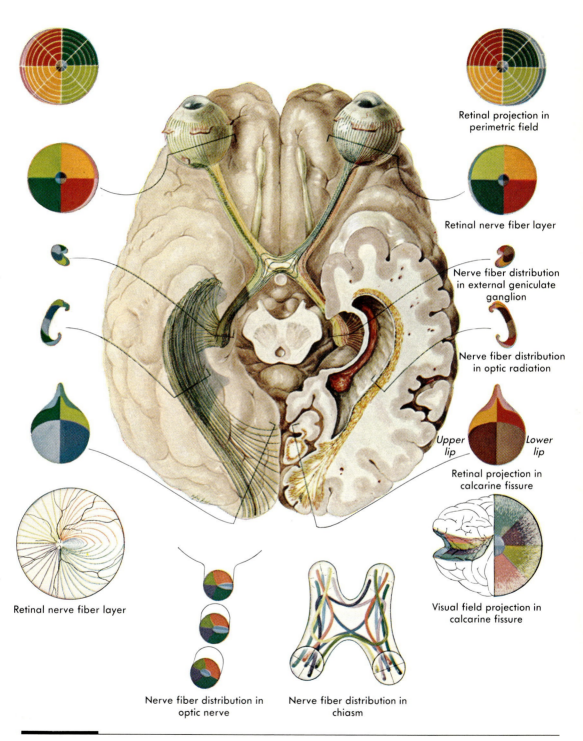

Retinal projection in
perimetric field

Retinal nerve fiber layer

Nerve fiber distribution
in external geniculate
ganglion

Nerve fiber distribution
in optic radiation

*Upper
lip*   *Lower
lip*

Retinal projection in
calcarine fissure

Visual field projection in
calcarine fissure

Retinal nerve fiber layer

Nerve fiber distribution in
optic nerve

Nerve fiber distribution in
chiasm

PLATE 1   Anatomy of visual pathway.

The optic radiations are supplied by the following arteries:
1. The anterior choroidal artery supplies the anterior portion, chiefly the optic peduncle after having passed through or under the optic tract and lateral geniculate body.
2. The posterior choroidal arteries give a fine network of branches to the optic peduncle.
3. The middle cerebral artery through its deep optic branch supplies the anterior and middle portion of the radiation where it lies lateral to the ventricle.
4. The posterior cerebral artery, through its perforating branches, supplies the posterior portion of the optic radiation before it enters the area of the calcarine cortex.
5. The calcarine artery, arising from the posterior cerebral artery, supplies the posterior portion of the radiation as it passes back of the lateral ventricle and enters the occipital lobe.

Smith and Richardson traced the course and origin of the arteries supplying the visual cortex of one hemisphere of 32 human brains. They found that the calcarine artery usually supplied most of the visual area but in three fourths of the specimens it was not the only vessel supplying this area, nor was its distribution restricted to this area. Branches of the posterior temporal artery helped to supply the visual cortex in half the specimens. These branches always supply a part of the macular area of the cortex and may be a factor in the preservation of central vision when the calcarine artery is occluded.

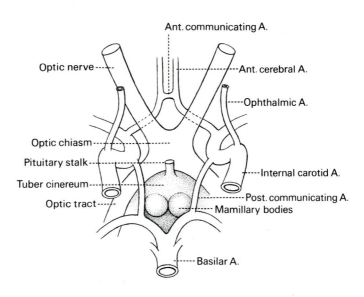

FIGURE 6-3   Relationships of chiasm to basilar arterial system of brain, pituitary body and pituitary stalk, tuber cinereum, and mamillary body, as seen from below.

In some specimens there was additional supply to the visual area from the parietooccipital artery and also a direct contribution from the middle cerebral artery. This overlapping of vascular supply with the calcarine branches of the posterior cerebral artery, posterior cortical optic branch of the middle cerebral artery, and the branches of the posterior temporal artery, all of which may supply a part of the macular area of the occipital cortex, is a reasonable explanation for the phenomenon of macular sparing in some visual field defects resulting from severe damage to the visual cortex.

VISUAL FIELD DEFECTS FROM VASCULAR LESIONS

Vascular lesions of the visual pathway that produce visual field defects are common, destructive, and have certain characteristics that differentiate them from other diseases affecting the visual pathway. They may affect any portion of the pathway from the retina to the occipital cortex. Sudden onset is the rule, although they may be preceded by a telltale constellation of symptoms. The resulting visual defects are usually dense, steep margined, and permanent.

Vascular lesions are categorized as follows:
1. Those which produce pressure on nerve fiber bundles of the visual pathway, such as an aneurysm or subdural hematoma
2. Those which destroy the nerve fiber bundles by hemorrhaging into them, such as retinal vascular lesions and intracerebral hemorrhage
3. Those which give rise to nerve fiber bundle infarction by arterial insufficiency and occlusion, such as retinal artery occlusion; general carotid and ophthalmic artery stenosis and occlusion; and middle and posterior cerebral artery occlusion with secondary cerebral infarction
4. Inflammatory lesions, such as giant cell or temporal arteritis

Such vascular lesions can be further subdivided according to their location within an individual pathway and will be considered separately under appropriate anatomic headings.

Aneurysms that directly compress nerve fiber bundles are most commonly located in the vessels of the circle of Willis and consequently involve the intracranial portion of the optic nerve, the chiasm, and the anterior optic tract. Aneurysms give rise to the unilateral scotomas, asymmetric bitemporal visual field defects, unilateral nasal or binasal field loss, and high incongruous homonymous hemianopsia.

Subdural hematoma may compress the visual pathway directly or may compress and obstruct the posterior cerebral artery by causing the hippocampal gyrus to herniate through the tentorial opening.

With indirect compression of the anterior visual pathway, the resulting contralateral homonymous hemianopsia is likely to have a sloping margin and to be incongruous. When posterior cerebral artery compression from temporal lobe herniation results in visual cortex infarction, the field loss is congruous, dense, and steep margined and is likely to be associated with ipsilateral third-nerve palsy of varying degree.

Hemorrhage into the nerve fiber bundles of the visual pathway may occur at any level. Retinal hemorrhages, either venous or arterial, produce visual loss and scotomas, depending on their size and location. Hemorrhage within the optic nerve, chiasm, and optic tract is rare. The classic example of extensive visual field loss resulting from hemorrhage is that occurring from the lenticular striate artery involving the posterior limb of the internal capsule, with contralateral homonymous hemianopsia and hemiplegia.

Intracerebral hemorrhage may occur from small arterioles in the temporal, parietal, and occipital lobes, giving rise to the characteristic homonymous hemianoptic field loss, depending on the site of the lesion. The field defects are sudden and usually quite dense. When the hemorrhage occurs in the temporal lobe, the resulting homonymous hemianopsia, if incomplete, is incongruous, whereas a very small hemorrhagic lesion of the calcarine cortex will produce exquisitely symmetric homonymous hemianoptic scotomas.

Arterial insufficiency and occlusion give rise to a wide variety of visual field defects that may be valuable in diagnosing and localizing the responsible lesion. Such occlusions are often preceded by periods of relative insufficiency and stenosis in the offending artery and its smaller branches. Attacks of arterial insufficiency give rise to transient visual loss, which may be monocular or homonymous and hemianoptic and are frequently associated with transient neurologic deficits.

These transient disturbances are often the result of small emboli passing through the cerebral and ocular circulation. Emboli arise from atherosclerotic plaques in the carotid, vertebral, and basilar arteries and have been photographed in the cerebral and retinal circulation. Two types of cerebral and ocular emboli have been implicated: fibrin platelet microemboli and lipid debris emboli.

A fibrin platelet microembolus that forms on an atherosclerotic plaque in the carotid artery may reach the small vessels of the brain and retina. These emboli are susceptible to lysis by plasma and therefore do not produce permanent visual loss.

A lipid debris microembolus discharged from an atherosclerotic plaque may lodge in a retinal or cerebral arteriole, producing infarction and permanent functional loss. These emboli are not lysed by fibrin and do not respond to anticoagulant therapy.

Emboli produce transient or permanent field defects that are characteristic of the site of the infarct as follows:

1. Occlusion of the ophthalmic artery or its branches, the central artery of the optic nerve, and the central retinal artery causes sudden, permanent, and marked monocular visual loss.

   a. If the embolus lodges in the anterior optic nerve near the lamina cribrosa, it often produces a nerve fiber bundle scotoma indistinguishable from an advanced open-angle glaucomatous field loss.
   b. When the central retinal artery is occluded, total visual loss usually results in that eye; but if the embolus obstructs only a retinal arteriole, the result is a sector-type or quadrantic visual field defect corresponding to the retinal areas supplied by the vessel in question.

2. Stenosis or occlusion of the middle cerebral artery may result from extension of the atherosclerotic process from the internal carotid artery or from emboli. These lesions produce cerebral infarction and typically cause contralateral homonymous hemianopsia, which is usually quadrantic and may be incongruous. If the ophthalmic artery is involved simultaneously, there may be a homolateral nerve fiber bundle or a Bjerrum scotoma combined with a contralateral homonymous hemianopsia.

3. Vertebral and basilar arterial disease frequently give rise to posterior cerebral and calcarine artery involvement with resulting visual cortex infarction and contralateral homonymous hemianoptic field defects of sudden onset. These defects may be total on one side, or they may take the form of a small central or peripheral homonymous hemianoptic scotoma, depending on the size of the occluded vessel and the area of cortex it supplied. These defects are congruous and invariably exquisitely symmetric in the two eyes.

4. Occipital cortical infarction is an uncommon complication of cardiopulmonary bypass surgery. It manifests itself by a postoperative complaint of defective vision varying from mild, transient blurring to total blindness. More frequently one finds deep, steep-walled, congruous homonymous hemianoptic defects, typical of occipital cortex involvement.

Transient or permanent neurologic defects are often found along with the visual disturbances just mentioned. The nature of these neurologic deficits depends on the artery involved. Noninvasive investigations (ophthalmodynamometry, blood pressure measurement, Doppler imaging, etc.) should be used when appropriate. Sophisticated neuroradiologic imaging, including computed tomography and magnetic resonance imaging are frequently diagnostic. Arteriography is the ultimate test, usually reserved for cases in which other tests are inconclusively negative or insufficient. Although arteriography has risks and limitations, it is invaluable in many circumstances. A close working relationship with the neuroradiology service is helpful in assuring that the right tests are performed and that the interpretation is appropriate.

Vascular lesions are among the most frequent producers of visual field defects. Several examples of visual field defects caused by vascular lesions appear in later chapters.

7 NORMAL VISUAL FIELD

If we refer once again to Traquair's concept of the island hill of vision (Plate 2), the visual field may be represented in three ways. Using kinetic perimetry, the outlines of the various contours of this hill may be projected on a map as contoured lines that, in the nomenclature of perimetry, are termed *isopters*. The central point from which these isopters are measured corresponds to the visual axis and is known as the *fixation point*. When charting the results of a tangent screen test, the isopters are designated by the size of the test stimulus and the distance at which it was viewed by the observer, expressed as a fraction. Thus the isopter for a 1-mm test object observed by the patient at a distance of 2 meters is expressed by the fraction 1/2000. The area within this contoured line designates the region of the visual field within which the patient was able to see the stimulus. When charting the results from a test performed on the Goldmann perimeter, the isopters are designated by the size and intensity of the test stimulus used. This is described in standard nomenclature by the designation of a Roman numeral, an Arabic numeral, and a lowercase letter (e.g., I4e), as explained in Chapter 2 (Figure 7-1). One need not designate distance in describing Goldmann isopters because the patient's head position is fixed at 33 cm from the perimeter bowl during examinations with this instrument.

In manual static profile perimetry, retinal threshold is determined along a visual field meridian. The graphic plot of these threshold values yields a profile section of sensitivity through the hill of vision (Figure 7-2). By this method of splitting the hill of vision and charting its profile, areas of decreased sensitivity are mapped as shallow to deep depressions, depending on the degree of visual field loss. Absolute scotomas, mapped with the largest and brightest available stimuli, are shown as deep pits extending down to the level of the sea of blindness (i.e., the normal blind spot).

The numerical threshold printout available from computerized perimeters depicts the island hill of vision as though viewed from above. The sensitivity values in decibels (dB) represent the height of the hill of vision at a given point. Most of the machines available currently operate over a dynamic

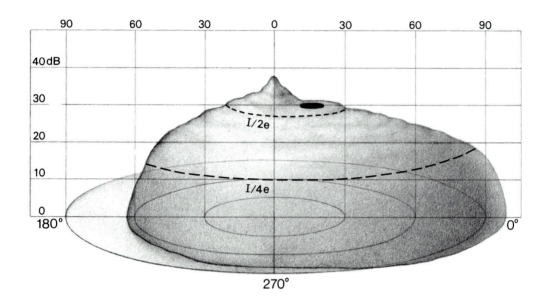

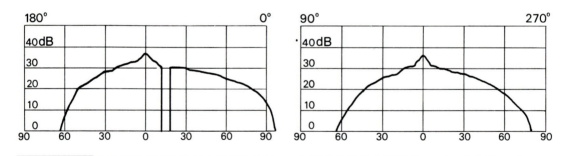

PLATE 2   Normal visual field. A schematic representation of "the island hill of vision." Peak sensitivity is between 30 and 40 dB and the temporal field is larger than the nasal field. The decline in sensitivity is abrupt from the fixation point to the paracentral area, and then rather gradual out to the midperiphery, where it once again becomes rapid. Scotomas would be represented as volume loss, analogous to a crevice or perhaps an eroded slope. The I/2e and I/4e isopters (from the Goldmann perimeter) are shown in their respective positions. In this model isopters represent a line surrounding the island demarcating seeing (within the borders of the line) from the nonseeing areas. The graphic representations below represent slices through the island hill taken at two meridians.

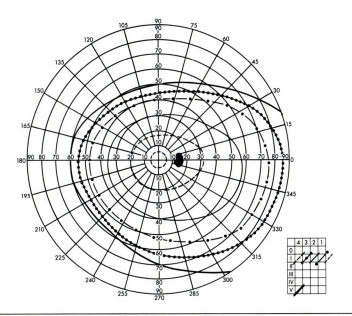

FIGURE 7-1   Normal isopters of young adults measured with Goldmann perimeter.

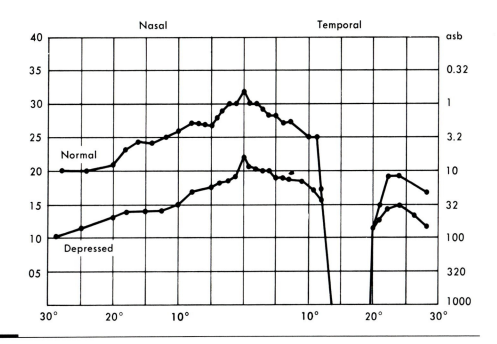

FIGURE 7-2   Static perimetry profile of normal and depressed visual field.

range of approximately 4 log units. On such a scale, measuring foveal sensitivity will generate a value that approaches 40 dB. Measuring an extremely deep or absolute scotoma will generate a value of 0 dB. Sensitivity 30 degrees from fixation generally averages approximately 25 dB.

For convenience, visual field charts are usually divided into four quadrants. A horizontal line passing through fixation divides the field into an upper and lower half, and these in turn are divided into quadrants by a vertical line also passing through fixation. In practice the upper and lower halves of the visual field are almost equal in size, but the nasal and temporal halves of the field are quite different because of the eccentric position of the fixation point; the temporal half is considerably larger than the nasal half (Fig. 7-1). The eccentricity of the field is largely due to the configuration of the orbit and limitation of the nasal field by the nose and brow.

The binocular field is made up of the overlapping uniocular fields. A central portion is common to both eyes with an average diameter of somewhat over 120 degrees. The so-called temporal crescent extends for approximately 30 degrees to each side of the paired portion of the binocular field. Occasionally, the clinical perimetrist is concerned with the temporal crescent in the interpretation of a homonymous hemianoptic defect, but for the most part it is the uniocular field that is important.

As mentioned previously, tangent screen visual fields are usually plotted with test objects of varying sizes at varying distances. Multiple isopters are examined with stimuli that have varying visual angles. By this means, the relative visual acuity within the visual field can be estimated quantitatively. Tangent screen isopters are designated by the fraction object over distance and numerically by 1/100, 2/2000, etc. This is readily converted to a visual angle in degrees or minutes by multiplying the fraction by the constant 180 divided by pi (which equals 57.3). For example, to convert the fraction 2/1000, multiply it by 57.3. The result is 0.114 degrees, or 6.84 minutes, the visual angle subtended by the 2-mm test object at a distance of 1 meter.

Many factors influence the overall size of the visual field and the precise sensitivity within areas of the field. The level of background illumination, patient age, target size, and other factors can have significant effects. Even the field of an individual normal patient can be different from one examination to the next if things like refractive error and pupil size are not held constant.

The normal blind spot, however, is reasonably constant in position and size. It is a vertical oval with steep edges. The center is located approximately 15 degrees temporal to fixation and about 1.5 degrees below the horizontal meridian. It averages 5.5 degrees wide and 7.5 degrees high. Surrounding the area of absolute blindness is a narrow zone of depressed sensitivity averaging about 1 degree in width. This zone has led to significant confusion among novice users of automated static perimeters. One commonly used grid pattern locates a test point at fixation and then each 6 degrees following the vertical and horizontal meridians. This system has test points at 0, ±6, ±12, and ±18 degrees horizontally. Since the blind spot is approximately 15 degrees from fixation and is just less than 6 degrees wide, in some patients it fits neatly between the ±12- and ±18-degree test point. One of two initially confusing results is obtained if this happens. In one scenario, the blind spot fits cleanly between the test points and there is little or no indication of a depression in this region (Figure 7-3). In the other scenario, the test points fall in the relative amblyopic zone that surrounds the blind spot. Under these circumstances, the value may be extremely depressed (down to 1 or 2 dB), nearly normal (25 to 26 dB), or anything in between (Figure 7-4). Obviously, all of these machines have programs that will allow one to place a test point squarely on the blind spot and thus generate a reassuring value of zero.

As has been mentioned, many factors enter into the determination of an individual's visual field. Because of this, a "normal" visual field does not

```
                                    Y
                                    21

                     22   23   23   23   23

                24   24   25   25   25   25   25

           23   25   26   27   27   26   26   25   25

           24   26   28   28   28   28   27   26   25

X    24    25   27   29   30   33   29   28   27   26   26   X

           25   27   28   29   29   29   28   27   26

           24   26   27   27   28   28   27   27   25

                24   25   27   27   27   27   26

                     24   25   26   26   26

                                    24

                                    Y
```

FIGURE 7-3   Numerical Octopus printout from left eye in which physiologic blind spot is straddled by test points at 12 and 18 degrees of eccentricity. Each test point on this printout is 6 degress from its horizontal or vertical neighbor.

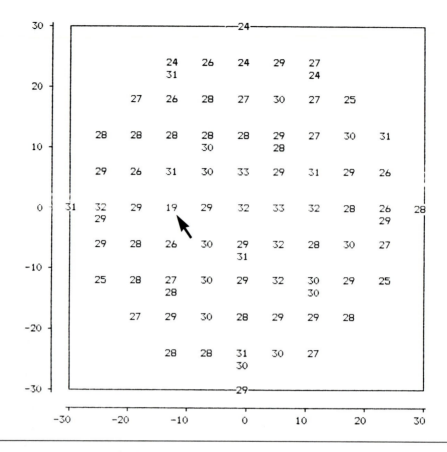

FIGURE 7-4   Octopus printout in which test point at 12 degrees left of fixation landed on outer edge of blind spot and generated single, moderately depressed value *(arrow)*.

represent an absolute value, but rather a range of responses distributed about a mean. In a given individual, the visual field varies according to age, the number of times a visual field has been examined previously, the state of health, the amount of fatigue at the moment of examination, pupil size, the amount of incident or stray light in the examining room, the ratio of background illumination to stimulus illumination, the subject's ability to concentrate during the examination, variations in response time, etc. In practice, these variables are extremely important and must be reckoned with, especially in serial examinations of a single individual's visual fields over time.

PHYSIOLOGIC FACTORS AFFECTING THE VISUAL FIELD EXAMINATION

Although we often stress that steady fixation is a requirement for reproducible perimetry, it should be remembered that if fixation were *completely* steady, all objects in the visual field would gradually disappear, those in the peripheral field more rapidly than those in the central field. Because complete fixation steadiness is impossible, there is a constant slight movement of the eye during a perimetric examination. Images in the peripheral retina move slightly with each of these fixation shifts, and therefore the question of retinal fatigue is of theoretic rather than practical importance.

The degree of dark or light adaptation of the eye is important in examining the visual field. When the eye is light adapted, vision is said to be *photopic,* and when it is dark adapted, vision is *scotopic.* During photopic vision the eye adapts to illuminations commonly met in good daylight or in good artificial light. Photopic vision is a cone function, and scotopic vision is a rod function. Light adaptation is a rapid process and is generally done within a minute or two. Complete dark adaptation is slower, however, requiring more nearly an hour. At illumination levels between complete light adaptation and complete dark adaptation, the retina makes an effort to come into equilibrium within a range of illumination, and thus both rods and cones are active. This intermediate zone of illumination is designated as *mesopic.* Active debate continues on whether it is preferable to test under photopic, scotopic, or mesopic conditions. Although controversy exists regarding the relative advantages of differing levels of background illumination during visual field testing, there is uniform agreement on the need for consistency in background illumination when performing serial testing.

Most commercially available visual field machines do not allow the examiner to vary background illumination. However, the standard level of background illumination used by different manufacturers can vary. In our clinics we have used perimeters with background illumination levels ranging from 4 to 315 apostilbs. Although it was difficult to determine whether one method was consistently superior to the others, it was clear that a patient's visual field looked dramatically different with different background illumination levels. For careful serial follow-up, such as that required in the research setting, it is probably reasonable to allow patients a consistent period for dark adaptation before beginning the visual field examination. This would be especially important when testing on machines that use the lowest background illumination levels.

For tangent field examinations one must attempt to control ambient light levels. This may be somewhat more difficult than with visual field examinations performed on a perimeter, because calibration equipment is not often readily available. Our practice has been to test in normal full-room illumination. For reasons mentioned previously, this may not be the ideal illumination level for visual field examination, but it is certainly the easiest to duplicate on serial tests. After completing a tangent screen examination with the room lights at their brightest level, it is certainly permissible to repeat the examination with the lights dimmed. Dimming the lights will make the test more sensitive as a given test object becomes more difficult to detect. The isopters will necessarily become smaller, and any scotomas will increase in size. If at all possible, one should use a consistent method for dimming the lights. We often turn off the overhead light and illuminate the room with a small incandescent spotlight aimed at the wall behind the patient so that indirect light falls evenly on the tangent screen.

The suggestion to allow patients some standard amount of time for dark adaptation is particularly important if tangent screen examinations will be performed serially using different illumination levels. This is much more critical when the patient is tested in bright light first and dimmer light second. The stimulus detection threshold, especially for relatively peripheral test objects, may change significantly within the first few minutes of dark adaptation. Whenever any of these testing parameters are varied—room illumination, dark adaptation time, etc.—a clear note should be placed in the patient's chart to facilitate meaningful comparison to past or future examinations.

In addition to altering background or stimulus illumination by modifying instrument parameters or room illumination, one encounters a form of physiologic stimulus intensity reduction if the transparency of the ocular media change. One would not expect to find the same visual field defects in a glaucomatous eye with a perfectly clear lens as in that same eye with cloudy media.

Such relatively simple movements as voluntarily or involuntarily narrowing the lid aperture during the examination may alter the visual field. This may be important in myopic patients or patients with high degrees of astigmatism who narrow their lid apertures habitually. These effects are probably most pronounced peripherally.

The contrast between an object and the object's background is a major factor in visual acuity determination, whether in the foveal area or in the peripheral visual field. The physiologic processes underlying form discrimination depend largely on image contrast. Visual acuity decreases with contrast reduction. Within certain limits a decrease in stimulus luminosity (or an increase in background luminosity) in a visual field examination will heighten test sensitivity. These considerations apply most directly to tangent field examination. In tangent field examination the contrast between the stimulus and the background depends on the color and size of the stimulus, the nature of the background, and the illumination level. In these examinations, within fairly wide limits, the room illumination and the resultant contrast vary directly with one another. With more room illumination, there is more contrast and the patient can detect test stimuli more easily; the test is less sensitive.

If the test is performed with instruments like the Goldmann perimeter or commercially available automated perimeters that use a dimly illuminated bowl for the background, different considerations apply. Under these circumstances, the background or ambient illumination is held constant, and the stimulus intensity is made to vary independently. The threshold sensitivity is determined by increasing the test object intensity until the contrast between the test object and the background is sufficient for the patient to detect the test object.

FACTORS INFLUENCING THRESHOLD OR ISOPTER SIZE IN THE NORMAL VISUAL FIELD

Age

Age gradually depresses the central and peripheral isopters. Measuring the rate of this decline is somewhat difficult because so many older patients have a small degree of media opacity or other changes that affect the overall visual field. We have found this particularly important when reading automated visual field charts from patients who are in their 80s and 90s. The age-matched normal standards published by most manufacturers leave something to be desired at this edge of the curve. Attempting to determine whether a small depression in such a patient is significant can be extremely difficult.

Miosis

It is well known that pupillary miosis depresses both peripheral and central isopters of a normal field and may exaggerate the size and depth of established defects. This effect is particularly noteworthy in patients being treated with miotics for glaucoma. It is important to note the pupil size on visual field charts from glaucoma patients and to be cognizant of pupil size when reading serial examinations. For the past several years, we have been routinely dilating patients' pupils to approximately 3.5 mm before a visual field examination.

Media clarity

Decrease in media clarity has a striking effect on the visual field. The presence of a cataract or vitreous opacification acts in the same way as a filter so that, in effect, the visual field is being tested under reduced illumination (reduced contrast), with consequent depression of the isopters and exaggeration of any defects.

Refractive errors

Uncorrected refractive errors affect the visual field in several ways. Areas of localized myopia (as in posterior staphyloma) or hyperopia (as in macular elevation) make so-called refractive scotomas, which disappear when the depressed or elevated area is brought into focus with lenses. We have seen several such refractive scotomas markedly enlarge blind spots or other defects. These enlargements disappeared when the proper local refraction was applied.

More commonly, one can find generalized depression in a visual field when the patient is examined with an out-of-date or otherwise inappropriate refraction. This has been measured quantitatively on both the Goldmann perimeter and a computerized static perimeter. This artifact is avoided simply by adhering to the rule to use a current refraction for all field patients.

Aphakia

Aphakic patients have always presented a challenge to the perimetrist. The prominent ring scotoma caused by lens-induced magnification of the central field makes it difficult to test the region between about 25 and 40 degrees from fixation. One can perform the entire examination without aphakic spectacles using very large test objects, but this will necessarily result in some compromise in sensitivity. Some have advocated fitting temporary soft contact lenses on aphakic patients and correcting any residual astigmatism with cylindric lenses in a trial frame or lens holder. Regardless of the exact method used, measuring and interpreting aphakic visual fields requires a great deal of care.

Pseudophakic patients and aphakic patients who normally wear contact lenses are examined in essentially the same fashion as phakic patients. The 8% to 10% magnification induced by contact lenses, however, will result in a field that is 10 or 15 degrees smaller than the phakic field for the same size object.

PSYCHOLOGIC FACTORS AFFECTING THE VISUAL FIELD EXAMINATION

The psychologic processes of vision are extremely important in considering perimetric techniques or in interpreting visual field charts resulting from those techniques. The subjective nature of visual field examination has been stressed repeatedly. These examinations are limited by the patient's capacity to respond; the perimetrist or physician ordering the test must be on guard constantly against making demands beyond the patient's capabilities. The responses of one individual to the examination may be entirely different from those of another. The time required for perimetric examination of different people with the same disease process may vary dramatically.

With experience, the perimetrist will be able to evaluate the patient's reaction times, ability to concentrate, and degree of suggestibility. Any or all of these factors may alter the visual field. They all must be considered carefully when making clinical decisions.

The perimetric chart should not be regarded as conveying a mathematically accurate and precise expression of the state of the peripheral vision. It indicates only the kind and degree of defect present at the moment of the examination. It must be interpreted with a knowledge of what perimetric techniques entail and of the psychologic background and condition of the patient.

Visual field variations of physiologic and psychologic origin can be compounded and exaggerated in direct ratio to the complexity of the examining technique. Excessive fatigue or malaise, caused either by the patient's underlying physical state or by an overly demanding visual field examination, can render the results of a visual field examination useless. Whenever possible, the simplest and most direct method of gaining the necessary amount of information should be employed.

The perimetrist must have knowledge of human anatomy, pathology, and psychology. This is important in manual perimetry, where the examination methods must be varied according to that knowledge, and also in computerized or automated perimetry, where explaining the test and helping the patient get started can be pivotal.

In many complex situations, especially with manual perimetry, the examiner may receive an impression of a visual field defect that is definite, but impossible to chart with accuracy. In such circumstances the statement of the impression is more valuable than plotting a chart, which may be highly inaccurate and may give a false impression of precise localization.

To interpret a visual field defect correctly, the examiner must, of course, analyze the defect in terms of its size, shape, and density. To be valid, this analysis must take into account the physiologic and psychologic parameters under which the examination was performed. All of these factors must be weighed intelligently if one is to make an appropriate clinical decision.

INTERPRETATION OF VISUAL FIELD DEFECTS

8 ABNORMAL VISUAL FIELDS

Visual field defects (Figure 8-1) are categorized as (1) contractions, (2) depressions, and (3) scotomas.

CONTRACTIONS

A true contraction is relatively rare. In the strict definition of a contraction, the defective area of the visual field must be totally blind to all stimuli no matter how bright or large. The defect's edge must be the same regardless of the stimulus intensity.

Contractions are usually peripheral defects (Figure 8-2, *A*), but a scotoma may fit the definition for a contraction if its boundaries are perpendicular (i.e., the same for all stimuli) and if its area is totally blind to all stimuli regardless of intensity. The normal blind spot (in its absolute portion) can be classified as a true contraction because it is totally blind to all stimuli within its area.

A characteristic of a true contraction is that if a very large test object is passed slowly across its border, moving from the nonseeing to the seeing portion of the field, the subject sees an increasingly larger portion of the stimulus as it comes into view. The stimulus has been described as a "moon rising over the horizon."

Contractions may have several forms: (1) general peripheral, (2) partial peripheral, (3) sector, (4) partial hemianoptic, (5) total hemianoptic, and (6) scotomatous. Each of these types of field loss will be discussed in detail later.

A true contraction can only be diagnosed with certainty after all possible stimuli have been used to test it, up to and including such things as a moving light or even a bath towel if necessary. One cannot state that a true contraction exists simply because a 100-mm test object is not visible in the defective field, if at the same time a test object 4 feet in diameter can be seen. Certainly, then, a visual field chart that shows a test for only one isopter should not be spoken of as a contracted field. It may, in fact, be a contracted field, but further isopters must be charted to prove this. Because automated perimeters are necessarily

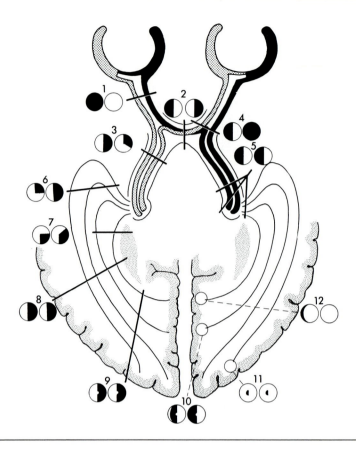

FIGURE 8-1 Abnormal visual field. Schematic representation of visual pathway showing sites of total interruption of nerve fibers and various abnormal visual fields produced by such interruption.

1. Optic nerve—blindness on side of lesion, with normal contralateral field
2. Chiasm—bitemporal hemianopsia
3. Optic tract—contralateral incongruous homonymous hemianopsia
4. Optic nerve—chiasmal junction; blindness on side of lesion with contralateral temporal hemianopsia or hemianoptic scotoma
5. Posterior optic tract, external geniculate ganglion, posterior limb of internal capsule—complete contralateral homonymous hemianopsia or incomplete incongruous contralateral homonymous hemianopsia
6. Optic radiation; anterior loop in temporal lobe—incongruous contralateral homonymous hemianopsia or superior quadrantanopsia
7. Medial fibers of optic radiation—contralateral incongruous inferior homonymous quadrantanopsia
8. Optic radiation in parietal lobe—contralateral homonymous hemianopsia, sometimes slightly incongruous, with minimal macular sparing
9. Optic radiation in posterior parietal lobe and occipital lobe—contralateral congruous homonymous hemianopsia with mascular sparing
10. Midportion of calcarine cortex—contralateral congruous homonymous hemianopsia with wide macular sparing and sparing of contralateral temporal crescent
11. Tip of occipital lobe—contralateral congruous homonymous hemianoptic scotomas
12. Anterior tip of calcarine fissure—contralateral loss of temporal crescent with otherwise normal visual fields

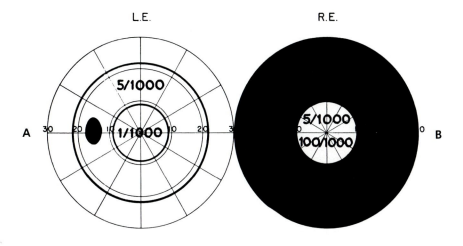

FIGURE 8-2 **A,** Generally depressed visual field. All isopters are smaller than normal and each isopter is different in size. **B,** Contracted visual field. Field loss is absolute for all stimuli, regardless of size, and all isopters are same size.

limited in their ability to present maximally large and bright targets, the most severe defects plotted on an automated perimeter are probably better termed *deep depressions* rather than true contractions. The numerical printouts of many machines will assign a value of 0 dB to those regions of the visual field where the machine's largest, brightest target is not perceived. The corresponding gray-scale, or halftone, printout will portray this area of the field as completely black. In such a format, these defects appear to be absolute and thus would appear to satisfy the definition of a contraction. It is important to remember that these defects may not be absolute in the strict sense of the word.

When found, a true contraction narrows the differential diagnostic possibilities. True contractions are usually associated with lesions that have a profound effect on the visual pathway, are stable or nonprogressive, and have a poor prognosis for recovery.

DEPRESSIONS

The great majority of visual field defects, both peripheral and central, are caused by depression of visual sensitivity within a given area of the field. This depression may be very marked or very slight. It may involve only the extreme periphery or only the most minute portion of fixation. It may take an almost infinite variety of forms. When examining the field kinetically, at least two isopters must be studied to determine that a visual field depression exists. The more stimuli used, the more visual angles employed, and the more isopters charted, the clearer will be the visual field depression and the greater its diagnostic value. To measure a depression using static perimetry, one must use a full-thresholding strategy or at least a multiple-zone screening strategy. Using a densely packed grid pattern and a full-threshold strategy will yield the clearest and most useful representation. Analyzing visual field depression is truly the raison d'être of quantitative perimetry.

Scotomas and peripheral visual field defects are often spoken of as relative. In fact, any visual field depression is relative in that it may be present for one stimulus but not for a larger one. Thus the field may be completely normal in size for the 20/1000 isopter, it may show a dim area in the Bjerrum region for a 5/2000 stimulus, and it may develop a broad and dense arcuate scotoma for a 1/2000 test object.

Visual field depressions are characterized as general or local.

General Depressions

With kinetic techniques, a generally depressed field is one in which all the isopters are smaller than normal, and some of the internal isopters may be missing. Visual sensitivity in all areas of the visual field is decreased, including the central portion; in fact, the central isopters are often the first and most

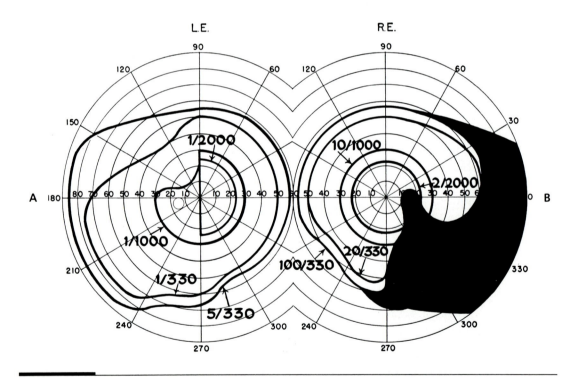

FIGURE 8-3 **A,** Example of depression in visual field due to pituitary adenoma. Peripheral isopters are normal to large stimuli. Defect increases in central isopters with weak stimuli. **B,** Example of contraction in visual field due to gunshot injury to optic nerve. Lower sector defect is absolute and is same size for all stimuli.

severely affected (Figure 8-2, *B*). In generalized depressions smaller and less intense stimuli reveal defects earlier than larger brighter stimuli (Figure 8-3).

Using the island hill of vision surrounded by a sea of blindness analogy to illustrate his point, Traquair likened visual field depression to a general sinking of the island into the sea. He pointed out that depression is less evident where the hill is steep and the contour lines are close together but becomes more evident on gently sloping areas of the hill, such as that between 5 and 25 degrees from fixation. Slight depressions, then, may be most readily detected by testing the flat part of the hill of vision. This is one reason why so many visual field defects are detectable within the 30-degree circle from fixation. In this regard, the central field reflects changes that occur in the periphery.

Static perimetry that maps the profile of the hill of vision shows areas of visual field depression even more clearly (Figure 8-4).

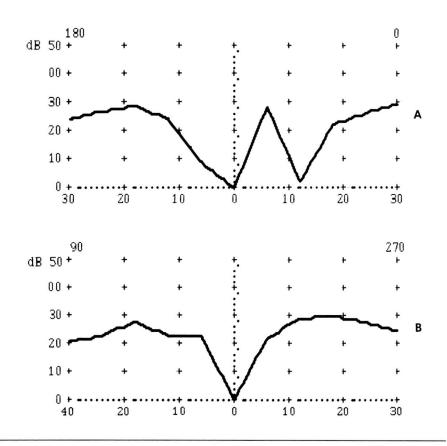

FIGURE 8-4 Profile cuts through **(A)** dense central scotoma and blind spot (horizontal meridian) and **(B)** through central scotoma alone (vertical meridian) show corresponding depressions clearly.

The visual field in a normal person may be generally depressed by decreasing the stimulus intensity. This may be accomplished by decreasing test object luminance or by increasing background illumination, or it may be accomplished by using gray or dirty test objects or by interposing filters between the eye and the stimulus. General depression of the normal visual field will also result from media opacities, miosis, or an improper refraction or near correction. In many of these same circumstances true visual field depressions are exaggerated.

In the case illustrated in Figure 8-5, it would have been impossible to be certain that the 1/2000 isopter with standard illumination had detected visual field loss, whereas the same isopter studied with reduced light would have revealed the characteristic bitemporal hemianopsia.

Local Depressions

In the past local depressions were considered the most common type of visual field defect. Current data indicate that the apparent relative frequency of local defects as compared to general defects may have been due in part to measurement error. A mildly generally depressed field can mimic a normal field quite effectively, whereas a mild localized defect, almost by definition, is usually recognized as such. Computerized perimetry, which has more sensitive data collection methods and more sophisticated data analysis techniques, can often indicate generalized depression in fields that might have been inter-

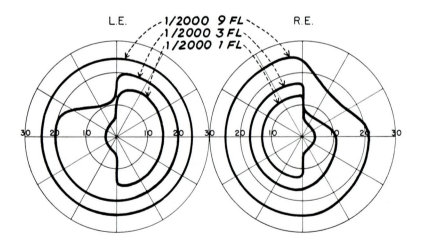

FIGURE 8-5   Effect of variation in test object luminance on visual field defect produced by chromophobic adenoma of pituitary gland. Note that size of test object (visual angle) remained constant but luminance decreased from 9 footlamberts to 1 footlambert with increasing defect in visual field.

preted as completely normal by manual techniques. Regardless of their true relative incidence, most localized depressions are recognized more easily than mild generalized depressions.

Localized depressions may take many forms, but certain characteristics should be studied in every case. Each visual field defect should be investigated and analyzed as to its (1) position, (2) shape, (3) size, (4) intensity, (5) uniformity, (6) margins, and (7) onset and course.

Position

The position of the localized depression may vary widely. It may be peripheral; central, involving only the fixation area, with a normal field about it (central scotoma); or a combination of both peripheral and central defects located in any quadrant or part of a quadrant. The defect may be bilateral or unilateral.

Shape

The shape of the local visual field depression is often of greater diagnostic value than its size or position. Besides scotomas the most common type of local defect is the sector defect. This may be monocular or binocular. It may be wedge shaped, regular, absolute, or relative, connected to or separate from the blind spot, and limited by the vertical, horizontal, or oblique meridian. The most common form of monocular sector defect is that found in patients with glaucoma in which the shape of the defect is determined by the fact that it is produced by physiologic interruption of retinal nerve fibers or nerve fiber bundles.

The typical binocular sector defect is the hemianopsia, which may be subdivided and classified according to characteristics as follows: (1) homonymous, total, (2) homonymous, partial (congruous or incongruous), (3) homonymous quadrantanopsia, (4) bitemporal, (5) binasal, (6) crossed quadrantanopsia, (7) altitudinal, (8) double homonymous, (9) macula spared, and (10) macula split.

Total homonymous hemianopsia. Total homonymous hemianopsia (Figure 8-6) is actually a contraction of the visual field rather than a depression. It is bilateral and left sided or right sided, which means there is total blindness in the temporal field of one eye and in the nasal field of the other eye. The dividing line between the seeing and the nonseeing portions of the field is vertical and passes through the field directly above and below the fixation point. The dividing line may split the fixation point or it may spare the fixation point by passing a few degrees around it. Because there is no vision in any portion of the defective half of the field, there can be no question of congruity or incongruity in the hemianopsia, regardless of the lesion location or stimulus intensity.

Total homonymous hemianopsia implies essentially total destruction of the visual pathway behind the chiasm on one side. The lesion may occur at

any level, from the optic tract to the occipital lobe. In the absence of radiographic identification of a specific lesion, a total homonymous hemianopsia
offers no localizing information in and of itself. Rather, one must rely on other
neurologic and neuroophthalmologic signs. Because total homonymous hemianopsia is usually due to widespread and severe cerebral tissue destruction,
it is frequently associated with other signs and symptoms. It is probably more
commonly seen in patients with vascular lesions than those with tumors, and
it is not an uncommon finding in patients with severe destruction of cerebral
tissue from trauma. Compared with other visual field defects, total homonymous hemianopsia is rather rare.

   Partial homonymous hemianopsia.   Partial homonymous hemianopsia
is by far the most common visual field defect resulting from damage to the
postchiasmal visual pathway. As the name suggests, a partial destruction or
physiologic interruption of the nerve fiber bundles occurs at any level from
the optic tract to the occipital pole. The defect may result from any type of
lesion in this area, but is most commonly found in patients with cerebral
tumor, hemorrhage, or infarct. In a partial homonymous hemianopsia, somewhat less than half of the visual field of each eye is affected. It is bilateral and
right sided or left sided. The dividing line between the seeing and the blind
portions of the field is usually vertical in either the upper or lower half of
the field and horizontal, slanting, or irregular in the other half (Figure 8-7).

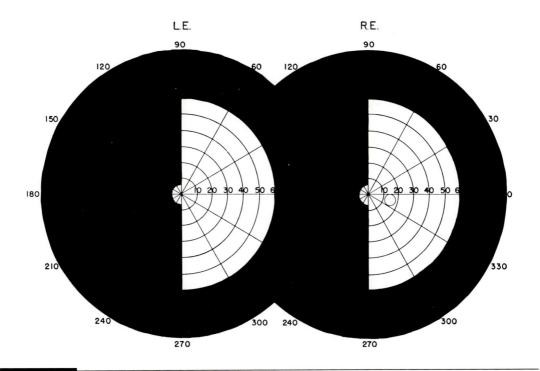

FIGURE 8-6   Total homonymous hemianopsia with small area of macular sparing. Defect is same
regardless of size of stimulus used.

Partial homonymous hemianoptic visual field defects may take an infinite variety of forms. The defect may involve only a small segment of one quadrant, an entire quadrant, an area within a quadrant in the form of a scotoma, or somewhat more than one quadrant. Because its margins usually slope, its shape will differ, depending upon the stimulus level used to test it. With relatively intense stimuli, a hemianoptic defect may appear quadrantric; when the eye is examined with a less intense stimulus, a total hemianoptic defect may be elicited.

Quantitative techniques are extremely valuable when examining and interpreting these defects. One should always use multiple isopters when examining such a field kinetically and multiple-level screening or full-threshold programs when examining such fields on computerized machines. A single isopter or screening strategy can often detect the presence or absence of the basic defect, but quantitative techniques are required to ascertain the true character of the field loss. For example, a partial homonymous hemianopsia with a markedly different size and shape in two or three of its central isopters indicates a sloping margin that may point to a progressive lesion. If, in addition, the two half fields are asymmetric or incongruous, the examiner may be able to localize the site of the visual pathway interruption and perhaps even make an intelligent guess as to the pathologic nature of the lesion producing the interruption.

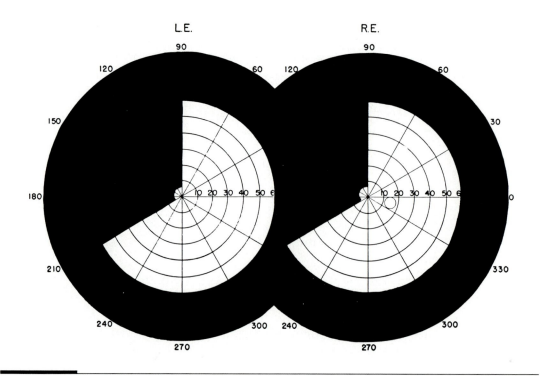

FIGURE 8-7   Congruous partial homonymous hemianopsia. Margins of defect are usually steep.

Partial homonymous hemianopsia may be congruous or incongruous. A *congruous* defect is one in which both half fields are symmetric or identical in size, shape, position, density, margins, and all other characteristics. If enough isopters are examined, absolute congruity for each stimulus is rare if not nonexistent, except in patients with damage to the calcarine cortex.

To show a complete congruity, each field must duplicate symmetrically its fellow field in all respects; each isopter or region tested in the right eye must be a carbon copy of the same isopter or region in the left eye, allowing for the size difference of the two fields caused by the temporal crescents. In total homonymous hemianopsia congruity cannot be determined because the dividing line between the seeing and nonseeing portions of the field is vertical. In partial homonymous hemianopsia, if one portion of the line dividing seeing and nonseeing fields slants away from the vertical, it is this portion of the margin of the field defect that may determine the symmetry or congruity of the defect.

Congruity in a defect may be determined by testing one isopter if that isopter shows a defect somewhat less than half the visual field. It may also be demonstrated in a visual field in which the margins are more sloping in one field than the other. But unless careful quantitative techniques are used to study these defects, an assumption of congruity in a given visual field is not justified.

An *incongruous* partial homonymous hemianopsia is one in which two fields are asymmetric in size, shape, or other characteristics (Figure 8-8). This definition, of course, does not apply to the natural and constantly occurring incongruity of the two visual fields caused by the temporal crescent. Incongruity in homonymous hemianopsia may vary from the slightest asymmetry in the two fields, one which is barely detectable by the most quantitative perimetric techniques, to a visual field defect that shows only the faintest depression of a portion of a quadrant in one eye and total loss of the homonymous field in the fellow eye. Minimal degrees of incongruity may be of some localizing value if associated with other neurologic signs, but they should not be allowed too much weight in diagnosis except as they indicate the right-sidedness or left-sidedness of a lesion. Gross incongruity or asymmetry in a homonymous hemianopsia may be of considerable localizing value and in fact may be the only neurologic finding that points to the anterior cerebral location of the lesion.

In general, the more extreme the asymmetry or incongruity in the two fields of homonymous hemianopsia, the more anterior in the postchiasmal portion of the visual pathway is the lesion producing it. The converse is also true. Perfectly congruous homonymous hemianoptic defects are generally caused by lesions that are more posterior in the postchiasmal visual pathway.

Lesions of the temporal lobe or optic tract can therefore be separated from lesions of the occipital cortex by the character of the homonymous hemianopsia they produce. Defects showing incongruity localize the lesion

anteriorly, whereas symmetric defects point to a location in the occipital cortex. In parietal lobe lesions the visual field character is less reliable, but if an inferior homonymous quadrantanopsia is associated with a positive or asymmetric optokinetic nystagmus, the lesion is almost certainly in the deeper portion of the parietal lobe.

Homonymous quadrantanopsia. Although homonymous quadrantanopsias (Figure 8-9) are considered separately, they are actually a form of partial homonymous hemianopsia. They may be congruous or incongruous. They may have steep or sloping margins. Depending upon whether the upper or lower quadrants are involved in a defect, it may point to a downward or upward progression of the lesion in the opposite cerebral hemisphere, or it may implicate the superior or inferior fiber bundles of the optic radiation. Superior homonymous quadrantanopsia is said to be diagnostic of lesions in the temporal lobe, but of course they may also occur as a result of a lesion of the inferior lip of the calcarine fissure. As a rule, however, an optic tract or temporal lobe lesion produces an incongruous superior homonymous quadrantanopsia, whereas a calcarine fissure lesion produces a congruous superior homonymous quadrantanopsia.

An inferior homonymous quadrantanopsia is most commonly associated with a lesion of the superior fiber bundles of the radiation in the parietal lobe

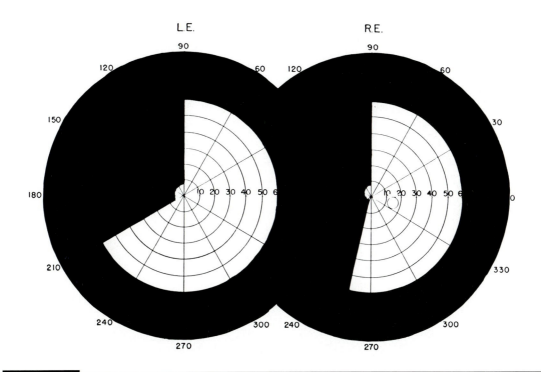

FIGURE 8-8   Incongruous partial homonymous hemianopsia. Margins of defect are usually sloping, so morphology of defect varies with isopter tested. Only one isopter is shown here.

or the upper lip of the calcarine fissue in the occipital lobe. Here again the symmetry or asymmetry of the quadrantic defects may assist in the antero-posterior localization, although the degree of incongruity in a patient with a parietal lobe lesion is likely to be slight and difficult to elicit.

Bitemporal hemianopsia.   Bitemporal hemianopsia (Figure 8-10) is a visual field defect in which part or all of each temporal field is insensitive to visual stimuli. The defect may vary from a slight depression of the upper temporal portion of the field to complete blindness in the temporal hemifield. This field defect implies an interruption of the decussating nerve fibers in the optic chiasm. The great variety of forms that bitemporal hemianopsia may assume is largely the result of the nerve fiber arrangement and vascular supply of the chiasm and also the intimate anatomic relationship of the chiasm to many other structures in the sella turcica region.

The classic bitemporal hemianopsia is produced by an adenoma of the pituitary gland expanding upward from the sella turcica and compressing the central decussating fibers of the chiasm from below. Radiographic techniques have shown that such a large extension, with the chiasm literally draped over the tumor mass, can still cause only subtle or minimal changes on the visual field examination. (See Figure 14-2.) Visual field damage usually begins on the upper temporal quadrants, with gradual extension to encompass the entire temporal field in each eye. In its late stages the visual field defect involves

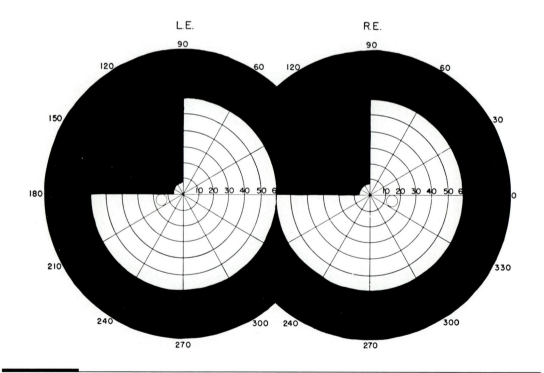

FIGURE 8-9   Homonymous quadrantanopsia.

the central area and lower nasal quadrants and then finally the upper nasal portion of each visual field. The progression of the defect is clockwise in the right field and counterclockwise in the left field. An anomaly in the suprasellar portion of the chiasm or any asymmetry in the tumor or its direction of growth usually produces an asymmetry in the visual field defects. Likewise, variations in the speed of tumor growth, the blood supply, the secondary pressure by contiguous structures, and even the cell structure of the tumor itself will be reflected in the size, shape, position, margins, and other characteristics of visual field defects. Extrasellar lesions that give rise to chiasmal pressure from directions other than beneath will produce a type of bitemporal hemianopsia that is quite different from the classic defect produced by intrasellar lesions.

Binasal hemianopsia. A binasal hemianopsia is not a true hemianoptic defect. It is usually produced by more than one lesion and is irregular and asymmetric in the fields of both eyes. It may, however, offer some diagnostic significance. This visual field defect implies an interruption of the uncrossed fibers in both lateral aspects of the chiasm or in both optic nerves or retinas. It therefore presupposes bilateral lesions, although they may have one etiology.

Binasal hemianopsia may be produced by symmetric lesions in the temporal halves of both retinas, such as severe retinal damage associated with diabetic retinopathy. It may be part of the visual field defect associated with postneuritic optic neuropathy and with the occasional bilateral retrobulbar

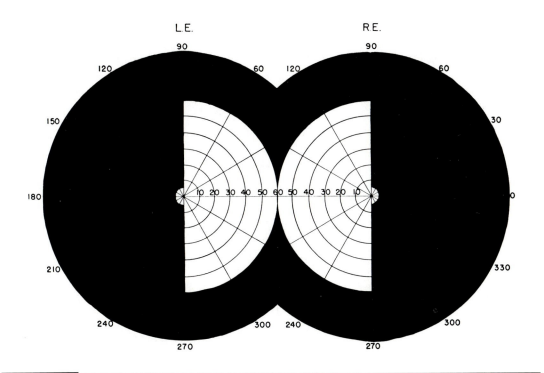

FIGURE 8-10 Bitemporal hemianopsia.

neuritis of multiple sclerosis. In this latter instance, the defect is often the result of a very large paracentral scotoma that involves the nasal field more than the temporal field. More or less symmetrically placed lesions lateral to the chiasm, such as adhesions resulting from opticochiasmic arachnoiditis, may produce binasal hemianopsia.

Most binasal hemianopsias are due to intraocular disease in both eyes. The nasal quadrant peripheral depression of glaucoma, when bilateral and reasonably symmetric in the two eyes, has been mistaken for binasal hemianopsia of central origin. Binasal hemianopsia can be produced by a tumor of the third ventricle with extreme dilation of the ventricle and downward pressure between the optic nerves, forcing them laterally against the carotid arteries. Similarly, an aneurysm of the right internal carotid artery may compress the chiasm laterally, destroying its uncrossed fibers on that side and producing a right-side nasal defect. This has been seen in association with a leftward shift of the entire chiasm, so that the opposite normal internal carotid artery had grooved the left side of the chiasm and produced a nasal defect on that side. This is an example of a binasal hemianopsia from bilateral lesions with a single etiology.

Crossed quadrantanopsia.   Crossed quadrantanopsia is a rare defect in the visual field in which an upper quadrant of one visual field is lost along with the lower quadrant of the opposite visual field. It can occur as part of the chiasmal compression syndrome, with the chiasm being depressed from beneath against a contiguous arterial structure and thus producing simultaneous pressure above and below. It may result from wide and coincidentally crossed sector defects in the two fields and, as such, may occur in association with glaucoma or inflammatory lesions such as juxtapapillary choroiditis. It is usually the result of asymmetric, bilateral, or double homonymous hemianopsia and occurs either as an incomplete bilateral hemianopsia or as its terminal stage. It is a rare phenomenon. Crossed quadrantanopsia may be explained by a lesion of the upper lip of the calcarine area on one side and the lower lip of the opposite calcarine cortex.

Altitudinal hemianopsia.   Altitudinal hemianopsia (Figure 8-11) may be unilateral or bilateral. A unilateral altitudinal hemianopsia is necessarily caused by a prechiasmal lesion. Injury to the vascular supply of the optic nerve will produce an altitudinal hemianopsia, usually inferior. The vascular supply of the anterior optic nerve is such that torsional forces, edema, or other injury may give rise to damage that produces a unilateral altitudinal visual field defect.

Unilateral or bilateral inferior altitudinal hemianoptic defects may be produced by lesions that press the chiasm up in its anterior portion, thus wedging the optic nerve against the superior margin of the optic foramen or against a sclerotic pair of anterior cerebral arteries. Olfactory groove meningiomas may extend posteriorly and downward, thus compressing the optic nerves in their short and vulnerable intracranial portion.

Intrinsic lesions of the optic nerve, such as the atrophy in ischemic optic neuropathy, tabes dorsalis, and, of course, that which accompanies advanced glaucoma, will produce unilateral or bilateral altitudinal field defects of an irregular type. These lesions have been noted in otherwise uncomplicated aphakic or psuedophakic patients within a year or so of cataract surgery.

Severe hypoxia resulting from exsanguination caused by injury or massive gastrointestinal hemorrhage may produce a glaucoma-like visual field defect that takes the form of an altitudinal hemianopsia. This type of defect has been seen in patients who have undergone major abdominal surgery and have experienced significant blood loss. It also has been seen in patients who have had prolonged periods of hypoxia following cardiac arrest and successful cardiopulmonary resuscitation efforts.

Rarely, double homonymous inferior or superior quadrantanopsia may result from injury or hemorrhage in the lower or upper lips of both calcarine fissures to produce a type of altitudinal hemianopsia.

Double homonymous hemianopsia.   Double homonymous hemianopsia (Figure 8-12) is a relatively uncommon visual field defect that is always the result of lesions of the occipital area and presupposes involvement of the striate cortex of both occipital lobes. Total destruction of both occipital lobes results in total blindness. Partial destruction of the occipital cortex on both sides from severe trauma with massive brain damage (such as in depressed

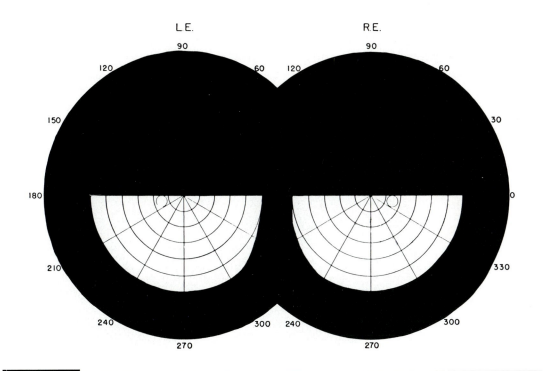

FIGURE 8-11 Altitudinal hemianopsia.

fracture of the occiput) or from bilateral vascular lesions involving a calcarine fissure will produce bilateral or double homonymous hemianopsia with macular sparing of a greater or lesser degree. This field defect simulates a gross concentric contraction of the visual field with loss of all peripheral vision to all stimuli. In these cases both hemianoptic field defects show great density and very steep margins, and the remaining small area of central vision represents the spared macular portion of both hemifields. Increased intracranial pressure may cause a shift of the uncal portions of the temporal lobe downward over the edge of the tentorium, with resulting compression of the posterior cerebral arteries and infarction in the calcarine cortex.

If the area of macular sparing in one homonymous hemianopsia is larger than that in the other homonymous hemianopsia, the spared central portion of the field can have small vertical steps above and below fixation where the two areas of macular sparing do not quite coincide. These steps may be likened to the unpaired double nasal steps seen on the horizontal meridian in cases of double arcuate scotoma in patients with glaucoma, except that they occur on the vertical instead of the horizontal meridian.

Most double homonymous hemianoptic field defects are vascular in origin, whether primary or secondary to severe trauma to the vascular supply of the striate cortex. Invariably they are congruous, dense, and steep margined. Bilateral or double homonymous hemianopsia may result from a stroke or infarction of one occipital lobe accompanied by complete homonymous hemianopsia with macular sparing, followed at a later date by infarction of the opposite occipital lobe, also with macular sparing. The size and shape of the remaining visual field depends on the degree of macular sparing. Conversely, there may be sudden and massive bilateral occipital lobe damage with cortical blindness resulting from trauma, anoxia, carbon monoxide poisoning, cerebral

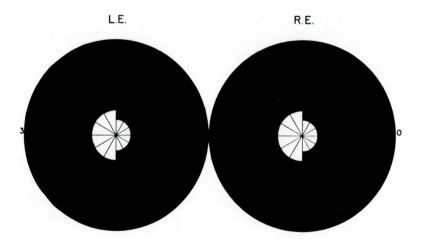

L.E.   R.E.

FIGURE 8-12   Double homonymous hemianopsia.

angiography, cardiac arrest, exsanguination, and other similar conditions. Partial recovery may leave a residual and permanent bilateral homonymous hemianopsia.

Macular splitting.   Macular splitting in homonymous hemianopsia is relatively uncommon. True macular splitting with an absolute bisection of fixation for all test objects is extremely difficult if not impossible to elicit because of constant minute fixation shifts during the test. These slight fixation shifts are physiologic and occur even in the most cooperative and intelligent patients.

Macular splitting is more likely to occur with homonymous hemianopsia produced by lesions in the anterior portion of the postchiasmal pathway, although it can occur with damage to the striate cortex.

Macular sparing.   Macular sparing in homonymous hemianopsia is the rule in instances of damage to the occipital cortex. Generally, it decreases in degree with more anterior lesions. This does not mean, however, that macular sparing is pathognomonic of a lesion in the posterior portion of the visual pathway. The degree of fixation sparing may vary from a minute area of less than 0.5 degrees to a major portion of the affected hemifield. Clinically, lesions of the anterior portion of the calcarine fissure that produce homonymous hemianopsia are more likely to leave a wide area of macular sparing than those involving the operculum, which will show a narrower area of retained central field. Even with slight macular sparing the central visual acuity may remain normal (Figure 8-13). Furthermore, normal vision may be retained with only one half of the macula functioning.

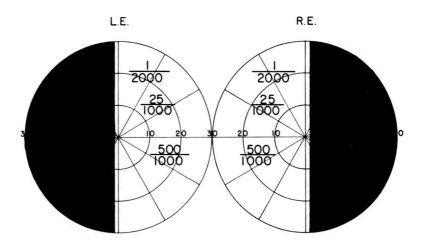

FIGURE 8-13   Total bitemporal hemianopsia with split macula and overshot field in patient who as infant had sustained severe frontal head injury with chiasmal rupture. Both temporal fields were completely blind, but central visual acuity was 20/20 in each eye, and patient was unaware of field defect at 17 years of age.

Macular sparing may occur in an interruption of any portion of the postchiasmal visual pathway. With anteriorly placed lesions, sparing is more likely to be present for large or intense stimuli only; the macula will appear to be split when small or dim test objects are used. The area of macular sparing produced in a homonymous hemianopsia caused by a lesion of the optic tract will have sloping margins, whereas that produced from an occipital lobe lesion will have steep margins and will be the same size regardless of the test objects used to elicit it. In a large sense macular sparing simply represents the border between the seeing and nonseeing areas of the visual field. As with any visual field defect, these margins may be smooth or irregular and congruous or incongruous when hemianoptic defects are involved. A congruous irregularity is further evidence of the cortical location of the responsible lesion.

Macular sparing may be an initial finding in the visual field loss that progressively involves the central field and finally macular splitting. The late involvement of macular fibers may result from the fact that there are so many more of them than there are peripheral fibers.

As noted earlier, each nerve fiber from the right half of each retina goes to the right occipital cortex, and the left homonymous retinas send their fibers to the left occipital cortex. These fibers traverse the cerebral hemispheres in a remarkably constant pattern. Despite this anatomic fact, it is not uncommon to find lesions totally destroying one visual pathway with resulting homonymous hemianopsia that is also total except for an area of macular sparing.

Much has been written and numerous theories have been proposed to explain this phenomenon. Each of these theories leaves some unanswered questions and there is probably no simple answer to the problem. A few of the theories that have been proposed are briefly described here.

In some cases of apparent total destruction of the occipital lobe with macular sparing, there may not have been total destruction. Small portions of the striate cortex may remain, even after extensive surgical procedures or trauma. Even complete interruption of the blood supply through the posterior cerebral artery may leave some cortical function. It is probable that the occipital cortex is supplied not only by the calcarine artery branches from the posterior cerebral artery, but also by deep optic or posterior cortical branches of the middle cerebral artery and, in a fairly high percentage of cases, by branches from the posterior temporal artery. All of these arteries may supply a part of the macular area of the calcarine cortex. This is probably an important reason for the high incidence of macular sparing in occipital lobe lesions.

It has been argued that macular sparing is only apparent and not real and that it is due to fixation shifts toward the blind field. Fixation shift is more noticeable in the central area and can rarely be detected in the peripheral parts of the visual fields. That the macula may be truly split, normal vision retained, and a true overshot field produced is best illustrated graphically. In Figure 8-13, traumatic rupture of the chiasm during infancy produced total bitemporal hemianopsia. The patient reached the age of 17 years and had little or no awareness of her visual field defect until it was detected accidentally in a routine visual test. She had compensated for her split macula by using half her fovea and by rapid and unconscious fixation shifts to develop the characteristic displacement of the vertical border of the visual field.

Hughes has demonstrated a simple way in which the overshot field may be differentiated from true macular sparing (Figure 8-14). If three large test objects are advanced simultaneously from the blind to the seeing field and a central one appears before the peripheral ones, then the macula sparing is real. If the sparing results from a fixation shift, then all three objects will appear simultaneously. Furthermore, at this same moment, an object placed in the blind spot on a tangent screen will also appear, showing that the whole field has shifted toward the blind side. This theory of macular sparing is supported by the clinical fact that the larger the occipital lesion, the more likely is macular sparing. It has been found that in about 70% of cases showing macular sparing, the lesion is in the dominant hemisphere. This apparent macular sparing due to field shift may be caused by associated damage to the visual association areas, resulting in disturbed orientation.

Bilateral representation of the macula has been suggested by several authors as a cause of macular sparing. Horseradish peroxidase studies have demonstrated a macular zone 1 to 3 degrees wide that includes fibers that terminate in both halves of the brain. A unilateral intracranial lesion will affect a certain percentage of the population of foveal fibers and thus spare fixation clinically.

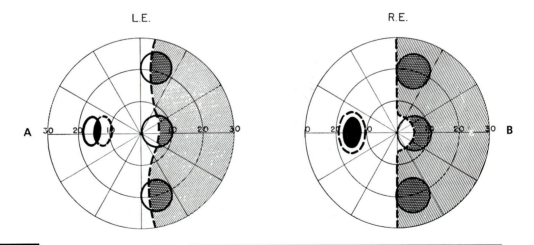

FIGURE 8-14 **A,** False macular sparing as demonstrated by three-disc test. If three white discs are advanced from blind to seeing portion of field, all three come into view simultaneously and normal blind spot shifts toward blind side. **B,** True macular sparing as demonstrated by three-disc test. If three white discs are advanced from blind to seeing portion of field, central disc appears first and blind spot does not shift. *(Adapted from Hughes B: The visual fields, Springfield, Ill, Charles C Thomas, Publisher.*

Regardless of the theoretic explanation of macular sparing, it remains a subject of much interest to the clinical perimetrist; its presence or absence and regularity or irregularity may be of considerable value. In examining patients with potential macular sparing, one must observe fixation carefully or use a multiple-object test on the tangent screen as suggested by Hughes. Under these circumstances, the greater flexibility and more precise fixation monitoring allowed by manual kinetic perimetry on the tangent screen are extremely helpful in separating artifactious from real changes.

Size

Generally the size of a visual field defect is of less diagnostic importance than is its shape or position. Size is of diagnostic value in scotomas, but in sector defects such as hemianopsia size is largely determined by the shape of the defect. The size of a glaucomatous sector defect is important in estimating the extent of damage at the time of diagnosis and the presence or absence of progression of the glaucomatous process during the follow-up period.

When examining the visual field quantitatively, the defect size will often be determined by the isopter tested. If the defect margins slope, then the defect will be larger when small or dim stimuli are used and smaller when more intense stimuli are used (Figure 8-15). For this reason, the defect size cannot be determined with certainty if only a single isopter is tested or if a one-level screening static program is used.

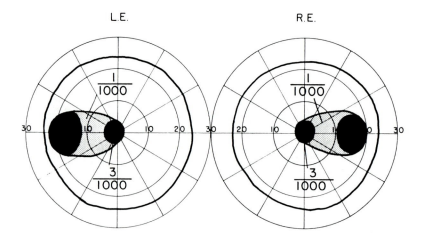

FIGURE 8-15   Example of apparent difference in size and shape of bilateral central scotomas when examined with different-size stimuli. The 3/1000 isopter shows only small central scotoma, whereas examination of 1/1000 isopter demonstrates rather large centrocecal defect. Defects are part of severe nutritional amblyopia associated with subclinical pellagra in chronic alcoholic patient.

The size of a visual field defect does not indicate the size of the lesion producing it, since very large field defects may be produced by minute lesions in areas of the visual pathway where nerve fiber bundles are closely packed together. Conversely, a large lesion in the optic radiations may produce a relatively small or mild visual field defect.

Intensity

The intensity of a visual field defect is determined by the visual acuity within its area (Figure 8-16). This is often referred to as the *depth of the defect.* The deficit may vary from total blindness to all stimuli, including light, to barely detectable or questionable field loss.

Absolute visual loss within the area of the defect is rare. If sufficient stimulation is presented, most defects are found to have some level of visual acuity no matter how faint. It is especially important to remember this when analyzing visual field charts produced by automated perimeters. A numerical printout that indicates a value of 0, or a gray-scale printout that demonstrates an area of confluent blackness indicates only that the patient did not see the size and intensity of stimulus projected to the area in question. In most instances, if a large enough and bright enough test object is used, some visual sensitivity is detected. There are, of course, instances in which absolute scotomas do occur. Surgical or traumatic destruction of a portion of the visual pathway, degenerative or inflammatory retinal destruction, and the normal blind spot are examples of pathologic and physiologic causes of an absolute scotoma.

A very dense visual field defect often indicates relatively complete conduction interference in the visual system. If the onset of the visual loss is

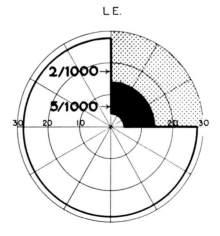

FIGURE 8-16 Example of variation in intensity within area of visual field loss. Quadrantanoptic scotoma is detected in 5/1000 isopter, whereas 2/1000 isopter breaks through into periphery and shows loss of entire quadrant.

sudden or rapid, a virulent, massive, or highly destructive lesion is indicated. In general, the more intense the defect, the poorer the prognosis for complete functional recovery.

On the other end of the scale, the defect may be of such low intensity as to be barely detectable by the most sensitive means available. Much of the thrust of automated perimetry is aimed at improving our ability to reliably detect the earliest visual field defects. Our ability to do this is limited mainly by the difficulty of separating minimally significant defects from transient depressions or physiologic fluctuations. Extensive study has demonstrated that the "line" separating a normal from a pathologic finding is really rather vague. Experience using automated perimeters for static threshold field testing shows that the visual sensitivity at a given point in the retina can change by as much as 10% or 15% over a period of only a few moments. The change can be either in the positive or negative direction, so that what appears to be a defect one moment might appear completely normal the next and vice versa. Fortunately, significant progress is being made in using computer-assisted statistical data evaluation to help the practitioner determine when the change seen represents a pathologic conditon and when it represents transient physiologic variation.

Uniformity

The uniformity of visual loss within a visual field defect may vary considerably, or it may be the same throughout the defect. Quantitative perimetric techniques are essential to analyze the defect correctly, not only as to its size and intensity but also as to its uniformity. The results of quantitative perimetry are often significant when examining glaucoma patients in whom a single-level visual field examination may indicate an altitudinal or quadrantic defect, but in whom multiple isopter or threshold testing indicates a more complicated pattern, such as an arcuate scotoma with peripheral breakthrough.

Static automated perimetry also reveals a characteristic and extremely nonuniform type of generalized depression in acute optic neuritis, such as that associated with multiple sclerosis. In these cases the island hill of vision is pockmarked randomly throughout its extent (Figure 8-17). Similarly, the general depression of a visual field from a patient with compressive optic neuropathy associated with thyroid ophthalmopathy may exhibit a dramatic lack of uniformity when tested appropriately (Figure 8-18).

Margins

The margins of a visual field defect are extremely important, not only in evaluating the progress of the disease producing it, but also in diagnosing specific lesions. In general, the margins of a visual field defect may be regular or irregular, sloping or steep; they may respect the vertical or horizontal meridians or they may not (Figures 8-19 and 8-20).

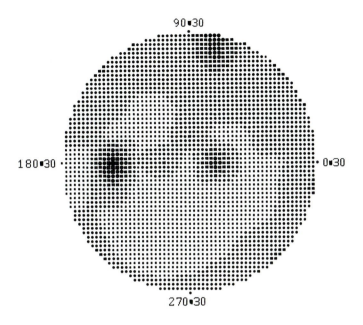

FIGURE 8-17   Generalized depression with irregular scotomas and enlarged blind spot in 37-year-old woman with optic neuritis.

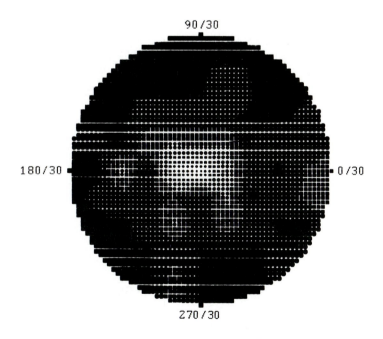

FIGURE 8-18   Dense irregular depression in patient with optic nerve compression secondary to thyroid eye disease. *(Courtesy Devron H. Char, MD)*

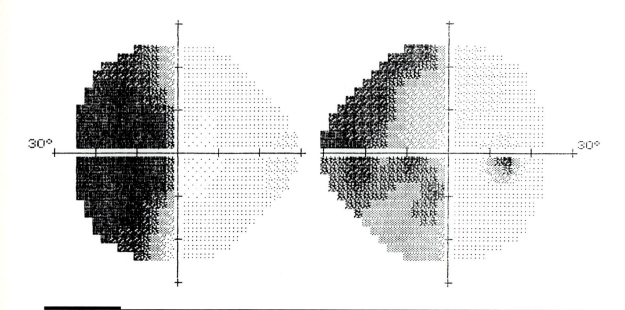

FIGURE 8-19 Left homonymous hemianopsia in woman with right-side carotid aneurysm. Field defect in left eye is uniformly dense, with steep margin. Field defect in right eye is less dense and shows sloping margins.

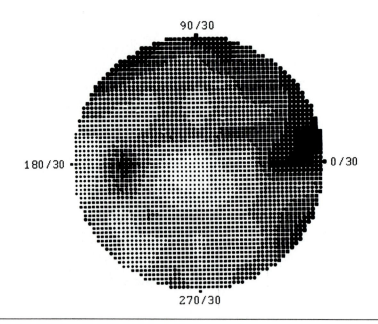

FIGURE 8-20 Computerized field from left eye of 57-year-old woman with open angle glaucoma. Irregular superior arcuate scotoma and superior nasal step have sloping margins. Nasal step defect respects horizontal meridian.

The regularity or irregularity of a visual field defect's margins are important in determining the size and shape of the defect and its degree of congruity.

Margin steepness relates to how abruptly the patient's sensitivity changes from normal to abnormal and secondarily the uniformity and intensity of the depression. Early defects in glaucoma tend to have relatively sloping margins, meaning that when they are tested with small dim targets the defects can appear rather large, but when tested with large bright targets the defects appear quite small or may disappear entirely. The opposite end of the spectrum is illustrated well by healed chorioretinal scars. In these cases visual sensitivity may be perfectly normal in the retina surrounding the scar, but the patient may have no light perception just a few degrees away, in an area where the retina has been destroyed totally (Figure 8-21).

Whether a defect's margins respect the vertical or horizontal meridians can be of pivotal diagnostic importance. The Bjerrum scotoma of glaucoma, for example, crosses the vertical midline, indicating that the lesion is present anterior to the chiasm, but the lesion does not cross the horizontal meridian

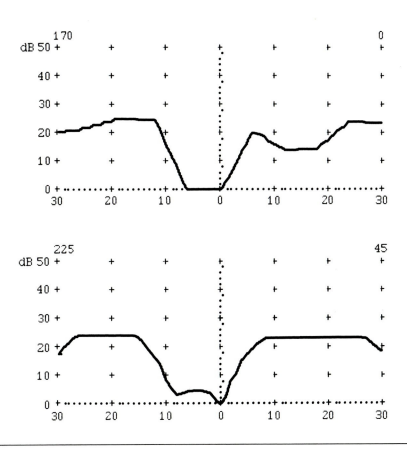

FIGURE 8-21 Dense central scotoma in patient with well-healed chorioretinal scar.

because of the anatomic restrictions of the retinal nerve fiber layer. Conversely, a right homonymous hemianopsia, such as produced by a retrochiasmal lesion, will respect the vertical midline, since each half of the brain only receives visual information from half of the visual field. A homonymous field defect will not respect the horizontal midline because it is not associated with the retinal vasculature or nerve fiber layer.

Measuring the visual field defect's margins can be important in assessing the activity level of the offending disease process. Sloping margins in the field usually indicate a lesion that is either actively progressing or regressing, whereas steep or perpendicular margins imply that the lesion producing the defect is relatively inactive.

Onset and course

The onset and course of visual field loss may be considerably important in diagnosing the pathologic process producing it. Generally a sudden onset is associated with vascular lesions, such as hemorrhage, embolism, or thrombus, or with infection or trauma. Slowly expanding lesions such as tumors are more likely to have a gradual onset and slow progress in the field defect. Sudden hemorrhage within a tumor may confuse the issue when only this characteristic of the field defect is considered.

The only certain way to trace the course and behavior of a field defect is through repeated observations. Sometimes, however, it is possible to determine in one examination the direction in which a field defect is progressing by using quantitative examination methods and analysis of the defect's margins. For example, examination with relatively dim targets may show a complete bitemporal hemianopsia in a given patient, whereas a very bright and large target may show only loss of the lower temporal quadrant. With computerized quantitative perimetry this defect would show up as a moderate to severe loss in the upper temporal quadrants and profound loss in the lower temporal quadrants. This would indicate that at its outset the defect was an inferior bitemporal quadrantanopsia, that it has progressed upward into each temporal field, that its margins are relatively steep, and that the lesion producing the defect is not growing very actively. The pathologic lesion that best fits this combination of circumstances is meningioma. Thus careful analysis of the characteristics of the field defect serves not only to localize the lesion in the visual pathway, but may also indicate its pathologic process.

SCOTOMAS

A scotoma is an area of partial or complete blindness within the confines of a normal or relatively normal visual field. In quantitative terms a scotoma is an area of decreased visual acuity or visual sensitivity within an area of normal or relatively normal sensitivity. Within a scotoma the vision is more depressed than in the areas of the visual field surrounding the scotoma.

Referring to the island hill of vision whose apex is at the fixation point, one can describe the scotoma as a depression on the hill's surface surrounded by a normal contour. The scotoma could be described as a lake, pit, or well, depending on factors such as shape, depth, and shoreline steepness. When mapped kinetically, the scotoma's contour lines, or isopters, surround it without interruption and do not normally extend to the hill's shoreline. When mapped with static profile perimetry, scotomas appear as sharp or shallow dips in the cross-sectional representation of the hill of vision (Figure 8-22).

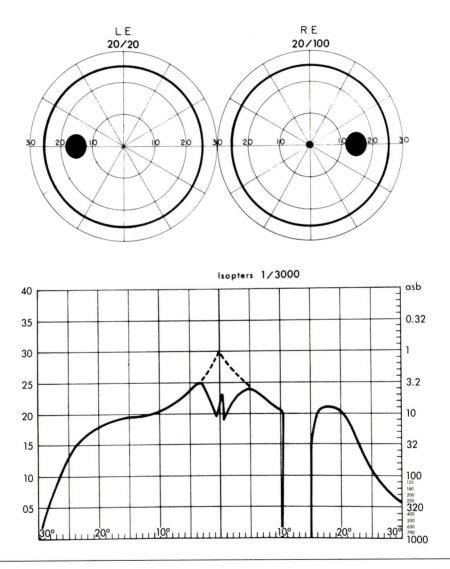

FIGURE 8-22 Tangent screen and static profile perimeter from 12-year-old patient with eclipse burn of fovea. Goldmann perimeter field was normal. Tangent screen field with 1-mm electroluminescent stimulus of 1 footlambert at 3 meters showed minute central scotoma. Threshold sensitivity test on Tübinger perimeter revealed sharp dip in profile at fixation. *(From Harrington DO: Trans Ophthalmol Soc UK 92:15, 1972, London, Churchill Livingstone, Ltd.)*

The "depth" of a scotoma is illustrated clearly by this method of plotting. A shallow depression is one that does not extend much below the normal surround; a deep depression extends far down into the substance of the island hill of vision and perhaps all the way to the sea of blindness below. If the scotoma extends to the periphery of the field, it is said to have "broken through." It may be likened to an inland lake whose walls have eroded away, making it contiguous with the sea.

As with sector visual field defects, scotomas may be unilateral or bilateral and should be analyzed as to their characteristics. These characteristics are generally the same as those for sector defects: (1) position, (2) shape, (3) size, (4) intensity, (5) uniformity, (6) margins, (7) onset and course, and (8) unilateral vs. bilateral.

Position

A scotoma's position is of considerable diagnostic importance and is described as peripheral and/or central.

Peripheral scotomas

Most peripheral scotomas result from localized areas of tissue destruction in the peripheral retina. Commonly such damage is caused by choroiditis or various forms of retinopathy. Bilateral or hemianoptic peripheral scotomas can be caused by lesions of the anterior portion of the lips of the calcarine fissure. Peripheral defects, such as temporal wedge defects or peripheral nasal step defects, can be the initial type of visual field loss in glaucoma.

The incidence of peripheral field loss in early glaucoma seems to depend somewhat on methodology. The peripheral field, that beyond 30 degrees from fixation, is usually not tested with a tangent screen; thus tangent field studies by definition would not detect peripheral field damage as an initial sign of glaucomatous field loss. Careful manual perimetry with the Goldmann perimeter has demonstrated peripheral lesions that are the initial form of field loss in glaucoma in approximately 10% of cases. Combinations of computerized threshold static and screening perimetry rarely show peripheral field loss in the absence of central loss. Several computerized field studies have shown peripheral field loss in early glaucoma, but these have commonly been associated with significant field loss within 30 degrees of fixation and revealed a high incidence of false-positive tests in normal control subjects.

This disagreement between computerized and manual static perimetry, and Goldmann static and kinetic perimetry, regarding the incidence of peripheral defects as a presenting sign in glaucoma is likely to have one of two circumstances as its cause: either manual kinetic perimetry is more sensitive in finding peripheral lesions than is computerized static perimetry, or computerized static perimetry is more sensitive in finding subtle central defects than is manual perimetry with the Goldmann apparatus. Currently the latter circumstance seems more likely.

Central scotomas

Central scotomas may be classified as central, paracentral, pericentral, and cecal. Among these positions, the central scotomas and the nerve fiber bundle defect, or paracentral scotoma, are the most common and affect vision the most profoundly. A central scotoma may be produced by a great variety of lesions. Its characteristics, other than position, are diagnostically helpful in localizing the lesion and in indicating the responsible pathologic process.

Central. Only the fixation area and the field immediately surrounding it are involved (Figure 8-23, *A*).

Paracentral. The area of depressed visual acuity is slightly eccentric from fixation, which is not involved. Paracentral scotomas may be classified further as to whether they are above, below, nasal, or temporal to fixation or in terms of the quadrant in which they lie. The normal blind spot may be considered as a type of paracentral scotoma (Figure 8-23, *B*).

Pericentral. The fixation area is relatively clear, and the field immediately and equally surrounding it shows a doughnut of depressed sensitivity (Figure 8-24, *A*).

Cecal. The area of the normal blind spot is involved. These scotomas may be simple enlargements of the blind spot or they may be pericecal or paracecal. In the latter instance, they are described as occurring above, below, nasal, or temporal to the blind spot.

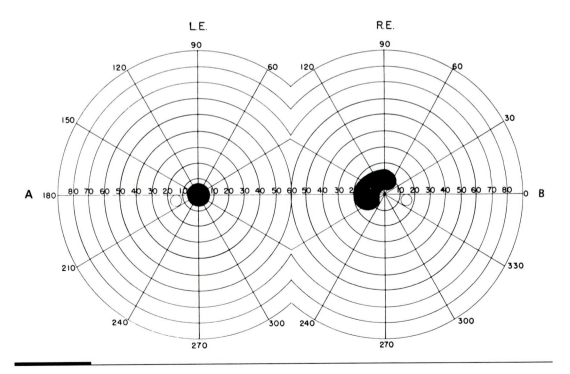

FIGURE 8-23 **A,** Central scotoma, left eye. **B,** Paracentral scotoma, right eye.

There are three forms of cecal scotomas: (1) the centrocecal defect, which extends from the blind spot toward or into the fixation area and is exemplified in the rather common papillomacular bundle defect seen in retrobulbar neuritis and in the scotoma of tobacco-nutritional amblyopia (Figure 8-24, *B*); (2) the angioscotoma, with its almost infinite variety of forms; and (3) the glaucomatous nerve fiber bundle or arcuate defect.

Shape

The scotoma's shape, regardless of its position, is extremely important. Whenever a depressed area is detected, careful quantitative means must be used to find its precise shape. What appears as an isolated irregular superior quadrant depression may reveal itself to be an arcuate scotoma or part of a superior quadrantanopsia with more thorough investigation. An irregular scotoma may be more indicative of a localized retinal disturbance than a retrobulbar or intracranial lesion.

A ring scotoma may be found in degenerative conditions, such as retinitis pigmentosa, as a late finding in patients with glaucoma, or may be associated with toxic or pharmacologic agents.

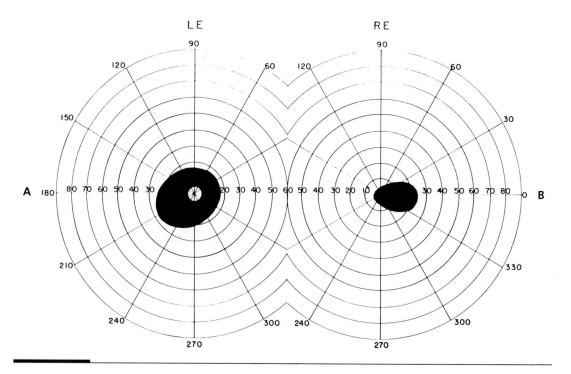

FIGURE 8-24   A, Pericentral scotoma, left eye. **B,** Centrocecal scotoma, right eye.

Nerve fiber bundle scotoma

This type of defect may also be known as an arcuate, scimitar, comet, Bjerrum, or Seidel scotoma. Characteristically, it follows the retinal nerve fiber pattern and consequently takes an arched form around fixation from the blind spot to the horizontal raphe in the nasal field, where it ends typically in a sharply demarcated horizontal nasal step (Figure 8-25).

Nerve fiber bundle defects may be incomplete, especially when examined with large or bright targets. The defect may appear to arise from the blind spot and follow the fiber pattern for a short distance before fading out into areas of normal vision. It may begin at the horizontal meridian in the nasal field, at varying distances from fixation, and arch temporally toward the blind spot but never reach it. It may appear as a curved, sausage-shaped defect lying directly above or below fixation midway between the blind spot and horizontal raphe. When such a curve is projected in either direction, it follows the path of the retinal nerve fiber bundles and invariably includes the blind spot. A series of small isolated paracentral depressions may appear in an area that has been referred to as the *Bjerrum region,* before coalescing into a typical nerve fiber bundle defect. This region is anywhere along an arc averaging about 15 degrees above or below fixation, from the blind spot around toward

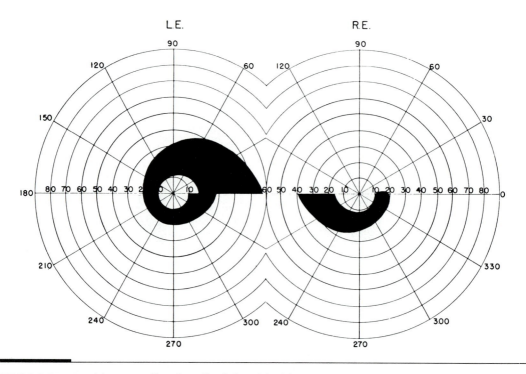

FIGURE 8-25 Double nerve fiber bundle defect (double arcuate scotoma) with nasal steps, left eye, and nerve fiber bundle defect (inferior arcuate scotoma), right eye.

the horizontal nasal raphe, and extending out along this horizontal raphe to 25 or 30 degrees or more from fixation.

Rarely, a nerve fiber bundle defect may extend temporally above or below the blind spot. These scotomas also follow the retinal nerve fiber bundle pattern but are straight or cuneate instead of curved and form narrow wedges of blindness extending into the temporal field.

In late glaucoma, a double arcuate scotoma will arise from the blind spot and arch above and below fixation to meet in the nasal field. Depending on the degree of peripheral breakthrough, the field is seen either as a ring scotoma or as only a central island of vision remaining. In the former case it is unusual to have symmetrically placed and perfectly equal nerve fiber bundle defects. Careful testing can practically always demonstrate a difference in the width and position of the superior and inferior defects, with the result that the meeting at the nasal horizontal meridian is asymmetric, and a characteristic wide or narrow double nasal step is formed. This pattern and the fact that the blind spot is always involved in the line of the ring serve to differentiate this type of double arcuate scotoma from the ring scotoma.

Although nerve fiber bundle scotomas may take a wide variety of forms and positions, certain constant characteristics help identify these defects readily. They arch around but do not involve fixation. Because nerve fiber

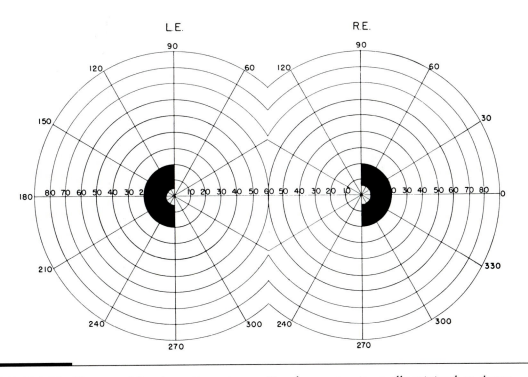

FIGURE 8-26 Bitemporal hemianoptic scotomas. Macular sparing is usually minimal or absent.

bundle scotomas are produced by lesions anterior to the chiasm, they tend to be asymmetric between the two eyes. They are associated with the retinal nerve fiber layer, retinal vasculature, or optic nervehead and therefore always appear to originate or terminate at or in line with the optic nervehead. Nerve fiber bundle scotomas do not respect the vertical meridian but do respect the horizontal meridian.

Certainly glaucomatous visual field defects form the overwhelming majority of arcuate field loss seen in clinical practice today. However, any lesion that interferes with the vascular supply to the anterior optic nerve in the region of the ring of Zinn-Haller may also give rise to nerve fiber bundle scotomas. The visual field defects these lesions produce may be indistinguishable from the field defect produced by glaucoma. A fairly large number of lesions may cause such confusion, and these will be discussed later.

Hemianoptic scotoma

Hemianoptic scotomas are bounded by the vertical meridian of the field. In reality, they are central hemianoptic defects. As is the case with peripheral hemianoptic defects, central hemianoptic defects can be homonymous, congruous or incongruous, quadrantic, temporal (Figure 8-26), cross quadrantic, or paracentral. They may spare or split fixation.

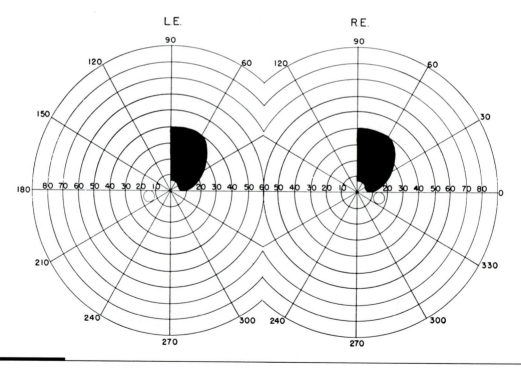

FIGURE 8-27 Homonymous hemianoptic scotomas. Vascular lesion of left occipital lobe involved inferior lip of posterior tip of left calcarine fissure. Note complete congruity of defects.

If the hemianoptic scotoma is bounded by a vertical and a horizontal meridian, it may appear triangular, with its apex at or near fixation (Figure 8-27). A temporal hemianoptic scotoma may be associated with blindness, a temporal hemianopsia, or a peripheral quadrantanoptic cut in the opposite field. This is one form of the classic junctional scotoma (Figure 8-28).

Careful analysis of the margins, intensity, and uniformity of a hemianoptic scotoma is necessary to reveal its true shape. When so studied, these scotomas may be extremely useful in indicating the location and pathologic process of an etiologic lesion.

Size

Although a scotoma's size may be of some value in indicating the virulence of the lesion producing the defect, size is generally less important diagnostically than is shape or position.

When considering the size of a given visual field defect, it is important to distinguish between apparent changes in size and real changes in size. Apparent changes in size are most commonly caused by changes in testing parameters or changes in the patient's distance from the target site.

When the visual field is tested by different parameters or under different conditions, the size of any defect will appear to enlarge or shrink based on

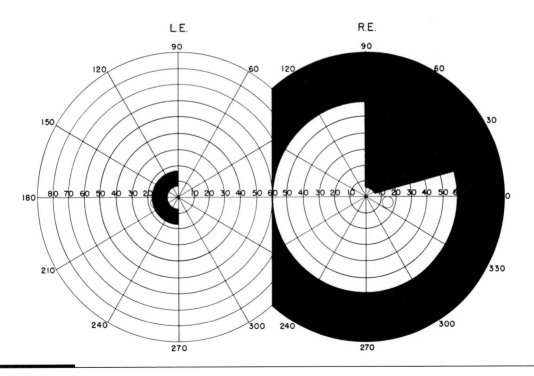

FIGURE 8-28 Junctional scotoma. Patient had aneurysm of left anterior cerebral artery with compression of left optic nerve and anterior chiasm.

a large number of factors. With manual kinetic perimetry the most obvious of these factors is the isopter tested. Any defect with a sloping margin will appear larger when tested with smaller dimmer objects than with larger brighter objects. Regardless of the field testing method, factors such as room illumination, pupil size, and accuracy of refraction can change the apparent size of a field defect if these parameters are not controlled carefully from one examination to the next.

In addition to these factors, when the visual field is plotted on a tangent screen or similar apparatus, one must be careful to note the patient's distance from the screen. Visual field defects subtend constant angles. As the patient moves closer to the tangent screen, the visual field defect will appear smaller, and as the patient moves further away, the defect will seem to enlarge. Of course, when plotted accurately, this apparent change in defect size corresponds perfectly with a symmetric enlargement or contraction of the entire visual field; the relative size of the defective portion of the field stays the same. Remembering this fact can be important when testing patients with functional field loss. In such patients the absolute size of the visual field will often stay the same, even though the patient's distance from the tangent screen is halved or doubled. Such an occurrence cannot be explained physiologically.

Real changes in the size of a visual field defect are generally associated with a physiologic or pathologic change.

A reversible transient change in the size of visual field defects is a ubiquitous finding. Even if all of the appropriate parameters have been controlled optimally, normal physiologic sensitivity fluctutation can make any defect appear marginally larger or smaller in just a few minutes. Furthermore, recent experimental evidence indicates that some patients may actually have an improvement of visual field loss from glaucoma when their intraocular pressures are lowered. Angioscotomas may be widened and intensified by raising the intraocular pressure transiently through digital pressure on the globe.

The most important reason for a change in a visual field defect size is a progressive pathologic condition. In general, the more rapid and profound the progression, the more virulent the pathologic process.

Intensity (Uniformity)

The intensity of scotomas can vary from absolute blindness to minimally detectable visual acuity loss. A scotoma's intensity may vary nonuniformly throughout its area. Highly intense and uniform scotomas are relatively rare; this is demonstrated easily by almost all forms of perimetry. Defects that require careful quantitative methods to demonstrate their true size, depth, and uniformity are much more common. Static threshold perimetry is particularly suited to this type of analysis, because its major thrust is measuring visual sensitivity (the converse of a scotoma's intensity) at multiple sites throughout the visual field.

It is certainly possible to accurately assess a scotoma's intensity using multiple isopters on the Goldmann perimeter. Depending on the size of the scotoma and the degree of intensity variation, this may be fairly straightforward or quite challenging.

Testing varyingly intensive scotomas on the tangent screen is fairly simple but requires a bit of ingenuity. As a general approach, one should consider varying the parameters and testing conditions in ways that make the contrast between the test object and the background less distinct. The tangent screen may have particular value in assessing the size of small central or paracentral depressions. When a patient is moved a considerable distance back from the screen, the projected size of even minute scotomas will increase and be easier to assess.

A method of demonstrating a minimal central scotoma is to use the principle of two-point discrimination. If a barely visible stimulus is chosen for fixation, a patient with a small central scotoma will be able to see it by constantly shifting fixation in order to bring the fixation point outside the scotomatous area. If a stimulus of the same size is brought slowly in to the point of fixation, an area may be demonstrated in which one or the other of the stimuli may be seen, but not both simultaneously. Such a technique may be necessary to demonstrate the minute central defect resulting from an eclipse burn of the fovea or the vague foveal edema associated with contusion of the globe or central serous retinopathy.

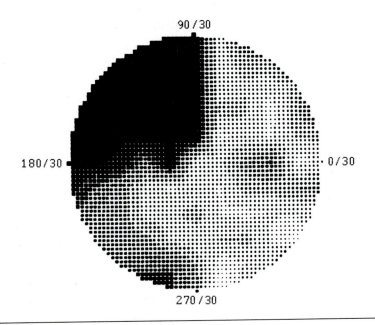

FIGURE 8-29 Quadrantanopsia. Halftone printout indicates somewhat sloping margin, when in reality margins were very steep. Apparent slope is artifact of algorithm used to generate display.

Scotomas are usually more dense in their centers than at their edges. This lack of uniformity often makes them appear to have one or more central or eccentric nuclei when examined carefully. This finding may be somewhat overemphasized on the gray-scale printouts of some computerized perimeters. Many of these perimeters are programmed to assume smooth progression from test point to test point within the field. The gray-scale printouts are generated to follow "best fit" lines drawn between adjacent test points. These lines may indicate a fairly gentle slope even though the field defect has a very steep wall (Figure 8-29). Careful analysis of the computer's numerical printout can be useful in evaluating such findings carefully.

Margins

A scotoma's margins usually slope but may occasionally be quite steep. In general a steep edge indicates a more static lesion, whereas a sloping margin indicates a more active process.

Onset and Course

The onset and course of a scotoma may be of great importance. There is a marked variation among different diseases. The onset of the scotoma associated with chronic open angle glaucoma tends to be gradual and its course tends to be slow, whereas the central scotoma resulting from multiple sclerosis may appear in a matter of hours and be gone again in a day. As is the case with peripheral defects, vascular lesions generally produce the most rapid onset of scotomas; inflammatory lesions produce defects with the most erratic course; and defects produced by chronic disease or by the pressure of intracranial neoplasms are the least variable.

Unilateral or Bilateral Scotomas

Scotomas may be unilateral or bilateral. Hemianoptic scotomas from lesions of the postchiasmal pathway are always bilateral, but it must not be inferred that all bilateral scotomas are postchiasmal in origin. It is not uncommon for the disease that affects one retina or optic nerve to affect the other. Advanced multiple sclerosis or glaucoma may give rise to bilateral or even symmetric field loss.

A unilateral scotoma may indicate the pathologic process that produced it, largely because of its shape, size, density, and other characteristics. Although unilateral scotomas are usually caused by diseases of the visual pathway anterior to the chiasm, the Foster Kennedy syndrome and also the junction scotoma found in certain anterior chiasmal lesions may be exceptions. Furthermore, with careful testing, what appears to be a unilateral scotoma may in fact be dramatically asymmetric field loss.

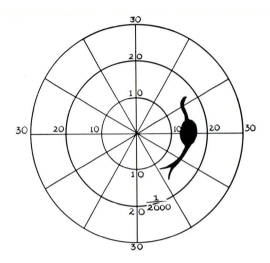

FIGURE 8-30 Normal angioscotoma as plotted on tangent screen with minimal stimulus and reduced illumination.

Angioscotomas

Angioscotomas have been described variously by many investigators.

Because angioscotomas are extensions from the blind spot, they may be considered as cecal, pericecal, or paracecal. These extensions follow the arborizations of the retinovascular tree (Figure 8-30). They can be difficult to map, especially as one travels any distance from the optic nervehead. Angioscotomas are produced in regions where the photoreceptors are obscured by the retinal blood vessels. Angioscotomas are difficult to detect because of their small size and unpredictable course and because even slight fixation deviations allow the patient to see what was concealed by the scotoma only a moment previously. Reproducing angioscotomatous defects requires optimal testing conditions and an unusually cooperative patient.

CONCLUSION

Implicit in the foregoing discussion is that the examiner should use the most sophisticated means possible to extract and record data regarding the characteristics of any visual field defect. The quality, accuracy, and reproducibility of the visual field defect relate directly to the quality, accuracy, and reproducibility of the testing circumstances. The perimetrist who examines a visual field exhaustively is in a much better position to use this visual field information to help make diagnostic and therapeutic decisions.

9

MEDIA OPACITIES (CORNEA, LENS, AND VITREOUS) AND THEIR EFFECT ON THE VISUAL FIELDS

Perimetry performed with relatively dim stimuli or reduced target-to-background contrast results in a generally depressed visual field in normal individuals. As dimmer and dimmer stimuli are used to test the visual field, the height and extent of the island hill of vision becomes smaller and smaller until at a certain level the stimulus is undetected. The island hill disappears into the sea. Given constant testing conditions, a filter in front of the patient's eye with a perimeter or reduced room illumination with a tangent screen will produce a correspondingly smaller visual field than testing with the same objects without filters or under normal illumination.

Any opacity of the ocular media reduces test object illumination. However, a failure to attempt a visual field examination is not justified simply because the media are so opaque as to preclude testing with routine parameters or commonly used test objects. When interpreting visual field defects in an eye with media opacities, one must make adequate allowance for the opacity's effect on the visual field chart.

If the cornea, lens, or vitreous is so cloudy that routine test objects are invisible, the perimetrist must use more light, larger test objects, or both. In extreme circumstances, when the largest and brightest test targets on Goldmann or computerized perimeters are not visible, useful information can be obtained with oversize targets on a tangent screen or by using a white bath towel or flashlight to test for large quadrantic or hemianoptic defects.

Visual field assessment can be an important part of the workup in patients with dense cataracts. Interpretation can be particularly difficult, however, when two diseases are present simultaneously. The most common combination we encounter is glaucoma and cataract. It can be difficult to tell if visual acuity loss results from an increase in the density of the cataract or from an encroachment on fixation by the glaucomatous visual field defect. Conversely, when one encounters an expanding glaucomatous visual field defect in a patient with a significant cataract, it is sometimes difficult to determine whether the field defect is progressing because of uncontrolled glaucoma or because of increased cataract density (Figure 9-1).

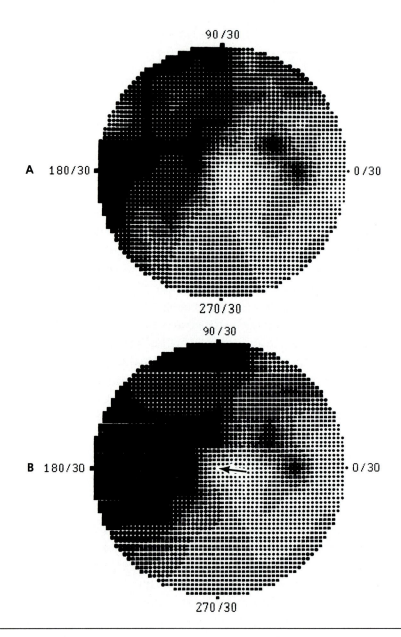

FIGURE 9-1 **A,** Dense superior arcuate scotoma with nasal peripheral breakthrough in 76-year-old woman with glaucoma and cataracts. **B,** Field from same eye of same patient 3½ months later showing increased consolidation of peripheral nasal defect *(arrow)*. It is impossible to tell if this increased field density is due to progression of glaucoma or to media opacity by examining visual field data alone.

Examination with a potential acuity meter or similar instrument may be helpful in some cases. We find that the most helpful way of assessing such patients is to keep copious and detailed records regarding the appearance and density of the media opacity, the condition of the optic nervehead, and the assessment of the visual fields. When reviewed serially these data can sometimes help the practitioner determine which if either disease is progressing more significantly.

When initially evaluating a patient with glaucoma and cataracts, it is particularly important to perform high-quality visual field studies. It is likely that the cataract will progress over time and that the examiner's ability to measure the visual field accurately will be diminished. The initial examination may, in fact, be the last good opportunity to assess the visual field adequately. This can be very important when monitoring the patient before surgery and, if cataract surgery is performed later, when comparing the subsequent visual field with the initial field to determine whether the glaucoma has been progressive during the interval. For optimal glaucoma management it is also important to meticulously record the morphologic details of the optic nerve before these details are obscured by progressive media opacity.

A decrease in pupillary size will decrease the overall size and sensitivity level of the visual field (Figure 9-2). In the presence of a cataract, vitreous opacity, or even a small central corneal opacity, the effects of a small pupil are magnified. In these instances it may be possible to obtain a more accurate estimate of the visual field with the pupils dilated than in their normal state. If the visual field is measured with the pupil dilated, it is important to use the same medications and the same size dilation for subsequent examinations.

If a patient demonstrates a generally depressed field in the face of moderate media opacity, one should consider using larger or brighter test objects. With manual perimetry this is fairly straightforward; the field is simply tested with more intense stimuli. With computerized static perimetry one may use a nonstandard parameter such as a 64 sq mm (Goldmann size V) test target (Figure 9-3). With this larger test object the computerized machine will map the visual field using increasingly intense stimuli, within the machine's technical limits. As with dilation, it is extremely important that any change in testing conditions (brighter illumination, larger targets, etc.) be recorded, and duplicated for subsequent examinations.

Reduced illumination seems to affect the visual fields for colors even more than it does for white. A true visual field defect in an eye with media opacities will be exaggerated when colored stimuli are used. The central field for blue is affected first, followed by green, yellow, and red in the more peripheral portions of the field. By projecting orange or red stimuli, it may be possible to diagnose retinal, choroidal, or optic nerve disease, including glaucoma, when ophthalmic examination of these structures is impossible because of the level of media opacification.

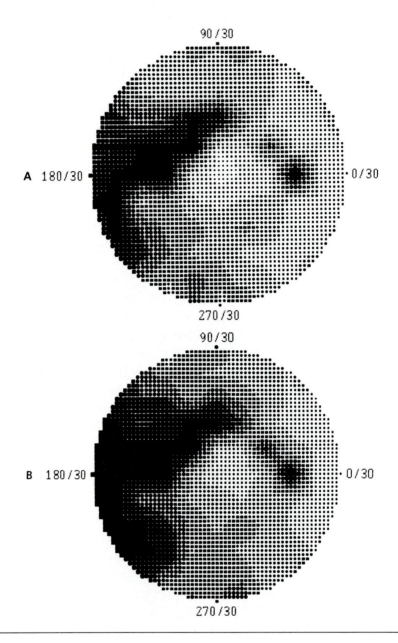

FIGURE 9-2   **A,** This patient with open-angle glaucoma was prescribed miotic therapy to reduce his intraocular pressure. Visual field taken before therapy shows dense superior arcuate scotoma and inferior nasal step. **B,** Visual field taken 2 months after miotic therapy began shows intensification of peripheral nasal defect because of effects of miotic pupil. Subsequent testing was done with pupils dilated, and those fields showed sensitivity similar to that shown in **A.**

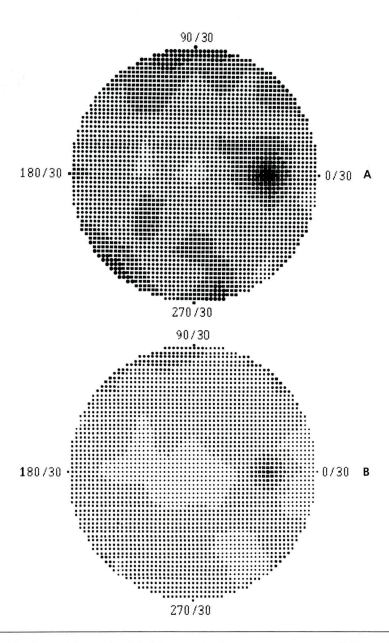

FIGURE 9-3 **A,** This field, taken with standard Goldmann size III target on Octopus field machine, shows mild to moderate generalized depression. **B,** When repeated 1 week later with nonstandard Goldmann size V target, overall sensitivity of entire field appears better. Apparent increase in sensitivity is due to use of larger test object.

In aphakic patients (but not pseudophakic patients), even those with clear media, the visual field may be contracted considerably. Unfortunately, this normal phenomenon is intensified further by the spheric aberration produced by cataract glasses. Cataract glasses magnify central images so that the patient's central field is projected over a larger area than normal. Depending upon the power of the glasses and the vertex distance, this magnification can range from 25% to 30%. If the patient can tolerate it and appropriate lenses are available, many practitioners have advocated testing aphakic fields while the patient's vision is temporarily corrected with a soft contact lens. The magnification of central images and the corresponding narrowing of the visual field is considerably less (approximately 7% to 10% magnification) with contact lenses than with aphakic spectacles.

Patients with successful intraocular lens implants (pseudophakia) do not experience the image size disparity and distortion that occur in aphakic patients with spectacle corrections, and to a lesser degree contact lens corrections.

10 CHOROIDAL DISEASE

Visual field studies in patients with choroidal disease can be useful both diagnostically and as a means of assessing the course and prognosis of the disease. Most choroidal disease that affects the visual pathway is visible ophthalmoscopically. The type, location, severity, and course of choroidal disease can be judged most effectively by careful ophthalmoscopic examination of the fundus, fluorescein angiography, and ultrasonography.

In general, choroidal lesions affect vision by extending to the retina, by producing secondary retinitis, by depriving portions of the retina of its vascular supply, by producing secondary retinal edema, or by promoting deleterious anatomic alterations such as nonrhegmatogenous retinal detachment.

Initially the visual field defects may be disproportionate to the observable fundus lesions. Precise quantitative perimetry is difficult with many of these lesions, however. The visual field defects may be variable, ranging from insignificant involvement to profound field loss. They can be irregular, particularly with inflammatory and vascular lesions. Recording visual field information from a patient with choroidal disease can be challenging and may result in a rather bizarre visual field chart. The information supplied by the visual fields should be correlated carefully with information gained from the physical examination and from office and diagnostic laboratory tests.

Choroiditis may affect any part of the fundus. Juxtapupillary choroiditis may affect the nerve fiber layer of the retina and may extend through the retina to affect the ganglion cell layer as well. The optic nervehead may be affected, resulting in characteristic visual field changes. When these findings are associated with exudation into the vitreous and a consequent clouding of the ocular media, the perimetric examination may help localize the lesion site.

Choroiditis of various types and locations may produce a variety of visual field defects: (1) general depression; (2) multiple scotomas, corresponding to the location of choroiditis and the area of overlying retinal lesions; (3) enlargement or extension of the normal blind spot; (4) an arcuate scotoma; (5) a sector defect; and (6) a central scotoma. These defects may coexist. A generalized depression of the smaller isopters may be associated with multiple peripheral scotomas detected with larger stimuli. The sector defect of juxta-pupillary choroiditis may take an arcuate form or may involve the fixation area at the same time that it enlarges the normal blind spot.

General depression or even marked contraction of the field often ac-companies acute and severe choroiditis, especially when there is vitreous exudation. Later, choroiditis may resolve into a mosaic of visual field loss. The visual field may have scattered multiple scotomas that correspond to the pigmented patches of healed chorioretinitis seen with the ophthalmoscope. At times these scotomas follow the pattern of the retinal vascular tree and can be demonstrated by angioscotometry.

When uveitis involves the optic nervehead, there is usually an enlarge-ment of the blind spot, a central scotoma, or both. This blind spot enlargement may vary within wide limits; it may appear as a simple overall enlargement in all its diameters, as an extension of the superior or inferior pole that simulates an early arcuate scotoma from glaucoma, or as the sector defect of juxtapupillary choroiditis; if the process involves the papillomacular nerve fiber bundles, a dense cecocentral scotoma may appear.

The true arcuate scotoma seen in patients with glaucoma is rare in choroiditis. When present, it implies involvement of the retinal nerve fiber layer. What may at first appear to be a nerve fiber bundle defect will, with careful study, often fail to reveal the characteristic nerve fiber bundle patterns, the nasal broadening, or the nasal step. More often the defect is irregular, dense, and steep margined, following the arcuate form only roughly.

Central scotomas are found commonly in patients with choroiditis. They vary from the most minute defect, encompassing less than 1 degree around fixation, to extensive central visual loss with little more than light perception remaining. If macular involvement is slight, the ophthalmoscopic appearance may be normal at first glance. Careful perimetry may demonstrate a minute scotoma that confirms the patient's rather vague symptoms of visual blurring. In such cases a repeat examination with the ophthalmoscope, a careful eval-uation of the macula with a slit lamp and contact (Hruby, or 90-diopter) lens, or careful examination of a fluorescein angiogram may reveal a localized area of retinal edema overlying a small patch of submacular choroiditis.

At times choroiditis can cause a positive scotoma that produces distressing symptoms out of proportion to the lesion size or the visual field defect size.

A rather common form of scotoma in patients with choroiditis is a peri-foveal defect in which the central part of the scotoma is less dense than the periphery. These scotomas evolve as multiple, small paracentral defects. They can be associated with trauma, central serous retinopathy, or any entity that produces foveal edema. Another variant of central scotoma seen with cho-roiditis is the minute paramacular defect that exists as a positive scotoma but fails to involve the fovea, with the result that central visual acuity, as tested by Snellen letters, remains good. In their early stages these lesions may produce retinal edema involving fixation, resulting in an irregular and eccentrically placed central scotoma and defective central vision. The defect margins are usually sloping. As the process regresses, the central field may clear, leaving a small permanent paramacular defect in the central field.

DISSEMINATED CHOROIDITIS

The field defects in disseminated choroiditis vary greatly, depending on the stage of the disease and its intensity. Usually there is a rather marked generalized depression, with later development of multiple peripheral scotomas (Figure 10-1). The macula may be involved, producing a central scotoma.

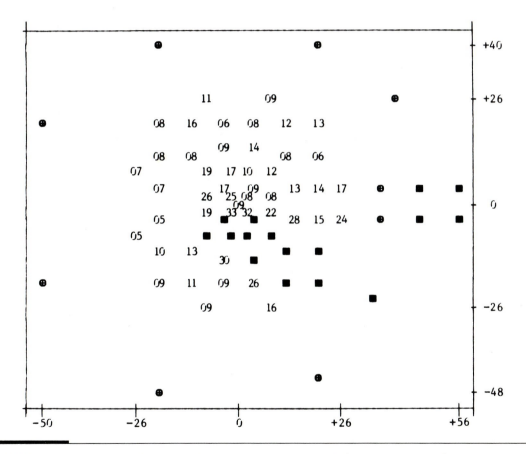

FIGURE 10-1 Sophisticated printout from computerized visual field examination of left eye of patient with uveitis and glaucoma. Black boxes represent no response or absolute loss. Dark circles around periphery indicate moderate loss. Cluster of numbers in central 26 degrees of field are from subtraction table and represent difference between patient's responses and normal. Absolute loss occurs in inferior arcuate pattern, and results from patient's secondary glaucoma. Diffuse loss represented by moderate to severe depressions within remainder of central field result from patient's chorioretinitis.

JUXTAPUPILLARY CHOROIDITIS

Juxtapupillary choroiditis is associated with arcuate, sector, or cuneate nerve fiber bundle defects that resemble arcuate defects from other causes, such as glaucoma. Juxtapupillary choroiditis can be localized exactly at the disc margin by the narrow sector type of nerve fiber bundle defect that it produces in the visual field. This defect varies greatly in size, shape, position, and other characteristics, but it always arises at the blind spot and extends in a nerve fiber bundle pattern into the peripheral field. In most cases it will break through, but in some instances it takes on the exact characteristics of the Bjerrum scotoma found in glaucoma, including the nasal step. A double arcuate scotoma, which may be common in advanced glaucoma, would be a rare coincidence in juxtapupillary choroiditis. Temporal extensions of the blind spot in the form of fan-shaped defects are more common in patients with juxtapupillary choroiditis than in patients with glaucoma. The location of the lesion is such that a small area of choroiditis involving only a few of the nerve fiber bundles may still produce an extensive visual field defect.

MACULAR CHOROIDITIS

With choroiditis limited to the macula, one may find central, pericentral, or paracentral scotomas.

SYMPATHETIC OPHTHALMIA

The visual field loss in sympathetic ophthalmia varies with the intensity of the disease. Peripheral choroiditis is relatively common and causes marked contraction of the field, especially in the periphery. The foveal area may also be involved in the sympathizing eye, with the resulting central scotoma.

AGE-RELATED MACULAR DEGENERATION

Age-related macular degeneration involves the choroid and the retina, depending on the specific subcategory of macular degeneration involved and the duration and extent of the disease. It affects the visual field through retinal damage. The usual field defect is a negative central scotoma of varying density. At times the fovea is affected late, so that in the early stages the scotoma may appear paracentral.

In the early stages of the disease it may be difficult to demonstrate a central scotoma. Evidence indicates that contrast sensitivity is down in these patients, and careful static perimetry may afford one the best chance of detecting a slight decrease in central sensitivity (Figure 10-2). As the disease progresses the scotoma becomes more dense. If the condition progresses to disciform degeneration, a sudden visual loss may occur, with hemorrhage into the macular area and a dense irregular central scotoma (Figure 10-3).

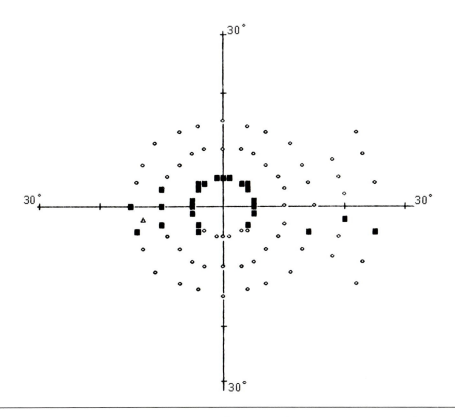

FIGURE 10-2 Field from right eye of patient with age-related macular degeneration. Central screening field performed on patient with involutional macular degeneration. Open circles represent normal responses, and black boxes represent depressed responses. Depressed responses here are clustered mainly in ring of points representing central 5 degrees of visual field. A few depressed points can be seen in region of blind spot to the left and in nasal periphery to the right.

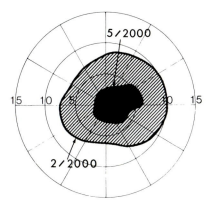

FIGURE 10-3 Large, irregular central scotoma with sloping margins in typical case of disciform degeneration of macula. Other eye showed early involutional macular degeneration with small paracentral scotoma. *(From Harrington DO: In Straatsma BR, et al: Retina: morphology, function and clinical characteristics. UCLA Forum in Medical Sciences, no. 8, Berkeley, 1969, University of California Press, © 1969 The Regents of the University of California.)*

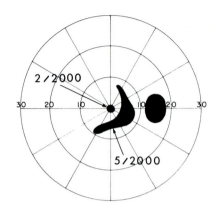

FIGURE 10-4   Crescent-shaped paracentral scotoma and small central scotoma from traumatic rupture of choroid. *(From Harrington DO: In Straatsma BR, et al: Retina: morphology, function and clinical characteristics. UCLA Forum in Medical Sciences, no. 8, Berkeley, 1969, University of California Press, © 1969 The Regents of the University of California.)*

CHOROIDAL RUPTURE

Choroidal rupture may follow a contusion injury of the eye. It is usually seen as a crescentic break in the choroid temporal to the optic disc. It may be accompanied by retinal hemorrhage and edema, which may involve the macula and produce a central scotoma (Figure 10-4). Sector defects may be produced by nerve fiber bundle interruption. The visual field defect generally corresponds to the size, shape, and location of the fundus lesion.

CHOROIDAL TUMORS

The visual field defects produced by choroidal tumors vary considerably according to the size and position of the tumor. Anterior choroidal tumors produce peripheral depressions or sector defects, whereas those of the posterior pole may produce central or paracentral scotomas. These defects are characterized by intensity and steep margins, in contrast to sloping edges and varying density of field defects in retinal detachment with subretinal fluid.

With meticulous perimetry, choroidal nevi may show visual field defects. When the visual field defect accompanying the nevus is clear, demonstrated easily, and progressive, it is reasonable to question the diagnosis. Such patients should be evaluated and followed up carefully.

Flindall and Drance studied 21 benign choroidal nevi. Using a Tübinger perimeter with both static and kinetic techniques, they found an 85% incidence of visual field defects localized to the site of the lesion. All of these defects were slight to moderate depressions and were more readily detected with

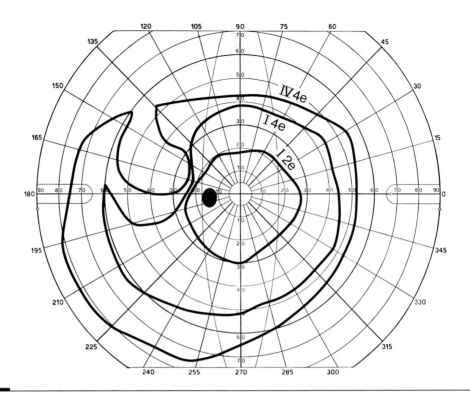

FIGURE 10-5   Dense superotemporal depression in patient with choroidal melanoma.

static than with kinetic perimetry. The field defects were the same size or smaller than the actual lesion.

Three eyes with malignant melanoma were studied by the same techniques. All three had some overlying retinal detachment, and all had absolute scotomas extending into the periphery beyond the limits of the tumor itself.

As a rule kinetic perimetry is more suitable for studying large choroidal tumors, than is static perimetry (Figure 10-5). Kinetic perimetry is valuable for the physician who is treating such tumor patients, particularly when the tumors are small enough that careful follow-up or radiation is the treatment of choice. In these cases careful visual field follow-up can augment data obtained by other means, such as ophthalmoscopic examination and ultrasound. Evidence of tumor growth, involution, or regression may be critically important in diagnostic and therapeutic decisions. Only by performing the visual fields personally will the physician be able to derive the maximal benefit from field examinations in such patients.

When choroidal tumors are accompanied by an overlying serous fluid, the visual field defect may take on some of the characteristics of simple retinal detachment. Usually the denser portions of the scotoma or sector defect correspond to the area of retina in contact with the tumor or overlying its highest point. The more dependent area of retinal detachment produces a sloping edge defect indistinguishable from a simple retinal detachment.

MYOPIA

Unless significant choroidal changes are visible with the ophthalmoscope, the visual fields in patients with myopia are usually normal. It is extremely important to correct for myopia accurately before subjecting these patients to visual field examination. A mild degree of blur can collapse the isopters with kinetic perimetry or depress sensitivity values with static threshold perimetry. Furthermore, in some patients with moderate to high myopia, bizarre or unexplainable "refractive scotomas" may appear even with a reasonably accurate correction in place. In such cases, adding one to a few diopters of minus correction may cause the scotoma to disappear.

In myopic choroidal atrophy the visual field changes usually parallel those seen with the ophthalmoscope. Peripheral degeneration produces general depression or contraction, and perimetry under dim illumination may reveal a quadrant defect involving the superior temporal quadrant.

Central visual field defects associated with myopia are (1) enlargement of the blind spot from extension of the myopic conus about the disc from associated colobomas of the choroid and optic disc (refractive scotoma) and from myopic atrophy adjacent to the disc; (2) central, pericentral, and paracentral scotomas resulting from macular atrophy, degeneration, and hemorrhages associated with Fuchs' black spot; and (3) Bjerrum scotomas due to nerve fiber bundle damage at the disc.

11 RETINAL DISEASES

Clinically, retinal function is measured by the ability of the rods and cones to detect stimuli and degrees of separation and luminance between stimuli within the visual field. Foveal vision is the function of the cones concentrated in the macular area and is measured by the recognition of standard stimuli such as Snellen letters at fixed distances and under constant illumination. Foveal/macular vision is best in daylight because the cones function most effectively under photopic conditions. The close relationship between photoreceptors and bipolar cells in this region results in very high resolution, or the ability to distinguish fine detail. Resolution is greatest at fixation and begins to fade noticeably only a few degrees away. Anatomically the normal fixation point corresponds to the foveola (the precise center is the umbo).

Peripheral vision is the function of the rods, which are diffusely spread throughout the retina except for the macular area. Rods are most effective under scotopic, or low light, conditions. Visual discrimination in the rod areas is low, partly because many rods may summate in a single bipolar cell. Such summation results in a visual sensitivity gain at the expense of visual discrimination.

Any disease process that damages retinal receptor organs can produce functional loss in the portion of the visual field corresponding to the affected retinal area.

The variety of visual field defects produced by retinal disease is almost limitless; no completely typical defect exists for a specific retinal lesion. However, careful analysis of these field defects often gives sufficient information to assist in the diagnosis and prognosis of retinal disease. When combined with other evaluations of retinal anatomy and function, such as indirect ophthalmoscopy, slit lamp–contact lens biomicroscopy, fluorescein angiography, and retinal electrophysiology, visual field charting can help establish the appearance and functional significance of various retinal lesions.

Retinal lesions that result in peripheral and central visual field defects are probably best classified according to the disease process, the retinal layers involved, and, when possible, the etiologic agents. Attention to the following broad categories can be useful in approaching the analysis of field defects produced by retinal lesions:

1. Vascular lesions affecting the arteries, veins, and capillaries of the retina and choroid
2. Inflammatory retinal and choroidal lesions
3. Degenerative retinal lesions, including hereditary, congenital, and acquired
4. Toxic retinopathies
5. Retinal trauma
6. Retinal and choroidal tumors affecting retinal function
7. Miscellaneous diseases

VASCULAR LESIONS

Retinal and choroidal vascular lesions are most important because of their common and devastating effect on retinal function. Frequent among these lesions are retinal arterial occlusion, both complete and partial, with resulting retinal ischemia and ischemic infarct; capillary insufficiency, occlusion, and leakage; special retinal vascular manifestations of diabetes, blood dyscrasias, and arteriosclerotic changes without frank occlusion; choroidal vascular disease affecting the overlying retina secondarily; damage to retinal function caused by intrinsic circulatory insufficiency; and retinal venous occlusion, both partial and complete.

Retinal Arterial Occlusion

The central retinal artery with its arborizations is an end artery, and its occlusion leads to complete ischemia of the retina and corresponding total visual loss. In cases of complete and irreversible injury the effects are sudden and permanent. If the patient is fortunate enough to have a cilioretinal artery arising from the choroidal circulation, the central area of the retina may be spared and a small island of central vision retained (Figure 11-1). On the other hand, cilioretinal artery occlusion can produce a total centrocecal scotoma with a normal peripheral field.

Obstructions of the retinal arterial system may be complete or may involve any part of the arterial tree from one half to a tiny macular twig. These obstructions may be embolic, atherosclerotic, or ischemic, or they may be due to vasculitis.

Embolic occlusion of the superior branch of the central artery before it bifurcates into its nasal and temporal branches produces sudden loss of most of the lower visual field (Figure 11-1, *A*), with ischemia and cloudy swelling of the affected superior retina. This cloudy swelling can be subtle clinically and is perhaps best detected with indirect ophthalmoscopy, comparing the unaffected half with the affected half of the retina. The same degree of cloudy

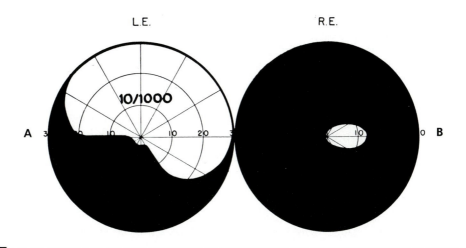

FIGURE 11-1 Visual field defects produced by retinal arterial occlusion. **A,** Occlusion of superior nasal branch of central retinal artery. **B,** Total occlusion of central retinal artery. Small remnant of centrocecal visual field results from persistence of cilioretinal artery.

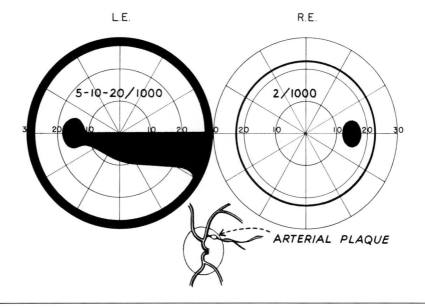

FIGURE 11-2 Arterial embolus of lipid-debris type occluding small branch of superior temporal retinal artery as creamy white arterial plaque and producing localized retinal infarct. Field defect is atypical Bjerrum or nerve fiber bundle defect with steep margins and great density. Patient had left internal carotid artery occlusion with reduced ophthalmic artery blood pressure and bruit.

swelling can affect the entire retina if the central retinal artery is occluded proximal to its division into superior and inferior branches. In some such cases the macular area is not affected by cloudy swelling, and a type of "cherry red spot" is noted because the more normal appearing macula stands out in contrast to the edematous retina. Often this extremely subtle sign is not detected. More commonly the unfortunate adage "the patient sees nothing and the doctor sees nothing" holds true.

When the embolus (which may be a fragment of an atheromatous plaque or a fibrin-platelet microembolus from the carotid circulation) lodges in an arteriole on the disc or in the anterior optic nerve, it may produce a typical or atypical nerve fiber bundle defect in the visual field (Figure 11-2).

Occlusions of peripheral branches give rise to irregular sector defects or isolated peripheral scotomas, depending upon the area of ischemic infarct in the retina. Although obstruction of a minute arterial twig near the macula may cause only a small or perhaps invisible infarction, the corresponding visual field defect may be positioned such that it results in considerable visual loss. Even if the scotoma is small, it is often positive and annoying.

Choroidal Obstruction

An embolus or obstruction of the choroidal vessels supplying the foveal area of the retina causes marked and permanent loss of central vision, with an irregular, dense central scotoma. Choroidal vascular insufficiency in the peripapillary area may be an important factor in the atrophy and excavation of the optic nervehead in glaucoma, with resulting nerve fiber bundle visual field defects.

Choroidal capillary insufficiency has been suggested as a causative factor in the loss of retinal function and consequent central scotoma seen in age-related macular degeneration. Whether this is because of changes in the microvascular system or deficient blood flow caused by faulty hemodynamics is not known precisely. Characteristically one finds an irregular, slowly progressing scotoma with sloping margins and variable density. Although unilateral onset is common, the lesions usually progress to involve both maculas.

Retinal Arterial Obstruction

Atheromatous obstruction of the retinal arteries produces sector defects in the visual field corresponding to the location of the affected arteries in the retinal vascular tree. Retinal ganglion cell layer death secondary to atheromatous occlusion of arteries relatively far removed from the retina may cause a variety of visual field defects. Thus occlusion of small arterioles supplying the optic nerve gives rise to segmental atrophy of the nerve and corresponding visual field defects, the most notable of which are typical and atypical nerve fiber bundle defects (Figure 11-2). These Bjerrum scotomas secondary to decreased blood flow in the nerve may be confused with typical glaucomatous field loss. They are rarely bilateral. They may bisect fixation and break through into the peripheral field as a true altitudinal hemianopsia. In such cases, except that the defect is unilateral, the field loss may resemble that seen in severe retinal ischemia following exsanguination or suffocation.

The same type of arcuate scotoma, often preceded by periodic and transient blackout of one eye, may result from gradual occlusion of the internal carotid artery. These attacks of amaurosis fugax occur with increasing frequency and duration until there is a prolonged obstruction, with retinal ischemia and either temporary or permanent visual field defects. The causative emboli in such cases are usually of the platelet-fibrin type. Frequently other neurologic defects occur, such as transient contralateral hemiplegia and homonymous hemianopsia. Other signs of carotid artery occlusion may be present, such as a bruit over the affected artery and lowered homolateral retinal arterial pressure as measured by ophthalmodynamometry.

Carotid angiograms will often show insufficiency or stenosis. Frequently the opposite, asymptomatic, arterial system will have some degree of occlusion as well. Fluorescein angiography may show markedly delayed filling of the retinal arterial tree on the affected side.

Retinal Arterial Spasm

Localized narrowing of retinal arteries may cause ischemia and secondary retinal edema. Visual field studies may reveal irregular scotomas with sloping margins and angioscotoma-like prolongations of the blind spot. If there is associated hypertensive retinopathy with retinal hemorrhage and exudates, one may expect to find corresponding visual field defects.

Central Serous Retinopathy

This condition, has also been known as central serous retinal detachment or central angiospastic retinopathy and is almost certainly of vascular origin. Fluorescein angiograms show that this disease is associated with small discrete choroidal vascular leaks.

The typical ophthalmoscopic picture is one of central retinal elevation. The edematous area is surrounded by a bright ring reflex. The macula appears deeper and darker red. There is loss of foveal reflex. Visual acuity may be reduced slightly or may be less than 20/200. Metamorphopsia is a frequent complaint and may be demonstrated on the Amsler grid.

The most characteristic field defect of central serous retinopathy is a small, relatively shallow central scotoma that is probably best demonstrated on the tangent screen at a distance of 2 to 4 meters. Because of the subtle nature of some of these defects, it may be necessary to examine the patient under reduced illumination. When such a macula is exposed to very bright light, as in the photostress test, the period of time required for vision to return to the pretest level is markedly prolonged, and the size and density of the accompanying scotoma is grossly exaggerated.

The ophthalmic picture and accompanying visual depression just described may result from a variety of causes, including those described in the following section.

Minute area of macular choroiditis

A minute area of macular choroiditis may cause overlying retinal edema that masks the inflammatory nature of the primary disease. As the edema subsides, the true nature of the underlying pathologic condition becomes evident. In such cases permanent scarring can cause considerable loss of central vision with a dense steep-walled scotoma.

Macular edema of commotio retinae

In its early stages the macular edema of commotio retinae closely resembles central serous retinopathy. Edema and functional visual loss depend directly on the severity of the contusion and the antecedent disruption of the outer retinal layers.

Thermal burn of the retina

Retinal burn, or solar retinopathy, such as that seen after exposure of an inadequately protected macula to a solar eclipse, may initially look like central serous retinopathy. Later stages reveal the minute hole in or immediately adjacent to the fovea and the tiny ragged central scotoma in the visual field. These holes are generally right at the point of fixation and may be quite tiny. In late stages a routine indirect ophthalmoscopic examination may miss such a burn because of the size of the lesion and the minified image afforded by indirect ophthalmoscopy. Slit-lamp biomicroscopy with an appropriate lens will reveal the characteristic macular lesion, however. Immediately after exposure there may be marked visual loss with intense after-image blindness, followed by the typical scotoma, which corresponds accurately to the visible retinal lesion.

These scotomas can be only fractions of a degree in size and may be difficult to detect, but careful tangent screen examination using small stimuli and the two-point discrimination method at 2 to 4 meters makes it possible to plot them accurately. Thermal burns have also been mapped satisfactorily with static perimetry on the Tübinger perimeter.

Solar retinopathy is seen more commonly after total or near-total solar eclipses. Under such circumstances the sun's brightness is reduced to the point where the unwary observer may be lulled into the mistaken impression that it is safe to gaze at the eclipse without protection for a prolonged period of time. In addition to seeing these lesions in unwary amateur astronomers, we have diagnosed solar retinopathy in former prisoners of war and in unfortunate individuals who engaged in prolonged periods of sun gazing while under the influence of hallucinogenic drugs.

Prolonged exposure to light

Numerous studies in subhuman primates have demonstrated the damaging effects of prolonged exposure to bright lights, such as those used by the slit lamp, indirect ophthalmoscope, and operating microscope. The syndrome of photic maculopathy has been described in patients who have been exposed to the operating microscope light during routine surgery. In some of these cases the surgery was unusually prolonged or complicated. Other patients have developed photic maculopathy after routine uncomplicated cataract extraction and intraocular lens implantation. Such patients may experience mild to moderate visual acuity loss and a small central or paracentral scotoma. The visual acuity loss may be difficult to demonstrate because almost all of these patients have poor acuity preoperatively.

Histologic studies in subhuman primates show permanent retinal damage.

We routinely reduce foveal light exposure during microsurgery by using the lowest appropriate illumination levels with the microscope and by using an opaque "corneal protector," most often a 1-cm gel foam disk, during those portions of the operation when direct intraocular illumination is unnecessary. Some operating microscopes have a dense built-in filter that can be flipped into place when a red reflex is unnecessary.

Hypertensive Retinopathy

Hypertensive retinopathy disturbs vision in many ways, and its visual defects usually reflect the picture seen with the ophthalmoscope. There may be isolated peripheral and central scotomas resulting from outer layer retinal hemorrhage and ischemic retinal infarcts. Venous occlusion secondary to arterial compression at an arteriovenous crossing may cause severe retinal destruction and widespread visual field defects.

Papilledema associated with hypertensive retinopathy may cause nerve fiber defects in the visual field, possibly from arterial obstruction in the nervehead. More commonly disc edema produces blind spot enlargement, which may take on the character of a centrocecal scotoma if the retinal edema extends far enough into the macular region. Occasionally blind spot enlargement may be so gross that most of both temporal fields become involved, simulating a bitemporal hemianopsia.

Retinal Vasculitis

Vasculitis or inflammatory involvement of the retinal vessels may take various forms. Most typical is giant cell arteritis in which central vision and visual fields are often affected. Loss of vision may be sudden, total, and permanent. Both eyes may be affected, one after the other. In some cases the presenting symptom has been bilateral blindness. When visual loss is incomplete, the fields may show a variety of defects, including central and arcuate scotomas. When optic nerve vessels are involved, the condition may be indistinguishable from any papillitis. The visual loss may be greater than would be expected from the appearance of the retinal vasculature alone. High-dose corticosteroid therapy has been associated with a favorable course in some cases.

Diabetic Retinopathy

Diabetic retinopathy is considered here because the main cause of visual loss is vascular in origin. In the early stages visual disturbance is uncommon. Relatively significant background retinopathy may be present with few or no visual complaints. If the macula is involved, especially by retinal edema, central scotomas may develop and visual acuity may decrease significantly (Figure 11-3). In cases of significant capillary nonperfusion and proliferative retinopathy there can be extensive visual field involvement. If complications such as vitreous hemorrhage or traction retinal detachment develop, functional vision may be lost.

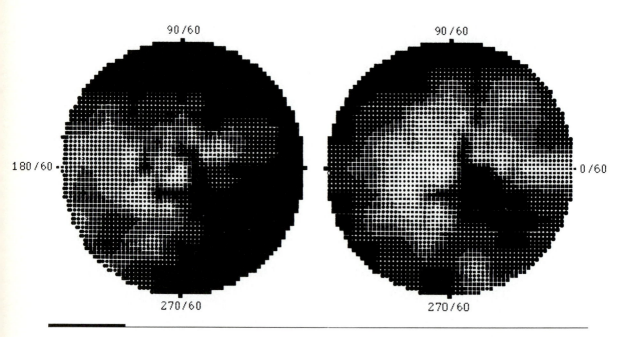

FIGURE 11-3 Patient with severe bilateral visual field loss due to diabetic retinopathy.

Retinal Venous Occlusion

Central retinal vein occlusion, occurring at or just behind the lamina cribrosa, produces severe hemorrhagic retinopathy with extensive deep and superficial retinal hemorrhages and edema. Visual loss is sudden and severe. The visual field defect is a central scotoma of varying size and density. The scotomas are usually dense centrally but have relatively sloping edges.

Branch vein occlusion is more common and is less visually destructive (Figures 11-4 and 11-5). A superior branch vein occlusion may leak blood and edema fluid down into the macular area, however, producing large irregular sector defects in the lower peripheral fields that extend up into the macular area to cause severe central visual loss.

Simultaneous involvement of the central retinal artery and vein at their site of entry and exit from the optic nerve produces the picture of retinal hemorrhage, retinal edema, and engorged retinal veins. Occlusion of the central retinal artery alone, however, produces a white retinal infarction with severe permanent visual loss and a corresponding visual field defect. Venous occlusion results in hemorrhagic infarction, with visual loss and a field defect. It may be difficult to discern the relative level of involvement of retinal arterial occlusion vs. retinal venous occlusion, especially in the early stages of the disease. Retinal arterial atherosclerosis may be the causative agent in either

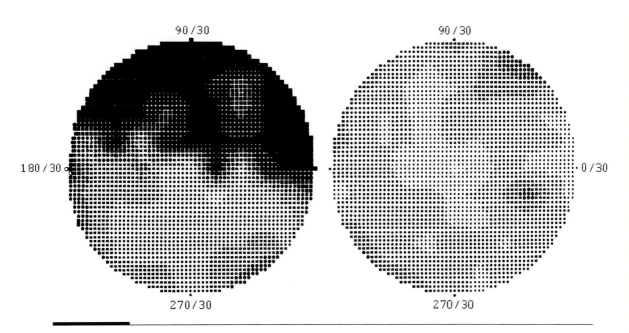

FIGURE 11-4 Visual field in left eye shows almost total loss of vision in superior half of field following retinal branch vein occlusion. Right eye is essentially normal.

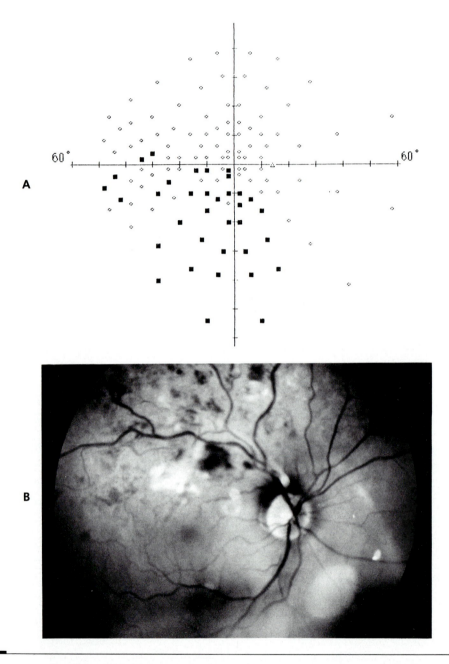

FIGURE 11-5 **A,** Two-level visual field from patient with branch vein occlusion in right eye. **B,** Fundus photograph of same patient showing typical hemorrhagic retinopathy.

case. Resolution of a good portion of the field defect may occur if venous obstruction alone predominates.

In addition to the acute and possibly reversible loss associated with retinal venous occlusion, a considerable degree of capillary nonperfusion can occur. Fluorescein angiography illustrates this clearly. Large or profound areas of capillary nonperfusion are significant because they may lead to rubeosis iridis and neovascular glaucoma. Although rubeosis may appear any time within the first several months after retinal venous occlusion, an interval of about 90 days is classic. We examine patients frequently after an occlusion in which significant capillary nonperfusion is demonstrated angiographically. In addition to careful slit-lamp biomicroscopy, it is important to perform careful gonioscopy to look for fine vessels that may appear first in the trabecular region of the anterior chamber angle. Iris angiography can also be useful. In our experience, the first sign of rubeosis iridis is an indication for urgent panretinal photocoagulation, if this has not been performed already. In several such cases we have been able to arrest the neovascular process before irreversible glaucoma occurred.

INFLAMMATORY LESIONS AFFECTING THE RETINA

Most inflammatory lesions affecting the retina are probably secondary to inflammatory disturbance of the choroid, with secondary destruction of overlying retina. As a rule these lesions produce a visible pathologic process. For a careful eye examination, indirect ophthalmoscopy, fundus photography, and fluorescein angiography are the examination and follow-up modalities of choice. Visual field changes will generally be useful to determine the level of disability and progression.

Harada's Disease

Harada's disease may give rise to a peculiar exudative retinal detachment, usually bilateral, affecting the lower peripheral retina and producing irregular superior quadrant or altitudinal hemianoptic visual field defects.

Toxoplasmosis

Toxoplasmosis is a common cause of unilateral and bilateral chorioretinal destruction, with dense, irregular, steep-margined, central and paracentral scotomas corresponding to the lesions seen on ophthalmologic examination (Figure 11-7).

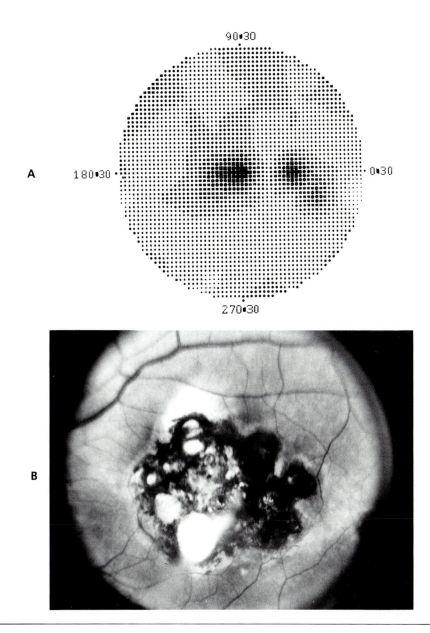

FIGURE 11-6   Dense central scotoma **(A)** in right eye of patient with well-healed chorioretinal scar **(B).**

Acute Multifocal Placoid Pigment Epitheliopathy (AMPPE) and Multiple Evanescent White Dot Syndrome (MEWS)

These two conditions are listed together because they are characteristic of a whole category of rare chorioretinal inflammatory conditions that may be viral or postviral in origin. These conditions occur in relatively young healthy people as a rule, they have been noted to follow viral illnesses by several weeks in many patients, and they produce significant but often transient visual loss and visual field defects. The visual field defects correspond generally to the lesions noted during ophthalmologic examination.

Interestingly, AMPPE was diagnosed with some frequency in the mid to late 1970s, but had largely disappeared by the end of the next decade. Multiple evanescent white dot syndrome seemed to appear about the same time AMPPE began to disappear. An intriguing speculation is that these conditions are caused by a similar agent or group of agents whose epidemiology and expression have changed over the years.

Recently Hoyt reported a series of patients with an enlarged blind spot of unknown etiology (Figure 11-7). Several authors have suggested that these patients have a form of multiple evanescent white dot syndrome, with the dots relatively transparent at the stage at which they were seen.

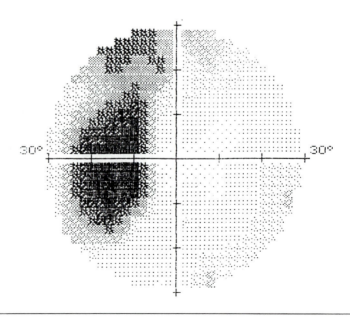

FIGURE 11-7 Large blind spot in patient with otherwise normal examination.

Luetic Choroiditis

The disseminated choroiditis of syphilis with overlying retinal destruction is responsible for profound visual loss when the macular area is involved. Peripheral and central islandlike scotomas occur from widespread patchy retinopathy. This condition is not seen commonly today.

Degenerative Retinal Lesions

Degenerative disease involving the outer retinal layers may cause marked and progressive visual loss, both central and peripheral. Except for retinitis pigmentosa, the usual visual field defect is a progressively enlarging central scotoma. These are bilateral conditions.

Because retinitis pigmentosa initially and primarily involves the rods, the earliest symptom is nyctalopia (night blindness) associated with a characteristic ring scotoma occupying the midperiphery of the visual field (Figures 11-8 to 11-10). This defect commonly starts as a group of isolated scotomas in the

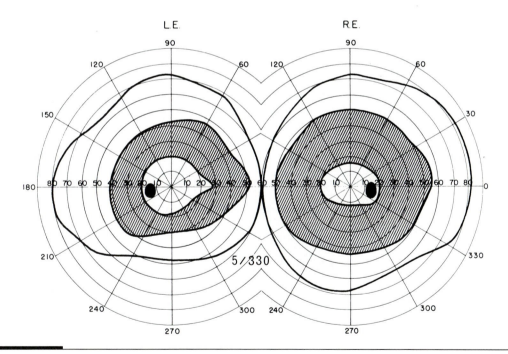

FIGURE 11-8   Typical equatorial ring scotoma in early case of retinitis pigmentosa. *(From Harrington DO: In Straatsma BR, et al: Retina: morphology, function, and clinical characteristics. UCLA Forum in Medical Sciences, no. 8, Berkeley, 1969, University of California Press, © 1969 The Regents of the University of California.)*

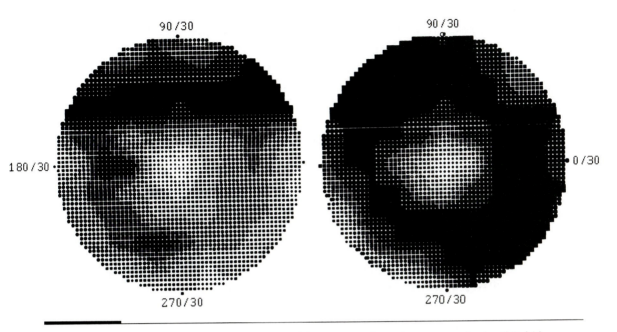

FIGURE 11-9   Retinitis pigmentosa in 32-year-old woman. Relatively asymmetric visual field loss may be seen in developmental stages of this disease.

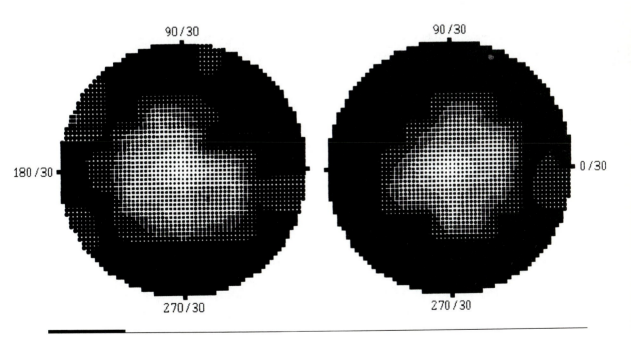

FIGURE 11-10 Advanced bilateral loss secondary to retinitis pigmentosa in 24-year-old man.

region 20 to 25 degrees from fixation. These scotomas gradually coalesce to form a partially and finally a complete ring. The outer ring edge may expand peripherally at a fairly rapid pace, whereas the inner margin contracts very slowly toward fixation. Long after the entire peripheral field is gone, a small oval remnant of intact central field, resembling the terminal defect of glaucoma, remains. Patients with these tubular fields may have excellent acuity with Snellen letters but may be able to see only one or two letters at a time. As such, a patient may have 20/20 vision but be functionally visually disabled.

Retinal pigmentary dystrophy characteristic of retinitis pigmentosa is seen at the end stage of several conditions. The ultimate visual outcome, and the rapidity of progression from mild to severe visual loss, are related to the specific subtype of retinitis pigmentosa involved.

Familial or Hereditary Macular Pigmentary Degenerations

Familial or hereditary macular pigmentary degenerations are a group of fairly common conditions that may affect several siblings or, more rarely, may affect several generations of a family. The visual loss is bilateral with gradual onset, usually in the second decade of life. Central visual loss and bilateral central scotomas with sloping margins occur early and progress slowly. Occasionally a minute area of vision is spared exactly at fixation, giving the scotoma the appearance of a doughnut.

Disciform Macular Degeneration

Disciform macular degeneration may occur at any age but is much more common after the sixth decade of life. In its early stages vision may remain surprisingly good, and scotomatous defects in the central fields may be vague and difficult to detect. The condition is always bilateral, although one eye may be seriously involved long before the other.

When hemorrhage from subretinal neovascularization occurs beneath or around the disclike, yellowish, elevated macular mass, central visual loss may be sudden and profound. The resulting central scotoma is irregular and dense. The visual loss and scotoma are due to the destruction of the outer retinal layers resulting from breaks in Bruch's membrane followed by hemorrhage associated with subretinal neovascularization.

Cytomegalovirus Retinitis

Cytomegalovirus (CMV) retinitis is an opportunistic infection seen predominantly in immunocompromised persons. Hospitalized patients and patients receiving immunosuppressive therapy accounted for a significant fraction of the cases through the early 1980s. Currently most diagnoses are made in patients with acquired immunodeficiency syndrome (AIDS).

CMV retinitis has had an important place in the medical management of AIDS patients. Because the appearance of CMV retinitis has been associated with an extremely poor prognosis for extended survival, the diagnosis is often made at a time when both patients and physicians are ready to try fairly aggressive experimental therapies. Because CMV retinitis is visible and the extent of the disease can be photographed, mapped with computerized retinal image analyzers, or visual field study, the behavior of CMV retinitis can sometimes be used as a yardstick by which one may measure the effectiveness of systemic medications being used to treat the overall syndrome.

CHOROIDAL TUMORS

Choroidal tumors with secondary effects on the retina were discussed in Chapter 10. Retinoblastoma is the most common intraocular tumor of childhood. Visual field studies are of no value for the most part because of the age of the typical patient.

Angiomatosis retinae (Hippel's or Hippel-Lindau syndrome) with or without cerebellar involvement causes severe visual loss and widespread visual field damage, both centrally and peripherally (Figure 11-11). Both eyes may

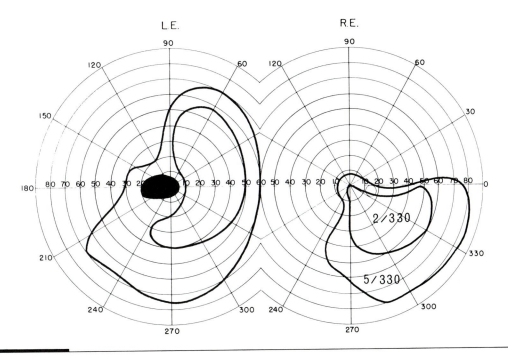

FIGURE 11-11 Visual field defects in case of bilateral Hippel's angiomatosis retinae. *(From Harrington DO: In Straatsma BR, et al: Retina: morphology, function, and clinical characteristics. UCLA Forum in Medical Sciences, no. 8, Berkeley, 1969, University of California Press, © 1969 The Regents of the University of California.)*

be affected. The lesions are usually in the peripheral retina, and the corresponding visual field defects are also peripheral; however, the central retinal area may be involved with an associated and disabling central scotoma. Unchecked growth of the tumor leads to total visual loss.

MISCELLANEOUS DISEASES AFFECTING RETINAL FUNCTION

Among the diseases that affect retinal function are staphylomas, abnormal protein retinopathies, the leukemias, retinal cysts, retinoschisis, and retinal detachments. Colobomas cause extensive loss of the superior field, usually involving fixation. The refractive scotoma of a staphyloma of the optic nervehead has been discussed previously.

Myopia with Retinal Stretching and Atrophy

High myopia with retinal stretching and atrophy may cause a variety of visual field defects. One may find a central scotoma associated with localized hemorrhage and Fuchs' black spot, a markedly enlarged blind spot associated with

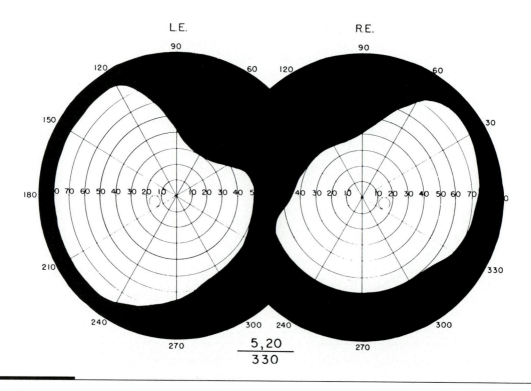

FIGURE 11-12 Retinoschisis. Binasal hemianopsia of considerable extent. Note that margins are steep and field defect is same size for both 5-mm and 20-mm stimuli.

an abnormal optic nervehead conus, and perhaps even nerve fiber bundle damage at the disc margin. As mentioned previously, care must be taken to differentiate refractive scotomas from other causes of visual field loss in such patients.

Retinoschisis

The visual field defect of retinoschisis is characterized by its density and steep margins, by its bilaterality, and by the fact that the nasal fields are almost always involved more frequently above than below (Figure 11-12). The patient may be unaware of the defect. Peripheral visual field examination may detect retinoschisis missed by other investigative means.

Retinal Detachments

Retinal detachment from whatever cause eventually destroys the outer retinal elements and results in visual loss in the separated area. Visual field studies may be of considerable importance. The actual extent of detachment may be

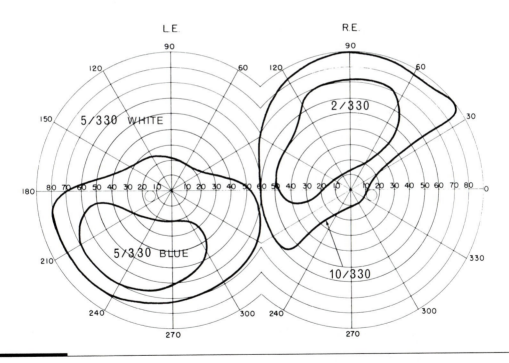

FIGURE 11-13 Two eyes with typical visual field defects resulting from retinal detachment. Note that defects have very sloping margins and that most marked deficit is demonstrated with blue stimuli. *(From Harrington DO: In Straatsma BR, et al: Retina: morphology, function, and clinical characteristics. UCLA Forum in Medical Sciences, no. 8, Berkeley, 1969, University of California Press, © 1969 The Regents of the University of California.)*

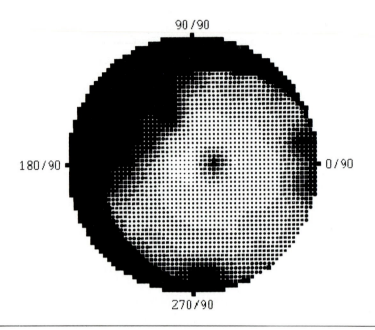

FIGURE 11-14 A 90-degree field from right eye of patient after repair of inferior retinal detachment. Large dense superonasal depression with sloping margin is seen. NOTE: A full-threshold computerized static test of entire 90-degree visual field tested by most machines is extremely tedious and time consuming. We almost always test large geographic defects such as one depicted here with manual kinetic perimetry on Goldmann perimeter or tangent screen.

judged more accurately by the field loss than with the ophthalmoscope, especially as it approaches the macula. If the visual field defect crosses fixation, the prognosis is generally poorer than when fixation is spared. When a very large bullous detachment of the superior retina hangs down over fixation, a period of bed rest for the patient may allow the detachment to flatten out. If the visual field defect is then quickly examined, the true area of retinal separation will be revealed. Visual field defects in retinal detachment often have sloping margins (Figures 11-13 and 11-14). These defects are usually best plotted by manual kinetic perimetry. There is no typical visual field defect in retinal detachment. Postoperative visual field studies are necessary for evaluating progress and prognosis and perhaps for comparing with preoperative fields for medicolegal evidence.

12 GLAUCOMA

The history of perimetry and the development of modern techniques of visual field examination are linked intimately with the study of glaucoma. Even with a better understanding of the disease through gonioscopy, tonography, stereo disc photography, nerve fiber layer photography, and an increasing knowledge of the physiology and dynamics of aqueous outflow, perimetry remains of paramount importance in the early diagnosis of the disease. Perimetry is of perhaps even greater value in assessing the progress and prognosis of glaucomatous eyes.

To fully understand a glaucomatous eye, one most investigate its many facets thoroughly and repeatedly. A single tonometric estimate of intraocular pressure is not sufficient to establish the diagnosis of glaucoma; nor is a single gonioscopic examination, a single tonographic measurement of the facility of outflow, or a first examination of the visual field or optic nervehead. The results of all these examinations must be weighed and correlated carefully before the total picture of the disease begins to form. To fully understand a glaucomatous eye and guide its treatment intelligently, one must first confirm these findings by repeated examination, estimate their degree of stability or oscillation, note their response to provocation of various types, and evaluate them in the clinical context of the total patient. Additionally, it is important to include pertinent demographic and historical data, such as the patient's age, race, and family history, in this evaluation. Given two patients with equal mild intraocular pressure elevation, the likelihood of diagnosing glaucoma in an elderly patient with large cup-to-disc ratios and a very positive family history will be much greater than the likelihood of diagnosing glaucoma in a young patient with normal cup-to-disc ratios and a negative family history. Certainly subtle or questionable visual field changes would have different implications in these two patients.

The primary concern with glaucoma is the loss of vision. The glaucoma patient is disturbed not by the fact that he or she has an increase in intraocular pressure, but rather by the possibility of impending blindness.

Functional loss in glaucomatous eyes is measured by careful, quantitative visual field study. Attention is focused primarily on the areas of the field that are likely to show the first changes characteristic of glaucoma, or, in cases of established glaucoma, on the characteristic defects themselves. Because central visual acuity is rarely affected until the late stages of disease, the patient may be completely unaware of functional loss. Only by measuring the visual field can one establish the degree of loss and its rate of progression.

A glaucoma patient may know that the disease can cause blindness, that drops may be necessary for the rest of his or her life, and that subsequent surgery is a possibility, yet may still not comprehend the reality of the visual loss until it is irreversible.

Interest in glaucoma was largely responsible for the development of quantitative examination methods of the central portion of the visual field. Reciprocally, these careful analytic methods have revealed much about the disease itself and contribute to our understanding and management of glaucoma.

There is perhaps no better way for the beginning perimetrist to learn finesse in the various techniques of manual visual field examination than to thoroughly analyze an eye with early but well-established glaucoma field defects.

Much of the knowledge of the character of visual field loss in glaucoma was obtained through quantitative study of the central portion of the visual field using the tangent screen. Study of the small isopters at 1 and 2 meters was particularly useful. This was because of the importance of the Bjerrum (or arcuate) region, which is readily examined with this technique, and because depressions in the peripheral isopters are generally reflected in similar central isopter depressions in the early stages of glaucoma. Later, the widespread use of Goldmann and Tübinger perimeters facilitated investigations of kinetic, static, and profile perimetry and encouraged refined experiments in perimetric examination with stimuli and backgrounds of varying luminance. All of these methods were applied extensively to studying the glaucomatous visual field. Historically, the two volumes of Ourgaud and Etienne and an earlier volume by Dubois-Poulsen greatly advanced knowledge of the nature and cause of the loss of central and peripheral vision in glaucoma. These monographs were published by the French Ophthalmological Society in 1961 and 1952, respectively. The earliest visual field defects in glaucoma are either isolated scotomas in the Bjerrum area or isolated nasal step defects. These defects are detected most consistently with minimal static threshold stimuli. Evidence suggests that inconsistent responses may precede frank scotomas in some patients. Therefore it is important to note an increased fluctuation or a wide intratest response variation in these areas.

Since the mid-1970s an increased emphasis on automating visual field examinations has spawned a variety of new perimeters and computerized perimetric systems. This has largely been in response to a desire for rapid, accurate detection and analysis of the visual field defects commonly found in the glaucomatous eye. These instruments make it possible to examine visual fields in a consistent and reproducible manner. The data are automatically recorded and can be computerized and stored for comparison with later findings. Obviously, however, not all patients are suitable candidates for automated perimetry; regardless of the excellence of the instruments used to record visual field defects, this examination must still be monitored by a technician, and the defects must be analyzed and interpreted carefully. Increasing demands on physicians' time support the tendency to relegate visual field examination and evaluation to a purely technical task, managed by office personnel. It is essential to remember that the usefulness of any visual field chart is limited, no matter how expensive or exquisite the apparatus that produced the chart may be. The results of this test, like any other test in medicine, must be evaluated in reference to the total patient.

TYPES OF PRIMARY GLAUCOMA

Excluding ocular hypertension due to uveitis, tumor, or other identifiable causes, two types of *primary* glaucoma must be considered with reference to visual field changes: (1) narrow-angle glaucoma, which may be associated with angle-closure glaucoma or acute glaucoma; and (2) open-angle glaucoma, also referred to as wide-angle glaucoma, chronic glaucoma, simple glaucoma, or glaucoma simplex.

Narrow-Angle Glaucoma

Narrow-angle glaucoma shows little if any visual field defect before the onset of frank angle closure. If the eye has been subjected to repeated bouts of high intraocular pressure with the symptoms of an acute glaucoma, visual field studies between the tests may reveal the following: (1) general isopter depression, (2) greater depression of the peripheral than of the central isopter, (3) particular depression of the superior nasal isopter, (4) blind spot enlargement, (5) widening of angioscotomas, and (6) nerve fiber bundle defects.

Clinical examination of a narrow-angle eye may reveal peripheral anterior synechiae in the anterior chamber angle, glaukomfleken, patchy areas of iris atrophy, or other signs of previous angle-closure attack(s). The intraocular pressure may be normal or slightly elevated. Patients who have gonioscopically narrow angles, along with signs of prior angle-closure attacks, are often referred to as having chronic or subacute angle-closure glaucoma. It is believed that in the initial stages of this disease the patient has intermittent attacks of angle-closure glaucoma, with or without recognizable symptoms.

With chronic or subacute angle-closure glaucoma, these attacks are self-limited and are terminated spontaneously before the onset of severe pain, redness, and loss of vision associated with a full-blown acute glaucoma attack. In some eyes repeated subacute attacks over the years may damage the drainage angle, and the intraocular pressure does not return to normal levels between attacks. These patients may have a diagnosis of "mixed mechanism glaucoma." In such eyes visual field study may reveal scotomas that will become more pronounced when the intraocular pressure is higher and correspondingly less pronounced between attacks.

With acute angle closure and sudden extreme elevation of intraocular pressure, the corresponding pain and visual loss make perimetric examination extremely difficult. Frequently the minimum visible stimulus is a bright light. When some semblance of visual field examination is possible, the upper nasal periphery is usually the most affected and the lower temporal quadrant the last to retain vision.

Once proper treatment has been initiated, a more careful visual field examination may be performed on patients whose media are relatively clear. Particularly with very high pressures, one may find the entire field extremely depressed, with frequent early loss of the central field (as opposed to the persistent retention of the central field in chronic glaucoma). These findings support a primarily vascular pathogenesis for the field loss. Harrington has observed macular and optic nervehead edema that persisted for a period of time after the rapid reduction of intraocular pressure in a patient with angle-closure glaucoma.

If the acute attack can be controlled, either medically or surgically, and the intraocular pressure can be normalized, the field may return to normal. Repeated attacks of short duration, however, will inevitably take their toll on vision, either central, peripheral, or both. If treatment is delayed, the vision may remain poor, with extreme depression of all isopters in the visual field or retention of only a small island of temporal vision, even though the intraocular pressure may eventually become normal. In chronic angle-closure glaucoma of longstanding duration, one may expect to find visual field changes of the same type as seen in chronic open-angle glaucoma. Such visual field changes are usually accompanied by corresponding optic nervehead cupping or atrophy.

In a study of visual field defects in acute and chronic angle-closure glaucoma, Douglas, Drance, and Schulzer show that after an attack of acute angle-closure glaucoma, more than half the patients retain a normal field with normal optic discs. Chronic angle-closure glaucoma presented a different picture. Increased intraocular pressure was likely to have been present for a prolonged period, and there was a high incidence of visual field defects of the nerve fiber bundle type.

Open-Angle Glaucoma

The characteristic field changes in chronic open-angle glaucoma include the following:

1. General depression of peripheral and central isopters
2. Widening and intensification of angioscotomas
3. Formation of a nerve fiber bundle defect
4. Formation of a nasal step defect
5. Rapid peripheral contraction, especially in the nasal field
6. Persistent retention of the central field until a very late stage of the disease
7. Loss of the central field and retention of a small, temporal island of vision
8. Blindness (Plate 3)

These defects may appear singly or in combination. They tend to progress relatively slowly at first, with months or years passing between the first sign of glaucomatous damage and the late stages of the disease. Once the late stages of the disease have been reached, however, the field loss may progress with disheartening rapidity.

Visual field changes may be monocular, particularly in cases of unilateral secondary glaucoma. Much more frequently, however, field loss occurs in both eyes. What at first is believed to represent monocular field loss is quite often found only to represent symmetric field loss. For this reason, the perimetrist should be scrupulously careful in the examination of the presumed unaffected eye and should be continuously alert for incipient visual field defects.

In confirmed or suspected glaucoma, it is always important to carefully examine the optic discs and to compare their appearance to the corresponding visual fields. Optic disc excavation and visual field defects should be assessed together as confirmation of the existence of glaucoma and also as part of the evaluation of the progress and treatment of the disease. Pathologic studies in animals and humans have shown that a substantial amount of optic nerve atrophy may precede the appearance of clinically significant cupping or visual field changes. It is important to evaluate these modalities carefully in patients who are at risk for developing glaucoma, particularly if the visual field or the optic nerve suggests an abnormality. One should pay careful attention to the morphology of suspicious optic nerve cupping in looking for corresponding visual field defects. For example, if one finds temporal inferior notching of the neuroretinal rim, one should look carefully for a superior arcuate scotoma. Conversely, if a well-established glaucomatous visual field defect is present, one should attempt to identify an anatomic correlate when examining the optic nerve. In the absence of appropriate optic nerve cupping, an arcuate

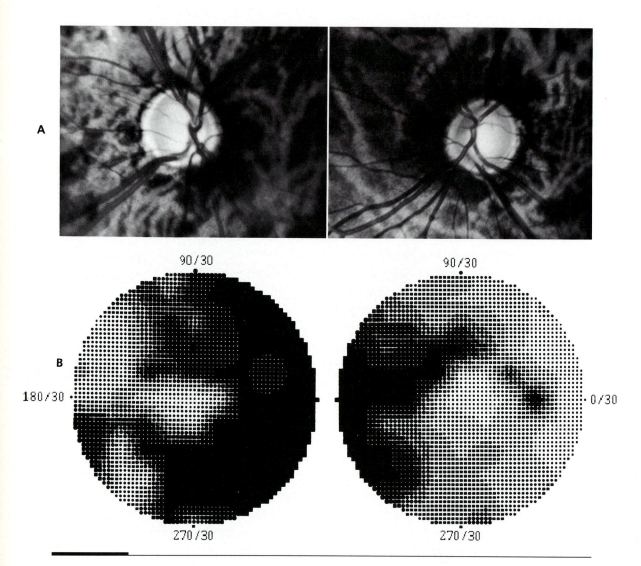

FIGURE 12-1   **A,** Fundus photography in patient with bilateral glaucomatous optic nerve atrophy clearly shows large cup-to-disc ratios, with cup extending as far as temporal rim bilaterally. **B,** Visual fields from same patient show corresponding dramatic glaucomatous field loss, with greatest damage occurring in nasal half of each field.

defect should alert one to look for other causes of nerve fiber bundle loss (e.g., an optic pit, optic nervehead drusen).

Careful manual perimetry or an intensified search with an appropriate grid on an automated perimeter may be necessary to reveal early changes in the Bjerrum region. A screening program, either because of an inappropriately wide spacing of test points or less than optimal sensitivity, may miss some of these early defects and thus give one a false sense of security. Only through careful and meticulous examination of the appropriate regions can one feel comfortable in ruling out a glaucomatous visual field defect.

When the diagnosis of glaucoma is confirmed or strongly suspected, it is a good idea to place a careful drawing of the optic disc in the patient's chart. This drawing should be constructed after examination with a contact lens, Hruby lens, or some other viewing system that permits a three-dimensional evaluation of the disc. In glaucomatous eyes, the degree of cupping is probably more important than the degree of pallor, and a monocular view would not allow one to assess the cupping optimally. If stereo fundus photography is available, serial stereo photographs of the optic nervehead can be useful for monitoring glaucoma patients over time. We have used this method for well over a decade now and find that careful analysis of a stereo slide pair or analysis of serial photographs taken months or years apart are often valuable (Figure 12-1).

High-resolution, black-and-white nerve fiber layer photography can also be useful in predicting glaucomatous visual field loss. Airaksinen, Drance, and others have investigated a large series of nerve fiber layer photographs and found a correlation between the nerve fiber layer photograph and the visual field. For the purposes of investigational study, these examinations were often carried out on photographs in which the image of the optic nerve had been masked or removed; however, when examining records in a clinical setting, one should examine the optic disc, nerve fiber layer photographs, and visual field in concert with one another in an attempt to make the appropriate diagnostic decision.

It is important that these parameters of visual function all support one another. If one finds a completely normal visual field in an eye that has significant optic nerve cupping or significant nerve fiber layer dropout, one should definitely reexamine the field, looking more carefully for appropriate defects. Conversely, if one finds a reliable visual field defect, one can expect to see a corresponding anatomic substrate. If any of these examinations do not agree with one another, one or perhaps the whole battery of tests should be repeated until a clear picture of the disease can be established.

DEVELOPMENTAL PHASES

In approaching the study of glaucomatous visual field defects, it is convenient to subdivide glaucoma into three developmental phases: (1) incipient glaucoma, (2) established glaucoma, and (3) terminal or end-stage glaucoma. Each of these phases has its characteristic field changes, although the defects typical of one phase may overlap into another. In established glaucoma all of the classic visual field defects may be demonstrated in a single field examined by careful quantitative methods.

Incipient or Early Glaucoma

In many centers the diagnosis of glaucoma requires that three components be present: (1) glaucomatous optic atrophy or cupping, (2) an intraocular pressure sufficient to cause or have caused the typical optic atrophy, and (3) typical visual field changes. These are the classic diagnostic criteria for chronic open-angle glaucoma; in practice they are often stretched somewhat. For instance, if one notices typical or asymmetric cupping in the presence of a high intraocular pressure, even though no visual field changes can be demonstrated, the patient should be considered glaucomatous. In some centers an extremely high intraocular pressure alone is sufficient to justify a diagnosis of glaucoma. In other centers some evidence of end organ damage, either in the optic nervehead or in the visual field, is required to establish the diagnosis.

Because of these definitions, establishing an initial diagnosis of glaucoma often depends on detecting early glaucomatous visual field loss. This is particularly true when one is examining a middle-aged patient who has no family history, an intraocular pressure in the low 20s, and a slightly enlarged cup-to-disc ratio. The decision to prescribe or withhold medication often rests on the results of visual field examination. These patients are common, and practitioners are often faced with making such a decision. Consequently, during the past several decades, a tremendous amount of energy has been devoted to determining the earliest reliable sign of glaucoma.

The earliest reproducibly detectable glaucomatous visual field defects differ, depending on the type of perimetry employed and the conditions and parameters of the examination. Regardless of the examination method, some general trends are common to early glaucomatous field loss. Testing by many methods and over many years has indicated that the earliest changes in glaucoma include mild generalized depression, shallow and perhaps fleeting paracentral depressions, baring of the blind spot, shallow peripheral nasal step defects, and shallow peripheral temporal wedge defects. These defects may appear different, depending on the testing method used. We will consider here the appearance of defects in early glaucoma in patients examined with (1) the tangent screen, (2) the Goldmann perimeter, and (3) computerized automated perimetry.

Tangent screen

The most important characteristic of the early changes seen in glaucoma is that they are subtle. In examining such a patient on the tangent screen one should attempt to maximize the test's sensitivity. The central fields should be tested with the smallest reasonable target. For the average patient this would be a 1-mm test target at a 2-meter test distance. The appropriateness of the test target size and examination distance can be evaluated first by mapping the blind spot. The target should be intense enough to be seen consistently in the area just temporal to the blind spot, but should be dim enough that it is not detected easily beyond about 25 or 30 degrees. The examiner may have to experiment with several targets to find one that meets these criteria for an individual patient. Selecting the target in this way assures that the patient is being examined with a test object that should be mildly to moderately suprathreshold in the region between 10 and 20 degrees from fixation, which is where most early glaucomatous defects are detected.

Once the proper initial stimulus intensity is determined, the examiner proceeds with normal tangent screen testing, using a combination of both static and kinetic techniques. One should first attempt to detect, and subsequently map in detail, any depressions in the central field, particularly in an arching region beginning at the blind spot and continuing at a constant radius from fixation out to the horizontal raphe and then out along the horizontal raphe to the midperiphery (Figure 12-2).

The typical early defects found in this area include shallow oval or ovoid depressions with a minimal diameter of perhaps 2 to 3 degrees that may occur alone or in small groups and may be quite subtle. Often the patient will only report a vague blinking or uncertainty about the presence of the test target as it traverses such a scotoma. The presence of the defect is established,

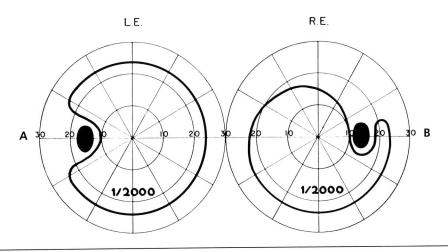

FIGURE 12-2 Baring of blind spot. **A,** False baring of blind spot. This defect is not characteristic of glaucoma and is found fairly frequently with small visual angles in normal individuals. **B,** True baring of blind spot. Early visual field defect in glaucoma is, in reality, incipient Bjerrum scotoma.

however, by the fact that the target is seen more easily in the region peripheral to the depression, as well as the region central to the depression.

The major difference between baring of the blind spot, Seidel's scotoma, a peripheral nasal step, and paracentral depressions is the location in which the scotoma appears. If one or more of these depressions appear adjacent to the blind spot, the patient has baring of the blind spot or, in a more intense state, typical Seidel's scotoma. If the depression appears first along the horizontal raphe at a distance of about 15 to 30 degrees nasal to fixation, then one has a shallow nasal step of Rönne. If the depression is located in the nerve fiber bundle arch before it reaches the horizontal raphe but after it has left the blind spot, one has a paracentral depression. The same is essentially true for the rather rarely seen early temporal wedge defect, except in this instance the nasal fibers are damaged first.

Mild generalized depression or collapse of the central isopters is also seen in early glaucoma. As discussed earlier, mild generalized depression can be caused by a wide variety of problems or circumstances and is fairly nonspecific. Furthermore, in many patients it is difficult to distinguish between small but normal isopters and mildly depressed central isopters. If one monitors a patient over time and sees that the isopters are collapsing in the presence of factors such as a dilated pupil, clear media, and normal acuity, then it may be fairly easy to deduce that change is taking place. On an initial examination, however, mild generalized depression can be overlooked easily.

To test the peripheral nasal step area the patient must be moved to 1 meter from the tangent screen. Visual sensitivity in the nasal periphery is less than in the central portion of the field, but the decreased testing distance may allow the examiner to continue to use the same 1-mm test target. If the patient cannot detect this target in the region between 30 and 60 degrees from fixation, a larger target should be used. When looking for a nasal step defect the examiner must determine whether the sensitivities above and below the horizontal raphe are similar. We commonly do this by a combination of static and kinetic testing in the region approximately 10 degrees above and below the horizontal raphe. It is important to remember that the receptor fields become larger as one extends further away from fixation, and the physiologic line separating the superior and the inferior field may not correspond precisely to the horizontal line drawn on the tangent screen. A true physiologic nasal step defect may violate the geometric horizontal meridian.

If the first pass at a tangent screen examination is normal and one seriously suspects glaucoma, the sensitivity of the test can be improved by examining the patient under reduced illumination. In this case all of the isopters will be smaller than in normal room light, and any scotomas will be larger.

The use of colored test objects has been investigated as a method of detecting glaucomatous field damage earlier. Glaucoma patients have been shown to have an increased incidence of defective color vision by a variety of tests. It makes sense that this defect might be exploited in creating a maximally sensitive visual field examination. It has been somewhat difficult, however, to standardize colored perimetric targets for hue, saturation, and stimulus intensity or to show that tests conducted under practical clinical conditions offer much diagnostic advantage over white-light testing with minimally suprathreshold targets.

Goldmann perimeter

Defects found on Goldmann perimetry mirror those detected with the tangent screen. They occur in the same regions and are about the same size and shape. In practice, early scotomas detected with the Goldmann perimeter are often smaller and more shallow than those seen with tangent screen examinations, but this probably reflects the differences in examination technique more than the ultimate sensitivity of the two instruments.

As with the tangent screen, it is reasonable to begin a Goldmann examination by mapping the blind spot. A Goldmann target I2e is a reasonable starting point. As with the tangent screen, we then establish the size and intensity of the target that would describe an isopter extending to approximately 25 degrees from fixation. Many techniques have been suggested for examining glaucomatous patients; the technique introduced by Armaly and modified by Drance is favored at our institution. In examining glaucoma patients on the Goldmann perimeter, one should proceed to test multiple isopters (Figure 12-3). This is similar to what we suggest with the tangent screen, but with the Goldmann perimeter one cannot change the patient-to-target distance or adjust the overall room illumination level, since these factors are standardized.

Although color perimetry is easier to standardize on the Goldmann perimeter than on the tangent screen, it is still not practiced widely.

Computerized automated perimetry

The overwhelming success of computerized automated perimeters in clinical practice is due to the value of these machines in testing and monitoring patients with glaucoma. The strengths of automated perimetry and the requirements for glaucomatous visual field study match up quite well. The literature abounds with studies on the sensitivity and specificity of computerized automated perimetry in detecting and following up patients with glaucoma. Although the results vary somewhat from study to study, the overall conclusion is straightforward: a basic, off-the-shelf, moderately sophisticated projection or LED-type computerized automated perimeter, in average hands and used under reasonable circumstances, can produce results that rival the best results obtainable by trained experts using manual perimetric techniques and instruments. Think of it—that's roughly equivalent to saying that with the proper clubs and a day's practice, the average golfer could shoot par at Pebble Beach!

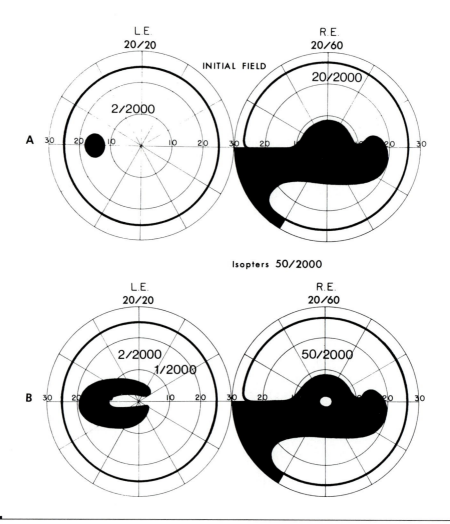

FIGURE 12-3 A, Chronic open-angle glaucoma secondary to prolonged use of topical steroids in treatment of uveitis. Initial field examination on tangent screen showed irregular cecocentral scotoma with nasal peripheral breakthrough in right eye. Left field was normal. Diagnosis was retrobulbar neuritis. Goldmann perimeter field was normal in left eye. **B,** Later examination with larger stimulus showed right field defect to be dense double nerve fiber bundle defect. Left field shows incomplete double arcuate scotoma. *(From Harrington DO: Trans Ophthalmol Soc UK 92:15, 1972, London, Churchill Livingstone, Ltd.)*

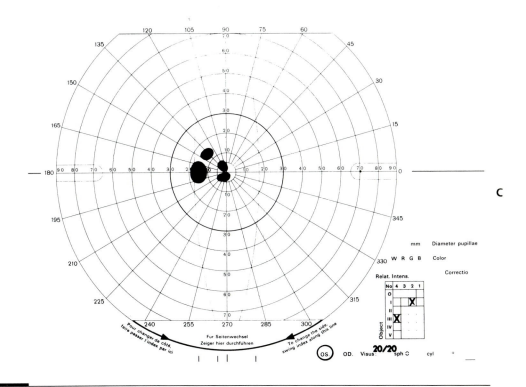

C

FIGURE 12-3, cont'd. C, Goldmann perimeter field shows small paracentral scotomas in Bjerrum areas of left eye. Defects were confirmed by static perimetry.

Detecting the earliest signs of glaucoma with computerized automated perimetry requires performing a full-threshold test. In our experience these changes have often been an increase in the local variability surrounding normal or slightly depressed values in the arcuate region. This "increase in baseline noise" has been seen before the appearance of consistently reproducible defects. Such defects seem to correspond roughly to the "blinking" or "on/off" responses seen with early defects detected by manual techniques with the tangent screen or Goldmann perimeter.

Mild generalized depression is easier to quantify with threshold computerized static perimetry than with manual kinetic perimetry. Many computerized perimeters will in fact give a numerical assessment of the overall height of the island hill of vision as part of their data printout (Figure 12-4). This "mean sensitivity" (the reciprocal value is "mean defect") allows one to establish at a glance whether the entire field is mildly depressed, making it easier for investigators and clinicians to attempt correlations between such factors as mild generalized visual field loss and changes in the cup-to-disc ratio or neuroretinal rim area or changes in the ophthalmoscopic or photographic appearance of the retinal nerve fiber layer.

Furthermore, as is the case in every phase of glaucoma, the ability to monitor a patient over time using the same test and testing parameters is of utmost importance. An area of questionable or inconclusive damage can be identified and followed up over months or years to see if it changes. The ability to use the same testing strategy and parameters from examination to examination, as well as the reduced impact of examiner variability, makes automated perimetry well suited for patients with early or questionable glaucomatous field loss.

The peripheral fields in early glaucoma

Some controversy exists about the incidence of peripheral field defects as the initial sign of damage in glaucoma. Although it appears that the overwhelming majority of new glaucoma field defects first appear within 30 degrees of fixation, a variety of reports show that between 5% and 15% of patients manifest their first damage in the region peripheral to 30 degrees. Drance and co-workers studied a large group of ocular hypertensive patients with

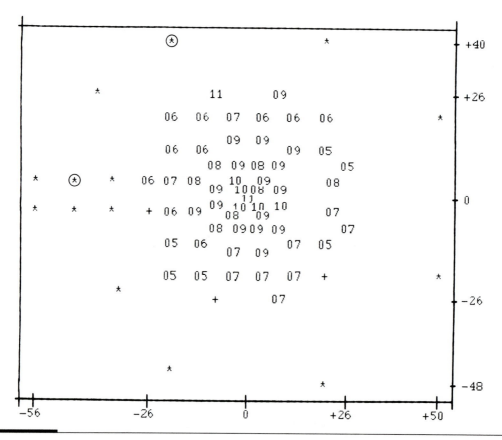

FIGURE 12-4 Subtraction table from right eye of 57-year-old man with chronic open-angle glaucoma. Each number represents difference between values generated during test and values obtained by averaging pooled data from age-matched normal controls. Note symmetric diffuse loss of between 5 and 11 dB per test site. We would describe this patient as having moderate generalized depression.

normal visual fields. During several years of follow-up, 22 of these patients developed glaucomatous visual field loss. In 20 patients the initial loss was within the central 30 degrees, and in two patients the initial loss was peripheral to 30 degrees. Thus in this series approximately 10% of the initial glaucomatous field changes occurred in the periphery.

Using a custom-designed static perimetric test, Caprioli and Spaeth found an 11% incidence of abnormal peripheral fields in patients with normal central fields. Their control group showed 12% false-positives (i.e., peripheral defects indicated in confirmed normal volunteers). We, too, have found that the incidence of false-positive defects in normal persons is similar to the incidence of isolated peripheral defects in patients diagnosed with glaucoma and in those in whom the disease is suspected. Our studies were performed using standard programs on a commercially available computerized static automated perimeter. We found a very low incidence—about 2% in combined series totaling 200 examinations—of confirmed peripheral defects in the absence of central defects in the glaucoma suspect or early glaucoma patients' eyes.

In separate studies by LeBlanc, Lee, and Baxter and Mills and Drance the incidence of initial peripheral defects in patients tested by computerized automated perimetry was also low. LeBlanc concluded that when very sensitive methods such as manual kinetic Goldmann perimetry are used, one may expect to find a small but substantial portion of initial field loss in the periphery. But when extremely sensitive methods are used, such as full-threshold computerized automated perimetry, the incidence of new peripheral defects in the presence of a normal central field is quite low. Mills concluded that peripheral static testing for routine neuroophthalmic patients should be deemphasized but not ignored.

We examine the central and peripheral field when testing glaucoma patients with manual kinetic perimetry. When using automated static perimetry, we currently use a full-threshold program for the central field and a threshold-related screening program for the peripheral field (Figure 12-5).

Nonstandard programs that test selected portions of the peripheral field quantitatively may be helpful clinically. Seamone and co-workers found that a custom quantitative program which tested the peripheral nasal field "provided valuable information in the detection of glaucomatous visual dysfunction additional to that provided by quantitative testing in the central visual field. Quantitative testing of the temporal periphery was less valuable."

Established Glaucoma

The perimetric approach to early glaucoma is significantly different from the perimetric approach to established glaucoma. In early glaucoma one is concerned with detecting visual field loss; in established glaucoma the emphasis is on progression of visual field loss. Testing strategies for early glaucoma must cover a fairly wide area of the visual field, because the examiner has no idea where an initial defect may appear. It is clear that certain regions are more likely to show the first change associated with glaucoma, but our preconceived notions about where a field defect is likely to occur may not be accurate for a given patient. The search for field defects is a methodical, organized, and somewhat tedious process, in which large areas of normal field must often be traversed in an effort to detect a shallow scotoma measuring only a few degrees in diameter. In established glaucoma the examiner can consult the patient's records and study the depth and extent of field defects. An essential question in perimetry performed on such patients is, Have the defects become more dense, have they enlarged, or both? If they have enlarged, are the defects now threatening fixation? Changes in the defect size, depth, or location can be critically important in managing patients with glaucoma,

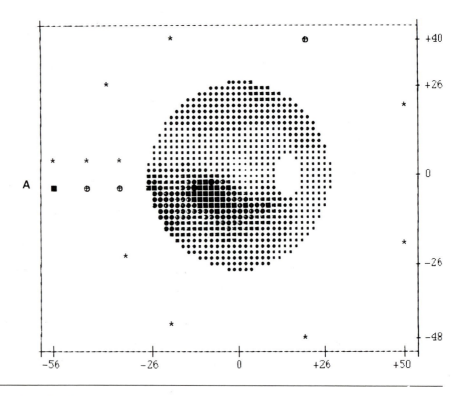

FIGURE 12-5 A, Moderately dense inferior arcuate scotomas. Halftone display represents central visual field to 26 degrees of eccentricity. In peripheral field, asterisk represents normal response, plus sign in circle indicates moderately depressed response, and small black square represents severely depressed response.

because one often makes medical, laser, or surgical therapy decisions based on such information.

The examiner must remember, of course, that new defects can appear as established glaucoma progresses, and thus many of the methods used for testing patients in the early phases of glaucoma must still be practiced in patients with established field loss.

Tangent screen

When testing patients with established glaucoma on the tangent screen, we usually prefer to have no knowledge, or minimal knowledge, of the prior field defects. In some centers the patients' prior fields are studied in detail

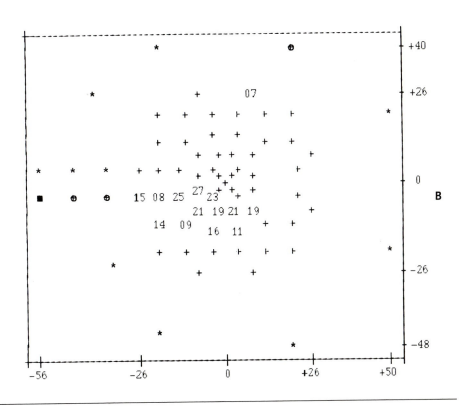

FIGURE 12-5, cont'd. B, Data from same field as represented in **A.** Instead of gray halftone display to represent central 26 degrees, plus sign indicates normal or near-normal response. If response was depressed significantly, depth of depression in decibels is printed at test site. Cluster of values in inferior arcuate region indicates points were depressed between 8 and 27 dB below normal.

before a follow-up examination takes place. This allows the examiner to concentrate energy on the specific margins of the visual field as detected by the prior examination. We generally prefer not to do this, however, because we feel a more objective examination can be obtained without intimate knowledge of the patient's prior field. A cursory knowledge of the patient's field is probably not harmful under such circumstances, but we usually try to determine the exact boundaries and depth of defective areas separately for each examination (Figure 12-6) and then compare a series of examinations side by side.

It is particularly important to note the examination conditions when performing repeat perimetry on a person who had field defects on an earlier examination. A patient with miotic pupils from medication or a patient who is not corrected properly or an examination that takes place in a more dimly lit room will make the field appear to be worse on the most recent examination. Furthermore, if media opacities such as cataracts have progressed in the interval between field examinations, scotomas will appear deeper and broader than they did before, even though there has been no progression of the glaucoma. Especially with manual perimetry, it is essential that one take the time to carefully note all of these factors in the patient's chart.

Multiple isopter perimetry is extremely important in follow-up examinations. Testing with only the very dim small targets used to detect initial field loss will not yield much information on the depth of a scotoma or the steepness

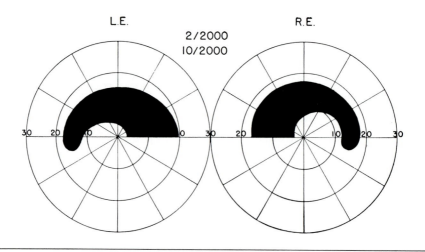

FIGURE 12-6   Typical bilateral arcuate scotoma or superior nerve fiber bundle defect in chronic wide-angle glaucoma. Intraocular pressure varied between 25 and 44 mm Hg, and there was bilateral glaucomatous atrophy and excavation of optic nerve. Central vision was 20/20. Defects were dense and steep margined, indicating stability in disease. More often scotoma lacks uniformity and has sloping margins.

of its margins. Since progression can be heralded by an increase in the depth, as well as in the area of a scotoma, it is important that one test these defects quantitatively. As with all scotomas, we try to define glaucomatous visual field loss using a combination of static and kinetic perimetry.

Once established, the nerve fiber bundle defect progresses as follows:

1. The lesion becomes more dense and generally more uniform so that it is easily detectable with relatively gross stimuli.
2. It broadens in width, expanding slowly toward fixation and more rapidly toward the periphery, especially in the nasal quadrant, where it eventually breaks through into the peripheral field or coalesces with a coexistent peripheral depression.
3. The defect lengthens until it connects at one end with the blind spot and terminates in a steep-margined and characteristic nasal step at the other.

Hoyt, Frisén and Newman have demonstrated a method of visualizing retinal nerve fiber bundle defects using ophthalmoscopy with red-free light. They studied the peripapillary nerve fiber layers in eyes with clinically elevated intraocular pressure and found that retinal nerve fiber atrophy corresponding to glaucomatous-type visual field defects can be seen with the ophthalmoscope and in fundus photographs (Figure 12-7).

The nerve fiber bundle atrophy appears as multiple fine shallow grooves or slits in the arcuate bundles of the retinal nerve fiber layer. These slits represent the effects of nerve fiber bundle degeneration. As the glaucomatous atrophy increases, the defect in the nerve fiber layer may resemble a wedge that tapers to the disc margin. In still later stages, these wedge defects expand to sector defects in which all nerve fiber bundle details are obliterated. There is generally excellent correlation between the ophthalmoscopic findings of degeneration and visual field defects in these patients.

More recently Airaksinen and many others have described various techniques of examining black-and-white fundus photographs to detect retinal nerve fiber layer defects. These defects generally occur in two forms: segmental and diffuse. Segmental retinal nerve fiber layer defects correspond roughly to localized visual field defects, whereas diffuse nerve fiber layer loss is associated with generalized visual field depression.

These techniques supplement visual field data and may have particular usefulness in the earliest stages of demonstrable glaucomatous damage.

Peripheral depression

Coincident with the development of nerve fiber bundle defects in glaucoma is a depression of the peripheral isopters, especially in the nasal quadrants. When examined carefully, this nasal depression may be one of the earliest signs of functional loss in glaucoma patients. When associated with a nerve fiber bundle defect, peripheral nasal depression is almost pathogno-

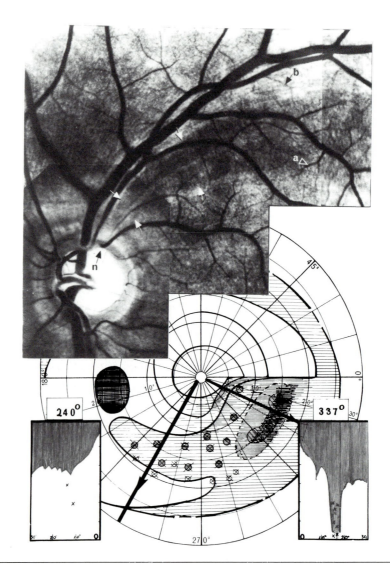

FIGURE 12-7 Funduscopy of nerve fiber layer defects. Glaucomatous nerve fiber layer defect between solid white arrows and peripheral arrows *a* and *b* appears as scimitar-like wedge joining disc margin at *n*. Borders of wedge conform to course of temporal arcuate bundles. Granular appearance throughout retina is caused by diffuse axonal attrition. Optic disc shows marked cupping with indenting of rim at *n*. Tübinger perimeter fields showed relative scotoma in Bjerrum area with nasal step. Static perimetry profile at 337-degree meridian showed general depression and dense scotoma at 15 degrees of eccentricity. *(From Hoyt WF, Frisén L, and Newman NM: Invest Ophthalmol 12:814, 1973.)*

monic of glaucoma, and its coalescence with the scotoma eventually results in the peripheral field breakthrough that is so characteristic of the terminal stages of glaucomatous field loss.

Once established, peripheral depression progresses relatively rapidly compared with changes in the central field, and in some instances may simulate a quadrantanopsia, especially when the depression has coalesced with an arcuate scotoma (Figure 12-8). When both upper and nasal fields are involved and the peripheral depression is symmetric in both eyes, the fields can mimic a binasal hemianopsia.

For the most part, the specific defects of established glaucoma represent a coalescence and intensification of the defects seen in early or incipient glaucoma. Thus the shallow paracentral defects that one might detect early join together to form the characteristic arcuate, or Bjerrum, scotoma. The Bjerrum scotoma (also called comet scotoma, scimitar scotoma, or nerve fiber bundle defect) was first described by von Graefe in 1856 as a paracentral scotoma characteristic of established glaucoma. But it was studied and analyzed in much more detail by Bjerrum in 1889. Since then the defect has been the subject of intensive investigation by numerous authors, including Landsberg, Peter, Meisling, Friedenwald, Sinclair, Traquair, Rönne, Dubois-Poulsen, Aulhorn, Harrington, Drance, and others. The Bjerrum scotoma is the classic

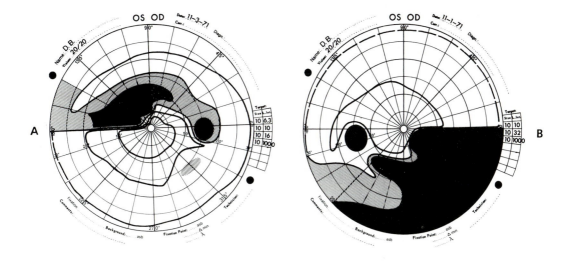

FIGURE 12-8 Right eye, **A,** and left eye, **B.** Nerve fiber bundle destruction following severe exsanguination from rectal bleeding. Kinetic examination with Tübinger perimeter was similar to tangent screen field for stimuli up to 30/2000. Both optic discs were pale. Intraocular pressure was 10 mm Hg. Field defect has remained stable for several years. Red-free ophthalmoscopy showed definite nerve fiber bundle atrophy in areas corresponding to field loss. Field from left eye **(B)** simulates quadrantic defect. *(From Harrington DO: Trans Ophthalmol Soc UK 92:15, 1972, London, Churchill Livingstone, Ltd.)*

visual field defect of glaucoma, and its presence and character are central to our understanding of the pathologic process of this disease.

As the Bjerrum defect arches around fixation to approach the horizontal raphe, it changes course and merges into central and ultimately peripheral nasal step defects. As the disease progresses further, this arching defect becomes absolute (Figure 12-5). What began as a series of small unconnected troughs or craters in the surface of the hill of vision, now is a deep crevice. By the time one sees a complete superior or inferior Bjerrum defect there is often at least some paracentral depression in the opposite hemifield. Finally, the defects will begin to break through into the periphery and ultimately will involve fixation.

Goldmann perimetry

Static and kinetic perimetry performed on the Goldmann perimeter in established glaucoma follows essentially the same pattern as that described for tangent screen perimetry. Again, it is important to perform quantitative multiple-isopter perimetry and to make sure that the machine and testing conditions are standardized. Goldmann perimetry offers advantages in that the periphery can be examined more carefully. Thus the full extent of peripheral breakthrough and peripheral nasal steps can be mapped, which may add valuable information to one's assessment of the progression of the disease.

Automated perimetry

As with the two methods mentioned above, static automated perimetry in established glaucoma is most useful if it is performed in a quantitative, threshold manner. Automated perimeters offer several advantages over manual perimetry in these circumstances. The exact same testing strategy and sequence used for detection of the initial defects can be duplicated each time the patient returns for a follow-up visit. This affords one an excellent chance to compare fields serially over time (Figures 12-9 and 12-10), which is important when trying to determine whether a field has changed. Most automated perimeters require that significant testing parameters be entered into the computer's memory before the test can proceed (Figure 12-11). This compels the examiner to monitor such things as pupil size and refraction and helps to ensure consistent testing conditions during serial examinations.

Another useful aspect of computerized perimetry is that the machines themselves can run statistical analyses of the data. Using the appropriate software, a series of fields can be analyzed and the machine's computer can evaluate statistically whether the field appears to have remained stable, worsened, or improved. Several of the more popular machines also print reduced renditions of prior field examinations, so that data from several examinations spanning many years can be compared on a single page. As these statistical programs become more widespread and further refined, they will become even more helpful in assisting practitioners in making therapeutic decisions.

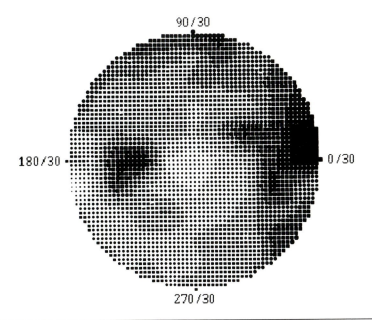

FIGURE 12-9 Visual field from left eye of 74-year-old patient with open-angle glaucoma. Note enlarged blind spot, dense superior nasal step, moderate incomplete superior arcuate scotoma, shallow incomplete inferior arcuate scotoma, and moderate generalized depression.

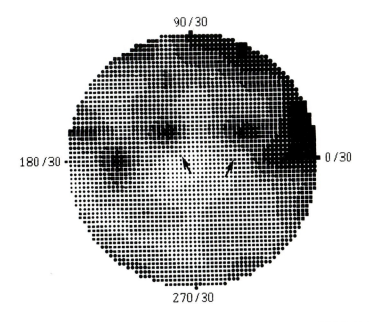

FIGURE 12-10 Field from left eye of patient in Fig. 12-9 approximately 1 year later. Overall generalized depression has remained about same. However, superior nasal step defect and, most specifically, two regions in superior arcuate region *(arrows)* have intensified dramatically.

Surname, given names:

Date of birth:

Patient number/eye:

Examination number, date, time:

Correction, (sph., cyl., + axis):

Diameter of pupil, head position:

Size of stimulus:

Fixation ring:

Program number:

FIGURE 12-11 Great benefit of computerized perimetry is that certain patient data must be entered before printout is generated. Besides patient's name, birth date, etc., many machines require that pupillary diameter, refraction, stimulus size, and other factors be recorded. These data make duplicating exact testing circumstances easier and allow better interpretation of previous test results.

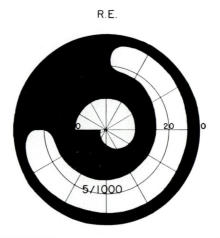

FIGURE 12-12 Chronic wide-angle glaucoma of right eye. Double nerve fiber bundle defects (arcuate scotoma) with characteristic double nasal step and breakthrough into peripheral nasal field. There is unusual finding of normal visual field, normal optic nerve, and normal intraocular pressure in other eye.

Late-Stage Glaucoma

As established glaucoma moves to the late stages, arcuate or Bjerrum scotomas develop on both sides of the horizontal meridian (Figure 12-12). This so-called double arcuate scotoma may meet at the nasal horizontal raphe; usually the nasal steps in this region do not correspond exactly, so even though broad defects are seen both above and below fixation, a central nasal step indicates that one is not simply dealing with a ring scotoma. These scotomas may ultimately encroach upon fixation and break through to the periphery.

Late-stage glaucoma is characterized by profound midperipheral and peripheral field loss, with often only a tiny island of vision remaining around fixation or a small preserved wedge of temporal field (Figure 12-13). In the ultimate case, the natural history of glaucoma is to progress until these last remaining areas too are destroyed and the patient is left sightless.

The central island of vision in late-stage glaucoma can measure only a few degrees from edge to edge. Patients with this vision may be able to read in the 20/20 to 20/40 range on the Snellen acuity chart, but may be unable to ambulate because they cannot see enough of a room at a time to traverse it safely. These patients invariably have dramatic cupping, with almost completely whitened nerves and cup-to-disc ratios greater than 0.9:1.

This remnant of the central visual field will retain certain characteristics of the glaucoma field until the very end. It is oval, with its longest diameter horizontal and in the centrocecal area. The field often shows a minute hori-

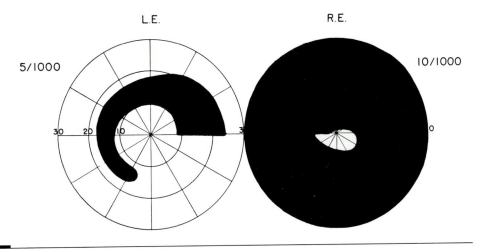

FIGURE 12-13 Chronic wide-angle glaucoma. Patient was unaware of visual loss, and central vision was 20/20 in each eye. There was typical glaucomatous atrophy of both discs. Right field shows extreme contraction with tiny nasal step. Left field shows typical arcuate scotoma ending at horizontal meridian.

zontal step just nasal to fixation, thus following the pattern of the retinal nerve fiber bundle. Final encroachment of the defect on fixation is usually from the nasal side; when fixation becomes involved the visual loss is sudden, severe, and dramatic.

As just mentioned, a small temporal area of vision is often retained in the peripheral field. The patient may be barely aware of this area before the central defect involves fixation, at which time he or she immediately becomes conscious of its value as a last hope. The small area of vision may remain for quite some time after all other areas are gone.

Tangent screen

Tangent screen examination is extremely useful in late-stage glaucoma. Because only a small area of central vision is spared, we often test such patients at a 2-meter distance from the tangent screen. This enlarges the preserved area in absolute terms and allows us to measure its borders more precisely. Goldmann perimeters and automated machines have fixation lenses or cameras in the central area that sometimes make it difficult to tell exactly how close a defect is coming to fixation. Because preserving fixation (central vision) is one of our primary goals in managing patients with late-stage glaucoma, monitoring the degree of encroachment on this vital area is extremely important.

Regarding the management of patients with late-stage glaucoma, most practitioners believe that more heavily damaged optic nerves require lower pressures to maintain their vision. For the 1981 R.N. Shaffer Lecture at the American Academy of Ophthalmology meeting in Atlanta, Grant reviewed the question of why people go blind from glaucoma. A striking finding in his studies was that the ultimate prognosis of glaucoma is closely related to the amount of visual field loss the patient has in the initial examination. Patients with field loss in all four quadrants had a much poorer prognosis than patients whose field loss was confined to one quadrant only.

Goldmann perimetry

The very reasons that make tangent screen examinations so valuable in late-stage glaucoma tend to make Goldmann perimetry not as useful. One is often looking at an area measuring only an inch or so in diameter, and it may be difficult to measure this with tremendous detail. Furthermore, there is often very little vision in the periphery, and the great advantage of being able to test the peripheral field quantitatively is of little value.

Static automated perimetry

Static automated perimetry can be limited in late-stage glaucoma. The static method does not allow efficient mapping of boundaries (Figure 12-14). Because of the time necessary to perform thresholding, minor fixation shifts can take place that change the boundaries of the preserved area projected on

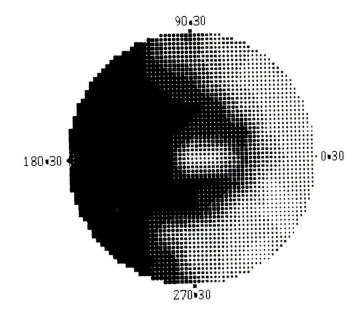

FIGURE 12-14 A 60-year-old patient with double Bjerrum scotomas breaking into nasal periphery. Temporal peripheral field is relatively spared.

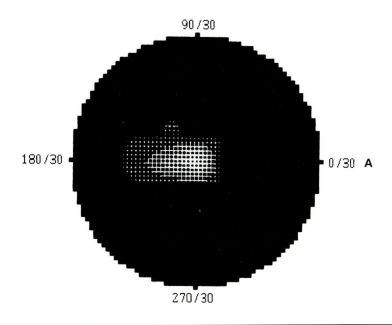

FIGURE 12-15 A, Late-stage glaucoma in left eye of 75-year-old man. Only small central island of vision remains.

Continued.

```
                              Y
                              0

                 0    0    0    0    0
                 0                   0
              0    0    0    0    0    0    0
           0    0    0    0    0    0    0    0    0
                          0         0
           0    0    0    1    0    0    0    0    0
B    X  0    0    0    6   14   28    0    0    0    0    0    X
           0                                   0
           0    0    0    0    0    0    0    0    0
                              0
           0    0    0    0    0    0    0    0    0
                 0                   0
              0    0    0    0    0    0    0
                 0    0    0    0    0
                              0
                              0
                              Y
```

```
24.5 24.5        28.5 25.5        2.5  2.5
24.5  0.0        24.5  2.6        2.5  0.0
24.5             23.5             2.5


18.5 17.5        20.5 21.2        2.5  4.0
19.5  2.6        20.5  1.2        9.5  4.9
14.5             22.5             0.0
   C

 0.0  0.0         0.0  0.0         0.0  0.0
 0.0  0.0         0.0  0.0         0.0  0.0
 0.0              0.0              0.0
```

FLUCTUATIONS (R.M.S.): 2.6 DB   LUM. INTERVAL: 2

FIGURE 12-15, cont'd. B, Standard numerical printout of same patient's field showing that only four points registered any sensitivity. Since each test point is 6 degrees from its nearest neighbor, however, it is impossible to tell how close field loss comes to fixation. **C,** Specialized program has concentrated points in central area at only 3 degrees apart. Each point is tested several times, and results are averaged to determine mean sensitivity and standard deviation. This concentrated grid pattern gives much more information about status of central field than does standard numerical printout.

the field chart from minute to minute. The most useful programs in these circumstances are those that concentrate a large number of test points in a very small area about the macula (Figure 12-15). We frequently augment our automated static testing with manual techniques using the tangent screen.

IMPORTANCE OF PERIMETRY IN GLAUCOMA

Visual field examination has a threefold value in glaucoma: diagnosis, prognosis, and therapy.

Diagnosis

The early visual field changes in glaucoma patients have been stressed. It is a simple matter to detect the established nerve fiber bundle defect or peripheral nasal step, since these are obvious even with relatively crude examination methods. It is of much greater importance to study and apply precise quantitative methods to detecting early functional loss so as to forestall further damage.

Visual field changes are indications of established glaucoma. In the strict sense, they are confirmatory evidence of the disease rather than diagnostic. They must be correlated with the other signs and symptoms of the disease.

With other evidence of glaucoma, such as optic disc cupping, nerve fiber layer atrophy, increased intraocular pressure, outflow facility, gonioscopic changes in the anterior chamber angle, and family history, the finding of early but characteristic glaucomatous visual field changes takes on added significance and may be the pivotal means of establishing the diagnosis. When the examiner has doubts about a given case, no method that will give evidence of functional loss in an eye should be neglected; the visual field examination may be of prime importance when all available examination techniques are used.

Prognosis

Visual field interpretation is of even greater value as a prognostic than as a diagnostic aid. In most cases the established visual field defect is associated with other signs and symptoms that are of great diagnostic value, but the progression of the visual field defect may tell more of the advance of the disease than any other single finding.

As in any visual field defect, a sloping margin and lack of uniformity indicate an actively changing process. In glaucomatous visual field loss, one more often finds sloping margins associated with early defects and increased density, uniformity, depth, and steepness of margins associated with the defects of well-established or end-stage glaucoma.

A sudden decrease in blood pressure in the vessels supplying the optic nervehead, even if only transient, may produce rapid deterioration of the visual field with a sudden appearance of nerve fiber bundle defects or exaggeration of previously existing defects (Figure 12-16). Such a drop in blood pressure and resulting decreases in blood flow may be initiated iatrogenically by too vigorous use of blood pressure–depressing drugs in the absence of adequate control of intraocular pressure. Glaucomatous visual field changes have also progressed rapidly in patients who suffer coronary artery occlusion, cerebrovascular accident, or severe gastrointestinal or other bleeding.

Optic nerve pallor and cupping are likely to closely parallel loss of visual field, but the examiner's judgment of an advancing atrophy may also be relatively inaccurate as compared with the record of visual field changes, unless photographs are used to record the disc changes.

Extreme care must be taken in assessing visual field change in the presence of simultaneous glaucoma and cataract. Any media clouding effectively reduces stimulus illumination or intensity and thus exaggerates the visual field defect. Some of the newer automated machines attempt to overcome this difficulty by including an analysis of the ability of the lens to transmit light in their data collection. Theoretically, the examiner will be able to objectively

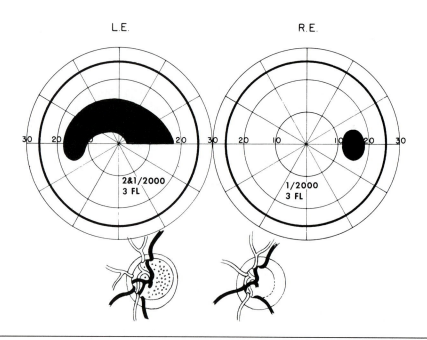

FIGURE 12-16 Nerve fiber bundle defect developing rapidly in eye with well-controlled glaucoma. Patient suffered mild cerebrovascular accident with sudden marked decrease in systemic and ophthalmic artery blood pressure. Both optic discs are cupped. Left disc is partially atrophic.

measure decreased lens transmission (or incresaed cataract density) and subtract this effect from the overall change in visual fields over a given period.
The result of being able to differentiate cataract changes from glaucoma
changes will be an improvement in our ability to monitor glaucoma, particularly among the elderly, who suffer from both diseases frequently.

Finally, we will stress again the importance of carefully controlling all
testing parameters for follow-up examinations.

Therapy

The proper therapy for glaucoma is obviously a large and rapidly evolving
subject. We will approach therapeutic decisions in glaucoma from the stand-
point of the visual field examination.

To a fairly large extent perimetry dictates glaucoma therapy. Without
functional loss in a given eye, most practitioners are comfortable with observation or conservative medical management. With moderate functional loss
or with extremely slow progression of visual field changes, the physician must
weigh other factors against the field when making decisions about how to
best treat the eye. For example, a slowly advancing loss in a relatively elderly
person with a reasonably controlled intraocular pressure might dictate one
course of action, whereas the same findings in a young person would call for
different therapy. In all cases one is really measuring the risks of therapy
against the benefits of halting or slowing progression of the disease. This is
an extremely difficult task in glaucoma management. The risks of long-term
(often lifelong) therapy are difficult to predict with certainty and may often
be underestimated. Furthermore, the benefits of treatment, in this case pressure lowering, are somewhat vague. We do not know precisely how a given
nerve will tolerate a given pressure level, or stated another way, how much
the pressure must be reduced to halt progression of the disease. Within the
practical ranges of pressure lowering achievable by modern therapy, some
investigators question the overall effectiveness of glaucoma treatment.

A dense arcuate scotoma proximal to the fixation area should be viewed
with great concern because even a minor change in the visual field can indicate
a poor future unless the intraocular pressure is normalized promptly.

Sudden, severe hypotony following fistulizing operations has been shown
to aggravate the visual field loss until later normalization of pressure arrests
this progress. Thus considerable visual field loss may occur for a short time
after successful surgery. If the preoperative field changes are severe, and
especially if they are proximal to fixation, this postoperative visual field loss
may obliterate the central visual area and nullify the benefits of surgery. In
other cases a rapid progression of visual field loss that obviously calls for
surgical therapy is only temporarily halted by operation and later resumes its
inexorable march toward blindness, despite a relatively normalized intraocular
pressure.

chronic open-angle glaucoma. Treatment with antiglaucoma medications tends not only to lower the average pressure in glaucomatous eyes, but also to damp to some degree the amplitude of the diurnal pressure curve.

The best way to determine whether a patient with low-tension glaucoma fits into this category is to hospitalize the patient and measure the intraocular pressure on an hourly basis for 24 to 48 hours. Because such intensive pressure measurement is usually thoroughly impractical, the concept of an "office diurnal curve" (meaning hourly measurements from about 8 AM until the early evening), or at least checking the patient's pressure at different times during the day during a series of visits, has gained wide acceptance.

The second type of patient that shows wide swings in pressure and may show normal pressures during visits is a perhaps underrecognized group of patients who have a type of chronic or subacute angle closure. These patients initially have relatively narrow angles, often with intermittent peripheral anterior synechiae. They show typical signs of glaucomatous damage at diagnosis. When treated, their intraocular pressures generally fall into an acceptable range. Unfortunately, longitudinal follow-up shows that visual field loss progresses, even though the pressures are usually in the high teens. The important characteristic of these patients is that from time to time the pressures during office visits may be quite high, reaching perhaps the low to mid-30s or more. Because of the history of a good response to medication, the physician assumes

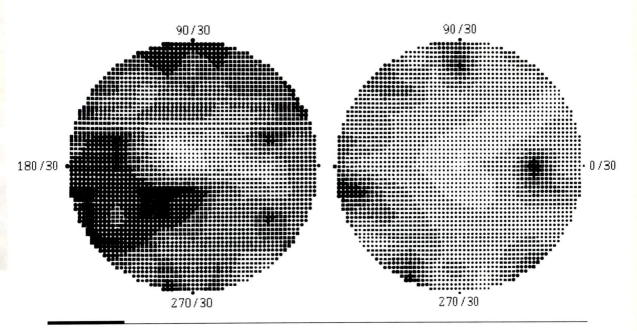

FIGURE 12-17 A 44-year-old woman with dense inferior arcuate scotoma with peripheral breakthrough and less dense superior arcuate scotoma. Although she has severe cupping bilaterally, her intraocular pressures have never been measured above 21 mm Hg.

that the problem is patient compliance, reinstructs the patient to take medications carefully, and schedules a follow-up visit for shortly thereafter. The pressure responds well and the physician's assumption of poor compliance is apparently confirmed. Careful gonioscopy during the pressure spikes, however, often reveals a component of angle closure. Thus the intermittent pressure elevations are caused not by poor compliance but by the chronic angle-closure nature of the patient's glaucoma. The relentless visual field progression occurs because of damage done to the eye during these periods of elevated pressure. Sometimes a peripheral iridectomy can be helpful in managing such patients.

The second category of low-tension glaucoma could also be termed "burned out glaucoma." These are patients with dramatic visual field and cupping changes who have had damage over past years with high pressures, and now, even though intraocular pressure is well controlled, damage continues. Thoroughly aggressive means of pressure control are often warranted; the prognosis must remain guarded.

The third category of patients includes those in whom some particular event, such as an episode of hemodynamic shock, has occurred that has resulted in a sustained period of diminished perfusion of the optic nerve. Drance has reported a series in which 93% of 41 eyes that fulfilled the criteria for low-tension glaucoma showed systemic abnormalities. Hemodynamic crises and low blood pressure occurred more frequently in this group than in a carefully selected and studied control series. Although these patients have cupping and visual field changes similar to other cases of advanced glaucoma, because the damage was caused by a remote and isolated set of events, the field changes and cupping should be relatively stable (Figure 12-18).

The fourth category, which might be termed simple or essential low-tension glaucoma, includes patients whose recorded intraocular pressure (including some type of diurnal curve), has never been above 21 mm Hg, who show no evidence of angle-closure glaucoma, and who give no history or indication of having suffered a hemodynamic crisis or hypotensive episode. Such patients are the subject of intensive study. Recent investigations indicate that they may have chronic mild circulatory peculiarities that may lead to some vascular insufficiency. Chronically cold hands and feet or other signs of peripheral "poor circulation" seem to occur more frequently in this group than in an age-matched control population.

A consistent finding in most patients with low-tension glaucoma is that they have evidence of established glaucoma, such as significant visual field changes and cupping, at the time of diagnosis. Rather than being a peculiarity of the disease, it is likely that this advanced state at diagnosis is simply the result of the disease not having been detected by more routine screening methods, such as intraocular pressure measurement. As our understanding of the relationship between intraocular pressure, intraocular pressure control,

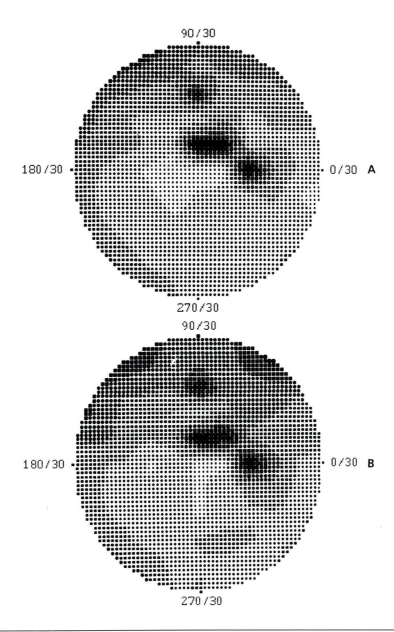

FIGURE 12-18 A, Visual field from 81-year-old woman with history of low-tension glaucoma secondary to catastrophic blood loss. Note position, size, and intensity of blind spot and nearby paracentral scotoma. **B,** Visual field from same patient at age 86. Superior paracentral scotoma has not progressed.

and glaucoma grows, hopefully we will develop more effective means of treating patients with low-tension glaucoma.

PATHOGENESIS OF THE GLAUCOMA FIELD

In 1954 Dubois-Poulsen and Magis suggested the the Bjerrum scotoma is not pathognomonic of glaucoma and showed that it may be associated with a wide variety of lesions affecting the visual pathway anterior to the lateral geniculate body. These included vascular lesions of the retina, choroiditis, optic neuritis, and optic nerve trauma.

These authors advanced the theory that the Bjerrum scotoma is not necessarily correlated to intraocular tension or to cupping of the optic discs. They state the Bjerrum scotoma corresponds to a well-separated nerve fiber bundle and that its cause must be vascular and extraocular. They believe that the actual lesion may be located immediately posterior to the eyeball in the arterial circle of Zinn-Haller or even further back in the optic nerve and that this "essential symptom of glaucoma" is not directly influenced by intraocular tension.

The vascular genesis of the Bjerrum scotoma (and the other visual field defects of glaucoma) was suggested by Traquair, Lauber, and Reese and McGavic; it has been elaborated on by Gafner and Goldmann in 1955, by Harrington in 1958, 1959, and 1964, and by Drance in 1961, 1968, 1970, and 1977.

Harrington has reported the sudden appearance of a nerve fiber bundle defect in patients with well-controlled glaucoma after their arterial hypertension had been iatrogenically lowered by excessive medication. He has also produced temporary nerve fiber bundle defects in the visual fields of patients with carotid artery insufficiency by artificially inducing very slight elevation in intraocular pressure through compression of the globe with an ophthalmodynamometer. Bjerrum scotomas have been produced or exaggerated in glaucomatous eyes by minimally elevating the intraocular pressure with a dynamometer, thus demonstrating that certain eyes are more vulnerable than others to increases in intraocular pressure.

Drance, Wheeler, and Pattullo studied a series of patients with uniocular glaucoma to determine which factors might influence the production of field defects. These eyes were subjected to visual field studies by kinetic and static methods of perimetry and were thoroughly studied for all possible evidences of glaucoma. Intraocular pressure, the degree of optic disc cupping and atrophy, tonographic data, and ophthalmodynamometer findings varied considerably in the 31 eyes studied. Those patients in whom intraocular pressure was normal or slightly elevated and who showed extensive optic disc and visual field deficits had a very high incidence of vascular disease, including myocardial infarctions, which produced a transient but pronounced drop in systemic blood pressure. In the group with low-tension glaucoma, two out of four patients gave a history of massive gastrointestinal bleeding with marked lowering of blood pressure. In the unaffected eyes of these patients with uniocular glaucoma, visual field tests on the Tübinger perimeter revealed paracentral scotomas in 14 eyes. All the eyes with badly damaged nerves and visual fields but with normal or very slightly elevated pressure had low diastolic perfusion pressures or had had a transient episode of very low blood pressure that would have resulted in a very low diastolic perfusion pressure at the time.

The authors concluded that the changes produced in chronic open-angle glaucoma can be the result, on the one hand, of markedly elevated intraocular pressure that embarrasses the circulation of the optic nervehead and retina independently of other factors and, on the other hand, of extreme circulatory events that do not require any elevation or change in intraocular pressure to cause extensive nerve and visual field damage.

Drance and Begg reported a case of chronic open-angle glaucoma with normal intraocular pressure and minimal paracentral scotomas in the visual field in which the patient sustained a sudden linear hemorrhage on the disc margin associated with enlargement of the optic cup and development of a dense new superior arcuate scotoma. They concluded that this hemorrhage occurred as a result of ischemic infarction in the nervehead, resulting from poor perfusion insufficient to maintain circulation under normal conditions of high tissue pressure at this site. The association of acute ischemic changes in the nervehead, manifested by sector hemorrhage, with the development of typically glaucomatous disc cupping and atrophy and advanced visual field defect, offers further evidence of the ischemic origin of the glaucomatous defect in the field (Figure 12-19).

Blumenthal and his co-workers investigated the effect of acute increases in intraocular pressure on the retinal, choroidal, and optic disc vessels by means of fluorescein angiography in normal human eyes. Their technique provided for controlled studies of intraocular pressure effects on the vascular bed of the eye. They demonstrated that flow ceases in the choroidal circulation at intraocular pressures significantly lower than those required to stop blood flow in the retinal vascular tree.

The optic disc capillaries were affected at the smallest increases of intraocular pressure and filled with dye only after the entire choroid had become fluorescent. In some instances the entire peripapillary choroidal area revealed a marked diminution in fluorescence. These findings imply that the peripapillary choroidal vessels and the optic disc vessels are the most vulnerable portion of the choroidal circulation when subjected to elevation of intraocular pressure.

Histologic evidence confirms the fact that the peripapillary choroidal vascular bed is the source of the blood supply to the pre–lamina cribrosa of the optic nerve.

Intensity of fluorescence in the optic disc capillaries has been assessed. A marked decrease in capillaries is seen with the increase in cup-to-disc ratio,

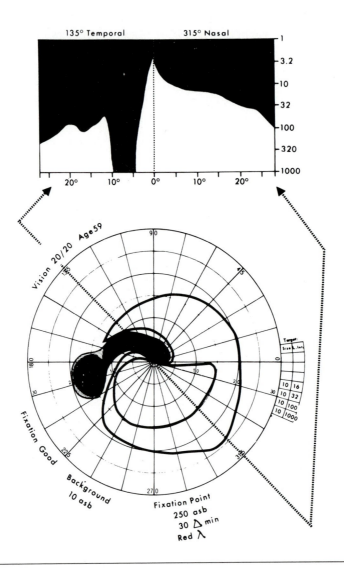

FIGURE 12-19 Static and kinetic visual field examination showing absolute arcuate scotoma in eye with sector hemorrhage and acute ischemic infarct in optic disc. Patient had medically controlled chronic glaucoma with minimal relative scotoma in superior Bjerrum area until sudden appearance of capillary hemorrhage on disc. *(From Drance SM and Begg IS: Can J Ophthalmol 5:137, 1970.)*

and the greater the visual field defects, the fewer the capillaries in the optic nervehead. It is possible to predict the visual field loss from the capillary distribution in the glaucomatous optic disc.

Ernest has written extensively and convincingly on the pathogenesis of glaucomatous optic nerve disease. His article carries an extensive bibliography. Ernest's studies described the vasculature of the distal segment of the optic nerve, measured the optic disc oxygen tension in monkeys, and measured the visual effects of induced elevations in the intraocular pressure in humans. He shows that the visual threshold in the Bjerrum area is elevated with an increase in the intraocular pressure but that the eye compensates when the threshold is reduced toward normal if given ample time. It is believed that glaucomatous optic nerve disease results when local homeostatic circulatory mechanisms fail to compensate for sustained elevation of the intraocular pressure.

Ernest concludes that the initiating pathogenic event in glaucomatous optic nerve disease is a breakdown in the homeostatic mechanisms responsible for normal perfusion and oxygenation of the optic disc; that the superior and inferior temporal nerve fibers are affected first, since these are in highest concentration relative to the optic disc blood supply; and that the first fibers affected in the superior and inferior nerve fiber bundles are those midway between the disc circumference and the central retinal artery, since this is the area of relatively lowest oxygen tension.

Studies by Anderson and Hendrickson of rapid axoplasmic transport in monkey optic nerve reveal that it is affected by intraocular pressure. There is a selective effect deep in the optic nervehead at the lamina cribrosa, and a partial effect can be detected even at moderate elevations of intraocular pressure. When intraocular pressure is moderately elevated, there is partial obstruction of axoplasmic transport in the region of the lamina cribrosa. When intraocular pressure is elevated to within 25 mm Hg of mean blood pressure, complete obstruction of transport at the lamina cribrosa occurs. Whether the obstruction is mechanical or secondary to reduced blood flow is controversial, and the exact relevance of these findings to the pathogenic mechanisms of glaucomatous cupping and visual field loss is unclear.

It seems logical to conclude, however, that such physiologic abnormalities would lead to functional deficits in the fields.

The same effect of increased intraocular pressure has been noted on slow axonal protein flow by Levy. He found marked initial reduction in flow with increased pressure and a gradual recovery as pressure returned to normal.

In contrast to these findings, Phelps and Phelps have succeeded in elevating systemic blood pressure by intravenous infusion of phenylephrine while simultaneously elevating intraocular pressure by paralimbal suction. They then measured the highest level to which intraocular pressure could be raised without obliterating perception of a slowly flickering stimulus in the nasal field of vision. Elevation of systemic blood pressure was accompanied in all subjects tested by a corresponding increase in the highest "safe" level of intraocular pressure. This observation supports the hypothesis that pressure amaurosis is the result of pressure-induced neuroretinal ischemia.

Pederson and Anderson have studied serial disc photographs of 259 patients with elevated intraocular pressures over periods up to 15 years. Twenty-nine eyes showed progressive enlargement of the optic cup. Expansion of the optic cup was the first change observed, typically preceding visual field loss by several years. They concluded that serial disc photographs are necessary for the earliest detection of optic nerve damage in ocular hypertension and that treatment is indicated for eyes exhibiting progressive disc cupping even in the absence of visual field defects. They noted that visual field examination is important in detecting early damage, since field loss can be present even when the disc is judged normal.

The histologic studies of Quigley and Addicks showed that dramatic glaucomatous optic nerve atrophy can occur, despite normal Goldmann perimetry. Their findings make a strong case for the presence of structural change before functional change, at least as we can measure.

13   TOXIC AMBLYOPIAS

Toxic amblyopias are generally classified as diseases of the optic nerve. In reality, the exact location and nature of the lesion producing the visual defect are often unknown. Some, such as methyl alcohol poisoning, appear definitely to produce optic nerve damage. Others, such as quinine or organic arsenic poisoning, result from retinal hypoxia and damage to retinal ganglion cells, with secondary optic atrophy. We will discuss the toxic amblyopias from the viewpoint of the type of damage caused by the individual toxic agents rather than attempting an anatomic classification based on the site of the lesion.

A wide variety of drugs and other synthetic and naturally occurring agents that patients ingest may affect the visual apparatus. This issue has been addressed in detail by many authors, including Grant in *Toxicology of the Eye,* ed. 2, and Fraunfelder in *Drug Induced Ocular Side Effects and Drug Interactions,* ed. 2.

From a perimetric viewpoint the toxic amblyopias generally fall into two groups: (1) those with central scotomas and (2) those with peripheral visual field loss or depression. The best known and most widely studied example of a toxic amblyopia associated with central visual field loss is tobacco amblyopia (variously described and grouped with other agents as tobacco-alcohol amblyopia, tobacco-alcohol-nutritional amblyopia, or acute malnutrition optic neuropathy). The most prominent example of a toxic amblyopia associated with peripheral visual field loss is quinine amblyopia.

BILATERAL CENTRAL SCOTOMA

Scotomas of varying size, shape, density, and position, always bilateral, may be produced by many agents, including (1) tobacco, (2) nutritional deficiencies, (3) ethyl alcohol, (4) methyl alcohol, (5) lead, (6) carbon disulfide, (7) oxtamoxin, (8) iodoform, (9) pheniprazine, (10) thallium, (11) epinepherine, (12) digitalis, (13) chloramphenicol, (14) streptomycin, (15) chlorodinitrobenzene, (16) sulfonamides, (17) ethambutol, (18) isoniazid, and (19) disulfiram.

Tobacco Amblyopia

Although tobacco amblyopia has been studied exhaustively, its pathogenesis and its very existence as a distinct entity remain controversial. Several factors conspire to make this the case. First, by any stretch, tobacco amblyopia is an extremely rare disease. Throughout 42 years of active practice with a large referral base, Harrington identified only eight cases. Similarly, a retrospective review spanning 25 years of case records from the Mayo Clinic produced only 22 patients who carried a diagnosis of tobacco amblyopia. Second, the diagnosis is necessarily retrospective based on obtaining a complete and accurate patient history; there are no disease-specific physical findings nor any biopsy or test results to confirm the clinical impression. Third, tobacco amblyopia is difficult to diagnose because the disease is one of chronic substance abuse and the subjective criteria (visual field studies) necessary for its diagnosis do not lend themselves to in vitro or laboratory animal study.

During recent years much has been learned by subjecting relatively rare chronic diseases to randomized prospective, double-blind, multicenter trials. Our knowledge of tobacco amblyopia would grow if such a trial were practical; it is not. Patterns of tobacco use—or abuse—have been changing over recent years. The numbers of elderly male pipe and cigar smokers who engage in these activities to the degree necessary to produce a toxic amblyopia are not large. Furthermore, to study the incidence of tobacco amblyopia per se, one must exclude individuals with a history of regular ingestion of alcohol, any hint of nutritional deficiency, or a history of ingesting other toxic agents, including those listed above. In addition, the treatment for visual loss caused by presumed tobacco amblyopia is extremely benign, consisting mainly of abstinence and B vitamins. This has been associated with dramatic improvement in many cases in the past. Because there is essentially no risk and potentially very great benefit to treatment in such cases, it would seem unethical to withhold a therapeutic trial whenever this diagnosis is entertained. Thus the entity of tobacco amblyopia seems destined to remain a mystery for some time to come.

Over the years careful observers have noted several features that describe or distinguish tobacco amblyopia. The visual disturbances of tobacco amblyopia occur mostly in elderly male pipe and cigar smokers. It has been reported in users of chewing tobacco and snuff. It is so rare in exclusive cigarette smokers as to be nonexistent or highly suspect.

Geographic variation has been noted, perhaps because of differential reporting or sensitivity or differences in the manner of tobacco consumption in different parts of the world. It is seen more commonly in the British Isles, especially Scotland, than in the United States. It was more common in the United States 50 years ago than it is today, perhaps because of a change in smoking habits.

In general, the more tobacco used and the darker and stronger the leaf, the higher the incidence of amblyopia, although some cases are seen in individuals consuming relatively small quantities. Although tobacco amblyopia is often found in individuals who are poorly nourished or are alcohol abusers, it has been seen in patients with neither of these complicating factors. It is doubtful if ethyl alcohol, even when consumed in large quantities, gives rise to a true toxic amblyopia. The designation *tobacco-alcohol amblyopia* has no clinical meaning. Certainly, tobacco amblyopia can occur in a person with alcoholism just as malnutritional amblyopia can occur in a person with alcoholism. There is some defense for the designation *tobacco-alcohol-malnutritional ambly-opia* if one uses this designation to describe the spectrum of clinical entities in alcoholic or malnourished smokers or both with a central or centrocecal scotoma. The descriptive term *malnutritional optic neuropathy* has also been applied to this entity. By no intrinsic virtue other than common usage, the term tobacco-alcohol amblyopia is likely to stay with us.

The typical visual field defect in tobacco amblyopia is a bilateral, centrocecal scotoma (Figure 13-1). The shape, size, and density of these scotomas vary with the amount and duration of the patient's tobacco consumption and with his or her susceptibility, but certain characteristics of the defect are constant and uniform. The defect is always bilateral. It may involve one eye to a greater degree than the other so that on first examination it appears to be unilateral, but when quantitative studies are performed, the fellow eye will almost always show at least a minimal defect (Figure 13-2).

A scotoma usually develops as a small area of visual loss midway between the blind spot and fixation on the temporal horizontal meridian. In its initial

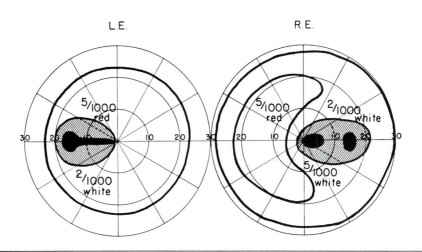

FIGURE 13-1 Tobacco amblyopia. Sloping margins of bilateral cecocentral scotoma and exaggeration of defect for red stimuli are clearly demonstrated.

stages, it is vague and indefinite. The patient is rarely aware of its existence. With time the scotoma extends both nasally toward fixation and temporally toward the blind spot. Its progress may be extremely slow. Coalescence with the blind spot may take place fairly early, with a dramatic loss of central vision; the patient often insists that his or her visual disturbance was of sudden onset. The defect may enlarge to take on a temporal hemianoptic character.

In the typical case, the centrocecal scotoma increases in its vertical diameter only slightly as it extends laterally. Thus it remains oval, usually regular in outline, but sometimes irregular or crenated. Occasionally, it may be slender.

The density of the scotoma is rarely uniform until the late stages of an untreated case. Usually there is a central island of greater density, and at times the entire scotoma appears fragmented when multiple isopters are plotted kinetically. This characteristic, along with the very sloping margins, can make plotting the scotoma difficult. Some patients in whom this condition is suspected are poor candidates for quantitative, subjective visual field study.

One of the most characteristic features of tobacco amblyopia is its effect on color vision, especially red perception. Patients may be aware of this for some time before there is any actual visual acuity decrease. Gold objects may

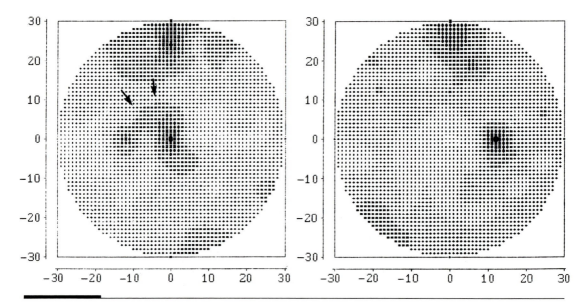

FIGURE 13-2 A 48-year-old man with history of bilateral visual field loss (left eye greater than right) over past several months. Approximately 8 years before onset of visual field loss a several-decade history of smoking several packs of cigarettes per day gave way to chewing large amounts of tobacco daily. Visual field shows central scotoma with centrocecal extension in left eye and no detectable defect in right eye. Manual tangent screen perimetry with a red test object showed central scotomas bilaterally, with defect in left eye simulating temporal hemianoptic defect.

appear silver, and friends and relatives may appear pale or even ill. One of Harrington's patients became so alarmed by the apparent pallor of his own normally ruddy complexion, as seen in the mirror, that he consulted his physician. The visual field defect for red is an exaggerated form of that found for white test objects. The centrocecal scotoma for red may become so large that it breaks through into the peripheral field and so broad in its vertical diameter that the field for red stimuli may simulate a bitemporal hemianopsia. Overemphasis on the defect for red without careful analysis with white test objects can lead to an erroneous diagnosis of pituitary adenoma.

With abstinence from tobacco and therapy with non–cyanide containing hydroxocobalamin (B_{12}) the scotoma begins to resolve in reverse order to its formation. Usually there is a retraction temporally away from fixation and a consequent improvement in visual acuity, which is very encouraging to the patient. As the defect shrinks in size and density it assumes its former position between the blind spot and fixation, and finally even this island melts away. Color vision is usually affected for a long time. Visual acuity may return to 20/20 within 3 to 6 months.

Prognosis for visual return is good if (1) tobacco use is stopped, (2) optic atrophy is not too marked, (3) the foveal portion of the scotoma is not too dense or too longstanding, and (4) compliance with the B_{12} therapy is good.

The pathogenesis of tobacco amblyopia is poorly understood. Evidence suggests that the primary lesion is a degeneration of the ganglion cell layer of the retina with secondary atrophy of the retinal nerve fiber layer and the papillomacular bundle. Apparently tobacco amblyopia is a toxic optic neuropathy caused by disturbance in the distribution of thiocyanate in body fluids; there is response to treatment with intramuscular hydroxocobalamin even when patients have continued to use tobacco.

Foulds and coworkers summarized their findings in a study of more than 100 cases of tobacco amblyopia:

1. All their patients smoked tobacco.
2. The patients were often elderly and had a diet poor in protein and B vitamins.
3. Twenty percent had addisonian pernicious anemia.
4. Forty percent had a demonstrable defect in vitamin B_{12} absorption.
5. Alcohol consumption per se played little or no part in the condition.

They concluded that tobacco amblyopia is a multifactorial disease in which tobacco consumption, an abnormality of vitamin B_{12} metabolism, including inadequate diet and malabsorption, and a diet low in protein are among the factors involved. The differential diagnosis depends on combining a detailed history with meticulous quantitative perimetric analysis of the bilateral scotomatous visual field defects and a favorable response to abstinence from tobacco or treatment with non–cyanide containing hydroxocobalamin (B_{12}).

Nutritional Amblyopia

Nutritional amblyopia is a deficiency disease rather than a form of toxic amblyopia, although it has certain characteristics that seem to classify it in this group. Permanent visual disturbances developed in some individuals held in military prison camps during World War II. Most of these cases, studied after release from prison, have revealed bilateral optic atrophy with dense bilateral central scotomas and normal peripheral fields. The scotomas were irregular in shape with steep margins and uniform density (Figure 13-3). In almost all cases there was severe malnutrition, but the degree of dietary deficiency did not always correlate with the visual loss. Some of these prisoners appeared fairly well nourished, whereas others were in the last stages of debilitation from lack of food. There appears to have been considerable variation in susceptibility to amblyopia. Besides optic atrophy, a few persons had a small, irregular, heavily pigmented macular choroidal lesion with central scotoma. It is not certain whether this lesion was nutritional in origin or the result of coincident central choroiditis.

Ethyl Alcohol Amblyopia

Although cases of ethyl alcohol amblyopia have been reported, it is difficult to establish the fact of toxic amblyopia from acute ethyl alcohol poisoning. The visual symptoms that occur with this condition may be the result of cerebral dysfunction resembling cortical blindness. Acute alcoholic amblyopia with optic atrophy and central scotoma can be produced when the ethyl

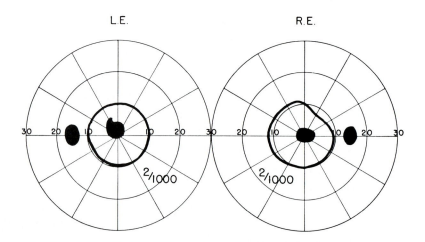

FIGURE 13-3 Nutritional amblyopia. Patient was prisoner of Japanese during World War II and demonstrated optic atrophy and central visual acuity of 20/200. Note bilateral depression of 2/1000 isopter and bilateral central scotoma.

alcohol is impure and unregulated. Low-quality whiskey and gin may contain quantities of various fusel oils sufficient to act as a toxic agent and produce this syndrome, but such poisoning should not be considered the result of ethyl alcohol ingestion. The amblyopia associated with chronic alcohol ingestion presents a picture identical with nutritional amblyopia. Although the visual loss is gradual, it may be noticed by the patient in its early stages. Vision is described as hazy, but later objects in the area of the scotoma are blotted out and the scotoma may be positive.

The characteristic visual field defect is a central scotoma that is usually slightly irregular in shape, varying in size from 2 to 5 degrees and in density from relative to absolute. The margins are often steep, even in the early stages of development, and density is fairly uniform (Figure 13-4). The scotoma occasionally extends temporally toward the blind spot and may coalesce with it to form a cecocentral defect. When this occurs, the area of greatest density within the scotoma is at fixation rather than in the cecocentral portion as seen with tobacco amblyopia. The amblyopia is bilateral, and the central scotoma is fairly symmetric. The peripheral fields are normal or slightly depressed.

Many of these cases have no history of tobacco consumption, but a careful inquiry into dietary habits will reveal gross deficiencies. Caloric intake may be limited almost entirely to the alcohol consumed. This syndrome, a nutritional type of amblyopia associated with chronic alcoholism, is usually seen in the category of alcoholics who "drink their meals" and neglect themselves in most other ways. Alcoholics who eat well rarely develop nutritional amblyopia.

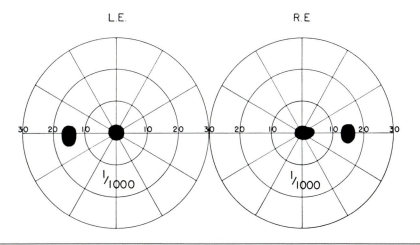

FIGURE 13-4   Amblyopia from chronic alcoholism with severe vitamin B deficiency and some signs of pellagra. Visual field defect is due to dietary deficiency associated with alcoholism rather than to toxic effects of ethyl alcohol.

Prognosis for return of useful vision is fairly good when adequate nutrition is restored, even in those individuals who persist in alcohol consumption. However, even though vision improves, it may not return to normal. Vitamin B_{12} is an important part of the therapy. Fortunately, although abstinence is desirable, it is not essential to significant recovery. Alcoholism severe enough to be associated with malnutritional amblyopia is an extremely serious life-threatening (or at least "life-ruining") disease. It demands aggressive and often long-term therapy.

Methyl Alcohol Poisoning

Methyl alcohol (methanol or wood alcohol) is a product of wood distillation used widely in industry as a solvent, antifreeze, and fuel, as well as other uses. It is extremely toxic to the eye; there is extensive literature on its effects on vision.

Poisoning is usually the result of deliberate consumption as a beverage, by inadvertent substitution for ethyl alcohol, or by criminal adulteration of stocks of cheap gin or whiskey. It may assume epidemic proportions.

As little as 10 ml may cause serious poisoning. Because methyl alcohol is metabolized very slowly, significant amounts may remain in the body for days. The symptoms are fairly typical: nausea, vomiting, abdominal cramps, and headache developing within 6 to 24 hours. Visual symptoms vary from slight haziness to total loss of vision. Severe poisoning leads rapidly to coma and death from respiratory failure.

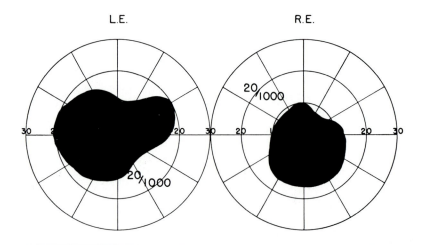

FIGURE 13-5   Methyl alcohol (methanol or wood alcohol) amblyopia. There was history of ingestion of 1 ounce of methyl alcohol followed by prolonged coma, severe bilateral optic neuritis, and finally optic atrophy and dense, irregular, steep-margined central scotomas.

In the acute phase of the poisoning, vision is reduced by the development of central or cecocentral scotomas (Figure 13-5). These scotomas may be transient but are usually permanent, the prognosis for vision depending on the density and size of the scotomas and the early appearance of the optic discs.

The optic discs are hyperemic in the early stages and later become edematous and elevated, with venous engorgement and with edema extending into the adjacent retina. The subsequent course depends on the severity of the poisoning and the adequacy of treatment and ranges from complete recovery to total and permanent optic atrophy and blindness. If vision has not improved markedly within 5 or 6 days of the onset of symptoms, the prognosis is poor and vision may continue to deteriorate for some time. With partial return of vision the bilateral central scotomas, which vary in size and density, persist. As optic atrophy develops, the peripheral field may also contract.

One of the most striking features of methyl alcohol poisoning is metabolic acidosis, manifested by dyspnea, acidic urine, and reduced carbon dioxide–combining power of the blood. The degree of acidosis closely parallels the severity of the poisoning, and its correction is the basis for successful treatment of the disease.

If the carbon dioxide–combining power of the blood remains more than two thirds of normal, the symptoms are mild and prognosis is good; but when it falls to below half of normal, the vision is usually poor and return of function is doubtful. During the acute phase of poisoning, therefore, it is important to quickly measure the blood electrolyte levels, with particular attention to the carbon dioxide–combining power. Metabolic acidosis should be corrected immediately with appropriate doses of sodium bicarbonate.

Methanol poisoning is a threefold disease, consisting of (1) narcosis, (2) metabolic acidosis, and (3) specific central nervous system involvement with retinal edema; fixed, dilated pupils; blindness; and basal ganglion necrosis. Ocular damage is believed to be caused by the slow oxidation of methanol to formaldehyde or a formaldehyde complex. This extremely diffusible substance affects oxidative enzyme systems, resulting in tissue anoxia, edema, and varying degrees of retinal degeneration. Addition of ethyl alcohol to the therapy may prevent or lessen the degree of metabolic acidosis and ocular damage by preempting the enzymatic site of methanol oxidation and allowing methanol to be excreted unchanged or to be oxidized minimally. Even with moderately severe poisoning, the patient may be too ill to cooperate with a visual field examination, but a rough estimate of the state of the field is usually possible. When vision is very poor or when pupils are dilated widely, the prognosis is poor.

By the time the patient has recovered sufficiently to submit to examination, he or she is usually in the chronic stage of the disease. Even at this point, the prognosis for return of vision is guarded. Acidosis may improve slowly but vision becomes steadily worse. Delayed visual failure may not begin for some weeks, and central scotomas may become progressively larger while the discs become chalky white. Treatment in this stage is of no avail.

Lead Poisoning

Lead poisoning is much less prevalent today than it was in the fairly recent past, largely because of precautions against the hazard in industry. It may still occur sporadically as an occupational disease in some painters, plumbers, workers in battery factories, and those who handle large quantities of leaded tetraethyl gasoline or gasoline additives; but when such cases occur, it is usually because factory-imposed or Occupational Safety and Health Administration precautions have been violated. During recent years lead poisoning has also been seen in children who inadvertently eat or suck on lead-based paint on the walls or baseboards of their homes. Demographically, this is seen more in children who live in poorly maintained, low-income housing in older buildings where lead paint applied many years ago is peeling or chipped.

For the most part lead poisoning is a chronic illness resulting from a gradual accumulation of small amounts of lead ingested over a considerable period of time.

All of the visual pathway from the retina occipital cortex may be affected. Increased intracranial pressure is not uncommon, especially in children, and optic atrophy may ensue from prolonged papilledema, as well as from the direct effect of lead on the optic nerve.

Occasionally the onset of symptoms is acute, with sudden amaurosis from which there is later recovery. More often there is gradually increasing visual loss with generally depressed peripheral fields or bilateral central scotomas or both. In such cases an associated optic nerve atrophy often develops and the visual field changes are permanent. In the acute cases with total or near blindness, one usually finds some degree of papilledema secondary to increased intracranial pressure.

Diagnosis of lead poisoning is established by a history of contact with lead, a lead line on the gum margins, a basophilic stippling of red blood cells, lead in the blood and urine, x-ray evidence of bony deposition of lead, and ocular and other clinical signs of lead intoxication in the nervous system. Treatment is directed to removing the lead from the blood by parenteral administration of edathamil calcium disodium.

Pharmacologic Agents

Given the amazing variety and number of compounds used to treat local and systemic disease, the number of pharmacologic agents associated with significant visual toxicity is impressively small. The following is a list of some of those agents. A list such as this is necessarily incomplete because cases of drug toxicity may be so rare, sporadic, and widespread as to defy categorization. Furthermore, pharmaceutical manufacturers are continually modifying their products and their product line. Drugs marketed in one region or nation may not be available in other areas.

The agents listed here are representative of the types of ocular toxicity one may see with certain pharmaceutical agents. When attempting to determine whether drug toxicity is an important etiologic factor in an individual patient's visual acuity or visual field loss, one should take a careful history and consult appropriate references or the manufacturer directly.

Carbon disulfide

Carbon disulfide is a product of the rubber vulcanizing and rayon industry that is absorbed chiefly through inhalation and through the skin. Poisoning is uncommon.

Amblyopia of varying degrees is an early sign, and the visual fields usually show bilateral, small, oval centrocecal scotomas. There may be concomitant peripheral field contraction. Color blindness and nyctalopia are frequent.

Octamoxin

The monoaminooxidase inhibitor octamoxin (Nimaol) has caused optic neuritis and retrobulbar neuritis, with centrocecal scotoma developing after several months of use. Vision usually returns after discontinuance of the drug, but partial optic atrophy may persist.

Iodoform

Since iodoform is used rarely today, either as a wound dressing or by mouth, iodoform poisoning is rare. Its use is somewhat more frequent outside the United States. It produces optic atrophy and an amblyopia caused by the presence of fairly large and dense central scotomas. Diagnosis is made by obtaining a confirming history.

Pheniprazine

Pheniprazine, a monoaminooxidase inhibitor, has been used for depressed patients and as an antihypertensive. It is avoided now because of its serious side effects, consisting of loss of vision, loss of color vision, and development of bilateral central scotomas. Symptoms are usually reversible with discontinuance of the drug.

Thallium

Thallium is a heavy metal used in large quantities as a soluble salt, thallium acetate or thallium sulfate, for exterminating insects or rodents. At one time it was also used as a depilatory. It is highly toxic.

The common ocular disturbance is optic neuritis, usually retrobulbar, occurring most often in chronic poisoning and producing bilateral central scotomas. Optic atrophy is the rule in chronic poisoning, and visual loss may be significant.

Epinephrine

When used in the treatment of glaucoma in aphakic eyes, epinephrine has been found to produce a maculopathy in a significant percentage of patients. Central visual acuity is reduced, the maculae show a definite but slight edema, and visual fields demonstrate a relative central scotoma. We generally avoid using epinephrine for treating chronic glaucoma in aphakic patients, except when the visual acuity is already in the range of 20/200 or worse from some form of irreversible pathologic condition or when the patient is at risk of an imminent blindness from glaucoma and is inoperable.

Digitalis

Ocular manifestations in patients with digitalis toxicity may be as high as 25%, and in many patients the ocular complications may occur before other symptoms of toxicity. The interval between the first dose of digitalis and the first symptom of toxicity may be as short as 1 day. More often the symptoms occur within the first 2 weeks of therapy, but they may not occur for several years after initiation of digitalis use. Symptoms usually disappear within 2 weeks of cessation of therapy and are rarely permanent. The most common ocular symptoms of digitalis poisoning are blurred vision and disturbed color vision. Objects may appear yellow (xanthopsia), greenish, or brown and may appear to be snow or frost covered. Photophobia, scintillating scotomas, light flashes, and sparks are common, and transient and persistent amblyopia may occur. Visual field studies reveal bilateral scotomas, which account for the blurred central vision. The scotoma may be secondary to retrobulbar neuritis or to the toxic effects of digitalis on the retinal receptor cells.

Chloramphenicol

Chloramphenicol (Chloromycetin) is a widely available antibiotic. It has been associated with optic neuritis and visual disturbances, edema of the optic discs, and bilateral central scotomas in a number of patients. Its use in the United States has been curtailed dramatically because of its association with serious and even fatal systemic side effects involving bone marrow suppression. Chloramphenicol illustrates the point made earlier regarding differential availability of drugs in different countries around the world; 20 years ago this potent antibiotic was included in over-the-counter formulations, including vitamins, in some countries.

Streptomycin

Toxic effects of streptomycin on the visual pathway are probably rare but have been reported as producing a variety of visual disturbances such as xanthopsia, nerve fiber bundle–type scotomas, and a central scotoma associated with optic neuritis. Topical aminoglycosides are used routinely in ophthalmology, without producing the side effects. Severe and irreversible retinal toxicity has occurred when aminoglycoside antibiotics have been injected into the vitreous cavity in inappropriate doses.

Chlorodinitrobenzene

Chlorodinitrobenzene (Dinitrobenzene) and related compounds used in munitions manufacture cause central scotomas from inhalation and chronic exposure. Optic neuritis and atrophy are rare.

Sulfonamide sensitivity

Widespread use of the sulfonamides as antibiotics has made sensitivity reactions inevitable. For the most part these are neither serious nor severe enough to cause anxiety or even withdrawal of the drug.

Occasional cases of optic neuritis caused by sulfonamide therapy have been reported. These do not seem to be related directly to the drug dosage but rather to the patient's individual sensitivity. Visual loss may be sudden, rapid, and severe. There is edema of the optic nervehead and large, dense, irregular central scotomas. The prognosis is good once the patient is no longer given the drug.

Ethambutol

Ocular toxicity caused by ethambutol is characterized by (1) loss of central vision with bilateral central or bitemporal scotomas, (2) marked decrease in color vision, and (3) peripheral visual field defects without retinal lesions. The drug is used in treating tuberculosis, and its toxicity is dose dependent. Ethambutol is often used in combination with isoniazid, which may also produce optic neuritis. The toxic effects of both drugs may be synergistic.

Isoniazid

Isoniazid is employed in treating tuberculosis, generally in combination with para-aminosalicylate or streptomycin. It has produced optic neuritis and optic atrophy with bilateral central scotomas. Toxic effects are uncommon and are usually reversible once the patient is no longer given the drug.

PERIPHERAL FIELD DEPRESSION OR CONTRACTION

The following agents characteristically show their initial or most prominent effects in the perimacular or peripheral fields. In some cases, fixation may be involved in the late stages of the disease. The agents included in this section are (1) quinine, (2) chloroquine, (3) arsenic, (4) salicylates, (5) filixmas, (6) methyl mercury compounds, (7) hyperbaric oxygen, (8) carbon monoxide, (9) thioridazine, (10) piperidylchlorophenothiazine, (11) oral contraceptives, and (12) recreational illicit drugs.

Quinine

Quinine poisoning is rare. It occurs in susceptible persons from small doses of the drug or nonsensitive persons from a large single dose. In the former instance, the drug is usually given as an antimalarial prophylactic or for the relief of leg cramps. In the latter instance, it is usually used to induce abortion.

In quinine poisoning the onset of blindness is sudden and the degree of visual loss may vary greatly and may not occur for days after ingesting the drug. The visual loss may be transient or permanent. Total blindness is rare and almost never permanent. Partial blindness, however, is common and is often permanent.

Quinine affects the ganglion cells, nerve fibers, and retinal photoreceptors. There is marked attenuation of the retinal vasculature. A secondary optic atrophy follows.

The corresponding visual field changes are constriction or contraction of the peripheral field, varying from a slight peripheral depression to a contraction of the field to within a few degrees of fixation in all quadrants (Figure 13-6).

Quinine-induced optic nerve hypoplasia has been reported in infants whose mothers ingested large amounts of quinine early during the first trimester of pregnancy. Side effects in the mother included severe dizziness, headache, blurred vision, and nausea. This tragic constellation of events has occurred in cases where the mother has failed in a desperate attempt to induce abortion. Differentiation of the ganglion cell layer of the retina, whose axons

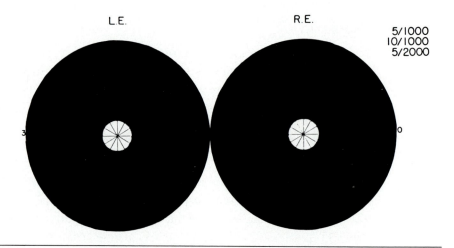

FIGURE 13-6 Quinine amblyopia. Visual loss was sudden after ingestion of approximately 40 grains of quinine in attempt to abort pregnancy. Contraction of visual fields is organic in type as opposed to tubular or cylindric visual field contraction of hysteria. There is partial optic atrophy and marked attenuation of retinal arteries.

extend into the optic stalk to form the optic nerve, occurs in the seventh to eighth week of gestation, this corresponded closely to the time of maternal quinine ingestion.

Chloroquine

Among the synthetic antimalarial compounds, chloroquine compounds have been used most widely in the treatment of systemic lupus erythematosus and other similar conditions. The dosages of the drug used for treatment in these conditions are considerably greater than that used for malaria. Numerous cases have been reported with corneal deposits and severe visual loss. These visual disturbances result from retinopathy that may involve the macular area, the midperipheral retina, or both. It is associated with marked narrowing of the retinal arterioles and eventually with pigmentary degeneration of the retina and optic atrophy.

Visual field defects vary from central scotomas to ring scotomas to peripheral contraction. The most characteristic visual field defect is probably a large central scotoma with a small island of slightly lesser visual loss in its center. When tested with large stimuli, the defect is a large, dense ring scotoma, sometimes breaking through into the periphery; when small test objects are used, the defect appears as a large central scotoma (Figure 13-7).

The dose of chloroquine usually required to produce retinopathy ranges from approximately 100 to 600 mg per day for 2 to 3 years, although damage may occur in a shorter time.

The symptoms of chloroquine retinopathy include reading difficulties, photophobia, blurred distance vision, and light flashes. Color vision testing

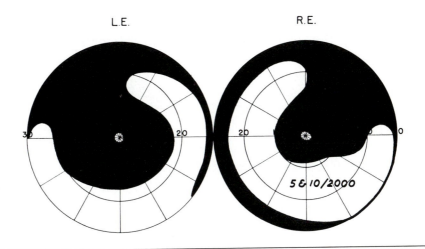

L.E.   R.E.

FIGURE 13-7   Chloroquine toxicity. Pigmentary degeneration of retina following 4 months' use of chloroquine in patient with lupus erythematosus. Minute islands of central vision are retained, surrounded by dense ring scotomas.

with pseudoisochromatic plates may be useful in detecting the condition early. The effects of chloroquine toxicity may not appear until some time after drug use has been stopped. The finding of a central scotoma for red stimuli is an early sign of retinal damage.

Chloroquine is stored in the pigmented uvea and may be retained in the retinal pigment epithelium for long periods after discontinuation of the drug. This would account for the retinopathy and the permanence of the visual field defects. The incidence of chloroquine retinopathy is dose related; it is most likely to occur when the total dose exceeds 300 g over a 2- to 3-year period. Fluorescein angiography demonstrates the area of retinopathy dramatically.

Arsenic

Inorganic arsenicals used in industry and in various pest poisons are capable of producing severe poisoning and death, but they rarely if ever affect the optic nerve or retina. Organic arsenicals, which were used in treating syphilis in the preantibiotic era, are capable of initiating severe toxic amblyopia.

Trivalent arsenicals, such as arsphenamine and neoarsphenamine, may produce optic nerve damage and visual field contraction in susceptible individuals. The pentavalent arsenicals sodium arsanilate (Atoxyl) and tryparsamide are most dangerous. These latter drugs have been known to produce acute degeneration of the retinal ganglion cell layer with severe visual field contraction.

Salicylates

Salicylate poisoning resembles quinine poisoning in many respects. There is usually an individual sensitivity to the drug, but overdosage has been reported as a cause of amaurosis.

The pupils are dilated and fixed, and the visual fields may show marked contraction.

Filixmas

In filixmas, again, the toxic ocular symptoms resemble those from quinine. This drug has been prescribed in treating tapeworm infestation. Individual sensitivity to the drug, more than dosage, is responsible for toxic effects.

Visual field changes may be unilateral or bilateral and consist of concentric contraction of the peripheral and central fields. There is a gradual increasing pallor of the optic disc and a narrowing of the retinal arterioles.

Methyl Mercury Compounds

Methyl mercury compounds are used for protecting wood or seeds. Poisoning may occur from inhalation in manufacture and in industrial application or from eating treated seeds or contaminated meat or fish. A poisoning results in extreme contraction of the visual fields because of atrophy of the visual cortex. The contraction is greatest at the anterior end of the calcarine fissure, with relative sparing of the occipital poles. Blindness may result from extensive atrophy of the entire cerebral cortex. No recovery of the field loss has been reported.

Oxygen

Hyperbaric oxygen has been shown to produce peripheral constriction of the visual fields in young, healthy patients after prolonged breathing of pure oxygen at 3 atmospheres' pressure. After 4 hours, progressive contraction of the fields, impaired central vision, and mydriasis occur, all of which are reversible after discontinuation of the oxygen or return to normal pressures.

Carbon Monoxide

Poisoning from carbon monoxide, a colorless, odorless gas, may result from attempted suicide or from inadvertent inhalation of automobile exhaust fumes or manufactured heating or cooking gas.

Toxic signs and symptoms and death are caused by a conversion of a portion of the hemoglobin of the blood to carbon monoxyhemoglobin, with a reduction of the amount of hemoglobin available for oxygen transport. Small concentrations of carbon monoxide in air may reduce the oxygen-carrying capacity of the blood. When exposure is severe enough to produce unconsciousness, permanent damage to the central nervous system may result.

When consciousness is regained, blindness may be noted immediately. Pupils react to light and convergence, suggesting that the blindness is cortical in origin. Visual hallucinations and agnosia may occur. If cerebral hypoxia is not too severe, complete or partial recovery of vision may occur. With partial recovery the resultant visual field defect may be a double or bilateral homonymous hemianopsia with two small central islands of vision determined by the area of macular sparing in the two half fields.

Thioridazine

Thioridazine, a phenothiazine derivative employed in psychotherapy, has been found to cause decreased visual acuity and pigmentary degeneration of the retina when used in high doses. Visual loss varies from slight and transient to severe and permanent. Visual fields may show contraction or central scotoma or both. Electroretinograms are grossly abnormal.

Piperidylchlorophenothiazine

Piperidylchlorophenothiazine is a major tranquilizer that has been used in the treatment of psychoses. In fairly large doses of 400 to 800 mg per day for 2 to 3 months, patients have developed visual disturbances with contracted fields. Recovery is only partial with discontinuance of the drug.

Oral Contraceptive Pills

The most common visual field defects associated with oral contraceptive pill use are scintillating scotomas and irregular spreading hemianoptic depressions of classic or ocular migraine. Oral contraceptive pills have been known to precipitate migraine attacks in patients without a previous history of migraine, and they frequently cause the return of migraine attacks in patients who have experienced migraine in the remote past. Such an occurrence or history is grounds for discontinuing the drug.

Illicit, Illegal Recreational Drug Abuse

Patterns of illicit drug abuse change. An agent used widely during one decade may lose popularity in the next, different segments of the population may be involved, and the routes and means of administration may vary. The one constant is that illicit drug abuse routinely produces devastating effects.

The ocular toxicity found in systemic illicit drug abusers is frequently due not so much to the drug itself as to the method by which the drug was prepared or administered. Specifically, intravenous drug abuse via shared, nonsterile needles is associated with a variety of ocular and systemic side effects. Some of these result in blindness and some in death.

As of this writing the most prominent and severe visual loss seen in illicit drug abusers is that associated with cytomegalovirus retinitis in patients with acquired immune deficiency syndrome (AIDS). A less common cause of irregular peripheral scotomas is a showering of septic emboli that may be associated with subacute bacterial endocarditis.

An interesting condition often seen in heroin addicts is the crystalline retinopathy associated with intravenous injection of crushed amphetamine or amphetamine-like tablets. This was described in the 1970s as "Ritalin retinopathy." In such cases, a series of small yellow white crystalline deposits are seen in the perimacular region (Figure 13-8). The deposits, and the corresponding retinopathy and mild central scotoma, are not caused by the drug itself, but rather by the insoluble fillers and binders (talc and cornstarch) used in formulating the tablets for oral ingestion. These fillers and binders present no problem when the pills are taken correctly: they simply pass unabsorbed through the alimentary tract. However, when the pills are crushed and placed into an aqueous suspension, so that the compound can be injected intravenously, the insoluble particles circulate through the body until they encounter a capillary bed sufficiently small to trap them. This trapping initially takes place in the lungs but after large quantities of the drug have been injected, the capacity of the pulmonary capillaries to absorb these 7- to 10-μm particles is compromised. Internal shunts develop within the lung, and the insoluble particles are thus able to bypass the pulmonary capillary bed and gain access to the right side of the heart and subsequently the systemic circulation. Pulmonary function tests performed at this stage will reveal restrictive lung disease.

Once the insoluble particles can bypass the lung, they find their way to susceptible capillary beds throughout the body, including the retinal capillaries and the perimacular region. Their appearance in the retinal capillary bed is characteristic, especially when a history of drug abuse can be obtained. Visual symptoms are usually relatively mild, with acuity dropping to the level of 20/70 or so with minimal to mild macular edema. Shallow central scotomas may be detected.

The ocular symptoms represent only the tip of the iceberg in such patients. Many of these individuals have died from respiratory complications or from other complications from either amphetamine injection or heroin addiction, which usually coexists. If the patient undergoes a major alteration in life-style, partial or complete visual recovery is the rule.

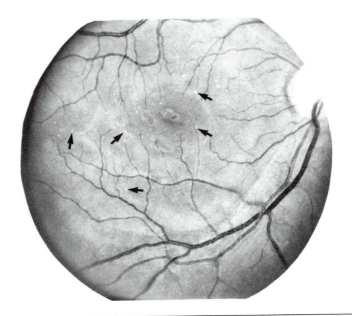

FIGURE 13-8   Right eye of intravenous drug abuser. Multiple tiny white dots *(arrows)* at end of perimacular vascular net are insoluble talc deposits that result from injecting a suspension of crushed tablets. *(Courtesy Dr. H. Schatz.)*

In cases of acute intoxication with stimulant drugs such as cocaine, a hypertensive crisis may ensue. Papilledema, retinal nerve fiber layer hemorrhages, and retinal artery or arteriolar spasm may occur, producing a corresponding blind spot enlargement and scattered small or large scotomas.

Finally, another type of visual field loss is seen in systemic drug abusers. In this case, the term should be extended to include chronic and acute alcoholism. A fair number of these patients experience significant trauma during episodes of acute intoxication. Head trauma with loss of memory associated with the trauma itself or with a drug-induced stupor may occur. In such cases patients may have traumatic retinal, optic nerve, or cerebral damage that produces a corresponding visual field defect. The patient may have no recollection whatsoever of the causative event and may not be aware of the visual field defect until it is elicited on a routine examination.

14 OPTIC NERVE

Except for visible changes in the optic disc and the retinal nerve fiber layer that are observable ophthalmoscopically, we test pathologic processes that affect the optic nerve primarily with perimetric examination. The optic nerve is the first portion of the visual pathway that cannot be visualized during a routine office examination. The ophthalmoscope, the slit lamp, fluorescein angiography, and even ophthalmic ultrasound cease to be sufficient; we must rely heavily on perimetry.

Even visible changes in the optic nervehead are likely to be so nonspecific that visual field examination is necessary for correct interpretation. The morphologic difference between papilledema and papillitis may be so slight that a perimetric examination is essential for diagnosis.

Not only is the visual field examination important in localizing lesions within the optic nerve, but also it is valuable in indicating the nature of the pathologic process, the prognosis, and the treatment.

Perimetric studies that localize a lesion in the intracranial portion of the nerve must be correlated with other clinical and radiologic findings and may be the most important consideration in the neurosurgeon's decision to explore the questionable region. Perimetric studies performed before neuroradiologic investigation can help point one's attention toward the most likely site of the lesion. This will aid both ophthalmologists and radiologists in ordering and performing the correct tests and in interpreting the test results accurately.

The most frequent visual field defect in patients with optic nerve disease is the central scotoma. Scotomas may be bilateral, as in certain systemic diseases and the toxic amblyopias, but more often they are unilateral. There may be many clues indicating a scotoma's presence, such as a positive defect noticed by the patient, a severe deficiency in vision without noticeable curtailment of the ability to get around, walk, and so on; and a characteristic manner of reading the Snellen chart in which letters are skipped over or the letter can be seen only if the patient looks at the one next to it. Color vision may be affected markedly. The presence of an afferent pupillary defect (Marcus Gunn pupil) is a valuable sign of optic nerve conduction disturbance.

Bowl perimeters such as the Goldmann perimeter or the majority of current automated perimeters generally locate their fixation or monitoring lenses or cameras at the point of fixation. This renders them unable to test sensitivity right at the point of fixation unless one uses a specific macular or foveal testing procedure relying on off-axis fixation. When testing patients with suspected optic nerve disease, it is extremely important that central sensitivity be measured. Often a tiny central scotoma is so small that it is missed by testing strategies that stop 2 or 3 degrees away from fixation.

The tangent screen and Amsler grid are well suited for measuring central sensitivity manually. The technique of two-point discrimination with the tangent screen (Chapter 11) is perhaps the quickest and most sensitive method for measuring minute central scotomas. Additionally, with the tangent screen, the patient can be moved back several meters from the screen, which will increase the absolute size of the projected scotoma and allow very careful measurement.

CLASSIFICATION OF OPTIC NERVE LESIONS

It is customary to consider optic nerve lesions that produce visual field defects according to their anatomic location. To this end the nerve is arbitrarily divided into three parts: the optic nervehead or papilla, the retrobulbar optic nerve, and the intracranial optic nerve. Each of these portions may be divided further into the axial and peripheral portions of the nerve. Within each of these divisions the nature of the lesion producing the defect must then be considered. These are generally classified as inflammatory, compressive, vascular, traumatic, or toxic lesions. With this anatomic and pathologic classification in mind, we now consider the various visual field changes associated with optic nerve disease.

OPTIC PAPILLA, NERVEHEAD, AND OPTIC DISC

Optic nervehead abnormalities seen with the ophthalmoscope are usually diagnosed by this means. Visual field findings may confirm such a diagnosis and in some instances may be the only means of differentiating two morphologically similar lesions.

Myelinated Nerve Fibers

Myelinated nerve fibers at the nervehead may be mistaken for juxtapupillary choroiditis or even papilledema from increased intracranial pressure. Even in extensive myelinization, however, the field can be normal. When a corresponding field defect is plotted, it is static. The visual field changes correspond to the anatomic location of the myelinated fibers and to their density and thickness. Nerve fiber bundle interference may rarely produce an arcuate

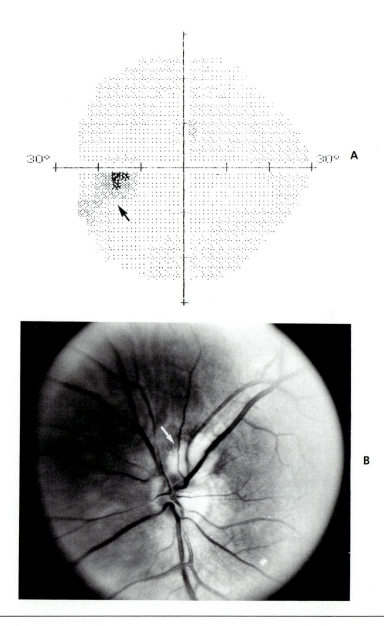

FIGURE 14-1 A, Mildly enlarged blind spot, with field loss corresponding to location of, **B,** my-elinated nerve fiber *(arrow).*

defect resembling that found in glaucoma. Occasionally one finds irregular blind spot enlargement (Figure 14-1) or perhaps a somewhat irregular paracentral scotoma.

Optic Nerve Coloboma

Optic nerve colobomas are readily demonstrable with the ophthalmoscope. Their associated visual field defects (Figure 14-2) do not necessarily correlate with their appearance. Often large colobomas show surprisingly little visual loss, and at times a minimal nervehead lesion produces extensive damage to the visual field.

Most commonly the visual field changes associated with the condition resemble those of glaucoma, with dense nerve fiber bundle defects and superior nasal depression. When associated with deeply cupped optic discs, the differentiation from glaucoma may be difficult. Both the appearance of the discs and the visual field changes, however, are stationary as opposed to the progressive visual field loss in glaucoma. Occasionally, with very large inferior colobomas, the entire upper field will disappear in a superior altitudinal

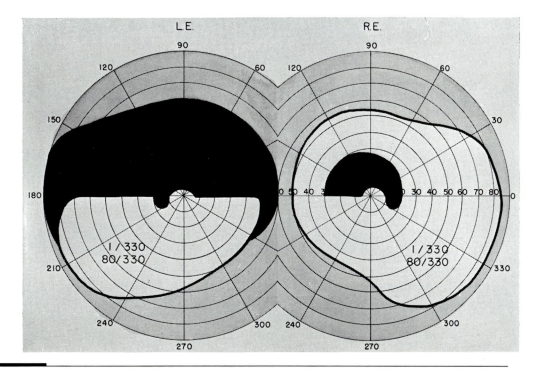

FIGURE 14-2 Colobomas of optic nerves. There was history of defective vision from childhood. Central vision was 20/20 in each eye. Visual field defects resembled those of glaucoma but remained unchanged in 5 years of observation. Intraocular pressure was repeatedly normal.

hemaniopsia. When the coloboma is associated with a significant myopic change, it is important to retest any scotomas with a few to several diopters more minus correction than the patient usually wears.

Congenital Optic Nerve Hypoplasia

Visual field defects associated with congenital optic nerve hypoplasia vary from total blindness of one or both eyes to a minimal paracentral scotoma. Binasal or bitemporal hemianopsia may also be seen (Figure 14-3). The condition is seen either as a singular ocular abnormality or in association with anterior midline central nervous system defects such as chiasmal malformation and dysgenesis of the anterior medullary velum and the septum pellucidum. In the latter case the result is a monocular temporal field loss or a bitemporal hemianopsia.

Many optic nerve hypoplasias that appear to be unilateral may, on closer study, be bilateral. The disc changes are often extremely subtle, and unless there is a field deficit or some decrease in central visual acuity, it is easy to miss the diagnosis. In many cases the condition is frankly bilateral, and in these patients the field loss may be binasal or bitemporal. Subtle bilateral optic nerve hypoplasia may be completely overlooked unless one's index of suspicion is sufficiently high. Optic nerve hypoplasia should be considered when otherwise unexplained extraocular muscle imbalance or nystagmus is present.

The retinal ganglion cell and nerve fiber layer are spare or absent with hypoplasia of the optic nerve. Examination or photography with red-free light is useful in detecting this circumstance.

Optic nerve hypoplasia may be misdiagnosed as optic atrophy, and yet visual acuity, although not normal, may be quite good. The patient may be completely unaware of even a dense visual field defect, as is often the case with congenital defects, and the extent of the field loss will be discovered by accident or during routine examination. Functional loss may be closely correlated with visible defects in the retinal nerve fiber layer. Maternal phenytoin (Dilantin) ingestion can be a significant etiologic factor in congenital optic nerve hypoplasia (Figure 14-4).

Optic Nervehead Drusen

Drusen, or hyaline bodies, in the optic disc may produce extensive and slowly progressive visual field defects; these may take decades to develop fully. The ophthalmoscopic appearance may give little indication of the visual field loss present. In most cases central vision is good and visual field defects do not appear until the drusen are extensive. In many such cases the diagnosis of pseudopapilledema is made and there is gross enlargement of the blind spot. Occasionally the condition is mistaken for true papilledema. This often occurs

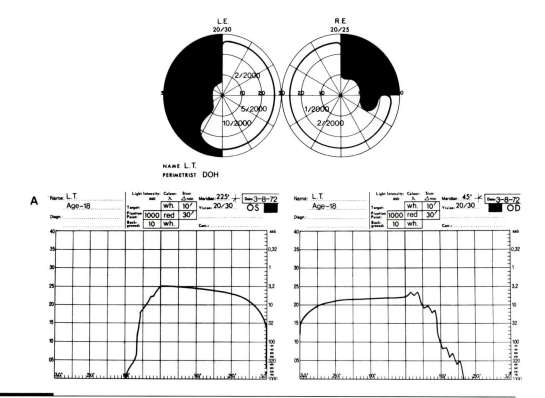

FIGURE 14-3   A, Bilateral congenital optic nerve hypoplasia with irregular bitemporal hemianopsia. Visual field deficit associated with vertical and lateral nystagmus and complicated vertical and lateral extraocular muscle imbalance. Despite its density, patient was unaware of field deficit when examined on tangent screen and by static perimetry. Field defect has remained stable since time of discovery. *(From Harrington, DO: Trans Ophthalmol Soc UK 92:15, 1972, London, Churchill Livingstone, Ltd.)*

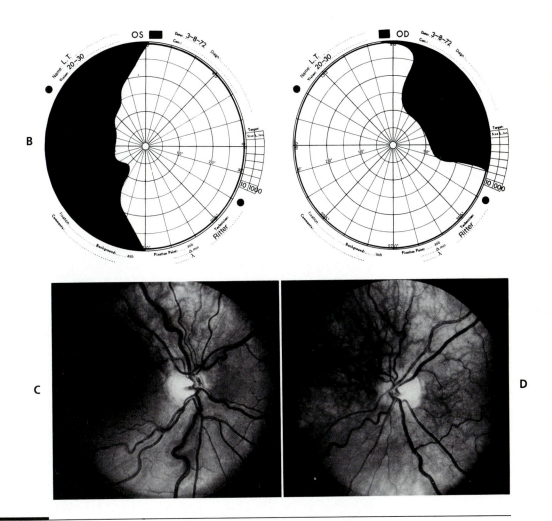

FIGURE 14-3, cont'd. B, Goldmann perimeter field of patient shown in **A. C,** Right and, **D,** left eyes of patient seen in **A.** Fundus photography with red-free light reveals bilateral optic nerve hypoplasia with sector atrophy. Degeneration of ganglion cells and nerve fiber layer of nasal hemiretinae produced congenital bitemporal hemianopsia.

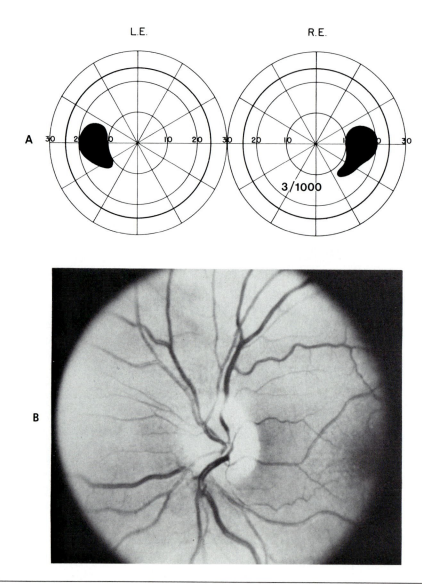

FIGURE 14-4 **A,** Congenital optic nerve defect. Moderate optic nerve hypoplasia with bilateral inferior extension of blind spot. **B,** Optic nerve abnormality responsible for field defect shown in **A.** Identical finding in both optic nerves.

when a good internist or family practitioner examines the optic nervehead with the ophthalmoscope, notes the distinctly blurred optic disc margins, and perhaps even detects a slightly elevated appearance to the optic nervehead.

Visual field changes usually take the form of nerve fiber bundle scotomas (that may closely resemble a typical glaucomatous visual field defect), blind spot enlargement, or irregular peripheral contraction (Figure 14-5).

Drusen may be embedded deeply in the optic nerve and not easily visible to the ophthalmoscope and yet may give rise to extensive visual field defects. Such cases constitute a considerable diagnostic problem. Careful high-resolution computerized tomography is very useful for demonstrating embedded drusen (Fig. 14-6). A number of cases have been reported with hemorrhage into or adjacent to the drusen, and these may adversely affect the visual field (Figure 14-7).

Visual field loss may progress slowly, and loss of central vision is rare except in those cases just mentioned with vascular damage at the disc edge and subsequent leaking of blood or edema fluid into the macula.

Optic Nervehead Pits

Optic nervehead pits are a fairly common congenital abnormality. They appear as small gray, black, or yellow depressions at the disc margin, most frequently located at the inferior or inferotemporal border of the nervehead. The defect is congenital but, because it may not cause any visual loss, may not be noticed until late in life either as part of a routine ophthalmoscopic examination or

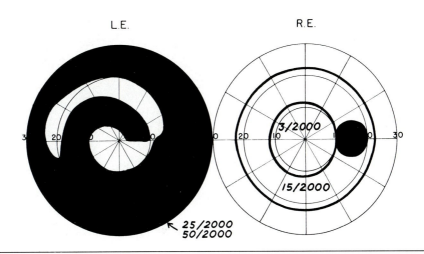

FIGURE 14-5 Drusen of both optic discs, more marked on left, with double nerve fiber bundle defect and nasal step. Defect is steep margined and dense, indicating its static nature. Right field shows central depression and gross blind spot enlargement.

because of the development of a retinal detachment or visual field defect. When viewed stereoscopically the pit is deep and steep sided.

Central visual field loss in the form of an irregular, sloping margined scotoma occurs in about 50% of cases as a result of serous macular detachment. The incidence of macular detachment appears greatest when the pit is located on the temporal disc margin.

Visual field defects vary considerably, depending on the location and size of the pit and the presence or absence of retinal detachment. Gross blind spot enlargement may occur, with or without macular involvement.

Isolated paracentral scotomas in the form of steep-margined nerve fiber bundle defects or Bjerrum scotomas may occur and remain stable throughout life. They are usually attached to the blind spot and are readily detected on perimetric examination because of their density and their prominent location in the central field. They are indistinguishable from a glaucomatous nerve fiber bundle or arcuate defect.

A third type of field defect seen with optic nervehead pits is a broad dense nerve fiber bundle scotoma that has a very steep-margined nasal step and peripheral nasal breakthrough. When associated with a close encroachment on fixation, this field defect may simulate an altitudinal hemianopsia (Figure 14-8).

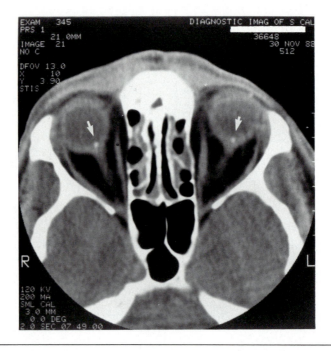

FIGURE 14-6 CT scan from patient with bilateral optic nerve head Drusen *(arrows). (Courtesy Johnson Lightfoote, M.D.)*

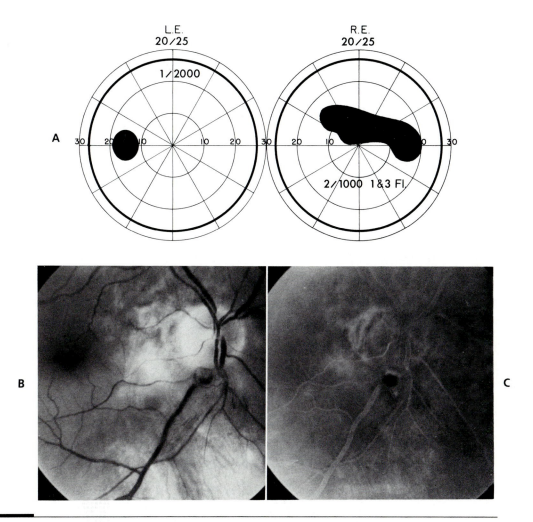

FIGURE 14-7 **A,** Retinal vein aneurysm at lower margin of right optic disc. Sudden loss of entire superior field in right eye associated with marked rise in systemic blood pressure. Gradual partial resolution of field deficit with resulting atypical, permanent, nerve fiber bundle defect. Lesion producing field loss is seen in **B** and **C. B,** Aneurysm of inferior retinal vein, right eye, photographed with red-free light and giving rise to superior nerve fiber bundle defect seen in **A. C,** Fluorescein angiography, full venous phase.

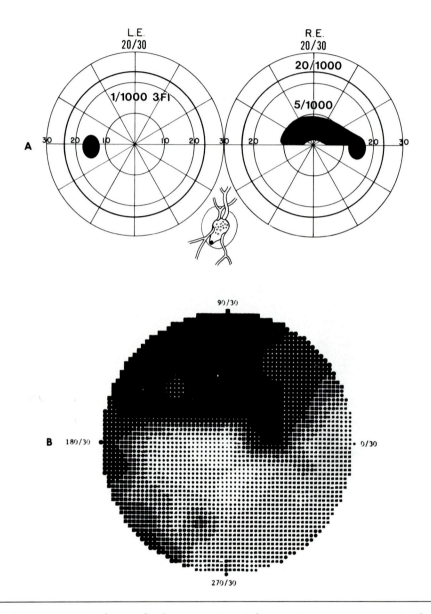

FIGURE 14-8 **A,** Optic nerve pit plus ocular hypertension, right eye. Dense, steep-margined nerve fiber bundle scotoma. Scotoma later expanded into superior nasal periphery. **B,** Octopus perimeter system visual field defect of case in **A** showing expanded and very dense scotoma. *(Courtesy Johnson Lightfoote, M.D.)*

Papilledema

Edema of the optic nervehead secondary to increased intracranial pressure produces generalized enlargement of the blind spot with certain characteristic features. In most cases, changes in the nervehead are visible ophthalmoscopically by the time the visual field defect is detectable.

Mild or moderately severe nervehead edema from increased intracranial pressure causes generalized blind spot enlargement in all directions. In most severe edema there will often be some exudate and hemorrhage on the nerve; in chronic papilledema there may be considerable gliosis. These will all affect the degree of blind spot enlargement.

Disc edema has a strong tendency to spread into the retina toward the macula. This enlarges the blind spot toward fixation in the form of a ceco-central type of scotoma with sloping edges and variable density (Figure 14-9). The area immediately adjacent to fixation sometimes shows a small island of increased density joined to the enlarged blind spot by a narrow neck of relative scotoma. This type of visual field defect is sometimes difficult to distinguish from the papillomacular bundle defect seen in optic neuritis, although central visual acuity is usually much worse in the latter condition.

Pseudotumor cerebri, or benign intracranial hypertension, may produce a variety of visual field defects. Significant visual field findings occur in approximately half of patients. A transient visual loss is common. Papilledema is the rule, and an enlarged blind spot, arcuate scotomas, and generalized depression of the peripheral isopters are not rare (Figure 14-10). Severe

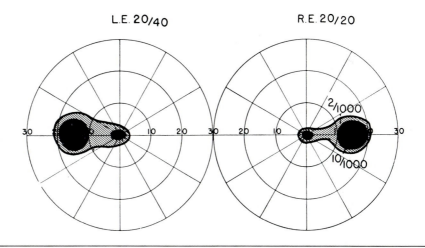

FIGURE 14-9   Papilledema. Bilateral disc edema of 5 diopters in case of cerebellar tumor showing absolute blind spot enlargement and relative scotoma extending toward fixation. Involvement of fixation area is probably caused by extension of edema into macula.

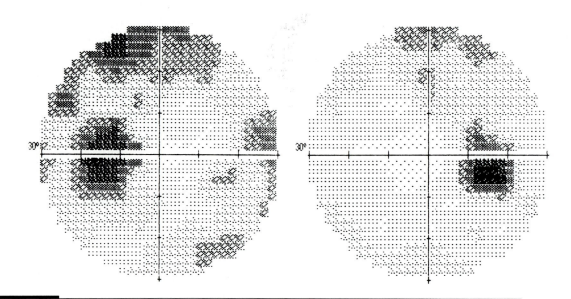

FIGURE 14-10 Right eye shows moderately increased blind spot with mild peripheral depression, and left eye shows a more substantially increased blind spot with moderate peripheral depression in 24-year-old woman with diagnosis of pseudotumor cerebri.

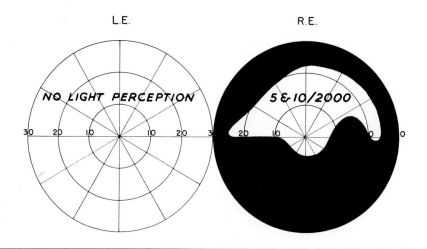

FIGURE 14-11 Chronic papilledema with gliosis and optic atrophy resulting from left acoustic neuroma. There was involvement of eighth, seventh, sixth, and fifth cranial nerves on left, along with almost total left optic atrophy and partial atrophy of right optic disc. Altitudinal field loss is caused by peripheral breakthrough of nerve fiber bundle defect.

chronic papilledema may result in ischemic optic neuropathy with sudden visual loss and altitudinal visual field defects.

Severe papilledema with the gross blind spot enlargement may be seen in patients with space-occupying lesions of the posterior fossa and tumors of the third and fourth ventricles.

Secondary Optic Atrophy

With prolonged papilledema, gliosis takes place in the optic nervehead, and optic atrophy, known as secondary or consecutive atrophy, gradually develops. The visual field change associated with this condition is peripheral contraction, especially in the nasal field, caused by destruction of the peripheral nerve fibers by the progressive gliosis. Eventually the entire nerve is involved and blindness supervenes. The peripheral field defect is absolute and slowly progressive (Figure 14-11).

Compression of nerve fiber bundles and their arterial supply may produce glaucoma-like nerve fiber bundle defects, altitudinal hemianopsia, irregular constriction, and finally no light perception.

Once field contraction has become well established, the prognosis for return of vision after removal of the intracranial lesion is poor.

Papillitis or Optic Neuritis

The term *papillitis* refers to inflammation of the optic disc. In the strict sense, it confines the lesion to the intraocular portion of the nerve, and because this is a rare if not impossible condition, the term is perhaps inaccurate. Optic neuritis, on the other hand, is too all inclusive, embracing as it does the entire nerve. For practical purposes papillitis is an inflammation of the optic nervehead involving the anterior portion of the nerve accompanied by ophthalmoscopically visible changes in the disc in the form of edema, exudate, venous engorgement, and sometimes hemorrhage. The visual field changes in papillitis are the same as those of inflammation anywhere in the optic nerve, that is, a central scotoma with or without peripheral depression or contraction, depending on whether or not the axial or peripheral portions of the nervehead are involved (Figure 14-12).

The neuritis is usually unilateral but may be bilateral in certain systemic conditions.

When nervehead edema is severe, the blind spot is larger. Nerve fiber bundle involvement may occur, leading to an arcuate scotoma. When a peripheral depression occurs, it often has steep margins and progresses rapidly. The combination of dense central scotoma coalescing with a peripheral contraction gives a poor prognosis.

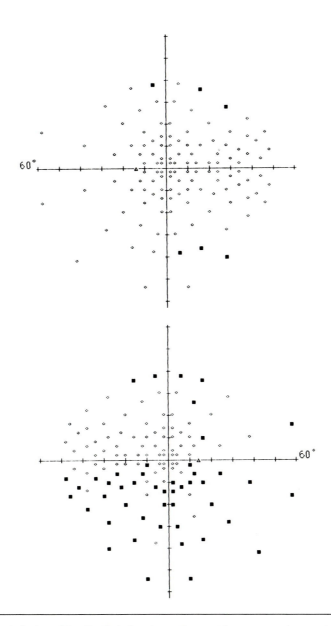

FIGURE 14-12 Right inferior altitudinal defect in patient with acute optic neuritis.

Vascular Lesions of the Optic Disc

Vascular lesions of the optic disc usually take the form of hemorrhage associated with venous thrombosis, severe papilledema, spontaneous subarachnoid hemorrhage, and trauma.

In arteriosclerotic optic atrophy with cupping of the disc and all the findings of low-tension glaucoma, the visual field changes usually include a peripheral depression and a glaucoma-like nerve fiber bundle defect. These are believed to be caused by atherosclerotic closure of the small arterial twigs to the periphery of the nerve.

Arterial emboli from atherosclerotic material in the vessels of the neck may occlude small arterioles in the optic nerve or on the disc, giving rise to sectorlike visual field defects or to typical Bjerrum scotomas. These arterial plaques may sometimes be visible ophthalmoscopically. At other times they may occur deeper in the vasculature and only become manifest through the changes they produce.

Anterior ischemic optic neuropathy may occur, usually in elderly patients with sudden onset of complete or partial visual loss and optic disc edema. When visual loss is partial, the visual fields may show central scotomas, sector defects, or large dense arcuate defects simulating altitudinal hemianopsia (Figure 14-13). These field defects are dense, steep margined, and permanent. Later the optic disc will show a characteristic sectorlike atrophy. Many of these patients have an elevated erythrocyte sedimentation rate; some show positive

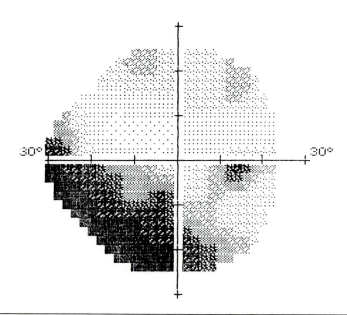

FIGURE 14-13 Inferior altitudinal loss in 51-year-old man with anterior ischemic optic neuropathy. Field in fellow eye was normal.

evidence of frank temporal arteritis. In suspected or confirmed cases of temporal arteritis, early treatment with corticosteroids is mandatory because this may prevent further visual loss.

Patients who have survived a subarachnoid hemorrhage may exhibit bright red preretinal hemorrhages extending out from the optic nerve and producing a corresponding dense visual field defect. This defect can take virtually any shape, but it generally takes the form of a fan-shaped lesion originating from the blind spot. In some cases this subarachnoid hemorrhage may break through into the vitreous. In such cases the condition is referred to as *Terson's syndrome.*

Trauma to Papilla

Direct trauma to the nervehead can occur as a result of avulsion of the nerve secondary to extreme compression or torsion of the globe. Rarely, an intraocular foreign body will cause direct trauma to the optic nervehead. In such cases a wide and atypical nerve fiber type of defect may occur if the patient is fortunate enough to have the injury repaired successfully and the retina remains attached.

RETROBULBAR OPTIC NERVE

Lesions within the trunk or orbital portion of the optic nerve present no ophthalmoscopic evidence of their presence until atrophy appears in a late stage of the disease. Their diagnosis, localization, pathologic process, prognosis, and indications for therapy therefore largely depend on the findings of careful quantitative perimetry and an analysis of the characteristics of their visual field defects.

Depending on whether the disease affects the axial or peripheral portions of the nerve, the visual field defects are central, paracentral, or centrocecal scotomas, or peripheral depression or contraction, or both.

The pathologic processes that affect this section of the optic nerve are (1) acute axial neuritis, (2) acute peripheral optic neuritis, (3) total transverse neuritis, (4) multiple sclerosis, (5) neuromyelitis optica (Devic's disease), (6) Leber's hereditary optic atrophy, (7) infantile optic atrophy, (8) luetic optic neuritis and atrophy, (9) hereditary cerebellar (Friedreich's) ataxia, (10) optic nerve trauma, (11) vascular optic nerve lesions, and (12) optic nerve compression.

Acute Axial Neuritis

Acute axial neuritis is characterized by a rapid onset of severe visual loss and a large and very dense central or centrocecal scotoma. Movement or rotation of the globe can be painful; the condition is commonly unilateral. The ophthal-

moscopic examination is normal. Diagnosis is made on finding a central scotoma. Return of vision is slow, and there may be a permanent central scotoma and loss of central vision. In the later stages of the disease optic atrophy may ensue, with peripheral contraction of the visual field. Rarely, the central scotoma takes an arcuate form, but whatever the form, its margins are steep and the density is uniform.

In many instances the causative agent is never known. In younger people, exhaustive neurologic examination may reveal evidence of multiple sclerosis. The effectiveness of therapy such as intensive corticosteroid therapy is judged by its effect on the scotoma. Central acuity may remain poor despite shrinkage of the scotoma. Even in cases where central acuity returns to normal a Marcus Gunn afferent pupillary defect may persist. Complete recovery is rare.

Acute Peripheral Optic Neuritis

When acute inflammation involves the peripheral fibers of the optic nerve, either as a primary process or secondary to disease of the pial sheath, the resulting visual field defect is a peripheral depression or contraction. Central vision remains intact until the onset of optic atrophy. Both eyes may be involved but usually unequally, and the neuritis is more often unilateral. Peripheral neuritis with concentric visual field contraction usually localizes the lesion in the posterior portion of the nerve, behind the point of entry of the central retinal artery. A differential diagnosis from tabetic optic atrophy may be difficult except that tabes is usually slow in onset, never regresses, is usually bilateral, and is accompanied rather than followed by optic nerve atrophy.

Total Transverse Neuritis

Fortunately, total transverse neuritis is rare. It may accompany nonspecific or influenzal acute encephalitis and gives rise to a total amaurosis of sudden onset or to large and dense central scotomas with almost complete loss of vision. The prognosis is poor.

Multiple Sclerosis

Multiple sclerosis is probably the most common cause of acute retrobulbar neuritis. Retrobulbar neuritis has been reported in 8% to 75% of all cases of multiple sclerosis, with an average incidence of about 50% in the statistical analyses of different authors. Recent evidence indicates that much of the literature may underestimate the chance that multiple sclerosis will develop eventually in a young patient with an otherwise unexplained onset of optic neuritis. This evidence suggests that as length of follow-up increases to 10 or perhaps even 15 years after the initial symptoms, most patients who remain in the study develop signs of more generalized demyelinating disease.

The characteristic visual field defect of retrobulbar neuritis is a central scotoma (Figure 14-14). It may take a wide variety of forms: bilateral or unilateral, sloping or steep margins, large or small, and round, oval, or irregular. Computerized threshold static perimetry shows a characteristic undulating pattern in which relatively normal areas are adjacent to mild to moderately depressed areas in an irregular and unpredictable pattern (Figure 14-15). When the lesion extends into the chiasm or the optic tract, the visual field changes may take on the characteristics of other disturbances of the visual pathways in those areas.

Frequently the scotomas in patients with multiple sclerosis are vague, relative, and ephemeral or fleeting in appearance, present on one examination and absent a few days later. Consequently, evaluating the success of therapy is extremely difficult, and great caution should be exercised in attributing a cure to any current form of treatment. Some patients report that a hot bath or even prolonged sunbathing causes a noticeable transient decrease in vision. In well-established multiple sclerosis a characteristic thinning and atrophy of retinal nerve fiber bundles occur. These "slits" in the nerve fiber layer can be observed with red-free ophthalmoscopy.

An inconstant central scotoma that fades after a few days only to reappear days, months, or even years later is highly suggestive of multiple sclerosis. A history of transient diplopia or other cranial nerve involvement more certainly confirms the diagnosis. When the neurologic examination reveals peripheral motor or sensory involvement, abnormal deep and superficial reflexes, emotional instability, and finally optic atrophy, the diagnostic criteria are complete.

Multiple sclerosis is an extremely variable disease. In some patients the only finding is a transient and recurrent central scotoma in one or both eyes. Some individuals have lengthy remissions between attacks of retrobulbar neuritis, and optic atrophy with bitemporal pallor of the optic nerveheads may ensue. In other cases retrobulbar neuritis, with initial typical transient scotoma, may precede general neurologic findings of multiple sclerosis by 10 to 20 years. When the central scotoma is progressive from onset, it is often quickly followed by optic atrophy and the prognosis for visual return is poor.

Visual perception is delayed after an attack of retrobulbar neuritis. In addition to delayed visual evoked response (VER), critical flicker fusion frequency is reduced in a high proportion of multiple sclerosis patients. Demyelinization impairs the patient's ability to detect the fact that two closely following light flashes are double rather than single. The time interval between the two flashes must be increased to restore the patient's perception of a double flash. This abnormality is large and rather easily detected and may be present before visual field defects develop. It may remain even though Snellen acuity returns to normal.

In many cases the only finding may be a delayed VER in one eye or, more often, both eyes. This abnormal latency may precede the onset of a frank and measurable visual field defect, or it may persist for a long time after the scotoma resolves.

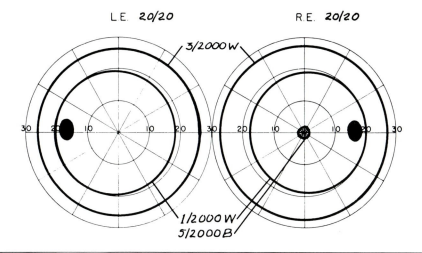

FIGURE 14-14 Retrobulbar neuritis associated with chronic ethmoiditis accompanied by fistulous tract into posterior orbit. Central scotoma was demonstrated with luminescent monochromatic blue test object even though visual acuity was blurred 20/20 in right eye. Two-point discrimination was shown to be defective when two 1-mm targets were brought together on 2-meter tangent screen. Color vision was deficient.

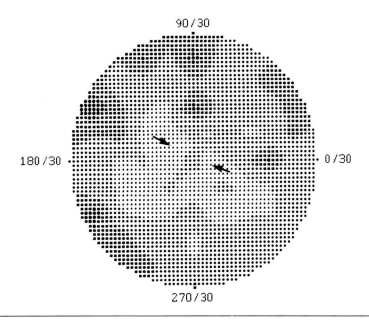

FIGURE 14-15 Mild irregular loss in right eye of 32-year-old patient with optic neuritis, who subsequently developed characteristic signs and symptoms of multiple sclerosis. Note slight but significant central depression *(arrows)*.

The reliability of the VER, especially its latency, makes it particularly sensitive to alterations in conduction velocity in the visual pathway, so that it has gained diagnostic value in evaluating patients suspected of having demyelinating disease. The usefulness of the VER is enhanced by the fact that the optic nerves are among the earliest and most frequently involved sites in multiple sclerosis.

On the other hand, it has been demonstrated that careful visual field examination can be quite sensitive in picking up early scotomas in patients with multiple sclerosis. Visual field examination is much less expensive and much more widely available than VER and certainly should be included in the workup of any patient suspected of having demyelinating disease.

Neuromyelitis Optica

Neuromyelitis optica (Devic's disease) is a severe bilateral optic neuritis. It is associated with transverse myelitis and accompanied by central scotomas and paraplegia. The disease most frequently occurs in adolescents or young adults but has been seen in elderly persons.

In about half of the cases the myelitis precedes the appearance of the scotomas. In about one fourth of the cases, the onset is with retrobulbar neuritis followed by paraplegia. The remaining cases show a simultaneous onset of myelitis and ocular signs.

Optic neuritis may involve the papilla or may be entirely in the axial portion of the retrobulbar nerve. The scotomas are usually large and very

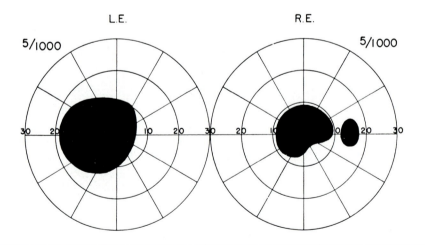

FIGURE 14-16 Neuromyelitis optica (Devic's disease). There was bilateral optic disc edema with poor vision and central scotomas. Visual disturbances were sudden in onset and followed in 2 weeks by complete paraplegia. Both optic neuritis and myelitis partially cleared after 4 months.

dense. Peripheral field involvement may be seen and the lesion may extend into the chiasm or the optic tracts (Figure 14-16). Bitemporal or homonymous hemianopsia may be produced. The prognosis is poor. The disease may be confused with, and is perhaps related to, acute disseminated encephalitis of Schilder.

Leber's Hereditary Optic Atrophy

A familial bilateral optic atrophy, Leber's disease usually becomes evident in the second or third decade. Acute loss of central vision, with large, dense, steep-margined, bilateral central scotomas, and optic atrophy occur. The disc changes and visual field loss are permanent.

In the acute stage of the optic neuropathy in Leber's disease, Smith, Hoyt, and Susac found three characteristic fundus changes: (1) swelling of the nerve fiber layer around the disc, (2) circumpapillary telangiectatic microangiopathy, and (3) absence of staining on fluorescein angiography. The initial changes mimic disc edema, but the rapid visual loss and scotomas coupled with the familial inheritance pattern help to point to the correct diagnosis.

The scotoma may assume many different forms, but it is always central. Occasionally the scotomas regress, but in most the visual loss is permanent. Total blindness is rare. Some peripheral depression or contraction of the field is common in the later stages.

Infantile Optic Atrophy

Aside from Leber's hereditary optic atrophy, Kjer and C. Hoyt have described a number of cases of infantile optic atrophy with an autosomal dominant inheritance mode.

Visual acuity is not severely affected unless nystagmus is present. The age of onset is early in life, but the condition often goes unnoticed until detected in a routine school screening program. The degree of optic atrophy varies.

The characteristic visual field defect is a cecocentral scotoma; its density varies greatly. The cecocentral defect may enlarge to encompass a large area of temporal field and simulate a bitemporal hemianopsia. Some cases show a nerve fiber bundle defect. Tests with colored stimuli exaggerate these defects.

Luetic Optic Neuritis and Atrophy

Diagnosis of luetic optic neuritis and atrophy depends on correlating a number of findings: appearance of the optic disc, visual field changes, and clinical and serologic evidence of syphilis.

In its more acute stages the disease more properly should be called luetic optic neuritis, whereas its more chronic and familiar form is an optic atrophy.

The degenerative changes may involve the axial portion of the nerve, but they are found more commonly in the peripheral nerve fibers. They are secondary to luetic inflammation. Papillitis is rarely present. In most cases the nerve is affected in its posterior orbital or intracranial portion. The same pathologic process may be seen in tabes dorsalis and in general paresis.

The visual field defects associated with luetic optic atrophy depend on the portion of the nerve involved by the process:

1. Peripheral or concentric inflammation is followed by nerve fiber degeneration that advances slowly toward the center of the nerve and gives rise to a gradually contracting visual field with steep margins. Central vision may be maintained for some time, but eventually fixation is involved and ultimate loss of light perception is the rule. The contraction may not be concentric but may spare one quadrant long after the rest of the visual field is gone. Occasionally the shape of the visual field is quite bizarre.

2. Sectorlike degeneration may occur with wedge-shaped areas of visual field loss pointing their apices at fixation. Optic atrophy in these patients may appear to involve the entire disc; when both eyes are equally involved, the visual field defect sometimes takes on hemianoptic characteristics, which may make them difficult to differentiate from chiasmal and postchiasmal lesions.

3. Luetic retrobulbar neuritis followed by degeneration of the axial portion of the nerve gives rise to central scotomas. These may be sudden or gradual in onset. They are of various forms and are progressive. The peripheral visual field may remain unaffected for a long time but is usually involved eventually.

The visual field defects of tabetic optic atrophy may simulate those of almost any disease of the visual pathway. In the decades since the advent of penicillin, optic nerve damage is less common.

The diagnostic criteria are the bilaterality of the condition, the optic atrophy, the prolonged course, and the inexorable advance of the visual field loss toward blindness.

Hereditary Cerebellar Ataxia

Visual field changes are not uncommon in hereditary cerebellar (Friedreich's) ataxia and have been variously described by different authors as concentric contraction, annular scotoma involving the blind spot, and central scotoma, all in association with optic atrophy.

Optic Nerve Injury

Direct injury to the optic nerve, such as may occur in avulsion of the nerve or in a gunshot wound to the head, usually causes immediate, total, and permanent visual loss. Indirect injury of varying degrees may occur and produces visual field defects in keeping with the degree of nerve damage.

Walsh has classified optic nerve and chiasmal lesions associated with indirect trauma as follows:

1. Primary lesions
   a. Hemorrhages in the nerve, dura, and sheath spaces
   b. Tears in the nerve or chiasm
   c. Contusion necrosis of the nerves and chiasm
2. Secondary lesions
   a. Edema and swelling of optic nerves and chiasm
   b. Necrosis from systemic circulatory failure or local vascular compression
   c. Infarction in the optic nerve or chiasm related to vascular obstruction from thrombosis

This classification was based on microscopic studies and is not concerned with visual field defects resulting from such lesions. In most instances, lesions were of such severity as to preclude visual field evaluation.

A number of cases have been reported in which gunshot wounds of the temporal region have damaged the optic nerve by the concussive effect of the bullets passing near but not through the nerve. In these cases the damage is generally greatest on the side where the bullet exits because of the greater concussive effect on that side. Indirect optic nerve injury can occur even

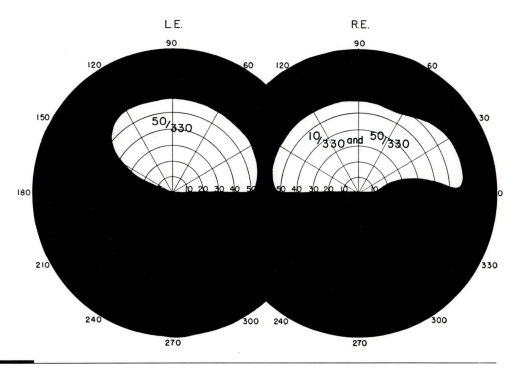

FIGURE 14-17 Concussion injury to optic nerve. Rifle bullet passed through right frontal lobe above and anterior to orbital apices. Path of bullet was obliquely upward from right to left, at considerable distance from optic nerve. Retina was normal.

though the bullet passes a considerable distance from the nerve itself (Figure 14-17).

Skull fracture with basilar fracture in the area of the optic foramen may give rise to optic nerve injury with unilateral or bilateral altitudinal hemi-anoptic field defects. Occasionally only a small portion of the lower visual field will be depressed, and in some instances this slight peripheral depression will be accompanied by a nerve fiber bundle defect.

The type of field defects produced by these indirect injuries, the nature of the injuries themselves, and evidence from operative exploration of some patients all indicate that the lesion producing these defects may involve damage to the vascular supply of the nerve rather than damage to the nerve fibers directly.

The nerve at this point is movable within its dural sheath, which is firmly attached to the periosteum of the optic canal. Torsion or pulling of the nerve in any direction would tend to shear the tiny vascular twigs that enter the nerve at right angles from the pial sheath. The blood vessels supplying the upper half of the nerve are shorter than those to the inferior portion of the nerve and are more vulnerable to the shearing action. Thus inferior visual field defects are more common in this type of injury.

Fractures of the optic canal or displaced bony fragments are extremely rare. They require careful radiologic evaluation. Some of these lesions may be amenable to surgical intervention, but the prognosis remains guarded even in the best of circumstances.

Vascular Optic Nerve Lesions

Arteriosclerotic disease of the small arterioles that supply the optic nerve may give rise to circulatory embarrassment and chronic hypoxia with resulting defects in the visual fields. These may take the form of gradual peripheral depression or, when the axial portion of the nerve is involved, vague and irregular central scotomas. Frequently there are nerve fiber bundle defects as described in the discussion of low-tension glaucoma.

When the arterial occlusion is more acute, as in thrombosis or embolism, sector defects or large dense central scotomas may develop.

As mentioned previously, the visual defects associated with indirect injury to the optic nerve are probably vascular in origin; possibly those produced by compression of the optic nerve are also, at least in part, caused by circulatory failure.

The type of visual field loss most frequently produced by vascular disturbance in the optic nerve is horizontal or altitudinal hemianopsia. A second type of field defect commonly associated with vascular disease is the nerve fiber bundle defect.

Optic Nerve Compression

The orbital portion of the optic nerve may be compressed by tumors impinging on it from four sides and from within the nerve itself. Optic nerve compression by aneurysm produces a generalized depression (Figure 14-18). Optic nerve compression can be an ominous occurrence in thyroid ophthalmopathy. Visual field defects may arise from direct pressure on the nerve fibers or from interruption of the vascular supply by compression of the arterioles supplying the various portions of the nerve. Offending lesions may involve the nerve in the anterior, middle, or posterior part of the orbit. Tumors in the anterior and middle parts of the orbit rarely give rise to visual field defects, whereas posterior orbital tumors compressing the nerve in its more fixed portion as it enters the optic canal give rise to characteristic visual field defects. When the visual field defect is unilateral and remains so, the pressure is probably intraorbital; when the defect is bilateral, the lesion is more likely to be intra-cranial.

The most common visual field defect produced by compression of this portion of the nerve is a central scotoma, often with certain hemianoptic features. The scotoma may involve an area of 10 to 20 degrees around fixation; but when measured quantitatively with multiple isopters, an area of greater density will be seen in the portion opposite the direction of pressure. These areas of greater density are generally limited by the vertical or horizontal meridians, so that the densest area of the scotoma assumes a quadrantic or hemianoptic character. Thus pressure exerted on the upper temporal portion of the nerve just before its entrance into the optic foramen is likely to produce an irregular central scotoma whose area of greatest density is a quadrantic sector in the inferior nasal portion of the scotoma. Pressure on the medial side of the nerve gives rise to a unilateral hemianoptic scotoma on the temporal side of fixation.

Frequently the central scotoma extends toward the blind spot, but it rarely extends into the peripheral field. Peripheral depression of the field is a late development and is usually associated with advanced nerve atrophy, exophthalmos, and limited motion of the globe.

The visual field defects associated with compressive thyroid ophthalmopathy can be dense and bizarre. Orbital decompression can result in significant improvement in the visual field, although some degree of deficit may remain. During the acute phases of dysthyroid optic neuropathy visual acuity may decrease rapidly. In such cases urgent or emergent orbital decompression may be necessary.

Tumors within the optic nerve, usually gliomas, give rise to visual field defects through a combination of pressure, nerve fiber destruction, and vascular occlusion. The field defects tend to be larger, denser, and more variable than with external compression.

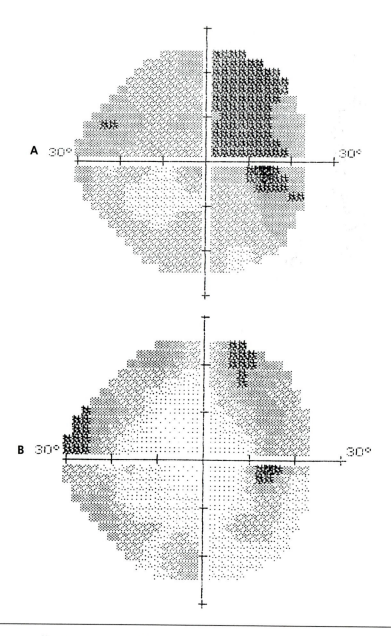

FIGURE 14-18 A, Generally depressed field from woman with optic compression from right carotid artery aneurysm. **B,** Field from same patient 1 week after surgical decompression.

The initial visual field defect in optic nerve glioma is usually a central scotoma that is rather steep margined and of uniform density. The scotoma enlarges with tumor growth and breaks through into the periphery in the form of irregular sector defects, which may occur in any area of the field. Eventually the chiasm may be invaded, with resulting involvement of the contralateral field, a so-called junctional scotoma.

INTRACRANIAL PORTION OF THE OPTIC NERVE

Precise localization of lesions affecting the intracranial portion of the optic nerve may sometimes be attempted because of the anatomic characteristics of the nerve and its surrounding structures. As the lesions progress, however, they invade the anterior angle of the chiasm and should rightfully be considered with diseases affecting that structure.

The classic example of a lesion of intracranial part of the nerve is seen in the Foster Kennedy syndrome in which there is visual loss, a central scotoma with hemianoptic characteristics, optic atrophy on the same side as the tumor, and papilledema in the opposite optic nerve (Figure 14-19). The tumor is usually an olfactory groove meningioma, but the syndrome may be caused by tumors of the frontal lobe; a cerebellar tumor with extreme third ventricle dilation; aneurysm of the ophthalmic artery, internal carotid artery, or anterior cerebral artery; arachnoidal cysts; or even intrinsic gliomas of the optic nerve that have not yet extended into the chiasm.

All these lesions together, however, are extremely rare. Much more commonly a pseudo–Foster Kennedy syndrome is seen in which asymmetric anterior ischemic optic neuropathy gives an appearance of optic atrophy with visual loss on one side and acute disc edema simulating papilledema on the opposite side. The clinical differentiation may be difficult in some cases. The presence of severe visual loss such as a dense arcuate scotoma that simulates an altitudinal hemianopsia may help direct one's thinking toward asymmetric anterior ischemic optic neuropathy as the cause; the presence of associated frontal lobe or other neurologic signs suggests true Foster Kennedy syndrome.

Figures 14-20 and 14-21 are examples of differential diagnosis and precise localization of a lesion involving the optic nerve in its intracanalicular portion by quantitative visual field analysis. The initial defect was a small inferior paracentral scotoma. This expanded to involve the inferior temporal quadrant and finally to become an inferior altitudinal field loss. The horizontal margin of the defect and its progression suggested a lesion compressing the nerve from above. Simple x-ray films of the optic foramina were normal. A frontal craniotomy was performed, disclosing a small meningioma within the left optic canal that was compressing the optic nerve from temporally and above. The tumor lay on the left carotid artery and extended well into the optic canal, causing erosion of the canal with a small sequestrum of bone from the posterior lip of the canal. Complete removal of the tumor was accomplished.

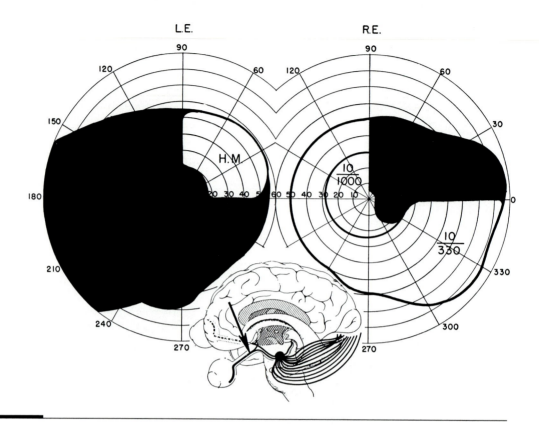

FIGURE 14-19 Visual fields in case of very large and slow-growing meningioma of left frontal lobe with schematic representation of site and direction of pressure on nerve and chiasm. Left eye was almost blind with advanced optic atrophy and small remnant of nasal field. Right eye showed temporal field loss and papilledema (Foster Kennedy syndrome).

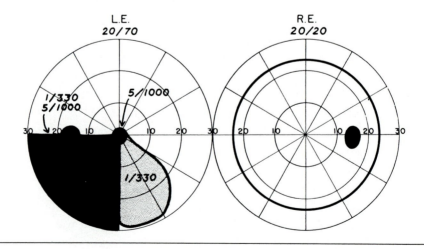

FIGURE 14-20 Inferior temporal quadrant defect with slight extension into inferior nasal field. Patient had small meningioma of posterior superior lip of optic canal.

Figures 14-22 to 14-24 are similar examples of precise tumor localization by careful quantitative perimetry. All initially involved one optic nerve and later, by extension, involved the chiasm. They initially affected vision in the visual field of one eye only. The hemianoptic character of the field loss indicates early chiasmatic compression, which may be missed without the most meticulous perimetry. Color perception may be impaired as an early sign, and the defects are exaggerated for red stimuli.

Knight, Hoyt, and Wilson have described the characteristics of the monocular syndrome of incipient prechiasmal optic nerve compression as slowly

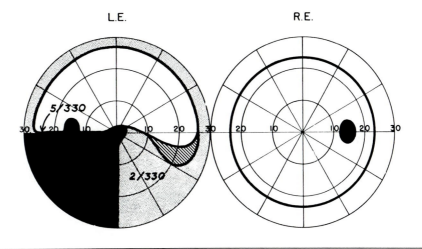

FIGURE 14-21 Extension of inferior field defect shown in Fig. 14-20 to become altitudinal loss. Progression occurred in 3 weeks.

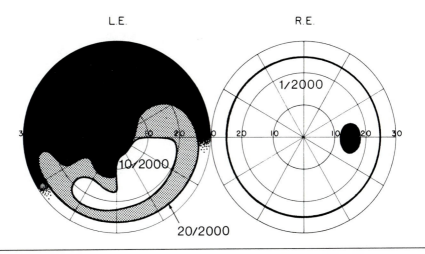

FIGURE 14-22 Superior temporal quadrant defect resulting from small meningioma arising from lip of left optic foramen under optic nerve and encroaching on chiasm and internal carotid artery. Advanced optic atrophy continued to progress after removal of tumor.

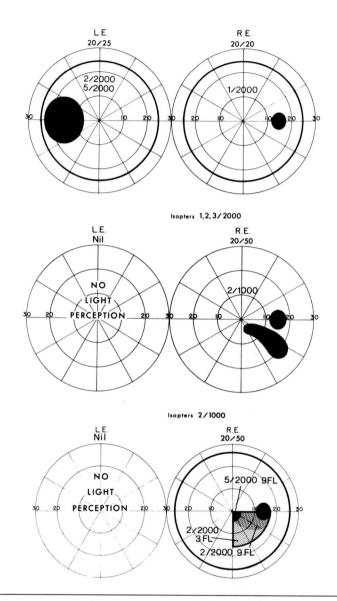

FIGURE 14-23 Prechiasmal pressure by meningioma involving left optic nerve caused complete blindness in left eye. Tumor was then extended across midline to compress right optic nerve at intracranial optic foramen. Note quadratic nature of right hemianoptic scotoma when tested with multiple stimuli. None 12-year lapse between first and last examination. Tumor was removed and vision in right eye was restored. *(From Harrington, DO: Trans Ophthalmol Soc UK 92:15, 1972, London, Churchill Livingstone, Ltd.)*

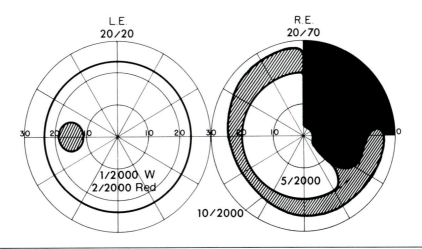

FIGURE 14-24 Suprasellar meningioma. Very gradual visual loss in right eye with hemianoptic superior temporal field deficit. Arteriogram and pneumoencephalogram showed large tumor impinging on tuberculum sellae. Tumor had invaded pial sheath of right optic nerve and markedly deformed left optic nerve. Tumor was successfully removed.

progressive dimming of vision, poor color perception, a positive Marcus Gunn pupillary sign, and a normal-appearing optic disc. The visual field studies show slowly progressive quadrantic defects similar to those seen in Figures 14-22 and 14-24. Even very small tumors in this area can now be detected by current neuroradiologic techniques. Microsurgical resection of these lesions ensures a chance for prompt visual restoration.

A case has been described in which an intrasellar tumor (chromophobic adenoma of the pituitary gland) had tilted the chiasm upward and kinked the optic nerve against the superior edge of the optic foramen, giving rise to a unilateral inferior altitudinal hemianopsia. The chiasm was postfixed and freely movable. This probably accounted for the lack of signs of inferior chiasmal pressure, even though the tumor was large and had produced radiographic evidence of erosion of the sella turcica. The opposite field was normal to the most careful quantitative examination.

Even before the contralateral visual field becomes involved, the disease may involve the chiasm. As in all tumors of this area, signs of involvement of contiguous structures are of utmost importance. Radiographic evidence of calcification within the tumor or of unilateral enlargement of the optic foramen should be obtained when possible. Computerized axial tomography and magnetic resonance imaging scans may be quite helpful in such cases.

15 CHIASM

No portion of the visual pathway offers a better opportunity for exact correlation between anatomy and function than the chiasm. The nerve fiber pattern in the chiasm is responsible for characteristic changes in the visual fields that are pathognomonic of lesions in this area and this area alone.

Binocular vision begins in the chiasm, which is the first portion of the visual pathway where a single lesion produces a simultaneous defect in both visual fields. This double, or hemianoptic, visual field defect is seen typically as a bitemporal hemianopsia.

Although the nerve fiber pattern of the chiasm is remarkably constant, other factors must be taken into account when interpreting visual field changes associated with chiasmal pathologic findings. These factors give rise to the large number of possible variations in hemianoptic morphology. At first some of the field changes may seem confusing, but usually they can be explained adequately by a knowledge of the chiasmal fiber architecture, vascular supply, and contiguous structures. Variations in chiasmal position, bony structure in the chiasmal area, and the anatomic relationship between the chiasm and the vessels of the circle of Willis, pituitary body, pituitary stalk, third ventricle, tuberculum sellae, and sphenoid ridge may each play an important role in the etiology of a given field defect.

Study of the complicated nerve fiber pattern within the chiasm makes it obvious that pressure at different points and from different directions will give rise to varying patterns of visual field loss. Further consideration of the large number of contiguous structures that may directly compress or give rise to indirect pressure on the chiasm makes it clear that a thorough knowledge of the area is essential for reasonably accurate visual field interpretation.

Although perimetry is the most valuable examination method for diagnosing chiasmal lesions, one should take full advantage of any other diagnostic procedures that might clarify the clinical picture. Some of the more important of these examinations include the following:

1. Radiologic and neuroradiologic examinations of the chiasmal region, sella turcica, optic foramen, sphenoid ridge, and tuberculum sellae.

Important advances in neuroradiologic technique have made it possible to localize even small tumors accurately. Alone or in combination, cerebral angiography, computerized axial tomography, and magnetic resonance imaging afford an excellent means of examining the chiasmal region.

2. Endocrinologic studies, both clinical and laboratory, for detecting pituitary dysfunction.

3. Neurologic examination, with particular reference to the function of the other cranial nerves.

4. Ophthalmoscopy, including an examination of the retinal nerve fiber layer with red-free light. Evaluation of optic nerve pallor is often difficult, and discs may appear normal in the face of advanced bitemporal hemianopsia. However, in some patients with bitemporal hemianopsia, a characteristic "bow tie" or band atrophy of the optic disc occurs. This pattern is caused by loss of fibers subserving the nasal retina (temporal field) and relative preservation of fibers subserving the temporal retina (nasal field). Thus the pallor is concentrated in a horizontal band across the optic nervehead. Careful examination of the retina with red-free light will show nerve fiber layer dropout or slits in the regions where nasal fibers are normally found.

When all these methods have been used, perhaps with negative results, the perimetric examination may be left as providing the only positive finding that implicates the chiasm. In many cases we have found it necessary to repeat laboratory studies or radiographic examinations that yielded negative results in the face of visual field evidence of an abnormality in the chiasmal region. The need to do this, particularly in the case of negative radiologic studies, is lessened tremendously by communicating actively with the neuroradiologist before ordering the test. This allows the radiologist to choose the most appropriate examination method, to focus the test on the proper region, and to examine this area with particular care when reading the results.

Frequently the first symptom of chiasmal disturbance is visual, and the first physician consulted is the ophthalmologist. In other instances, vague signs and symptoms of endocrine dysfunction may implicate the pituitary gland, and the endocrinologist may request the assistance of a visual field examination to support his or her impression of disease in this organ. A careful visual field examination can provide useful data in either situation.

PERIMETRIC TECHNIQUES FOR CHIASMAL LESIONS

Except when there is a central scotomatous element in the visual field defect, the patient may be completely unaware of an advanced bitemporal hemianopsia. When the macula is spared, the nasal field of one eye overlaps the defective temporal field of the other eye, so that even tasks requiring excellent vision are performed easily. Gross examination methods such as confrontation testing may miss early chiasmal field defects. One must use fairly dim, small targets when testing the field manually or use a full-threshold program on a computerized perimeter (Figure 15-1).

In addition to standard perimetry on the Goldmann perimeter or tangent screen, we use two modifications when examining patients whom we suspect may have a chiasmal field defect. First, because we are searching for a bitemporal defect, we carefully map the isopters on either side of the vertical midline. Receptor fields may overlap, especially as one is progressing peripherally, so we carefully map a fairly wide range corresponding to the region between about 2 degrees and 10 to 20 degrees from the vertical midline in either direction. Additionally, because the superior field is most often involved first (pituitary lesions), we spend more time testing the superior field than the inferior. After we have established the isopters for a given stimulus by using our normal method of moving the stimulus in a radial or meridional pattern from nonseeing to seeing and from seeing to nonseeing, followed by testing the area with static targets, we change the approach and compare stimuli from one side of the vertical midline to the other. For instance, we would start with a stimulus that is just suprathreshold in the nasal field and then pass this stimulus into a corresponding area in the temporal field to see if it is detected. Conversely, we might take a stimulus that is just infrathreshold in the temporal field and then test a corresponding area in the nasal field to determine whether or not the stimulus can be detected.

When using the tangent screen, one can place two stimuli of equal intensity, such as two 2-mm white targets, on the testing wand 20 to 25 cm apart. One can then hold the wand in such a way that one stimulus is in the superonasal field and the other is in the superotemporal field, equidistant from the vertical midline. By rolling the testing wand in the normal fashion used for presenting static targets, one can test for the extinction phenomenon with double simultaneous presentation in the two quadrants. A patient with a temporal quadrantanopsia would only see one of the targets under these circumstances.

The second special method we use for patients with suspected chiasmal syndromes is a test of the perifoveal region with a red object. This can be done with the normal array of red test objects that are used with the tangent screen or, in a pinch, with any other handy small red object, such as a red mydriatic eyedropper bottle top. In this test the red object is placed a few degrees from fixation in the temporal or nasal field and then moved slowly back and forth across the vertical midline. We use an arcing motion, as though we were moving along the circumference of a circle of constant radius with its center at fixation, but this is probably not critical. The object is moved back and forth, first comparing the temporal and nasal superior or inferior quadrants and then the superior and inferior quadrants in either the temporal or nasal field. A positive response to this "red desaturation test" occurs if the

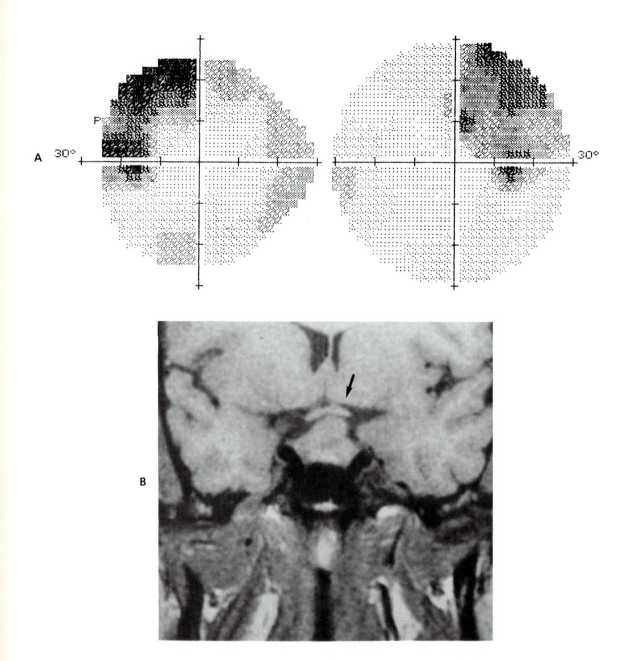

FIGURE 15-1 **A,** Visual field chart from 38-year-old woman with prolactin-secreting tumor but no visual complaints. Referral was made by her endocrinologist. Vision was 20/20 bilaterally, with confrontation fields reported as normal. **B,** Magnetic resonance imaging revealed large pituitary mass, with the chiasm draped over it *(arrow)*.

patient notices that the target is bright and red in a nasal quadrant or hemifield, but pink or grayish in the corresponding temporal quadrant or hemifield. Furthermore, the superior and inferior temporal quadrants may show differential red desaturation, depending on the direction of chiasmal pressure.

When visual field defects are found it is important to analyze their character by testing them carefully with appropriate computer programs or with multiple isopters. Among many reasons for such careful analysis are the following:

1. A hemianoptic scotoma is usually associated with a peripheral temporal cut in the field of the same or the opposite eye. It is important to search diligently for this second defect in order to differentiate a chiasmal from an optic nerve lesion.

2. In an apparent total bitemporal hemianopsia it is important to test with large bright objects to determine whether the densest portion of the anoptic field is in the upper or lower quadrant, thus indicating the location of the initial field loss and the probable direction of pressure on the chiasm (Figure 15-2).

3. Sloping margins in a bitemporal field defect are more indicative of progressive visual field change; steep margins and uniform density are signs of a static lesion.

4. An incomplete nerve fiber bundle type of scotoma can mimic a temporal quadrantic defect. It is important to examine the vertical meridian carefully to determine whether the defect crosses or stops at the midline. Nerve fiber bundle defects such as those seen in glaucoma respect the horizontal midline, whereas hemianoptic defects respect the vertical midline.

5. When a temporal hemianoptic defect is found in one field, the contralateral field should be searched carefully for a similar defect.

6. In view of the extraordinary variation in the morphology of bitemporal hemianopsia, numerous errors and misinterpretations of these visual field defects are possible. Careful attention to detail is essential if one is to avoid these errors.

VISUAL FIELD DEFECTS PRODUCED BY CHIASMAL LESIONS

The typical chiasmal field defect is a bitemporal hemianopsia. Binasal, altitudinal, and homonymous hemianopsias are also seen in chiasmal lesions.

Bitemporal Hemianopsia

Classically, bitemporal hemianopsia is either scotomatous or nonscotomatous.

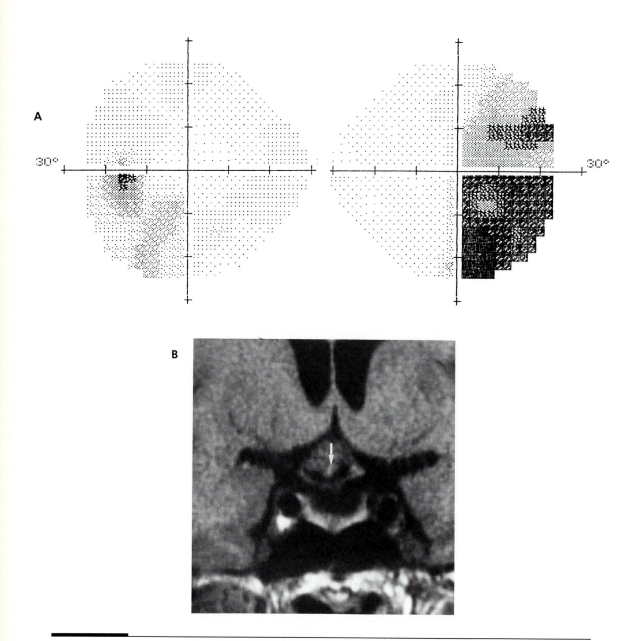

FIGURE 15-2 **A,** Incongruous bitemporal hemianopsia. Inferior quadrant of right eye is more severely involved than left. In left eye inferior quadrant shows significant loss but superior temporal quadrant is within normal limits. **B,** These field defects were produced by craniopharyngioma depressing chiasm from above. *Arrow* points to mass lesion; chiasm is displaced inferiorly below mass.

Scotomatous bitemporal hemianopsia

Hemianoptic scotomas occur rather rarely with chiasmal disease. These defects are explained by the "little chiasm within the chiasm" formed by macular fibers and described by Traquair. They are usually associated with a hemianoptic scotoma of the opposite field, a temporal peripheral defect in the same or opposite field, or both. Almost any combination of scotoma with peripheral depression is possible. The scotoma may be quadrantic or hemi-anoptic, it may be uniformly dense or may have sloping edges, and it may be isolated or may break through into the periphery. It may extend toward or even engulf the blind spot. Its one constant characteristic is that it stops at the vertical meridian (Figure 15-3).

When the chiasm is flattened and tilted upward, causing traction on the optic tracts, a bitemporal hemianoptic scotoma may result, signaling the presence of an intrinsic lesion within the third ventricle such as a cystic cranio-pharyngioma, a small invasive metastatic tumor, or a pituitary apoplexy. These defects are most readily detected within 20 degrees or so of fixation. They may split or spare the macula, usually the former. Bitemporal hemianoptic scotomas often indicate a rapidly progressing lesion (Figure 15-4).

A quadrantic scotoma in which the upper field is involved to a greater extent than the lower indicates that the chiasm is being damaged by pressure from below. In this circumstance the progression of the scotoma is from the upper temporal quadrant, across the horizontal meridian, and into the lower temporal field. At the same time, it may expand outward slightly and may fuse

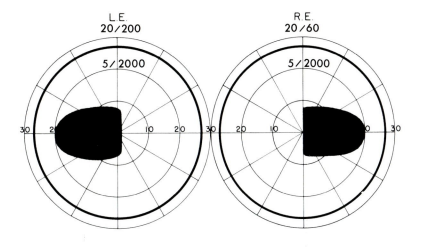

FIGURE 15-3 Pituitary apoplexy. Hemorrhage into large pituitary tumor. Sudden onset of bitemporal hemianoptic scotomas with macular splitting and decreased central vision. Analysis of bilateral cecocentral scotomas revealed steep vertical hemianoptic borders characteristic of chiasmal involvement. Large hemorrhagic cyst evacuated with restoration of vision.

or break through into a gradually progressing peripheral temporal defect. Having reached the inferior temporal quadrant, the hemianoptic scotoma may remain relatively static for some time before beginning the next stage of progression into the lower nasal field and finally into the upper nasal quadrant or across the midline into the nasal field, with macular involvement and resulting loss of central vision. By this time, there is usually some optic atrophy and general depression of the peripheral field, especially in the upper temporal quadrant.

Progression of the bitemporal hemianoptic scotoma, then, is typically clockwise in the right eye and counterclockwise in the left eye. The two visual fields may show symmetric defects, but more often this is not the case. In some instances, the asymmetry is extreme. When one field presents a temporal hemianoptic scotoma and the other shows a peripheral defect, the findings indicate a lesion involving the anterior portion of the chiasm with the scotoma on the side of the lesion. This type of field defect was termed a *junction scotoma* by Traquair. The scotoma has the same characteristics as those resulting from optic nerve compression, but the temporal depression of the opposite field indicates chiasmal involvement. Peripheral temporal loss is caused by compression of the fibers from the contralateral optic nerve as they loop into the ipsilateral nerve before passing backward into the body of the chiasm. The lesion is most often medial to the nerve, arising between the two optic nerves and pressing backward and laterally.

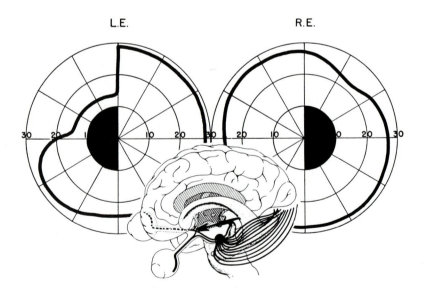

FIGURE 15-4   Bitemporal hemianoptic scotomas with superior temporal peripheral defects in case of pituitary adenoma. Subjective visual disturbance was rather sudden in onset, although other signs and symptoms of endocrine imbalance had existed for at least 6 months.

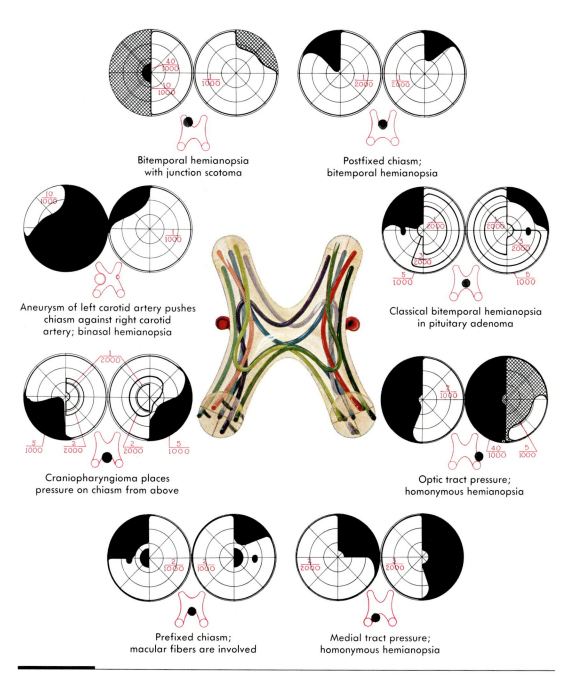

Bitemporal hemianopsia
with junction scotoma

Postfixed chiasm;
bitemporal hemianopsia

Aneurysm of left carotid artery pushes
chiasm against right carotid
artery; binasal hemianopsia

Classical bitemporal hemianopsia
in pituitary adenoma

Craniopharyngioma places
pressure on chiasm from above

Optic tract pressure;
homonymous hemianopsia

Prefixed chiasm;
macular fibers are involved

Medial tract pressure;
homonymous hemianopsia

PLATE 3   Perimetry of chiasmal lesions.

As described, the strictly defined junctional scotoma of Traquair is rare. More often one may find severe field loss in one eye, indicating optic nerve involvement, in association with temporal loss in the opposite eye. Lesions such as this are termed junction scotomas in common usage because the visual field loss indicates involvement of the optic nerve on one side and the crossing fibers from the other side. This type of lesion is seen in intrinsic optic nerve disease that infiltrates the chiasm. It is not as precise a lesion as that of the original designation, however, because two lesions or a diffuse lesion could lead to blindness in one eye and a temporal hemianoptic field cut in the other. These limitations notwithstanding, we have found this junctionlike scotoma useful in directing our attention toward the anterior chiasmal region as we progress in examining a patient with this type of visual field loss.

Nonscotomatous bitemporal hemianopsia

The nonscotomatous type of bitemporal hemianopsia is similar in essentially all respects to the scotomatous type, except that the changes are largely peripheral and no scotoma is present. Central visual acuity is good, and in the early stages the defect is usually only detectable with small stimuli in the area beyond 10 degrees. In its typical form, resulting from median chiasmal pressure from below, the upper temporal quadrants of the field are depressed symmetrically and the defects progress slowly into the lower temporal quadrants before finally crossing the vertical midline into the lower and, ultimately, the upper nasal quadrant. As with the scotomatous type, great variation and marked asymmetry may occur in the two fields.

The progression of a bitemporal hemianopsia may be studied in two ways: (1) by periodic examination of the visual field using the same test parameters, which may require months or even years, or (2) by quantitative analysis of an advanced defect: smaller test objects will show late changes in the field with earlier loss being demonstrated by progressively increasing stimuli (Figure 15-5). In the latter case, the assumption is that the larger stimuli will produce visual field results that resemble the results smaller stimuli would have produced earlier in the patient's course. In essence, one is attempting to look back into time to try to determine better where the lesion began.

After surgical removal of the tumor, the visual field defect resolves in the opposite direction from the field loss. When nerve fiber layer destruction is incomplete, return of retinal function is first noted in the lower nasal field, then in the lower temporal quadrant, and finally in the superior temporal field. Generally, if the temporal field loss is absolute, restoration of the visual field does not occur or, at best, is incomplete. In these patients, the defect becomes static with steep margins and uniform density.

The wide variation in the visual field morphology in chiasmal lesions makes more accurate localization of these lesions possible. Thus a tumor that compresses the chiasm from the right anterior-superior direction is likely to produce a different type of bitemporal hemianopsia from what a tumor pressing upward in the midline would produce.

The ability to localize the pressure site with some accuracy in the anterior, middle, posterior, and lateral portions of the chiasm may make possible a reasonably intelligent estimate of the pathologic process producing the pressure. This is so because certain types of lesions are known to arise from certain structures adjacent to the chiasm, and when pressure is exerted from the direction of these structures, they and their more common pathologic conditions become suspect.

Tumors and other mass lesions affecting the chiasmal visual pathways most likely do so by compromising the vascular supply to the area in question. Direct pressure, even from surprisingly large lesions, may simply displace the chiasm without having much effect on visual function (Figure 15-6). A relatively small lesion that affects the blood supply, on the other hand, can have significant visual sequelae. With this in mind, one can see that too precise a localization of the pressure is not desirable. What is being localized may not

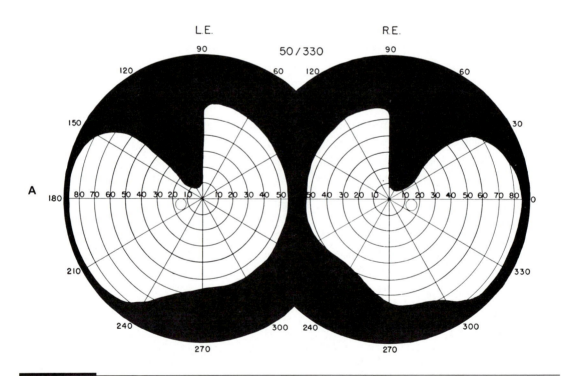

FIGURE 15-5 **A,** Progress in development of bitemporal hemianopsia from pituitary adenoma. This was demonstrated by visual fields taken on same day using multiple stimuli subtending different visual angles (multiple isopter technique of quantitative perimetry). Field for the 50/330 isopter shows only small superior bitemporal sector-type defect. (See also **B** to **E.)** Same mode of progression may be demonstrated by visual field examinations at regular intervals over period of time.

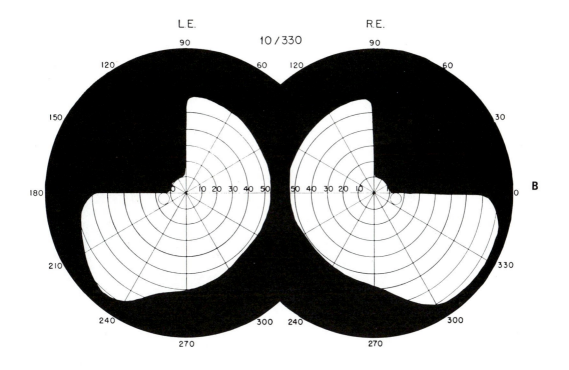

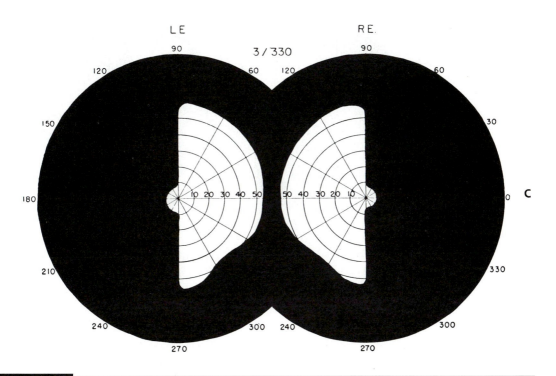

FIGURE 15-5, cont'd. B, Field for 10/330 isopter shows superior bitemporal quadrantanopsia. **C,** Field for 3/330 isopter shows total bitemporal hemianopsia.   *Continued.*

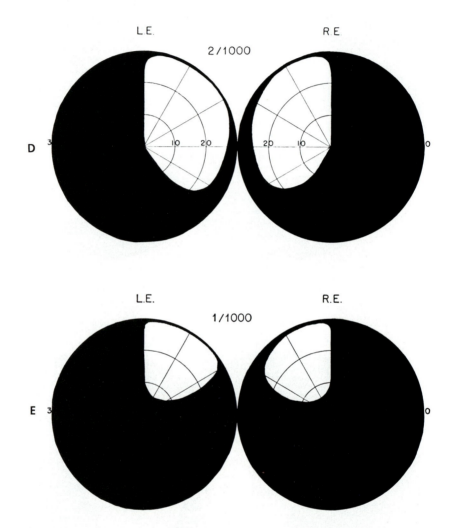

FIGURE 15-5, cont'd. D, Field for 2/1000 isopter shows early involvement of both inferior nasal fields. **E,** Field for 1/1000 isopter shows only remnant of two superior nasal fields. Mode of progression of visual field defect is well demonstrated by use of diminishing stimuli in visual field examination.

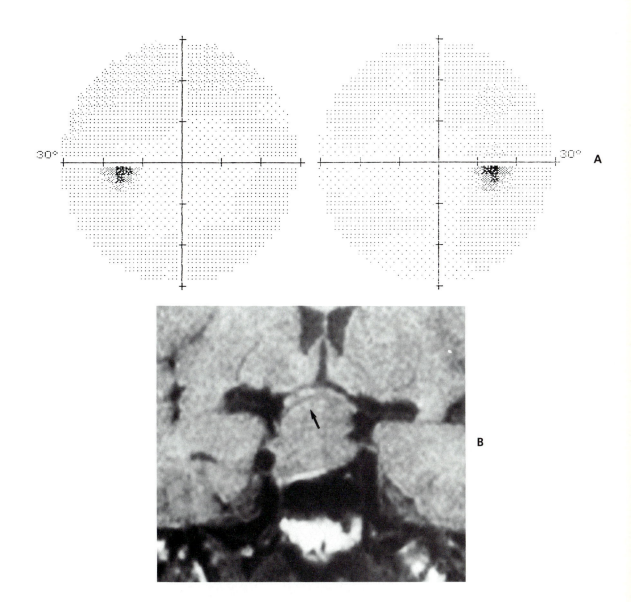

FIGURE 15-6 Computerized static perimetry reveals *very* subtle superior bitemporal field loss **(A)** despite large lesion **(B)** identified by magnetic imaging scan. Arrow is on pituitary mass and points to chiasm draped over lesion.

be a point of pressure on the nerve fibers themselves, but rather the point at which the blood supply has been interrupted. Fortunately, these areas are rarely far removed from each other, and clinical localization of the lesion may be accomplished in most instances almost as though the nerve fiber dysfunction were the result of direct compression.

Actual invasion of the chiasm, optic nerves, or optic tracts may take place with certain tumors. Irregular and bizarre visual field defects result from such infiltration, which may occur in craniopharyngioma, glioma, and metastatic tumors of the chiasm.

Binasal Hemianopsia

Binasal hemianopsia implies two lesions, compressing the chiasm from each side (Figure 15-7). Such situations are rare. It must be remembered, however, that certain diseases characteristically involve both optic nerves and may produce visual field defects that are predominantly binasal. Among these are (1) glaucoma, (2) diabetic optic atrophy, and (3) multiple sclerosis with plaques in both optic nerves or in the chiasm, (4) an aneurysm of one internal carotid artery with displacement of the chiasm against a normal artery on the opposite side (Figures 15-8 and 15-9), (5) opticochiasmatic arachnoiditis (Figure 15-

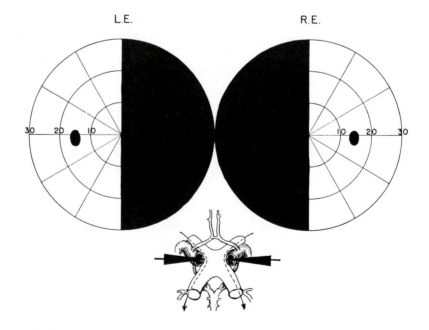

FIGURE 15-7   Binasal hemianopsia. Note direction of pressure lateral to chiasm. This may be produced by calcified and sclerotic internal carotid arteries or by aneurysm of one internal carotid artery with shift of chiasm against normal opposite carotid artery. (See also Plate 3.)

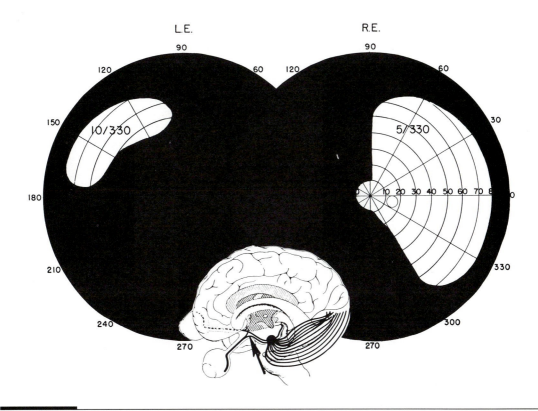

FIGURE 15-8 Binasal hemianopsia produced by large aneurysm of left internal carotid artery. Left eye was blind for 1 year before visual field defect was noted in right eye. Aneurysm was demonstrated by arteriography, and subsequent operation revealed shift of chiasm to right side against normal right internal carotid to produce right nasal field loss. Note site and direction of pressure lateral to chiasm.

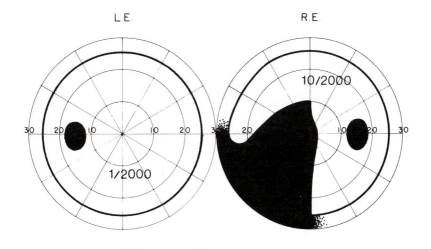

FIGURE 15-9 Inferior nasal quadrant defect produced by large aneurysm of right internal carotid artery. Visual loss was gradual. Arteriogram confirmed diagnosis of aneurysm lateral to chiasm. Artery gradually occluded, with return of visual field to normal.

10), (6) infratentorial tumors with ventricular dilation and hydrostatic compression of the chiasm (always accompanied by papilledema), (7) intraventricular tumors, especially those involving the third ventricle, and (8) meningiomas, particularly those arising from the region of the lesser wing of the sphenoid bone.

Altitudinal Hemianopsia

Altitudinal hemianopsia may occur rarely as the result of a chiasmal lesion (Figure 15-11). This visual field defect, which involves both upper or both lower quadrants with the hemianoptic border of the field on the horizontal line, has been dealt with elsewhere. Its etiology is often obscure, but it most often results from inflammatory or vascular lesions.

Homonymous Hemianopsia

Homonymous hemianopsia, which may be scotomatous or nonscotomatous, is encountered in chiasmal conditions when the lesion is in the posterior portion or angle and involves the beginning of one or both optic tracts. If the lesion compresses the inner side of the tract, it produces a temporal loss in

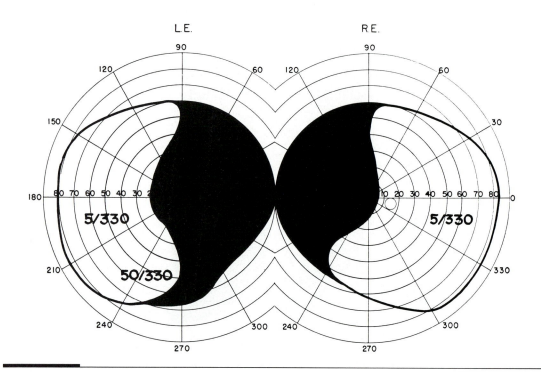

FIGURE 15-10 Binasal hemianopsia resulting from chiasmal adhesions in case of opticochiasmatic arachnoiditis.

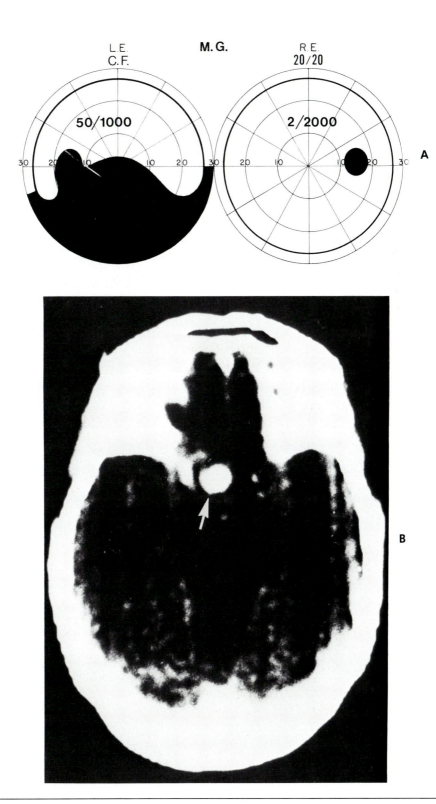

FIGURE 15-11 A, Steep-margined left inferior altitudinal hemianopsia resulting from chiasmal pressure by giant supraclinoid left internal carotid aneurysm. Patient complained of severe headache and rapid loss of vision. **B,** Computerized tomography of lesion in **A** shows giant aneurysm *(arrow)* next to clinoid and slightly to left. Findings confirmed by cerebral angiography.

the contralateral field and a nasal field loss on the side of the lesion (Figure 15-12). If the compression is from the lateral side, nasal field loss occurs first on the side of the lesion and is followed later by loss of both temporal fields so that there is a blindness on the side of the lesion, with a temporal hemianoptic defect on the contralateral field (Figure 15-13).

If medial tract pressure and the body of the chiasm are involved simultaneously, both the temporal and nasal fields will be lost on the side of the lesion. It is therefore not always possible to precisely localize the lesion medially or laterally to the tract, since either may give rise to blindness on the side of the lesion, with temporal loss in the opposite field. The radiologist can be useful in helping with precise localization.

INTERPRETING VISUAL FIELD DEFECTS ASSOCIATED WITH CHIASMAL LESIONS

The clinical importance of careful visual field study is obvious from the preceding discussion. Perimetry may be valuable because it supplements the findings of endocrinologic, neurologic, and radiographic study; or it may be the only method that reveals disease in the area of the chiasm. Having considered the general characteristics of visual field loss in chiasmal lesions, we

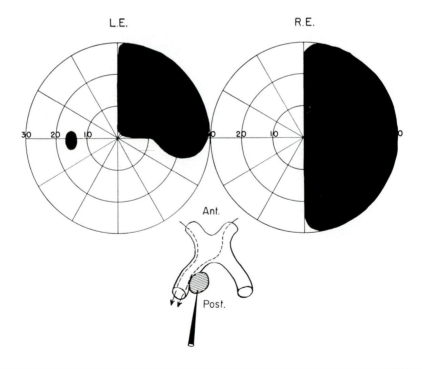

FIGURE 15-12 Homonymous hemianopsia produced by pressure medial to left optic tract in posterior chiasmal angle. Major field loss is contralateral to lesion.

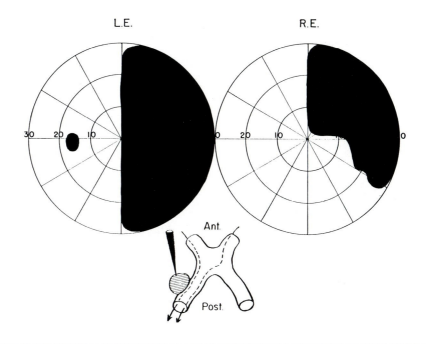

FIGURE 15-13 Homonymous hemianopsia produced by pressure lateral to left optic tract at chiasmal junction. Major field loss is on side of lesion.

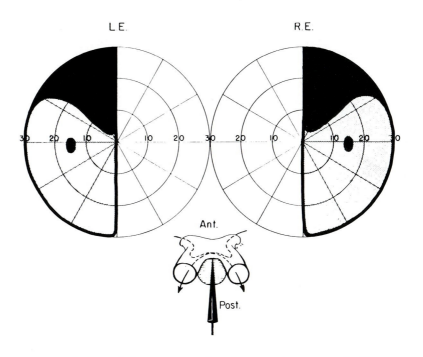

FIGURE 15-14 Bitemporal hemianopsia produced by pressure from directly beneath chiasm in midline. This is typical visual field defect associated with chromophobic adenoma of pituitary. Field defect begins in superior temporal quadrants and progresses downward.

will now concentrate on changes associated with more specific localization and pathologic processes.

For the clinician (as well as the patient!) the site of fiber interruption and the pathologic condition of the lesion producing the dysfunction are important. Because they are closely related, the localization, direction of pressure, and probable pathologic findings of certain specific lesions are discussed as a group.

Infrachiasmatic Lesions

Pituitary adenomas, which exert their pressure in the midline from below, vary in their exact sites of involvement, depending on whether the chiasm is prefixed (short optic nerves), in the middle position, or postfixed (long optic nerves). The classic visual field defect of pituitary adenoma is a symmetric bitemporal hemianopsia of either the scotomatous or the nonscotomatous variety. When the defect is scotomatous, either a rapidly growing tumor is indicated, or a prefixed chiasm with pressure on the posterior angle, or both.

Pituitary adenomas

Pituitary adenomas are the most frequent type of infrachiasmatic tumors. They tend to grow rather slowly, producing sloping-margined, bitemporal, superior quadrant, visual field defects (Figure 15-14). The patient may not

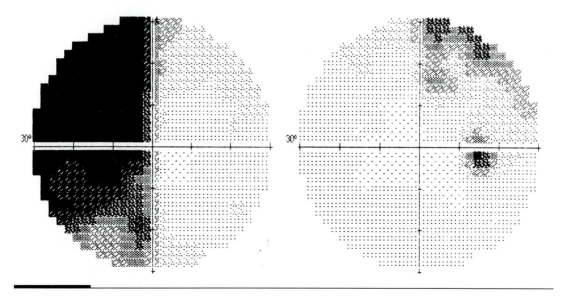

FIGURE 15-15 Incongruous bitemporal hemianoptic defect. Left eye shows nearly total loss of function in temporal hemifield, with superior loss greater than inferior loss. Right eye shows loss in superior temporal quadrant, but inferior temporal quadrant is normal. This is characteristic of damage produced by a pituitary mass compressing chiasm from below.

have visual complaints until substantial field loss has occurred. This is in part caused by the slow-growing nature of many of these lesions and thus the slow progression of the visual field loss, as well as by the fact that patients generally seem to be less aware of superior peripheral field loss than they are of inferior or certainly central visual field loss. A patient complaining of visual loss from a pituitary adenoma may give a vague history of "blurred" or "dimmed" vision; a young man with a pituitary adenoma recently consulted our clinic because he believed his "glasses needed adjusting" (Figure 15-15).

By the time patients experience visual symptoms, the pituitary adenoma is usually large. There is an average of approximately 1 cm between the inferior chiasm and the dorsum sellae. As a rule, then, one needs about 10 mm of suprasellar extension before the chiasm is encountered. Obviously, variations in anatomy and remote compromise of the chiasmal blood supply create exceptions to this rule; suffice it to say that we have been impressed (most recently by magnetic resonance imaging) with the relative paucity of symptoms in a patient with a large pituitary adenoma (Figure 15-16).

Depending on the age group involved, somewhere between half and two thirds of patients with pituitary tumors are first seen with signs of endocrine abnormality. These abnormalities are the result of the secreting or nonsecreting (hormonally active or hormonally inactive) nature of pituitary adenomas. In the past, pituitary adenomas were classified as chromophobic, acidophilic, or basophilic based on the light microscopic characteristics of the tumor's most prominent cell type. This system has given way to a series of classifications based on clinical hormonal activity, immunohistochemistry, and electron micrographic findings. Neuroradiology has supplanted perimetry as a method of confirming the presence of a pituitary adenoma. Perimetry maintains an important role, however, in assessing the level of functional disability such tumors can cause and in assessing morbidity or functional recovery associated with medical, surgical, or radiation treatment. Visual field studies are an important part of the assessment and follow-up of pregnant women and others treated with bromocriptine. Periodic visual field examination is an important addition to routine repeat neuroradiologic studies as a means of assessing tumor regrowth or recurrence after a therapeutic intervention.

Pituitary apoplexy

Under certain circumstances, such as infarction of or hemorrhage into the parenchyma, a pituitary tumor can expand rapidly. Such an event is often characterized by a rapidly developing symptom complex that includes sudden profound visual loss, headache, and double vision associated with single or multiple cranial nerve palsies. The event may or may not be associated with signs of subarachnoid hemorrhage. Such patients are often initially diagnosed as having suffered a ruptured intracranial aneurysm. Pituitary apoplexy should be considered in patients with a compatible history, that is, preexisting knowl-

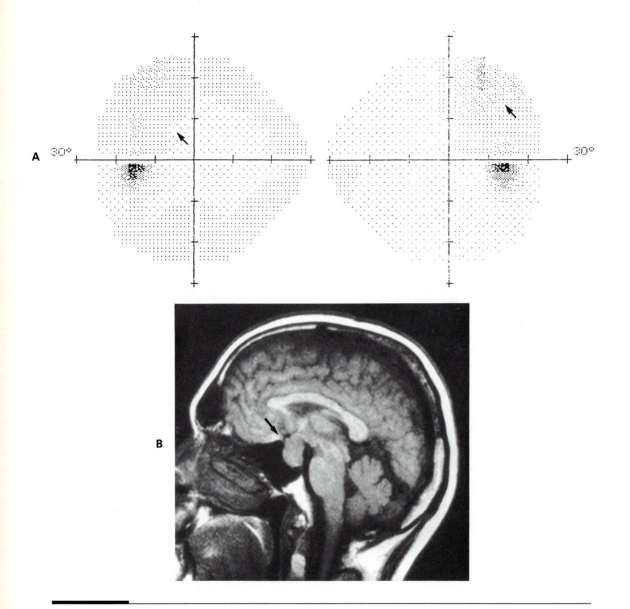

FIGURE 15-16 A, Mild symmetric superior temporal field loss *(arrows)*. This patient with 20/20 vision complained only of difficulty in reading his computer terminal at work. **B,** Magnetic resonance imaging revealed substantial pituitary lesion.

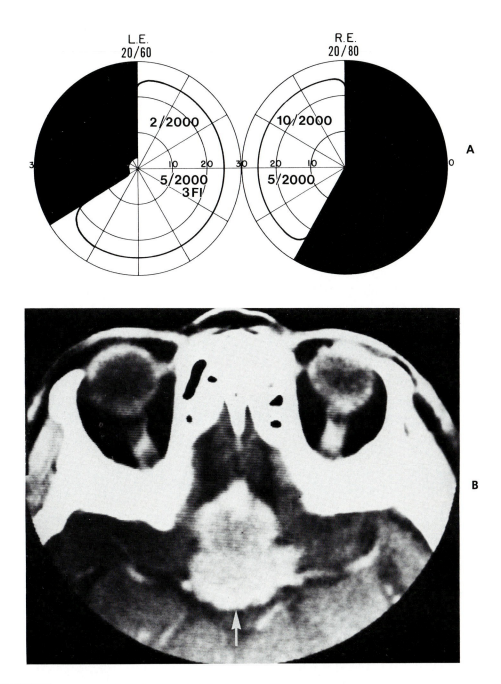

FIGURE 15-17 A, Bitemporal hemianopsia in patient with very large suprasellar meningioma. Field
defect much denser in right eye. Left field quite normal on Goldmann perimeter.
Skull roentgenograms and tomograms of sella turcica were normal. **B,** CAT scan of
patient in **A.** Enlarged and enhanced computed tomography shows enormous tumor
overlying sella *(white arrow).*

edge or signs of a pituitary tumor or radiologic evidence indicating a pituitary mass lesion or both. A particular variant of pituitary apoplexy is Sheehan's syndrome, which is characterized by multiple endocrine abnormalities associated with postpartum intraparenchymal pituitary hemorrhage.

Suprachiasmatic Lesions

A variety of lesions may attack the chiasm from above. As opposed to pituitary lesions, which progress from below upward, lesions that impinge the chiasm from above tend to cause *inferior* bitemporal quadrant defects. The pituitary is not involved, so that there are no radiologic signs of sella enlargement or suprasellar extension or any associated pituitary endocrine abnormalities (Figure 15-17).

Suprachiasmatic lesions may impinge on the chiasm from the anterior-superior direction or from the posterior-superior direction (Figures 15-18 to 15-21).

Meningiomas

The tumors most frequently affecting the anterior-superior aspect of the chiasm are the meningiomas. These can arise from the olfactory groove, the tuberculum sellae, or the lesser wing of the sphenoid bone. Somewhat less commonly, meningiomas can involve the intracranial lip of the optic foramen and give rise to unilateral optic nerve compression. Meningiomas tend to be

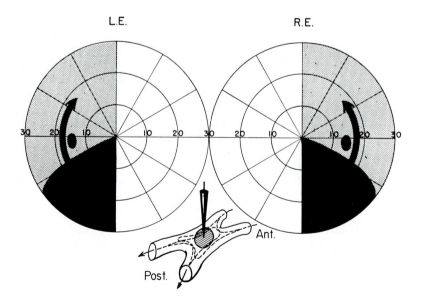

FIGURE 15-18 Pressure from above downward on center of chiasm producing bitemporal hemianopsia with initial loss in inferior temporal quadrants, later expanding upward.

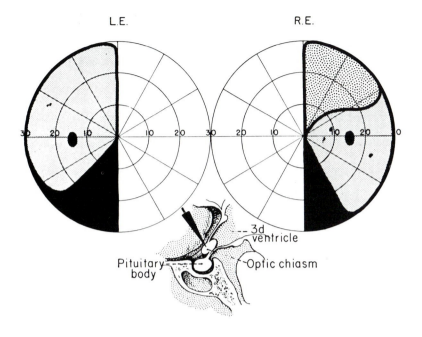

FIGURE 15-19 Inferior bitemporal hemianopsia resulting from pressure on chiasm from above and in front. Direction and site of pressure are shown in sagittal section.

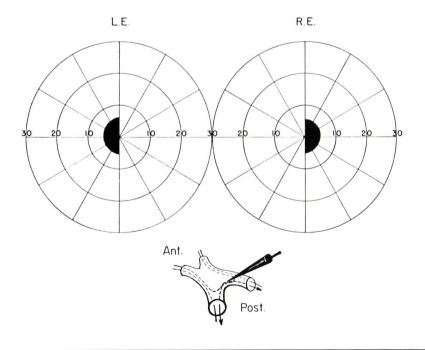

FIGURE 15-20 Bitemporal hemianoptic scotomas resulting from pressure on decussating macular fibers from posterior and above. Scotomas are rarely as symmetric as shown.

slow-growing tumors, and visual impairment is often the presenting sign (Figure 15-22). Meningiomas can cause bony calcification or hyperostosis, which helps to identify them radiologically. Clinically, other signs such as involvement of the third through sixth cranial nerves and unilateral exophthalmos can be helpful in diagnosis and localization.

Olfactory groove meningiomas are one of the causes of the classic Foster Kennedy syndrome of optic atrophy on the eye on the side of the tumor and papilledema in the contralateral eye. Meningiomas arising from the tuberculum sellae may involve the lateral aspect of the chiasm along with the posterior portion of the optic nerve, resulting in a junctional scotoma (Figure 15-23). Meningiomas arising from the lesser wing of the sphenoid bone characteristically produce irregular, asymmetric chiasmal defects. Prominent bony involvement may lead to prominent radiographic changes (Figure 15-24).

Gliomas

Gliomas are generally slow-growing tumors that involve the optic nerve, the chiasm or hypothalamus or both, and the third ventricle. The typical patient is a child under the age of 10 or 12 years. Glioma is frequently (about 25% of the time) associated with neurofibromatosis. When the tumor involves structures associated with the frontal lobe, the classic Foster Kennedy syndrome may occur.

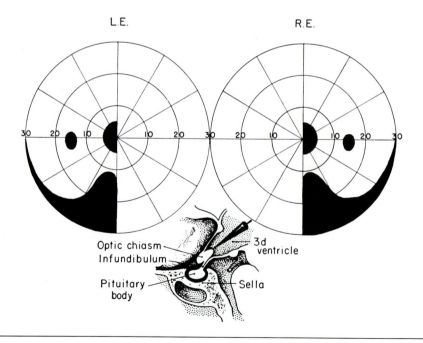

FIGURE 15-21 Inferior bitemporal quadrantanopsia and bitemporal hemianoptic scotomas resulting from pressure on chiasm from region of third ventricle. Direction of pressure from above and behind is illustrated in sagittal section.

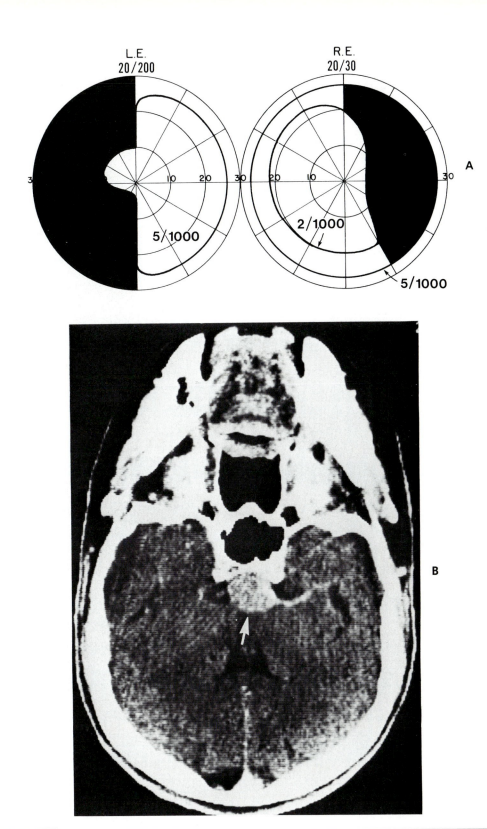

FIGURE 15-22 A, Suprasellar meningioma with bitemporal hemianopsia. Note temporal pallor of both optic discs. Patient had defective color vision. **B,** CAT scan of patient in **A.** Suprasellar mass strongly enhanced with contrast medium *(white arrow).* Marked improvement in visual field defects after tumor removal.

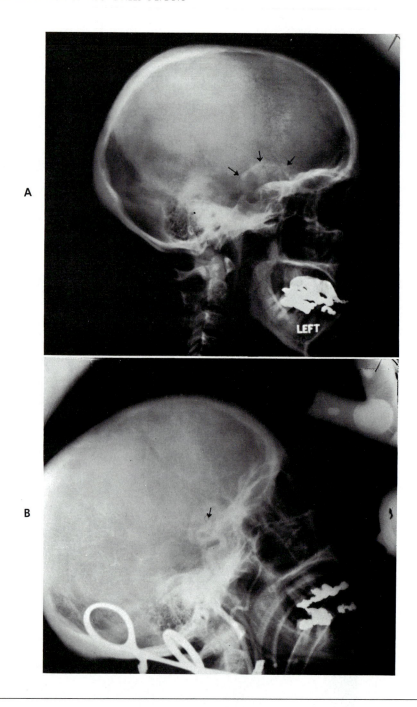

FIGURE 15-23 A, Lateral roentgenogram of skull showing calcified meningioma of tuberculum sellae. **B,** Angiogram of same tumor. Point of entrance of external carotid artery into tumor can be seen in sudden vessel arborization, resulting in blush of tumor area. (*A and B courtesy Thomas Fullenlove, M.D.*)

Mental status changes associated with frontal lobe involvement may make it difficult to examine such patients. For example, patients may be belligerent, forgetful, or euphoric. These mental status changes may be relatively subtle but may significantly affect the patient's course. We recently examined a young adult who was appropriately concerned and agreed to follow-up tests when informed of his possible diagnosis. He failed to show up at several scheduled visits with neuroradiology despite telephone follow-up and repeated urgings. On a subsequent visit to the eye clinic, he was escorted to the computed tomography (CT) suite by our staff. A CT scan revealed a frontal lobe lesion. The differential diagnosis of a pseudo–Foster Kennedy syndrome with poor compliance vs. a true Foster Kennedy syndrome with organic brain syndrome was resolved in favor of the latter entity.

Intrinsic chiasmal or optic nerve glioma can be manifested by a wide variety of visual field findings, including a classic chiasmal field cut, a junction scotoma, or a dramatically asymmetric bitemporal inferior hemianopsia (Figure 15-25). Precise quantitative visual field studies may be difficult with this entity because many of the patients are below 10 years of age. Nevertheless, with appropriate investigating techniques, substantial information can be gleaned concerning the condition of the visual fields.

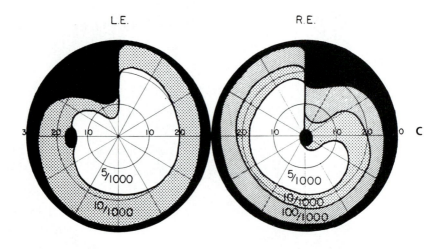

FIGURE 15-23, cont'd. C, Visual field defects produced by same tumor. It was meningioma arising from tuberculum sellae, anterior to right clinoid process. It compressed right optic nerve from below and spread through anterior chiasmal notch to compress anterior aspect of chiasm and encroach inferiorly on left optic nerve.

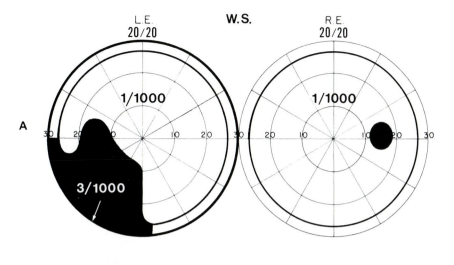

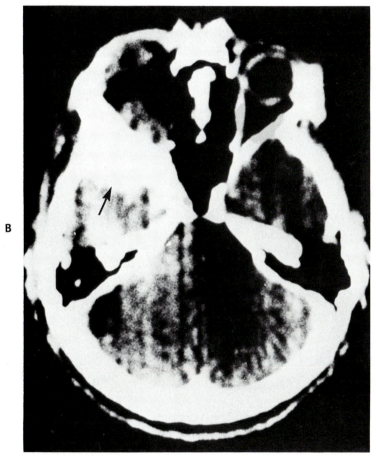

FIGURE 15-24 A, Recurrent meningioma of left orbit and middle fossa with proptosis of left eye and inferior quadrant field loss. Note sharp vertical border to field defect. **B,** CAT scan shows marked thickening and hyperostosis of lateral wing of left sphenoid bone *(arrow)*.

Aneurysms of the anterior cerebral or anterior communicating artery

Aneurysm of either the anterior cerebral or the anterior communicating artery may give rise to visual field changes that closely simulate tumors of this area. These lesions are rare. Symptoms associated with aneurysm often appear suddenly and may be caused more by extravasation of blood than by direct pressure.

Craniopharyngioma

Craniopharyngiomas are slow-growing tumors that arise from the remnants of Rathke's pouch. In their initial stages of growth, craniopharyngiomas, or Rathke's pouch tumors, are in close contact with the posterior portion of the chiasm. Visual complaints may be an early sign of their presence. They occur most often in childhood or youth and may reach considerable size, compressing the chiasm before giving evidence of their presence. They are occasionally seen in adults in the fifth and sixth decades of life.

The growth pattern of a craniopharyngioma is notoriously erratic and therefore so is its effect on the visual fields. Although a bitemporal hemi-

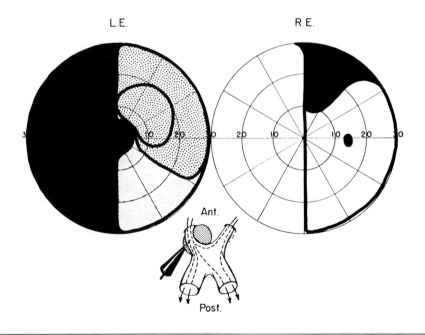

FIGURE 15-25 Pressure on chiasm from in front on left side with involvement of left optic nerve and later compression of anterior decussating loop of fibers from right optic nerve. Left eye was blind and showed advanced optic atrophy for considerable time before right field defect could be demonstrated.

anopsia, denser inferiorly, is probably the most common presenting visual field defect (Figure 15-26), wildly incongruous tract lesions are also seen.

A high percentage of patients have radiographic evidence of suprasellar calcification and, in the very young patient, a widening of the suture lines with fingerlike areas of radiolucence in the cranial vault. The sella turcica may be flattened from above with erosion of the posterior clinoids. Intrasellar craniopharyngioma produces ballooning of the sella with extension into the sphenoidal sinus. Computerized axial tomography has been quite useful in determining the size and the precise location of such tumors, although some tumors may be missed by this modality because the radiodensity of the craniopharyngioma is similar to that of normal brain.

Increased intracranial pressure and papilledema are common in children but rare in adults. Secondary optic atrophy often ensues, with generalized depression of the visual field, sometimes complicating the interpretation of visual field defects. Rupture of a Rathke's pouch cyst may give rise to meningeal irritations simulating bacterial meningitis.

Clinical findings in patients with a craniopharyngioma include headache, visual disturbances, and endocrine abnormalities. Some patients, especially in the adult population, exhibit mental status changes.

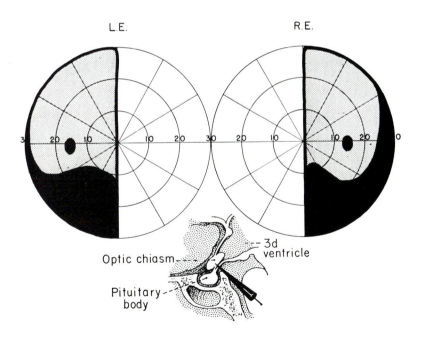

FIGURE 15-26 Inferior bitemporal hemianopsia from pressure on chiasm from behind in case of craniopharyngioma. Visual field defects in this tumor are rarely as regular as shown here. Site and direction of pressure are demonstrated in sagittal section.

Perichiasmatic Lesions

Perichiasmatic lesions are largely inflammatory and usually attack the chiasm from the anterior-inferior direction.

The chiasm is covered inferiorly by the pia mater. The subarachnoid space below and anteriorly is expanded into the cisterna chiasmatica. This area may be involved in infectious processes such as luetic basilar meningitis or inflammatory processes associated with traumatic basal meningitis. Any of these syndromes may lead to chronic arachnoiditis and the so-called optico-chiasmatic arachnoiditis.

The role played by arachnoidal adhesions around the chiasm is controversial. Numerous case reports attest to the presence of bitemporal or other visual field defects, which regress after removal of these opticochiasmatic arachnoidal adhesions. Patients have been operated on for suspected pituitary adenoma, and the arachnoidal adhesions were an incidental finding in an otherwise normal chiasmal area. This diagnosis is relatively rare currently because modern neuroradiologic techniques have reduced the number of surgical explorations of patients with normal-appearing chiasmal regions.

The visual field changes in this condition are extremely variable as would be expected, since the lesion may attack only a small part of the chiasm or

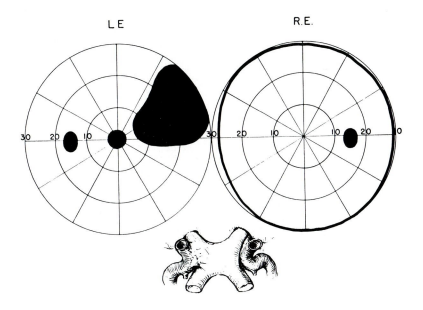

FIGURE 15-27 Nasal hemianoptic scotoma in 11-year-old girl resulting from adhesions between left optic nerve and left internal carotid artery in opticochiasmatic arachnoiditis exposed through left frontal osteoplastic flap. Location of major area of adhesions is shown in anatomic sketch. There was some return of vision and restoration of visual field following operation.

may envelop the entire region. The following field changes have been reported: (1) bitemporal and homonymous hemianopsia, (2) central scotoma and hemianoptic scotomas, (3) concentric contraction of the peripheral field, and (4) binasal hemianopsia.

The postoperative improvement in visual field defects after separation of the adhesions from the chiasm is the best argument for the role of these adhesions in the production of these defects (Figure 15-27).

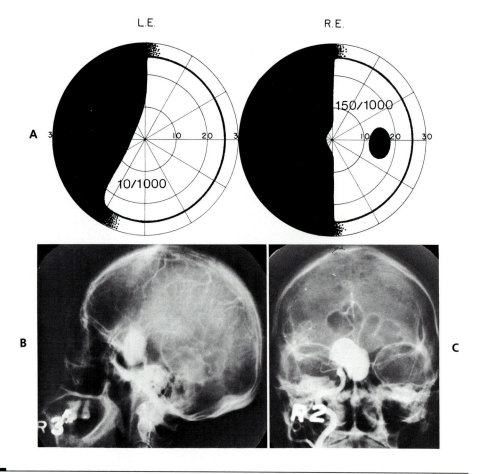

FIGURE 15-28 A, Homonymous hemianopsia resulting from large aneurysm of right internal carotid artery. Dense nasal field defect with optic atrophy of right eye indicated lateral pressure on chiasm and nerve and suggested diagnosis of aneurysm. Left field defect cleared after ligation of aneurysm. **B,** Arteriogram, lateral view, showing big lobulated aneurysm that produced field defect in **A. C,** Arteriogram, anterior-posterior view, of same aneurysm. It was at takeoff of ophthalmic artery from right internal carotid artery and extended toward midline to completely fill sella turcica and produce field defect seen in **A.**

Vascular Lesions

The intimate relationship between the chiasm and the basilar arteries of the brain in the circle of Willis makes these structures important potential causes of pressure on the chiasm and its blood supply.

Aneurysms may arise at almost any point in the circle and give rise to chiasmal compression simulating that produced by tumors. The variability of the visual field defects is in itself an important diagnostic sign of aneurysm. Visual field defects that suggest aneurysm include (1) a nasal defect with a scotoma on the side of the lesion and a temporal defect in the contralateral field, (2) inferior bitemporal quadrantanopsia, (3) a unilateral nasal hemianoptic defect, and (4) homonymous hemianopsia (Figure 15-28).

Combinations of bilateral visual field defects that do not conform to the usual patterns explained by the fiber architecture of the chiasm suggest an aneurysm. The most frequent aneurysm encountered in this area is an aneurysm of the internal carotid artery. Visual field changes resulting from pressure of these aneurysms on the chiasm are typically scotomatous, with early and severe visual loss on the side of the lesion and temporal field loss in the opposite eye (Figure 15-29).

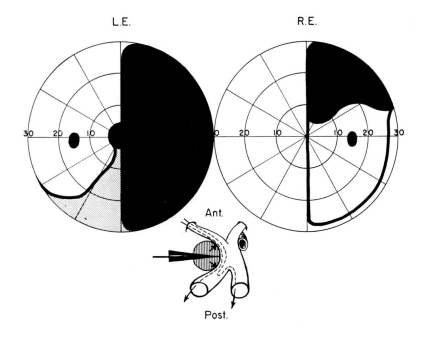

FIGURE 15-29 Aneurysm of left internal carotid artery with pressure on left optic nerve and chiasm, accompanied by left nasal and central field loss. Upper temporal field loss on right is from involvement of anterior decussating fibers from right optic nerve, as they loop into left optic nerve before passing backward through chiasm and into optic tract.

In practical terms, an aneurysm or another vascular lesion producing findings typical of chiasmal field loss as its only clinical manifestation is uncommon. The diagnosis is made after a neuroradiologic workup for a neoplasm or other mass lesion is negative. Cerebral angiography is an invasive procedure with significant morbidity, and in cases where there are no other signs of an aneurysm, subjecting the patient to this test is not a trivial decision. More commonly, an aneurysm is diagnosed via arteriography following a more classic symptom complex, such as a painful third nerve palsy or a violent headache and loss of consciousness. An astonishing number of aneurysms show up as incidental findings at autopsy or as silent lesions on radiographic studies ordered for other reasons.

Trauma

Direct trauma to the chiasm is rare. Surgical splitting of the chiasm was reported by Cushing, and we have seen one such case, in which total bitemporal hemianopsia resulted.

Indirect chiasmal trauma is less rare. Numerous cases have been reported. The responsible injury is usually direct, severe, frontal head trauma. Such severe trauma is usually associated with other signs of serious neurologic damage. We have seen these visual field defects in patients who have survived head-on automobile accidents or, in two cases, in patients who were thrown from moving vehicles and struck their heads on concrete (Figures 15-30 and 15-31).

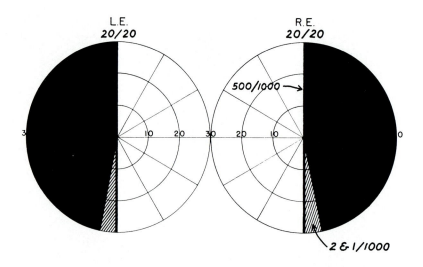

FIGURE 15-30 Traumatic bitemporal hemianopsia resulting from severe frontal head injury (automobile collision) with rupture of chiasm or injury to its blood supply. Defects are total to all test objects except for narrow inferior wedge detected only with small stimuli. Note that vision is 20/20 despite macular splitting.

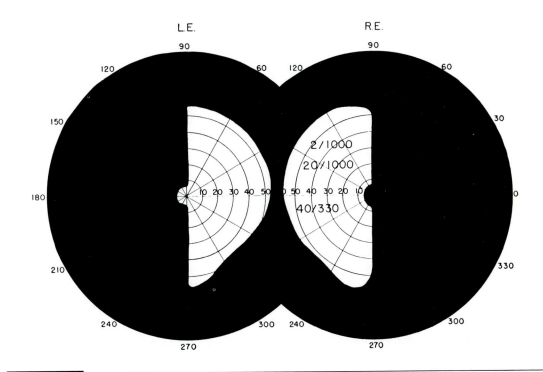

FIGURE 15-31 Traumatic rupture of chiasm with total bitemporal hemianopsia resulting from blow to frontal region of skull in automobile accident. There was skull fracture in frontal area and contrecoup fracture of base of skull.

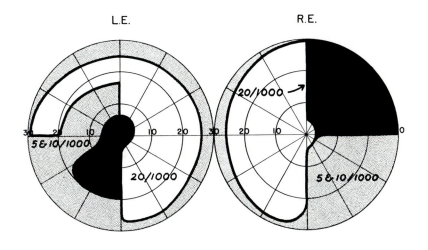

FIGURE 15-32 Bitemporal hemianopsia from multiple sclerosis with chiasmal involvement. There was history of transient visual loss and extraocular muscle palsies at age 27 years. Later, pyramidal tract signs, speech impairment, emotional instability, characteristic reflex changes, and visual field defects developed.

Interestingly, there may be some variation in the course of visual field loss in patients with traumatic chiasmal involvement. In the routine case, if the patient is tested as soon as recovery permits, a steep-walled bitemporal field defect is found. The defect is partial or complete, depending on the extent of damage. In other cases, the initial visual field will appear somewhat worse than later tests because of the effects of pressure associated with the acute injury. Finally, in rare cases, the defect will intensify over time, presumably as a result of scarring and adhesions that develop in the chiasmal region, as discussed previously.

Chiasmal Neuritis

Extension of retrobulbar neuritis from the optic nerve into the chiasm is quite rare, but several cases have been seen.

A central scotoma that starts on one side and subsequently involves the second field as a temporal hemianoptic scotoma should suggest this lesion. One might also consider chiasmal neuritis in a sudden bitemporal hemianoptic scotoma without other signs in a young person (Figure 15-32). Careful longitudinal follow-up in such patients may eventually reveal the classic signs and symptoms of multiple sclerosis.

In instances of multiple sclerosis involving the chiasm, the prognosis for return of vision may be good, just as in the case of retrobulbar neuritis from the same cause.

16 POSTCHIASMAL VISUAL PATHWAY

The visual pathway is divided into a prechiasmal and postchiasmal portion on clinical grounds. The following is a classification of visual field defects produced by a single lesion in the visual pathway:

1. A prechiasmal lesion gives rise to a monocular visual field defect.
2. A chiasmal lesion gives rise to a bitemporal visual field defect.
3. A postchiasmal lesion produces a homonymous hemianopsia.

Anatomically the postchiasmal visual pathway is made up of four parts: (1) the optic tracts, (2) the lateral geniculate nucleus, (3) the optic radiations, and (4) the striate cortex of the occipital lobe.

The first portion of the postchiasmal visual pathway, the optic tract, is simply a continuation of the third neuron. Although its fibers have decussated and represent the corresponding halves of the two retinas, the postchiasmal pathway is indistinguishable from nerve fiber bundles of the chiasm and optic nerve, except in the architectural arrangement of the fibers. Injury to a fiber within the optic tract will lead to degeneration of that fiber from the point of injury forward through the chiasm and optic nerve to the ganglion cell layer of the retina.

The lateral geniculate body is a true ganglion, and as such represents the end station of the third neuron. Anatomically, then, the optic tract and the lateral geniculate body should be included in the discussion of the chiasm and optic nerves.

The optic radiation and its end station, the striate cortex of the occipital lobe, represent the fourth-order neuron and should be considered separately from the optic tracts and the lateral geniculate. That they are not is for practical reasons, because lesions affecting all four postchiasmal areas produce the same type of visual field loss: homonymous hemianopsia.

Homonymous hemianopsia is bilateral and consists of visual loss in the two right or two left halves of the visual fields. Thus a temporal portion of the field of one eye is destroyed simultaneously with a nasal portion of the field of the other eye. As is the case with bitemporal field loss associated with chiasmal lesions, homonymous hemianopsias exhibit extreme morphologic variation. This variation may be diagnostically useful in localizing the lesion and also in indicating its pathologic process.

Of course the central localizing feature of homonymous hemianopsia derives from the anatomic fact that the visual fibers from each optic nerve undergo partial decussation in the chiasm. Because of this, fibers in the right postchiasmal pathway carry visual information from the left half of each visual field, and fibers in the left postchiasmal visual pathway carry visual information from the right half of each visual field. The optic tract represents the region where the visual information from half the field of vision in each eye first comes together. On clinical if not anatomic grounds, the fibers from corresponding areas of the two fields seem to be widely separated in this region. Thus optic tract lesions lead to dramatically incongruous homonymous hemianopsias. As one proceeds more posteriorly through the visual pathway, congruity tends to increase until one reaches the occipital cortex, where nearly precise congruity is the rule. In general, anterior lesions in the postchiasmal pathway produce less congruous lesions than do posterior lesions.

In each pathway, right and left, there is a group of fibers from the extreme nasal portion of the contralateral retina that have no counterpart in the opposite pathway. These fiber bundles are responsible for the temporal crescent in the visual field and give rise to a form of incongruous homonymous hemianopsia when they are spared by a given lesion.

By careful investigation, analysis, and interpretation of these variations it is possible not only to place the lesion on the right or left side, but also, within limits, to estimate the anteroposterior position of the lesion. The results of careful quantitative perimetry, when combined with the patient's history and physical findings, afford the practitioner an excellent opportunity to localize intracranial lesions accurately. At the very least this is important to help ensure proper neuroradiologic evaluation. These findings may be particularly important in areas where the full range of ancillary tests is not readily available or when the progress of a diagnosed lesion is being monitored over time.

The postchiasmal visual pathway comprises approximately two thirds of the entire visual system. All of it is intracranial. It passes in intimate juxtaposition to numerous vital centers in the brain, and its vascular supply in many places is the same as that which supplies other sensory and motor areas of the brain. Because of the long and complicated course of the visual pathways, a vast number of intracranial events have a measurable effect on the visual system. This is an extremely important point in localizing lesions precisely. Certain characteristics of a given binocular field defect may indicate whether it is the result of a lesion in the anterior or posterior portion of the postchiasmal pathway, but a more important and exact localizing sign would be some other neurologic disturbance that, in conjunction with the field defect, pinpoints the site of the lesion. A classic example of this is the association of homonymous hemianopsia with hemiplegia in lesions affecting the posterior limb of the internal capsule. Furthermore, precise localization often makes possible a more exact etiologic diagnosis.

In addition to neurologic, radiologic, and laboratory evidence, certain ocular signs and symptoms other than visual field defects are valuable in localizing intracranial lesions. These include the following:

1. Symptoms of visual loss noted by the patient usually indicate some degree of macular splitting, which in turn is more indicative of an anterior than a posterior lesion. It must be remembered, however, that 20/20 Snellen acuity is possible even when only half the macula is functioning.

2. Diplopia, with bilateral sixth nerve involvement, may indicate only an increase in intracranial pressure and may be of little localizing value. When the third or fourth nerves are involved, the possible sites of interference are decreased considerably.

3. Monocular diplopia with homonymous hemianopsia indicates a lesion in the calcarine cortex.

4. Lightning streaks, colored lights, and other abstract visual hallucinations are usually evidence of visual cortex irritation. Most patients describe these light flashes as though they were in one eye only and are unaware of their hemianoptic character. The flashes are thus often confused with similar scintillations that occur monocularly with vitreous traction.

5. Formed visual hallucinations, such as people, familiar faces, landscapes, and animals, occur with lesions of the temporal and parietal areas.

6. Homonymous hemianopsias without other signs or symptoms usually indicate a temporal or occipital lobe lesion. Complete unawareness of the defect usually indicates a lesion of the parietal lobe, especially when the hemianopsia is elicited only with double simultaneous stimulation.

7. Papilledema with homonymous hemianopsia points to a space-occupying lesion of the suprageniculate pathway.

8. Optic atrophy with homonymous hemianopsia implies a lesion in the geniculate body or optic tract.

9. Hemianoptic pupillary reactions are theoretically valuable because the optic tracts carry pupillomotor fibers, whereas the optic radiations do not. Practically, however, the test is so difficult to perform that its result can be quite unreliable and it is rarely used clinically.

10. Optokinetic nystagmus is a basic ocular reflex in which the eye sequentially fixates on a series of targets moved before it. In some homonymous hemianopsias, targets brought into the visual field disturb the optokinetic reflexes.

An abnormal optokinetic response helps differentiate homonymous hemianopsia of a tract or temporal lobe lesion from one produced by a parietal lobe lesion.

When the patient views a series of moving stripes on a rotating drum, the resultant nystagmus is normally symmetric in the two sides. It is also symmetric in optic tract lesions, anterior optic radiations in the temporal lobe, and some occipital lobe lesions. With parietal lobe involvement, however, the optokinetic response is characteristically asymmetric to the two sides. There is a diminished or absent response, with rotation of the drum toward the side of the lesion, whereas rotation of the stripes toward the opposite side elicits a normal nystagmic response.

11. Aphasia, agnosia, astereognosis, and other evidence of temporal and parietal lobe involvement in the dominant hemisphere indicate disturbance of the anterior optic radiation.

When examining an aphasic patient with manual perimetric techniques, it is important to remember that the patient's responses may be slowed because of the aphasia itself. Accurate results may be obtained, however, if the patient can respond using sign language.

Examination methods in patients with homonymous hemianopsia are essentially the same as field examinations in patients with other diseases. Careful quantitative perimetry gives the best and most useful information. This is fairly easy to do if the patient is examined with the tangent screen or on the Goldmann perimeter. One simply starts with relatively large bright test objects, outlines the basic field defect, and then looks with smaller and smaller test objects for increasing detail.

With quantitative static perimetry the approach may need some modification. Testing a patient with a homonymous defect using a full-thresholding

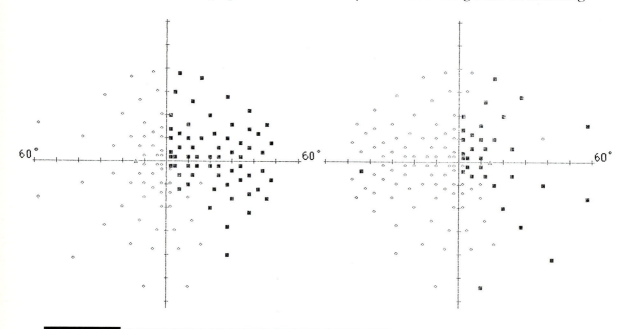

FIGURE 16-1 Threshold-related screening field from patient with pituitary mass lesion. Dark squares indicate points missed. Open circles indicate points seen. This test shows homonymous field defect with more loss in upper field than lower and more in left eye than right.

program with tight spacing of test points can be tedious, frustrating, and wasteful, and we do not use such an examination for the initial field test in a patient we suspect of having intracranial disease. Rather, we first evaluate the patient with manual techniques to get some idea of the lesion size and density. Manual techniques are useful in allowing the examiner to concentrate on the diagnostically important horizontal and vertical meridians. Valuable information can be obtained quickly. Once the presence of a defect has been established, and particularly when the defect seems less than "absolute," a follow-up examination with quantitative techniques will help determine such facts as whether the margins are sloping or steep, whether there are islands of preserved vision, or whether the apparently uniform defect is denser in one or another portion. This quantitative follow-up can be accomplished either by careful manual techniques or by computerized static threshold perimetry. We routinely perform quantitative computerized perimetry on patients with postchiasmal lesions who can tolerate the examination, but only after or in conjunction with manual perimetry.

If for some reason a "technologic inversion" has taken place and proper equipment and facilities for performing careful manual perimetry (other than confrontation perimetry) are not available, then we would use a full-field threshold-related screening program on the computerized perimeter as our first semiquantitative examination. Most computerized perimeters have a screening program that allows examination of the visual field with 100 to 200 test points. An examination such as this can usually be performed in 4 to 7 minutes per eye, depending on the patient and the level of disease. Information obtained from such a test can help direct further workup (Figure 16-1).

Because of the location and nature of lesions that produce defects in the postchiasmal visual pathway, a fair number of these patients may be bedridden, and therefore cannot be examined with the tangent screen or a perimeter. We have found it particularly useful to employ the double simultaneous presentation method of confrontation field analysis in these patients. We have examined these patients when Goldmann perimetry performed elsewhere showed full fields bilaterally, but the patient had radiographic and other evidence of a very large intracranial lesion. On several occasions examining the patient with confrontation methods using double simultaneous presentation has easily demonstrated a homonymous hemianopsia.

TYPES OF HOMONYMOUS HEMIANOPSIA

Homonymous hemianopsia may be partial or complete, relative or absolute; it may have steep or sloping margins; and its intensity may be uniform or variable. These variations depend in part on the anatomic location of the corresponding lesion and therefore are diagnostically valuable.

The basic types of homonymous hemianopsia follow:

1. Sector defects that are homonymous but less than a full quadrant
2. Homonymous quadrantanopsia
3. Partial homonymous defects that are more than a quadrant and less than total hemianopsia
4. Total homonymous hemianopsia
5. Congruous sector or partial homonymous hemianopsia
6. Incongruous sector or partial homonymous hemianopsia
7. Homonymous hemianopsia with macular sparing
8. Homonymous hemianopsia with macular splitting
9. Unilateral homonymous hemianopsia with temporal crescent involvement
10. Homonymous hemianopsia with temporal crescent sparing
11. Homonymous hemianoptic scotomas
12. Double homonymous hemianopsia

Sector Defects

Sector defects encompassing less than a quadrant are relatively rare. They occur in one field of a markedly incongruous homonymous hemianopsia, the other field of which shows a quadrant or greater than quadrant loss. They are usually depression-type defects with sloping margins, most often detected in the central areas of the field. These defects may require careful quantitative techniques.

When perimetry reveals an apparent unilateral hemianoptic field defect involving a quadrant or slightly more than a quadrant loss in one eye only and a normal field in the other eye, a careful search of the central area of the normal field with very dim stimuli may reveal a faint sector defect. This is in reality a grossly incongruous homonymous hemianopsia and indicates a lesion in the anterior portion of the postchiasmal pathway in the optic tract, geniculate body, or anterior part of the optic radiation.

Homonymous Quadrantanopsia

Homonymous quadrantanopsia is closely related to the sector defects just described. Again, one has a visual field depression with sloping margins, mainly in the central field. By definition a homonymous quadrantanopsia represents bilateral quadrantic field loss, and as such these defects are relatively congruous or symmetric (Figure 16-2). Stated differently, if the defect involves much less than a full quadrant, it is often termed a sector defect; if it involves much more than a full quadrant, it is called a partial hemianoptic

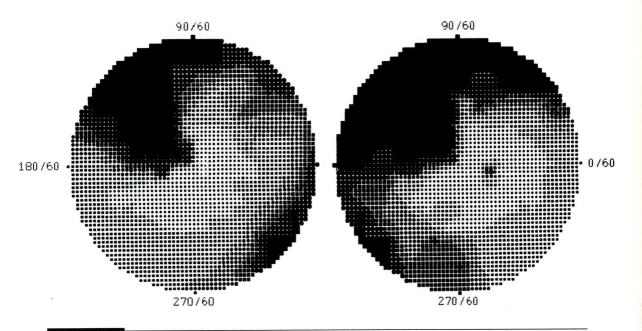

FIGURE 16-2 Moderately incongruous left superior quadrantanopsia.

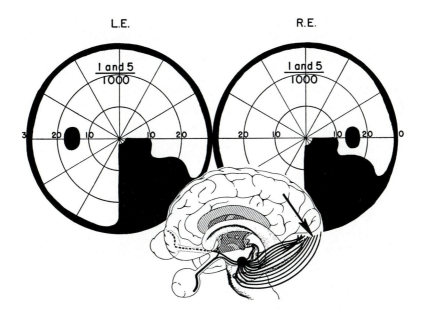

FIGURE 16-3 Completely congruous but irregular right inferior homonymous quadrantanopsia. Note that congruity extends even to irregularities of horizontal margin. This arose from vascular lesion of upper lip of left calcarine fissure. Site of calcarine cortical damage is illustrated in anatomic sketch.

defect. Homonymous quadrantanopsia may occur in lesions of the anterior radiation because of the wide separation of the upper and lower quadrant fibers. When the upper quadrants are involved, the lesion is usually in the lower part of the temporal lobe.

When the quadrantanopsia is sharp margined, dense, and congruous, the lesion is usually in the striate cortex of the occipital lobe (Figure 16-3). An upper quadrant defect implies a lesion of the lower lip of the calcarine fissure and vice versa. Macular sparing is the rule in this type of quadrantanopsia, and, when the lesion is far forward in the fissure, macular sparing may be quite wide.

In homonymous quadrantanopsia from lesions of the optic radiation, the horizontal margin is usually fairly straight. Cortical lesions may produce a more irregular horizontal margin that is completely symmetric in the two fields. This is particularly true in traumatic and vascular lesions.

Superior homonymous quadrantanopsia is more common in lesions of the radiations because of more frequent involvement of the temporal loop, whereas lower homonymous quadrantanopsia is the rule in occipital lesions, especially traumatic, since the upper calcarine area is more exposed to injury. Superior homonymous quadrantanopsia was referred to by Cushing more

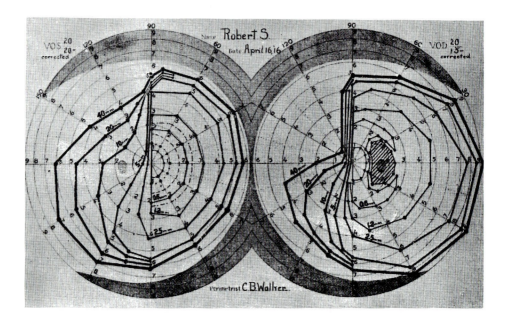

FIGURE 16-4   Demonstration of incongruous homonymous hemianopsia in case of gliomatous cyst of right temporal lobe. Note that greatest degree of asymmetry is shown in isopters for largest stimuli and that larger defect is on side of lesion. Case is Cushing's with precise quantitative perimetry performed by C.B. Walker in 1916. *(From Cushing H: Brain 44:341, 1922.)*

than 60 years ago in his discussion of tumors involving the temporal loop of Meyer (Figure 16-4).

Partial Homonymous Hemianopsia

In partial homonymous hemianopsia, as is the case with quadrantanopsia and a sector defect, we are dealing with an incomplete homonymous hemianoptic defect that may be either congruous or incongruous (Figure 16-5).

Asymmetric defects are frequently the result of compression of the nerve fiber pathway or of its vascular supply in the optic tract or radiation. They have sloping, straight, or slightly curved margins and may involve a quadrant or slightly more than a quadrant area of one field and a complete loss of the homonymous area in the the other field.

A screening field or a test with a single dim stimulus may indicate a total homonymous hemianopsia. However, quantitative testing or multiple isopter examination may reveal that the field loss does not have a uniform density.

When the two fields show symmetric but incomplete hemianoptic defects, the occipital cortex is the likely site of the lesion. Again, as in quadrantanopsias, a high degree of symmetry and wide macular sparing help confirm the diagnosis. Except for the mode of onset, the occipital type of incomplete hemianopsia is the same whether produced by tumor, injury, or a vascular lesion.

Partial homonymous hemianopsia can also take the form of a sloping-margined depression. This kind of incomplete homonymous hemianopsia most often results from an active lesion compressing the geniculocalcarine pathway fibers; a tumor is the most likely cause.

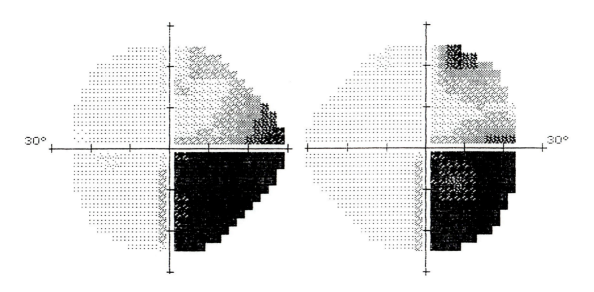

FIGURE 16-5 Slightly incongruous right partial homonymous hemianopsia in 42-year-old man after resection of left parietal lobe lesion.

Total Homonymous Hemianopsia

Absolute loss of visual sensitivity in the complete homonymous halves of both visual fields is due either to an extensive lesion in that portion of the postchiasmal pathway where the fibers are widely dispersed or to a destructive smaller lesion in those areas where the fibers are concentrated in a narrow bundle (Figure 16-6). Such a field defect might occur, for example, as a result of a widespread infiltrative or compressive lesion in the temporal or parietal lobe or from a relatively small hemorrhage in the knee of the internal capsule.

Optic tract or geniculate body involvement may produce such a field loss, with complete interruption of fibers, as may be associated with an intrinsic tumor, multiple sclerosis, or trauma. Lateral or medial tract pressure from a tumor in the posterior chiasmal angle rarely gives rise to total homonymous hemianopsia.

With total loss of homonymous half-fields no congruity or incongruity can be demonstrated. Thus the visual fields alone have no localizing value other than to indicate interruption of the right or left postchiasmal visual pathway.

Congruous Sector or Partial Homonymous Hemianopsia

When the visual field defects in each eye are completely symmetric in every respect, so that they appear to be carbon copies of one another, they are said to be congruous.

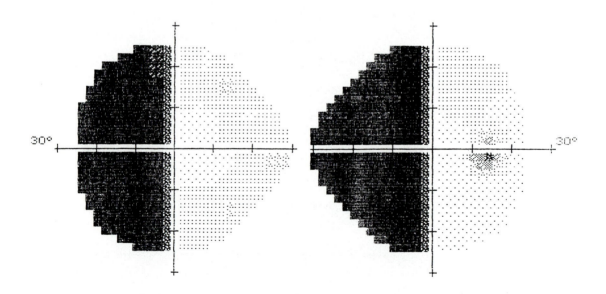

FIGURE 16-6   Left total homonymous hemianopsia in patient with left-sided paresis and right-sided cerebral atrophy after infantile illness.

To fulfill the strict diagnosis the field should be examined in each eye separately and then binocularly, and the hemianoptic border between seeing and nonseeing areas should be exactly the same for all three examinations.

Allowance must be made for the fact that the temporal field is larger than the nasal field because of the temporal crescent. It also must be remembered that one visual field will have a blind spot in its seeing area and the other will not. In the case of a quadrantanopsia, this blind spot may give rise to an apparent indentation of the horizontal margin of one visual field that is not present in the other (Figure 16-7).

Congruence is measured primarily in the oblique and near vertical meridians and is seen most clearly centrally. Particularly with sloping-margined lesions, the border between seeing and nonseeing areas for a given stimulus may be difficult for the patient to determine repeatedly. Other factors, such as mild fixation shifts, may make it difficult to record precise congruity in visual field loss.

Congruous homonymous hemianopsia is best and most frequently seen in lesions of the striate cortex and the occipital lobe. The classic example of this type of field loss occurs with injury to the posterior-superior lip of one calcarine fissure, resulting in irregularly shaped but completely symmetric inferior homonymous quadrantanoptic scotomas.

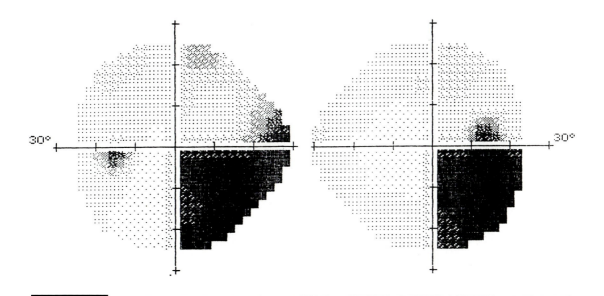

FIGURE 16-7 This right inferior quadrantanopsia is congruous except for presence of normal blind spot. Test program used for examination does not test temporal periphery past 24 degrees of eccentricity; thus peripheral nasal defect in left field has no apparent analogue in right field.

Incongruous Sector or Partial Homonymous Hemianopsia

An incongruous, or asymmetric, homonymous hemianopsia is the opposite of the congruous defect just described. The hemianopsia must be incomplete in order to detect the presence of asymmetry. Commonly this type of visual field defect involves a quadrant or sector loss in one field and a complete half-field loss in the other eye.

True incongruity, especially when it is marked enough to preclude stimulus response variation or unsteady fixation as its cause, indicates a lesion in the anterior portion of the postchiasmal pathway. The same type and degree of incongruity may be found in optic tract lesions or in anterior optic radiation lesions occurring in the temporal lobe.

Homonymous Hemianopsia with Macular Sparing

Numerous attempts have been made to explain the phenomenon of macular sparing that occurs in most cases of homonymous hemianopsia. These have been discussed previously.

Whatever the explanation, it is a clinical fact that most homonymous hemianopsias, regardless of their morphology, show some preservation of central vision. This is usually represented as a deviation of the vertical hemianoptic border a few degrees around the fixation point. True macular sparing may show enormous variation, with the area extending from a fraction of a degree to many degrees into the blind field. The areas of sparing may be congruous or incongruous; they may be perfect hemispheres or irregularly shaped.

In general, the more anterior the lesion in the postchiasmal pathway, the smaller the area of macular sparing. Although it is possible for a lesion of the posterior chiasmal angle to produce a homonymous hemianopsia with 5 degrees of macular sparing, a more common finding is a 2-degree area of macular sparing or less. Conversely, lesions of the striate cortex most commonly give rise to relatively large areas of macular sparing, often measuring 5 degrees or more. A tumor near the anterior end of the calcarine fissure may produce a homonymous hemianopsia involving only the peripheral field, and the central field is spared out to 30 degrees or more from fixation. On the other hand, a minute injury or vascular lesion at the tip of the occipital lobe may cause a tiny hemianoptic scotoma with macular splitting or an extremely small area of sparing.

Homonymous Hemianopsia with Macular Splitting

True macular splitting is probably rather rare in lesions of the postchiasmal pathway. It is certainly uncommon in lesions of the striate cortex, where, as noted previously, wide macular sparing is the rule.

Visual acuity as tested with Snellen letters is often not affected by hemi-anoptic field defects, even in those patients with macular splitting.

Unilateral Homonymous Hemianopsia with Temporal Crescent Involvement

Interference with the unpaired peripheral nasal fibers is the only explanation for a truly unilateral field defect resulting from a lesion of the postchiasmal visual pathway. The temporal field is larger than its homonymous nasal field because of the presence of these unpaired nasal fibers. In the normal field this pattern accounts for a spurious type of incongruity. It is reflected by the fact that the temporal field extends out to about 90 degrees, whereas the nasal field has its border between 60 and 70 degrees from fixation.

A unilateral temporal crescent scotoma in the visual field may indicate early disease of the posterior optic radiation or the anterior striate cortex (Figure 16-8). Such defects are rarely plotted.

Homonymous Hemianopsia with Temporal Crescent Sparing

Homonymous hemianopsia with temporal crescent sparing is a much more common visual field defect in which the temporal crescent plays a diagnostic

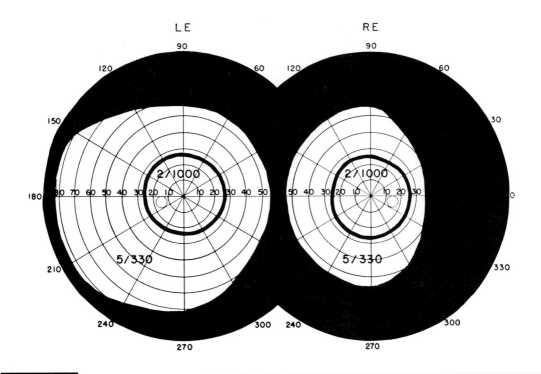

FIGURE 16-8 Apparent unilateral hemianopsia due to involvement of right temporal crescent.

role. It results from occipital lobe involvement and may be a valuable localizing sign. The entire crescent may be spared or only its upper or lower portion. The resulting field may thus give the appearance of complete hemianopsia in the ipsilateral nasal field, with a large homonymous hemianoptic scotoma in the contralateral temporal field (Figure 16-9).

Benton, Levy, and Swash have reported four patients with hemianopsias due to occipital infarction, well documented with visual field studies on the Goldmann perimeter and computerized tomography (CT) scans, in whom useful residual vision was retained in the unpaired temporal crescent. Moving stimuli were particularly well perceived in this part of the field. In each case preservation of the temporal crescent resulted in strikingly incongruous fields. These authors discuss the significance of a defect in this part of the visual field in relation to perception of movement, the fixation reflex, reports of residual vision in patients with lesions of the striate cortex, and the role of the monocular temporal field in striate and visual systems.

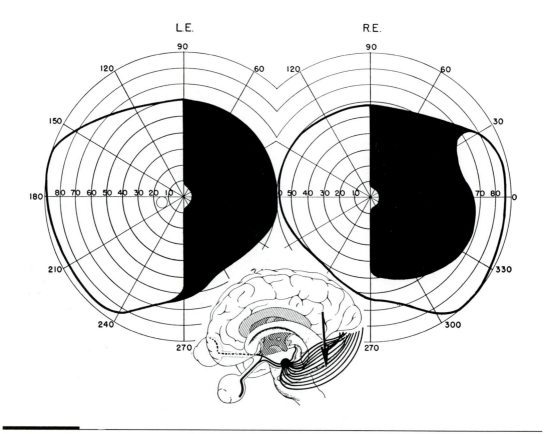

FIGURE 16-9   Right homonymous hemianopsia with preservation of temporal crescent from cerebrovascular accident. Location of lesion in central portion of left parietal lobe is shown in sketch.

Homonymous Hemianoptic Scotomas

Homonymous hemianoptic scotomas generally are considered to be extremely rare. We have seen several such fields, however. They are usually caused by a vascular or traumatic lesion. Commonly these lesions produce completely congruous paracentral homonymous hemianoptic scotomas. They are irregular in outline, steep-margined, and dense. None of those we have seen resulted from compression of the visual pathway by tumor, and all were static and permanent. These characteristics implicate the occipital cortex as the site of the lesion, and in traumatic cases this was easily verified (Figure 16-10).

Vascular lesions are probably caused by occlusion of small arterial twigs supplying the calcarine cortex (Figure 16-11). They are sudden and spontaneous in onset and noticed early by the patient because they interfere with reading, especially when they are in the right homonymous fields.

Traumatic lesions are often seen following severe concussive trauma with depressed fracture, cortical injury from bone spicules and minute intracranial foreign bodies. These injuries are often associated with patients who have been victims of armed conflict or others who have sustained sublethal explosive injuries.

In several patients with retained intracerebral foreign bodies (shrapnel fragments), it has been possible to localize the site of brain damage in the

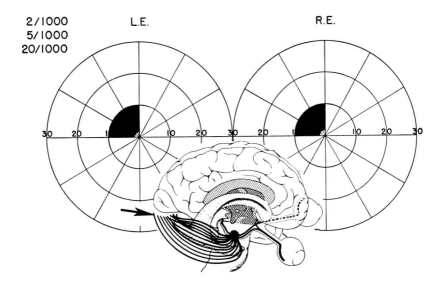

FIGURE 16-10 Homonymous quadrantanoptic scotoma from shrapnel wound of skull with depressed fracture over occiput. Debridement of wound revealed bone spicule penetrating dura over tip of right occipital lobe, with brain damage and hemorrhage in inferior lip of right calcarine fissure. Vision was 20/20 in each eye.

striate cortex by careful perimetry and to confirm the localization by means of a stereoscopic x-ray examination.

A few cases of incongruous homonymous hemianoptic scotomas have been reported. The lesion site in such cases is not known, but may be in the optic tract as a result of a minute vascular, demyelinating, or inflammatory disturbance.

Double Homonymous Hemianopsia

Bilateral lesions of both striate cortexes are not uncommon. They may be the result of direct injury or of a vascular accident (Figure 16-12). Severe head injury after automobile accidents is a prominent cause.

The sudden spontaneous development of double homonymous hemi-anopsia associated with signs of brain stem damage, such as nystagmus and internuclear ophthalmoplegia, is evidence of occlusive disease of the basilar artery system (Figure 16-13). Visual field defects in these cases can vary widely. If the upper lips of both calcarine fissures are damaged, the resulting field will be an inferior altitudinal hemianopsia with partial preservation of the macular area.

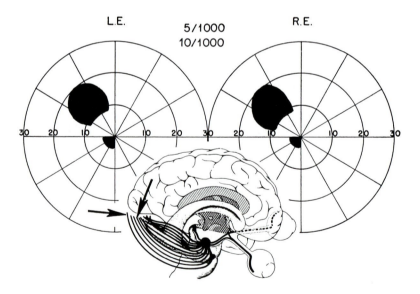

FIGURE 16-11 Double homonymous hemianoptic scotomas. Visual loss was sudden. Neurologic examination was normal. Scotomas resulted from presumed vascular lesion of right occipital lobe, with one small lesion in posterior tip of right superior calcarine lip and another in middle portion of lower lip of fissure. Note absence of macular sparing in inferior quadrantanoptic scotoma and rather wide macular sparing in superior paracentral homonymous hemianoptic scotoma.

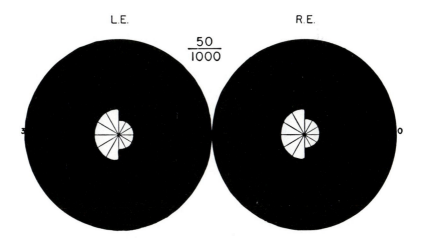

FIGURE 16-12 Double homonymous hemianopsia, caused by injury to occipital pole from falling weight. Remnant of visual field is result of bilateral macular sparing, area of left field being slightly larger than that on right. Note small vertical steps produced by this difference in size of spared areas.

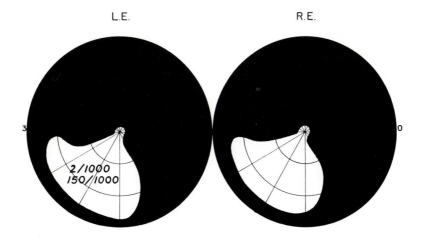

FIGURE 16-13 Double homonymous hemianopsia associated with thrombosis of basilar, vertebral, and posterior cerebral arteries. Note absolute congruity of defect margins for large and small stimuli.

If both calcarine fissures are involved extensively, the visual field will look like the end stages of a bilateral glaucoma field, with only central vision remaining because of bilateral macular sparing. The loss may be unequal in the two fields, resulting in somewhat wider macular sparing on one side than the other and steplike defects on the vertical meridian. Central vision may remain normal so that reading is possible if the area of sparing is sufficiently wide, but locomotion with such narrowed fields is difficult.

A related but rare type of visual field defect is crossed quadrant hemi-anopsia, which is actually a partial bilateral homonymous hemianopsia with the site of the lesions in the upper lip of one calcarine fissure and in the lower lip of the other.

ANATOMIC DIVISIONS OF THE POSTCHIASMAL VISUAL PATHWAY

Having considered the general morphology of homonymous hemianopsias resulting from lesions of the postchiasmal visual pathway, we will now discuss the visual field changes associated with each of its four anatomic divisions: (1) the optic tracts, (2) the lateral geniculate body, (3) the optic radiations or geniculocalcarine pathway, and (4) the striate, or occipital, cortex.

In each case proper analysis requires detailed knowledge of the anatomy of the area, not only of the fiber pathway but also of contiguous structures, vascular supply, and the more common pathologic lesions affecting the area. With this knowledge, visual field analysis can lead to a reasonably accurate diagnosis of the location and etiology of the offending lesion.

Optic Tracts

The characteristic visual field defect produced by optic tract lesions is an incomplete incongruous homonymous hemianopsia with lesions of variable density and sloping margins (Figure 16-14). The defect often begins with quadrantic loss and a small area of macular sparing. As the lesion progresses, it may encroach on fixation and involve more of the peripheral field, until finally there is a total homonymous hemianopsia with macular splitting.

In early hemianoptic lesions the asymmetry may be so marked that the defect at first appears to be unilateral; only after a careful search will the homonymous loss in the opposite field be detected.

Primary optic tract lesions are relatively rare, although the tract is oc-casionally the site of a glioma and may be affected in multiple sclerosis.

Chiasmal and postchiasmal involvement in patients with multiple scle-rosis is rare. As mentioned previously, we have seen several instances of bitemporal hemianopsia produced by extension of retrobulbar neuritis into the chiasm and of homonymous hemianopsia from tract lesions associated with well-advanced multiple sclerosis. Boldt and associates reported five such examples in a series of 365 cases of multiple sclerosis studied perimetrically.

The lesions that most frequently affect the optic tract are tumors of adjacent structures and aneurysms of the posterior arteries of the circle of Willis (i.e., the posterior communicating, posterior cerebral, internal carotid, and middle cerebral arteries). The proximity of the optic tract to the pituitary body, ventricular system, basilar vessels and meninges, temporal lobe, and basal ganglia may cause lesions of these structures to impinge on the tract.

Tumors affecting the tracts are more common; pituitary tumors occur the most frequently. Parasellar tumors, tumors of the third ventricle, basal ganglia, and transverse fissures may also affect the optic tract.

Tumors of the medial portion of the temporal lobe occasionally exert pressure on the lateral aspects of the optic tracts. In those cases it cannot be easily determined whether the visual field defects associated with these tumors are the result of pressure on the optic tracts or on the fibers of the optic radiation within the temporal lobe.

Anterior tract lesions are usually caused by pituitary tumors or lesions closely associated with the posterior chiasmal angle. They are frequently accompanied by signs and symptoms of pituitary disease. Midtract lesions may be accompanied by pyramidal tract signs and hemianesthesia on the same side as the hemianopsia or by involvement of the third, fourth, fifth, and sixth cranial nerves on the opposite side.

Sarcoidosis involving the nervous system has been reported by a number of authors. McLaurin and Harrington reported a patient with intracranial sarcoidosis involving the left optic tract and temporal lobe, with incongruous homonymous hemianopsia and a positive computed tomographic (CT) scan

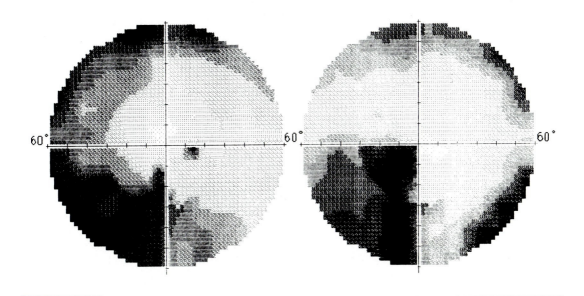

FIGURE 16-14 Incomplete incongruous homonymous hemianopsia of variable density and with sloping margins, characteristic of right optic tract lesion.

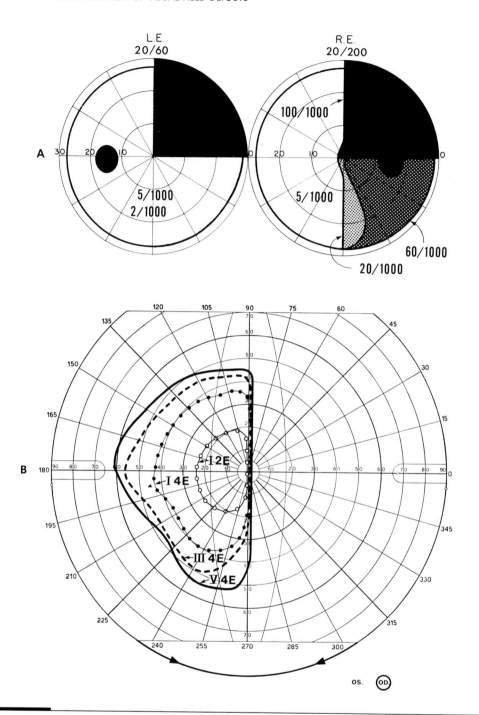

FIGURE 16-15 A, Intracranial sarcoidosis. Tangent screen field showing markedly incongruous right
homonymous hemianopsia with macular splitting. **B** and **C,** Goldmann perimeter field
of case shown in **A.** Markedly incongruous right homonymous hemianopsia due to
intracranial sarcoidosis involving left optic tract.

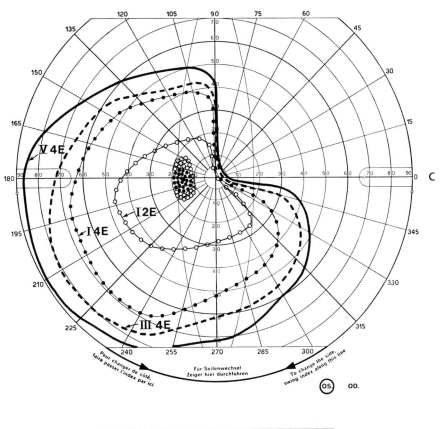

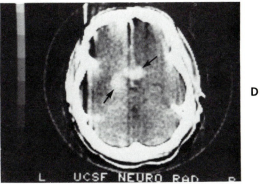

FIGURE 16-15, cont'd. D, CAT scan of case shown in **A.** Intracranial sarcoidosis involving left optic tract. Chest roentgenograms show extensive hilar adenopathy. Lymph gland biopsy was positive for sarcoid, and slit lamp shows evidence of chronic anterior uveitis.

(Figure 16-15). The diagnosis was substantiated by radiologic evidence of bilateral hilar and peritracheal adenopathy. Furthermore, the patient had a past history of recurrent uveitis, and a mediastinal lymph node biopsy was positive for sarcoidosis. The CT scan indicated a large lesion in the suprasellar cistern, with extension into the left temporal lobe along the optic tract. Intensive corticosteroid therapy resulted in restoration of vision, marked improvement of the visual field defect, a decrease in the pulmonary hilar adenopathy, and almost complete resolution of the temporal lobe lesion.

Posterior tract lesions have symptoms associated with the basal ganglion and are generally indistinguishable from disease affecting the lateral geniculate body.

When pressure is exerted lateral to the tract, the field is generally most affected on the side of the lesion, whereas the contralateral field is most severely affected by lesions between or medial to the tracts. Optic atrophy eventually ensues, although it may require months to develop.

Hoyt and Kommerall found objective evidence of homonymous hemiretinal atrophy, documented by red-free fundus photography, in patients with homonymous hemianopsia resulting from optic tract lesions. Injury leads to retrograde degeneration of the involved nerve fibers as far as the retinal ganglion cells. Two of their patients had sustained a laceration of the right optic tract, whereas two other patients had presumed early injury of the right occipital lobe with transsynaptic degeneration through the lateral geniculate body into the retina. In the eye with the blind nasal hemiretina (temporal hemianopsia), an atrophic band was found running diagonally over the papilla. In the eye with the blind temporal hemiretina (nasal hemianopsia), an oval papillary excavation similar to a glaucomatous alteration was seen. These optic disc changes correspond to the areas of retinal nerve fiber bundle and ganglion cell atrophy. Homonymous hemiretinal atrophy may appear as early as 2 to 3 months after optic tract injury, whereas many years are required to develop retinal nerve fiber atrophy after injury to the visual cortex.

Lateral Geniculate Body

It is rarely possible to diagnose lesions of the lateral geniculate body during life. The characteristic visual field defect is an incongruous homonymous hemianopsia identical to that produced by a lesion of the posterior part of the tract or the anterior part of the optic radiation (Figure 16-16).

Gunderson and Hoyt have reported quantitative perimetric studies in two patients with involvement of the lateral geniculate nucleus with strikingly incongruous defects in the contralateral homonymous visual field. One patient had an astrocytoma proven at autopsy, and the other had a small arteriovenous malformation demonstrated by vertebral arteriograms. The patterns of these hemianopsias correlated anatomically with the patterns of retinal projections within the six cellular laminae of the geniculate body. Their studies confirmed earlier findings that crossed retinal projections terminate into geniculate laminae 1, 4, and 6, whereas uncrossed projections terminate in laminae 2, 3, and 5.

Frisen and co-workers have reported two patients with sectorial optic atrophy in homonymous horizontal wedge-shaped sectoranopsia. Neuroradiologic investigations localized the visual pathway lesions to the lateral geniculate body. The peculiar nature of the field defect and the optic atrophy could be explained by ischemia in the territory of the ipsilateral carotid artery.

The close association of the external geniculate body with the thalamus may cause hemianesthesia on the side of the hemianopsia. Involvement of the nearby pyramidal tract may cause motor weakness or hemiplegia on the side opposite the lesion. These symptom complexes may also be found in patients with lesions affecting the internal capsule and the beginnings of the optic radiation in association with homonymous hemianopsia

Optic Radiations or Geniculocalcarine Pathway

The optic radiations constitute the fourth and final neuron in the visual pathway. They are the longest, most widespread, and, except for the chiasmal decussation, most vulnerable portion of the visual pathway. Because of the tortuous course of the geniculocalcarine pathway and the wide area that it occupies in the cerebral hemisphere, it is subject to interruptions at many points and from lesions of many types. For this reason, the morphology of its

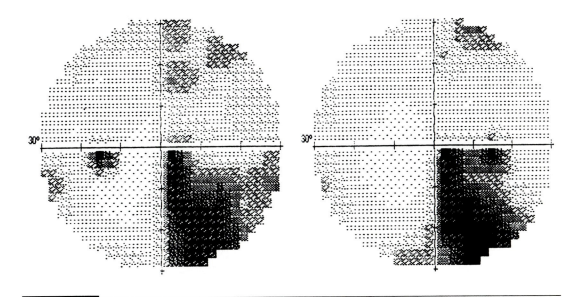

FIGURE 16-16 Incongruous right inferior quadrantanopsia in 44-year-old patient with multiple sclerosis. Magnetic resonance imaging (MRI) revealed lesion in region of left lateral geniculate body.

visual field defects is extremely variable, and the interpretation of these variations is diagnostically important.

A brief review of the anatomy of the optic radiation shows it leaving the lateral geniculate body to run laterally through the retrolenticular segment of the internal capsule behind the sensory fibers in a compact mass, the optic peduncle. The fibers then fan out rapidly in the medullary optic lamella, so that the fibers from the upper and lower retinal quadrants are separated by the macular fibers between them.

The fibers from the medial aspect of the lateral geniculate body that have come from the upper retinal quadrant run dorsally in the optic lamella in a straight course through the white matter of the parietooccipital lobe and then descend in a horizontal fan over the caudal end of the calcarine fissure to enter the cortex in the dorsal portion of the striate area.

The fibers from the lateral aspect of the lateral geniculate body that have come from the lower retinal quadrant run in the ventral portion of the lamella that runs forward in the temporal lobe to form Meyer's temporal loop. This may reach far forward to envelop the temporal horn of the lateral ventricle and then pass along its body and around its posterior horn to end in the ventral portion of the calcarine cortex.

The macular fibers run from the dorsal part of the lateral geniculate ganglion in a flat bundle between the dorsal and ventral fibers, to end in the posterior pole or operculum of the occipital cortex. (See Figure 5-9.)

For convenience the optic radiations may be divided into three parts:
1. The anterior radiation and, in particular, that portion within the internal capsule
2. The midportion of the radiation, which includes the wide band of fibers traversing the temporal and temporoparietal lobes in the external sagittal stratum
3. The posterior radiation, made up of that portion of the fibers in the external sagittal stratum of the parietal and parietooccipital lobes

Lesions of the forward portion of the internal capsule may not affect the optic radiations, producing only motor and sensory changes. Lesions in the posterior limb of the internal capsule almost invariably affect the optic peduncle and give rise to homonymous hemianopsia of the opposite side and are usually associated with hemianesthesia or hemiplegia or both.

If the area of fiber interruption in the internal capsule is posterior and small, the hemianopsia may be accompanied by hemianesthesia alone.

Because of the compact area occupied by the optic peduncle, small lesions usually produce total homonymous hemianopsia, and the congruity or incongruity of the field defects cannot be determined.

The lesions most commonly affecting the internal capsule are vascular. Obstruction of or hemorrhage from the lenticulostriate and lenticulooptic branches of the middle cerebral artery (the arteries of cerebral "stroke") account for most of these cases. The visual field defects produced by such damage are usually permanent, although a small area of field recovery may occur in some patients.

In most vascular lesions, whether caused by hemorrhage, thrombosis, embolism, or angiospasm, the onset of symptoms is sudden. Tumors and injuries of the internal capsule are rare.

Intracranial space-occupying lesions with unilateral cerebral edema occasionally give rise to herniation of the hippocampal gyrus over the edge of the tentorium into the tentorial hiatus. This gives rise to rapidly developing third nerve palsy associated with signs and symptoms of an acute rise in intracranial pressure, homonymous hemianopsia, and development of brain stem compression, hemorrhage, coma, and death. The visual field defect may result from interruption of the fiber bundles in the temporal lobe or from calcarine cortex ischemia and infarction caused by compression of the posterior cerebral artery. The lesion producing the temporal lobe herniation may be far removed from the site of the hernia.

The exact course of the fibers of the optic radiation immediately after they leave the optic peduncle has been the subject of much debate. From both the anatomic and the clinical points of view, the majority of observers favor the concept that the fibers fan out widely in the external sagittal stratum. The dorsal fibers run laterally for a short distance to the outside of the lateral ventricle and then straight back to the occipital lobes. The ventral fibers run forward for a distance in the temporal lobe, passing around and over the temporal horn of the lateral ventricle in the temporal loop of Meyer before turning backward in the lower part of the temporal lobe, where they are closely applied to the lateral wall of the body and posterior horn of the lateral ventricle, until they reach the occipital lobe. The macular fibers run between these two bundles.

The chief controversy seems to center around the degree of forward looping of the fibers in the temporal lobe. Harrington has found variation among individual brains. In most brains, however, the temporal loop was fairly easy to demonstrate and, in fact, was probably even more extensive than could be shown readily in the average gross dissection.

Because of this widespread disposition of the visual fibers in the temporal lobe, tumors of various portions of the lobe may obstruct the fibers, giving rise to homonymous hemianoptic visual field defects of widely varying morphology.

Lesions of the extreme anterior tip of the temporal lobe may not encroach on the visual pathway and thus do not cause a visual field defect. If only a few of the ventral fibers are involved, however, the result is a homonymous hemianopsia. Tumors of the temporal lobe have a great tendency to produce a depressional-type field loss in which the typical characteristics are an incongruous upper homonymous quadrantanopsia with sloping margins. Such typical visual field defects have been repeatedly demonstrated by many observers in proved lesions of the temporal lobe. One of the outstanding features

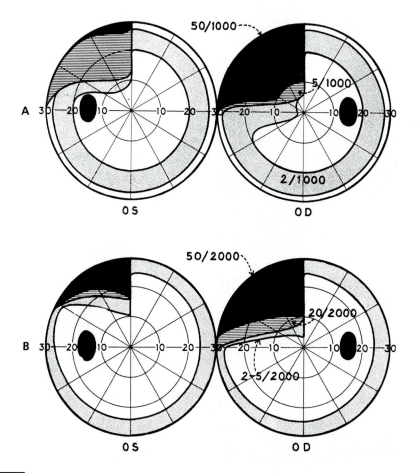

FIGURE 16-17 A, One month after temporal lobe resection. Tangent screen examination shows incongruous left homonymous quadrantanopsia. Incongruity is most clearly demonstrated in isopters for large stimuli (50/1000). **B,** Ten months after right temporal lobectomy. Tangent screen examination shows slight regression of quadrantanopsia, which is still markedly asymmetric.

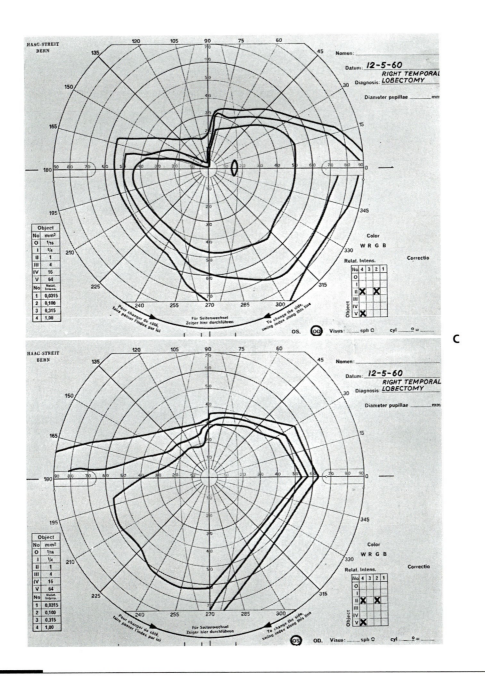

FIGURE 16-17, cont'd. C, *Above,* Right eye field. *Below,* Left eye field. Goldmann perimeter examination showed incongruity best in larger isopters.

of the homonymous hemianopsias in these cases is their incongruity (Figure 16-17).

Clinical data from a large number of cases reported in the literature by various observers generally confirm the incongruous character of temporal lobe visual field defects and the exquisite symmetry of those defects produced by occipital lobe lesions. But some authors take exception. Holmes and Lister illustrated case after case of occipital area injury with precisely symmetric homonymous defects in the visual fields. Dubois-Poulsen illustrated an incongruous homonymous hemianopsia following a partial temporal lobectomy. The largest and most intense stimuli on the Goldmann perimeter show the asymmetry to best advantage.

Spalding's study of wounds of the visual radiation and striate cortex beautifully illustrated the anatomic distribution of the geniculocalcarine fibers in the radiation and the visual field representation in the occipital cortex. He did not comment on the congruity of defects after injury to the radiation, but all six of his field studies showed some degree of incongruity, and in some

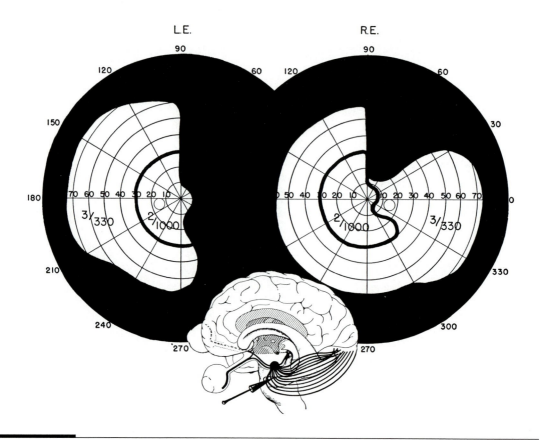

FIGURE 16-18 Typical incongruous right homonymous hemianopsia in case of glioma of left temporal lobe. Tumor was large, and patient had had a seizure disorder, headache, increased reflexes in right arm and leg, and severe papilledema.

the asymmetry was considerable. In his study of the striate cortex, the congruity of the homonymous scotomas was striking.

Smith concluded from a study of his cases that lesions of the temporal lobe produce basically incongruous homonymous hemianopsias, whereas occipital lobe damage causes basically congruous visual field defects.

Walsh and Hoyt stated that most of the partial homonymous upper quadrantanopsias resulting from lesions of the temporal lobe are incongruous; and they agreed with Harrington that the field defects from occipital lobe lesions are congruous.

Van Buren and Baldwin studied the visual fields of 41 patients after a temporal lobectomy for relief of epilepsy. Thirty-three patients showed major defects in the fields; ten of these demonstrated homonymous congruous defects and 23 developed incongruous deficits. The incongruities were most obvious in the larger isopters. These authors believe that "all fibers derived from a given retinal point do not lie close together in the optic radiation." They believe that lesions affecting the occipital area give rise to entirely symmetric field defects in the two eyes and that "in the posterior portion of the optic system, fibers from homologous areas of the two retinas must lie side by side."

Harrington's clinical data (Figures 16-18 and 16-19) suggested that the incongruity so often seen in homonymous hemianopsia in temporal lobe lesions is best explained by the dissociation in the temporal lobe of fibers from corresponding retinal points, and that this separation of homologous fibers persists in lessening degree throughout the optic radiation as far posterior as the postparietal area.

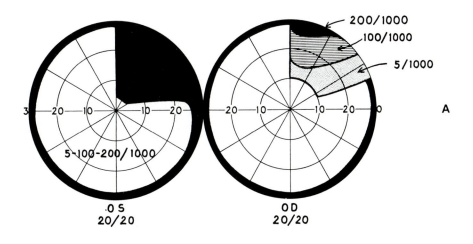

FIGURE 16-19 A, Tangent screen 4 years after left temporal lobectomy for relief of epilepsy. Resection did not enter ventricle. Gross incongruity is most evident in larger isopters.

Continued.

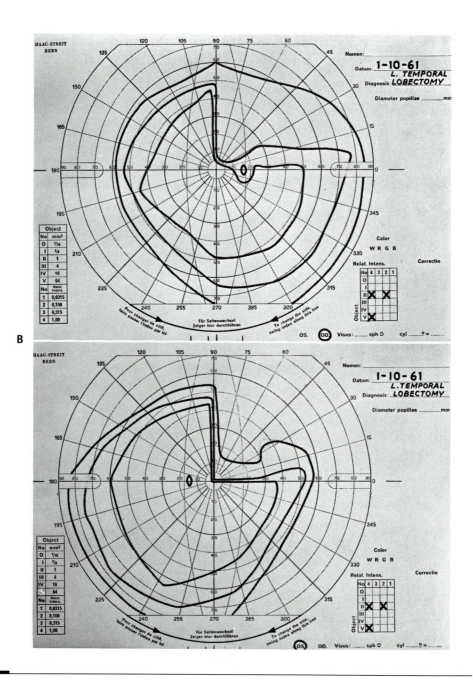

FIGURE 16-19, cont'd. B, *Above,* Field for right eye. *Below,* Field for left eye. Goldmann perimeter examination of patient shows incongruity best with largest and brightest stimuli.

Regardless of its cause, asymmetry or incongruity of incomplete homonymous hemianopsia is a clinical entity quite regularly present in visual field defects resulting from lesions of the temporal lobe (Figure 16-20).

Vascular and traumatic lesions are less common in this area than tumors (Figure 16-21). Brain abscess of otogenic origin may involve the temporal lobe and give rise to typical visual field defects through visual fiber compression.

Certain other neurologic signs and symptoms of localizing value may accompany the characteristic homonymous hemianopsia described previously:

1. Complex partial seizures, in which the patient complains of abnormal smells or taste and occasionally of complex visual hallucinations of persons, animals, or known objects. This aura is often followed by localized seizures involving the arm and the leg on the side opposite the lesion. These episodes are associated with involvement of the uncinate gyrus beneath the temporal lobe (Figure 16-22).
2. Aphasia occurring in right-handed persons with tumors of the left temporal lobe.
3. Papilledema caused by a general increase in intracranial pressure.
4. Signs such as weakness of the facial muscle, conjugate deviation of the eyes, and partial third nerve palsy caused by involvement of nearby structures.

The parietal lobe is large, and the optic radiation occupies a wide flat band close to the lateral wall of the body of the lateral ventricle. It is bounded anteriorly by the central sulcus, laterally by the sylvian fissure, posteriorly by the parietooccipital fissure, and medially by the cingulum. Its vascular supply is principally through the ascending and posterior parietal branches of the

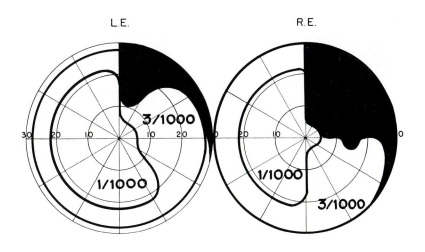

FIGURE 16-20 Large cystic tumor mass in lower portion of left temporal lobe produced incongruous right homonymous quadrantanopsia. Encapsulated tumor was removed with partial resolution of visual field defect.

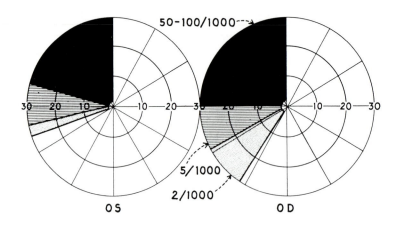

FIGURE 16-21 Incongruous homonymous quadrantanopsia resulting from intracerebral hematoma in right temporal lobe. Margins of defect were unusually straight and exact for each isopter studied.

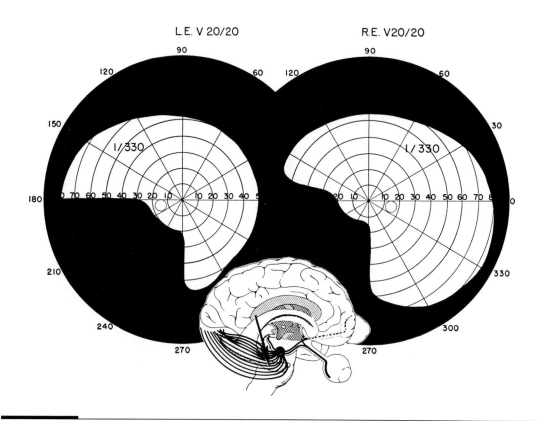

FIGURE 16-22 Left inferior homonymous quadrantanopsia produced by degenerative lesion of right temporoparietal area. Patient had a seizure disorder preceded by aura of formed visual hallucinations of bright, multicolored geometric figures in left visual field.

middle cerebral artery laterally and branches of the anterior cerebral artery medially.

The clinical manifestations of parietal lobe disease are among the most interesting in neurology and are often associated with characteristic visual difficulties and field deficits (Figures 16-23 to 16-26). The precise function of the various areas of the lobe is poorly understood, but in general lesions of the anterior and lateral portions of the lobe give rise to somatic disorders, whereas those located posteriorly and superiorly cause visual imperception.

The syndromes related to parietal lesions display a disorder of awareness of the disturbance no matter where the lesion. The patient is neglectful of and fails to perceive the nature of the disability. This behavioral defect applies equally to somatic and visual perception disorders (Anton's syndrome).

It is with lesions of the parietal lobe that the extinction phenomenon becomes most manifest. The patient may easily detect a moving finger or even a small test object held consecutively in each quadrant of the visual field, thus demonstrating that simple sensation is preserved. When stimuli are exposed simultaneously in both sides of the visual field, the patient fails to recognize the one in the field contralateral to the lesion even though it may be a gross one easily detected when presented alone. Often these patients are unable to maintain a central fixation and involuntarily shift their gaze to the finger or other target in the normal field.

When asked to bisect a horizontal line, the patient crosses the line well to the side of the unaffected field (i.e., away from the lesion). Writing and drawing often deviate from the horizontal, and constructional apraxia may be manifested by the inability to copy a cube or draw a clock face.

All these visual manifestations may be associated with somatic perceptual disorders such as extinction of tactile stimuli on one side when the other side of the body is tested simultaneously, astereognosis, and even unawareness by the patient of his or her own limb.

Many left cerebral lesions with visual perceptual disturbance are complicated by aphasia, which interferes with examination of the patient. Reading and writing disability is common, and visual acuity may appear to be grossly depressed because the patient fails to recognize letters on the Snellen chart. When numbers or the illiterate E chart are used, vision may be normal.

Visual loss is usually more severely affected in the lower quadrants, and the most common visual field defect is an inferior homonymous quadrantanopsia, with perhaps a slight degree of incongruity. This defect is most clearly demonstrated on the tangent screen using simultaneous double stimulation. Superior quadrant loss associated with parietal lobe disease is so rare as to be suspect and is more likely to result from temporal lobe involvement.

The association of homonymous hemianopsia with pain in the eye and orbit has been reported as a symptom of vascular accident in the parietooccipital area. The pain, which occurs on the side of the lesion, is presumed to be mediated through the dural branches of the first division of the fifth nerve.

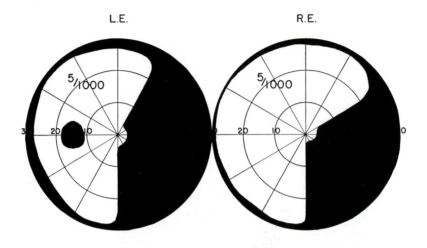

FIGURE 16-23 Fracture of parietal area of skull with bone spicules from inner table of skull penetrating dura and brain produced this slightly incongruous right homonymous hemianopsia. There was moderate aphasia.

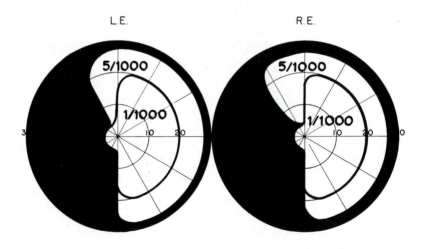

FIGURE 16-24 Large tumor of upper portion of right parietal lobe produced left homonymous hemianopsia.

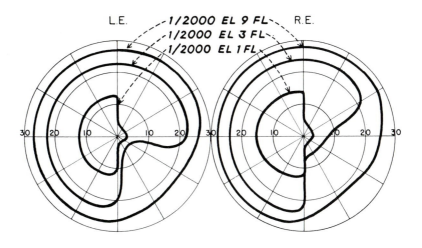

FIGURE 16-25 Varying degrees of right homonymous hemianopsia produced by left parietal lobe tumor as demonstrated with electroluminescent stimuli of varying luminance from 9 footlamberts to 3 footlamberts to 1 footlambert.

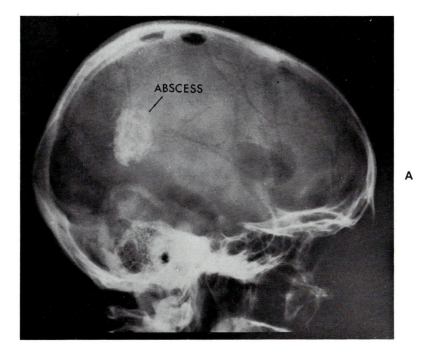

FIGURE 16-26 A, Roentgenogram of Lipiodol-injected right parietal lobe abscess.

Continued.

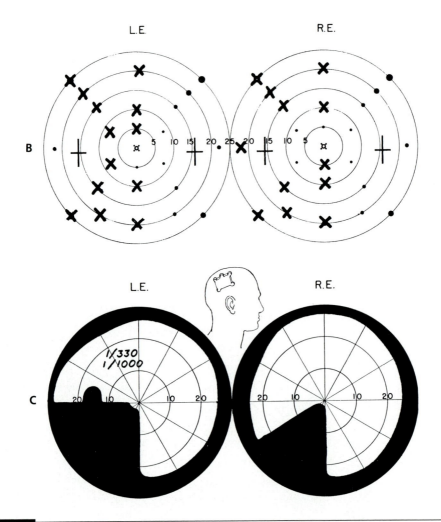

FIGURE 16-26, cont'd. B, Multiple pattern visual field examination in case of parietal lobe abscess. Total homonymous hemianopsia is due to simultaneous double stimulation used in this test as compared with single stimulation. **C,** Tangent screen field defects were produced by parietal lobe abscess shown in **A**. Note that defects involve inferior quadrant and are incongruous.

In two cases observed by Harrington, severe pain was the presenting symptom, leading to detection of the contralateral homonymous field loss of which the patient had been unaware.

Bilateral parietal disease is not uncommon as a complication of diffuse cerebrovascular disease. It results in devastating visual disability. Patients become lost in familiar places, fail to recognize friends, and finally lose all evidence of visual function. The facial expression becomes vacuous and the patient appears to be blind. Pupillary reactions to light and accommodation are retained, however.

Mooney has reported a series of most unusual and vivid visual hallucinations in a patient with a parietooccipital meningioma. The patient was an artist and was able to reproduce his various hallucinations in brilliant color. Some of them were abstract and some were distortions of human figures. All were in the nonseeing right field of vision, and quantitative perimetry revealed an irregular but congruous homonymous hemianopsia.

A positive or asymmetric optokinetic nystagmus response is found present in homonymous hemianopsia due to parietal lobe lesions.

Striate Cortex

The characteristic visual field defect associated with lesions of the striate cortex is a congruous homonymous hemianopsia, either complete or incomplete, with macular sparing, steep margins, and uniform density. Tumors and vascular lesions of the occipital lobe frequently involve adjacent cerebral areas so that pure striate area involvement is unusual. Injuries, on the other hand, sometimes involve relatively small and isolated areas of the occipital cortex and thus give rise to discrete and isolated central and peripheral homonymous field defects that localize the site of damage precisely.

The most common vascular lesion involving the occipital lobe is thrombosis of posterior cerebral or calcarine artery (Figures 16-27 and 16-28). This lesion usually causes extensive damage in the cortex with complete homonymous hemianopsia. The macula is frequently spared. A thrombosis or embolism of small branches of the posterior cerebral artery may produce homonymous hemianoptic sector defects, quadrantanopsias, or scotomas. The macular portion of the occpital cortex, supplied in part by the middle cerebral artery, may escape damage and thus accounts for the widespread area of macular sparing seen in these patients. Bilateral or double homonymous hemianopsia is not uncommon.

The appearance of bright orange-yellow cholesterol crystals in the retinal arterioles (Hollenhorst plaques), with or without episodes of transient visual loss (amaurosis fugax) or transient or permanent homonymous hemianoptic

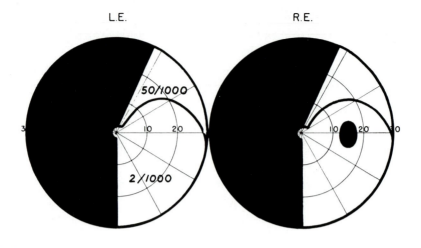

FIGURE 16-27 Right calcarine cortical cerebrovascular accident with completely congruous left homonymous hemianopsia and evidence of partial involvement of left striate cortex. Field loss was sudden in onset. There are other evidences of cerebrospinal and vascular syphilis, including Argyll Robertson pupils.

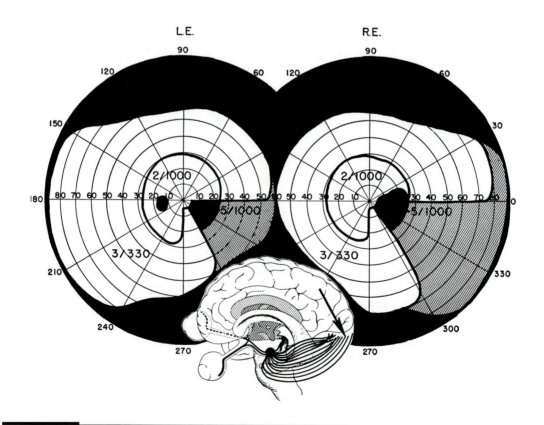

FIGURE 16-28 Congruous right homonymous quadrantanopsia with homonymous quadrantanoptic scotoma resulting from thrombosis of branch of left posterior cerebral artery. Apparent incongruity in scotomas is due to inclusion of blind spot in right field defect.

visual field defects, indicate the possibility of an extracranial embolic source. In most patients ipsilateral carotid artery disease is implicated, but such emboli may also arise from a cardiac source. It has been said that the glistening intraarterial plaques arising from carotid disease are more yellowish than the whitish plaques associated with cardiac disease, but this is at best a subtle distinction that is unlikely to be useful in the hands of the average practitioner.

Considerable controversy exists concerning the proper workup and management of patients with amaurosis fugax. Certainly such patients require a careful systemic cardiovascular workup. At the very least the workup should begin with an evaluation of and an attempt to eliminate or modify risk factors for cardiovascular disease, such as obesity, hypertension, smoking, and hypercholesterolemia. The physical examination should include an evaluation for the presence of carotid bruits.

The next step is not so clear. For decades carotid angiography has been practiced as the reference standard test for determining the presence of operable carotid disease. Unfortunately, carotid angiography in and of itself carries a small but significant morbidity and mortality. Many centers are now evaluating patients with noninvasive techniques, such as real-time B-scan imaging, Doppler ultrasound, and photoangiography. In some laboratories a combination of these noninvasive techniques is used to maximize sensitivity and specificity.

Even when "significant" carotid disease is established, there is still considerable controversy about how it should be managed. Carotid endarterectomy has become a fairly common procedure in the United States; approximately 100,000 are performed annually. However, the procedure carries a significant morbidity and mortality, especially in elderly patients, for surgical teams that perform few such procedures. When combined, the total "perisurgical" morbidity and mortality of carotid angiography followed by endarterectomy can be substantial, averaging about 10% in a study by Dyken and Pokras. This alarmingly high figure includes high-risk patients in surgical centers where such procedures are not performed routinely. Under better circumstances perioperative morbidity and mortality range from about 1% to 3%.

Many experts simply recommend systemic anticoagulation therapy, commonly with a single daily aspirin tablet.

Unfortunately, it is difficult to compare precisely the efficacy of carotid endarterectomy vs. daily aspirin therapy because of the heterogeneity of the patient population, diagnostic and therapeutic criteria, and physicians who have contributed to our data base. Currently, the weight of evidence indicates that medical therapy may be appropriate for a significant number of these patients. It is hoped that more definitive data will be forthcoming shortly.

The ever-increasing resolution of neuroradiologic studies has improved our ability to correlate visual field defects with appropriate findings.

McAuley and Ross Russell studied 39 patients with various types of isolated homonymous hemianopsias resulting from ischemic lesions in the posterior parts of the cerebral hemispheres. All were examined by CT scanning. Most had localized low-density lesions within the distribution of the posterior cerebral artery. The lesion locations (deduced from a separate anatomic study of postmortem brains cut in the plane of the CT scanner) were correlated with visual field defects. Lesions giving rise to quadrantic defects were smaller than those with total hemianopsias. Lower quadrantic defects tended to occur in superior cuts and vice versa. Macular sparing was associated with survival of the occipital pole in some instances. Bilateral cases had more associated neurologic defects.

Congruous homonymous hemianopsia has occurred after cardiopulmonary bypass surgery with occipital cortical infarction.

Tumors of the occipital lobe may occur as the various types of infiltrative or cystic gliomas, often arising in the parietal lobe and extending backward. These lesioins frequently involve the optic radiations before they reach the striate cortex. The field defects are therefore more or less identical with those found in the postparietal area.

Meningiomas frequently affect the occipital cortex. The tumor may involve any part of the occipital lobe and occasionally attains enormous size before producing neurologic signs other than vague visual defects. When such meningiomas begin their growth at the posterior pole or operculum, they produce depression-like homonymous hemianopsias that are seen best in the central field. The peripheral field may be normal in such cases until late in the disease.

When the tumors are farther forward, they usually compress the radiations before they reach the cortex, except for an uncommon meningioma arising from the falx. Tumors of the falx may give unique opportunities for diagnosis and localization and are one of the few examples of pure striate cortex involvement.

They occur in the midline and may compress the calcarine fissure on either or both sides. They usually grow to one side and indent the calcarine cortex, causing ischemia and cellular destruction. When located posteriorly the tumor may be associated with hemianoptic scotomas. Quadrants only are involved if the tumor compresses the upper or lower lip of the calcarine fissure unequally. Inferior quadrantanopsia is more common than superior quadrantanopsia. Wide areas of macular vision may be preserved. Statokinetic dissociation is an interesting finding in which patients perceive movement without perceiving form (Figures 16-29 and 16-30). A patient who exhibits this phenomenon has a larger visual field with kinetic testing than with appropriately similar static testing. Formerly this sign was considered evidence of occipital lobe disease. More recent evidence has shown that it is associated with lesions virtually anywhere in the visual pathway. The incidence of this

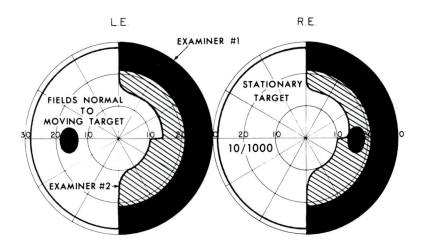

FIGURE 16-29 Homonymous hemianopsia from lesion of striate cortex of occipital lobe demonstrating statokenetic dissociation (Riddoch phenomenon). Note that field defect varies in size with rate of movement of test object. Stationary stimuli (as used in static perimetry) show complete homonymous hemianoptic deficit. Field defects differ between examiner No. 1 and examiner No. 2 because of difference in speed of stimulus movement in kinetic examination. Anoptic portion of visual field responds to motion but not to form.

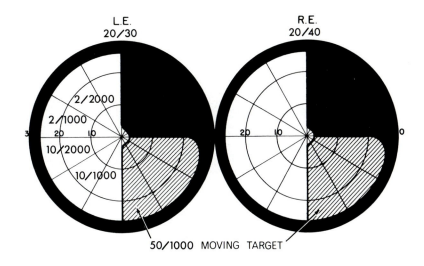

FIGURE 16-30 Homonymous hemianoptic hypoplasia. Left cerebral hypoplasia with optic disc hypoplasia and hemianoptic retinal nerve fiber atrophy detectable with red-free ophthalmoscopy. Visual field defect first noted during routine perimetry 6 years earlier. Patient was unaware of deficit. Nystagmus, alternating esotropia, and psychomotor epilepsy have been present since childhood. Left side of each optic disc shows segmental atrophy.

finding is difficult to determine, because it requires testing with both static and kinetic stimuli. Adding a few static test points to kinetic examinations in appropriate patients will reduce the frequency of missing this phenomenon.

Traumatic lesions of the occipital cortex are fairly common. Depressed fractures of the occiput with bone spicule penetration of the dura is seen after violent crimes or automobile accidents. Gunshot and shrapnel wounds have afforded military surgeons the opportunity to carefully study the effects of sharply localized lesions of the occipital cortex.

When brain damage is extensive, the degree of visual field changes reflects the degree of brain damage (i.e., total homonymous hemianopsia). Extensive brain injury sometimes causes the disturbing double homonymous hemianopsia mentioned previously. On the other hand, small areas of brain damage may occur occasionally, giving rise to minute irregular complex but congruous homonymous hemianoptic or quadrantanoptic defects.

The upper portion of the radiation and occipital cortex appear to be more vulnerable to injury, hence the higher incidence of inferior homonymous damage than traumatic lesions. When both sides of the lips of the calcarine fissure or the occipital pole are injured, the resulting visual field defect is likely to be a superior altitudinal hemianopsia or scotoma that is symmetric in each half-field (Figure 16-31). Severe injury to the lower occipital lobes is often fatal.

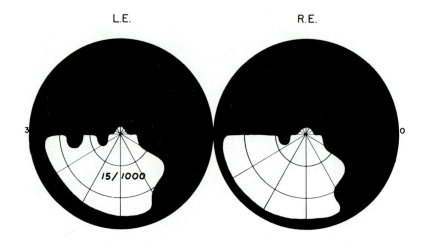

FIGURE 16-31 Double homonymous superior quadrantanopsia resulting from inferior calcarine fissure infarction secondary to basilar artery thrombosis with bilateral posterior cerebral artery involvement. Note complete symmetry of defects carried into smallest irregularity. Patient had transient right hemiplegia, aphasia, and facial weakness with repeated attacks of amaurosis fugax. Diastolic pressure in ophthalmic artery was lower on right side.

Occipital trauma characteristically gives rise to defects with steep walls rather than defects with sloping margins, although either may occur. The sloping margins seem to be associated with edema or other transient sequelae of the injury. The ultimate degree of recovery depends on the amount of actual cellular damage. When the transient effects of injury have dissipated, the remaining defect is typically dense and steep margined (Figure 16-32).

Injury to both occipital lobes with production of double or bilateral homonymous hemianopsia has been seen with gunshot wounds that traverse the two occipital areas. In most instances the visual field loss is inferior and the defect is a double inferior homonymous quadrantanopsia with or without macular sparing (Figure 16-33). Occasionally both upper and lower fields of both sides are involved, giving rise to an apparent concentric contraction, with only a small area of double macular sparing remaining. Injury of the posterior tip of both occipital lobes produces a double homonymous hemi-anoptic scotoma that appears in the visual field as a bilateral circular central scotoma with or without minute areas of macular sparing (Figure 16-34).

Crossed quadrant hemianopsia is a form of bilateral or double hom-onymous hemianopsia due to injuries to the upper lip of the calcarine fissure and the lower lip of the opposite cortex (Figure 16-35).

Visual phenomena associated with cortical lesions

Four visual phenomena should be considered when examining patients for disturbances of the visual cortex: (1) visual hallucinations, (2) cortical blindness, (3) paroxysmal scintillating scotomas and hemianopsia of migraine, and (4) light flashes and homonymous visual field dimming associated with occipital lobe arteriovenous malformations.

Visual hallucination.   A visual hallucination is the perception of an object or visual stimulus that is not actually present. As noted previously, such hal-lucinations may occur with temporal and parietal lobe lesions. They also accompany disturbances in the visual cortex of the occipital lobe.

Visual hallucinations are generally described as formed or unformed. Formed, or complex, hallucinations appear as specific objects or people, al-though they may occur as elaborate abstract patterns or landscapes. Because unformed, or simple, hallucinations may be interpreted by the patient as complex familiar objects, and conversely because formed hallucinations may simulate simple abstract patterns, it may be difficult to determine which phe-nomenon the patient is experiencing. In general, these hallucinations result either from abnormal stimuli to the neurons of the visual pathway or the retinal receptors and the end organ of the calcarine cortex or from irritation of the cortical association areas.

Unformed hallucinations consist of lightning streaks, pinwheels, explod-ing stars, or Roman candles in the anoptic half of a homonymous hemianopsia produced by a calcarine lesion. When unilateral, hallucinations are usually the result of local irritation of the photoreceptors. Care must be exercised in

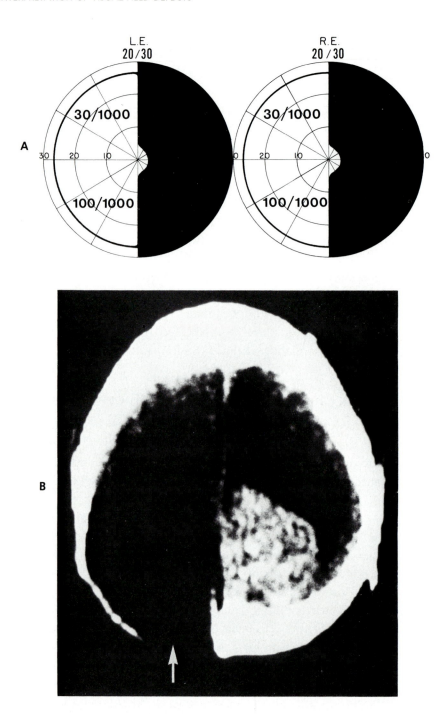

FIGURE 16-32 A, Total right homonymous hemianopsia, with macular sparing, resulting from extirpation of large meningioma of left occipital lobe. Defect same for all stimuli. Later removal of large meningioma of right occipital lobe produced total left homonymous hemianopsia with macular sparing so that few degrees of central vision were retained. **B,** CAT scan of case illustrated in **A** shows extirpation of tumor of left occipital lobe *(arrow)* and residual tumor in right occipital lobe.

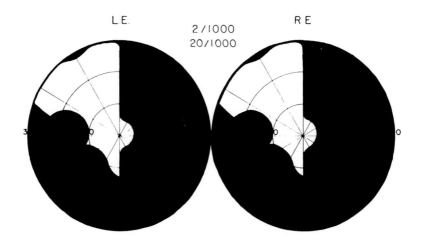

FIGURE 16-33 Completely congruous, irregular, double homonymous hemianopsia due to thrombosis of both posterior cerebral arteries with ischemia and degeneration of entire left occipital lobe and upper lip of right occipital lobe.

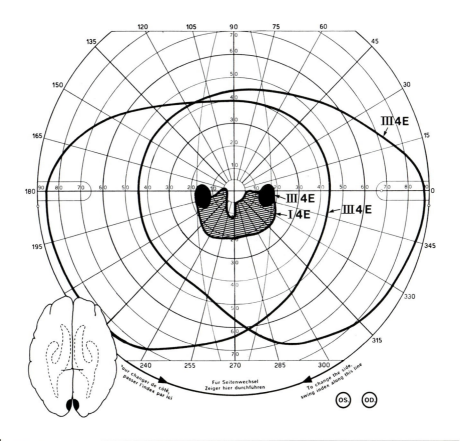

FIGURE 16-34 Double (bilateral) homonymous hemianoptic scotomas (two superimposed Goldmann perimeter fields) from small meningiomas of falx involving medial lips of both calcarine fissures at occipital pole.

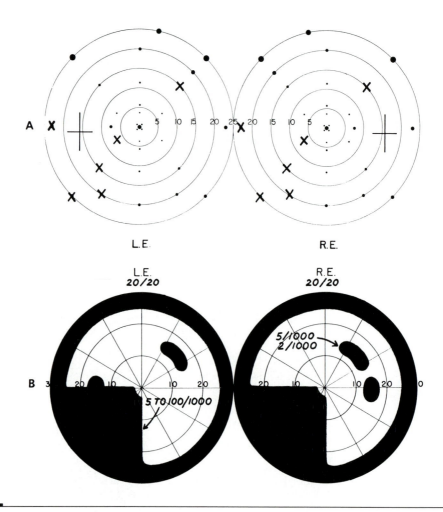

FIGURE 16-35 A, Routine multiple pattern visual field examination showing left inferior homonymous quadrantanopsia with small homonymous defect in opposite field. Patient was unaware of any visual disturbance. **B,** Tangent screen examination of visual field defect, same patient. This double homonymous nature, density, and complete congruity of defects is readily apparent with large and small stimuli.

obtaining a history because what may appear to the patient as a monocular scintillation in the left eye may be in fact a left homonymous hemianoptic hallucination.

Formed hallucinations appear as a familiar face, object, person, animal, or complete scene in the blind portion of the homonymous hemianopsia resulting from a lesion of the temporal or parietal lobe affecting the optic radiations.

Although these generalizations apply to most cases and are of some diagnostic value, it is important to remember that the very nature of a visual hallucination is so complex that there are many exceptions. Thus the hallucination of light when the optic nerve is cut is a well-known exception to these rules, whereas extremely complex visions are common in psychosis, delirium, and psychedelic drug abuse and are not necessarily the result of organic irritation of the optic radiation or associational pathways.

Cortical blindness.   Unlike double homonymous hemianopsia, cortical blindness is total loss of vision caused by bilateral destruction, either transient or permanent, of the occipital visual area. Removal of the visual end organ (occipital cortex), usually because of vascular or traumatic accident, results in a striking and unusual visual loss in which the patient is unaware of the blindness. Pupillary responses to light are normal. Furthermore, the patient may deny visual loss and even supply confabulatory accounts of what is seen (Anton's syndrome). This is in contrast to the strong sense of blindness exhibited by patients after loss of both eyes.

Anton's syndrome also may occur with patients whose cortical lesions produce a homonymous hemianopsia. Although only half the vision is gone, the patient suffers from partial cortical blindness and is not conscious of the one-sided visual loss until he or she repeatedly bumps into objects on that side. Also, because of the completion phenomenon, patients with this type of homonymous hemianopsia often accurately complete images, only half of which are actually seen.

The clinical features of complete cortical blindness are (1) complete loss of vision, often without awareness of such loss, (2) loss of reflex closure of the lid on sudden exposure to light or danger, (3) normal pupillary reaction to light and convergence, (4) normal ophthalmoscopic appearance, and (5) normal ocular rotations.

Frequently these signs and symptoms are associated with various forms of aphasia, visual memory loss, spatial disorientation, amnesia, and mental deterioration; in fact, the entire symptom complex may be considered as a form of visual agnosia.

Recovery from cortical blindness may occur when cell destruction has not been too great. Such a recovery is most likely to take place in cases of traumatic or concussional damage. Return of vision is gradual, with a vague sense of brightness followed by an ill-defined light perception and finally by the return of the form and color sense. Vision may return slowly while a variety of degrees of amnesia, spatial disorientation, anxiety, and nervous fatigue persist.

From the foregoing discussion it is clear why cortical blindness is often misdiagnosed as functional or malingering amaurosis. The total loss of vision with the preservation of pupillary light reactions; the bizarre and inappropriate affect, including confabulation; and the lack of funduscopic changes, may all be confusing. When this is compounded by the patient's loss of recall regarding the concussive force that led to the visual loss and the fact that a significant number of these patients may recover vision, differentiating organic disease from functional loss may be challenging indeed.

Migraine.   Migraine is a paroxysmal disorder in which transient scintillating scotomas and homonymous hemianopsia are prominent symptoms. The syndrome of ocular migraine consists basically of a visual aura, followed by or associated with a hemianoptic area of spreading depression that may occur with or without headache.

Migraine in its various forms occurs commonly. Various surveys have indicated that 20% to 25% of adult respondents believe they have had at least one migraine episode.

The typical migraine attack comprises several parts: an aura, visual blurring or a scintillating scotoma, homonymous hemianopsia, and headache.

The patient experiences an *aura* of vague uneasiness or increased activity or depression. Chronic migraine sufferers recognize the signs of an impending attack.

Visual blurring or a *scintillating scotoma* may start near fixation and then grow to involve a larger portion of the hemianoptic fields of both eyes. Many patients may describe these scotomas as occurring in one eye only. Scintillating scotomas assume many forms and are actually a type of simple visual hallucination. More commonly they occur as jagged or sparkling light streaks. They have been referred to as a fortification specter because of their resemblance to maps of old fortification systems. Other patients describe the scotomas as ill-defined circles of whirling light or as exploding balls of light that fill the homonymous half-field with brilliant color. At times the scintillating scotoma is barely perceptible, as though objects were seen through a heat haze rising from an asphalt pavement. Some patients describe the visual disturbance as ripples of light on a pond into which a stone has been cast. All of these visual perception disturbances occur in the half-field of vision that subsequently develops the homonymous hemianopsia. Other disturbances reported include macropsia, micropsia, distortion of straight lines, diplopia, polyopia, the pulsation phenomenon, and loss of stereopsis. The scotoma generally lasts only a few minutes, and its place is occupied by an area of visual loss, either relative or complete.

The scintillating scotomas in homonymous hemianopsia are occasionally accompanied by other sensory disturbances such as transient aphasia, hemianesthesia, and paresthesia.

Homonymous hemianopsia associated with migraine is a transient visual field defect that may vary in duration from a minute to several days. Cases have been reported in which, after many transient attacks, a permanent hemianopsia develops. The usual duration of the field defect is 15 to 20 minutes. The homonymous hemianopsia may be total or partial and may involve or spare the macula. The defects tend to be absolute for very small objects but relative for larger stimuli. This common description is born out by visual field examination on those rare occasions when the field could be examined before the defect disappeared. Because of the transient nature of the field loss in migraine attacks, much of our knowledge of these defects comes from examinations performed on medical personnel (including self-examination).

In Harrington's experience with migraine attacks, the homonymous hemianopsia spared a minute area around fixation and obscured test objects under 3 mm, but was relative for larger stimuli. In a series of patients Harrington examined during migraine attacks, the anoptic portion of the fields varied from total visual loss to a vague depression of vision through which the 1/2000 stimulus was seen dimly. One patient clearly demonstrated a dense homonymous hemianoptic scotoma close to fixation within a more peripheral field loss that was less dense for the same stimulus.

The homonymous hemianopsia of migraine appears to be a positive field. The patient is aware of the defect and can describe it accurately. Some patients insist that only one eye is involved, whereas others readily recognize the homonymous nature of the bilateral field defects.

The *headache* that follows the hemianopsia (and from which migraine takes its name from the French meaning "half head") characteristically involves the side of the head opposite the visual field loss. It has great variety. It may be so mild as to be overlooked unless specifically questioned for, or it may be totally debilitating. It may be localized to one small superficial or deep area, or it may involve the entire head. It may last from a few minutes to several days. Symptoms and signs frequently associated with migrainous headache are nausea and vomiting and marked vasomotor changes that are sometimes unilateral.

The cause of migraine is unclear. As mentioned previously, it is a common disorder and is diagnosed frequently in young, intelligent patients.

An ever-changing variety of therapeutic agents are used to treat, abort, or prevent recurrent migraine attacks. These agents meet with varying success. Conversely, oral contraceptive pills have precipitated migraine attacks in women who were previously free of migraine or have increased the frequency of attacks in women with previous migraine history. Many physicians avoid prescribing oral contraceptives in patients with a history of migraine.

Occipital lobe arteriovenous malformation.   The differentiation of migraine headache preceded by scintillating scotomas and transient homonymous hemianopsia from the occipital epilepsy produced by occipital lobe arteriovenous malformations may be difficult unless certain criteria for each condition are kept in mind.

Troost and Newton have reported the clinical and radiologic features of 26 cases of occipital epilepsy and occipital apoplexy resulting from occipital lobe arteriovenous malformations.

In occipital epilepsy focal seizures are fairly common, with visual auras indicating the focus in the occipital lobe. These consist of poorly formed episodic brief visual sensations unlike the scintillating figures of a migraine attack. Epileptic photopsias last only seconds or rarely for a few minutes before the onset of a generalized seizure. Typical seizure activity may not be present. Transient homonymous hemianopsia may or may not occur. A headache usually precedes the attack, unlike that which comes later in a migraine attack.

The syndrome of occipital apoplexy is characterized by the sudden onset of severe headache and homonymous hemianopsia produced by hemorrhage and hematoma formation within the occipital lobe. Some of the effects of compression can be reversed by prompt therapeutic intervention. The size of the arteriovenous malformation bears no relation to the presence of the homonymous visual field defect.

BEHAVIOR PATTERNS IN SPLIT-BRAIN ANIMALS

In any consideration of the interpretation of homonymous hemianoptic visual field defects, the split-brain experiments, which cast much light on the connections between the visual cortex and prefrontal cortex and between the right and left sides of the brain, should be mentioned.

If the chiasm is sectioned midsagittally so that all crossing fibers are cut, then the afferent connections from each eye go only to the hemisphere on the same side. When such an animal is trained to choose consistently between a circle and a square with one eye open, the animal retains the habit when the opened eye is closed and the previously closed eye is used. If both the optic chiasm and corpus callosum are sectioned, however, transfer of monocularly learned visual discrimination habits does not occur. Such sectioning isolates the two cerebral hemispheres from one another. With the left eye open and the right eye closed, all behavior dependent on visual stimuli will be determined by the left cerebral hemisphere and vice versa. In such a situation a unilateral cerebral lesion can be produced, and its effect determined by comparing the response of the animal to visual stimuli with either one or the other eye open.

In one experiment on a split-brain monkey, a right prefrontal lobe resection was performed. The right eye was left open and the left eye occluded.

Immediately the monkey displayed many of the behavior patterns described in animals with bilateral prefrontal lobe resections. Before the resection the animal bared its teeth and attempted to attack anyone approaching it; after removal of the prefrontal lobe the monkey responded placidly and peacefully to the approach of the person and accepted raisins from his hand. When the left eye was opened and the right eye was closed, the visual stimulus was projected to the undamaged side of the brain. The monkey's behavior abruptly reverted to the preoperative level, responding aggressively when the person appeared.

Other experiments have been performed in which the optic tract and corpus callosum have been sectioned, followed by a prefrontal lobectomy on one or the other side. In a split-brain monkey, if the right optic tract is sectioned and the right prefrontal lobe resected, the animal can see with both eyes and the remaining or left visual and prefrontal cortex are sufficient for learning to discriminate between a circle and a square. If, on the other hand, the right optic tract is cut, the corpus callosum is split, and the left prefrontal lobe is resected, the animal can still see with both eyes through the left visual cortex but neither visual cortex can communicate with either prefrontal lobe, and the monkey can no longer learn to solve new problems. In other words, at least one visual cortex must have connections with at least one prefrontal cortex.

17 PSYCHOGENIC DISTURBANCES

Until now we have been concerned with visual field defects associated with demonstrable organic lesions. One may also encounter visual field defects that do not have a demonstrable or conceivable physiologic basis. These visual field defects have variously been described as psychogenic, hysterical, supratentorial, or functional. We will refer to these as *functional defects*. Within the large category of field defects that do not have an anatomic substrate one must also include visual field defects found in malingering patients. In this chapter, we will differentiate functional field defects attributed to other causes from those seen in malingerers, which we will identify as such.

Functional field defects occur in patients with confirmed or at least categorically sound psychiatric diagnoses. Such patients may have a biochemical or hormonal abnormality that serves as the physiologic substrate for the systemic illness and therefore could be considered to be the lesion responsible for the visual field defect. Nevertheless, we will consider such field defects as functional field defects because they do not correspond to our current neuroanatomic knowledge.

Although patients with functional fields do not have a resectable lesion or a treatable infection, they have a real problem. It is important for the examiner and interpreter of the visual fields to remember this. Too often the conclusion "no organic disease" seems to imply that the patient is wasting everyone's time or in some way is abusing the health care system. At the very least, patients who have created or are experiencing such visual defects are signaling for help. We believe that it is most appropriate for these patients to undergo thorough evaluation, generally by the psychiatric service.

In monitoring such patients over time, one sees that the patient cannot just turn the defect on and off at will. The symptoms may change from moment to moment or may be vague and inconsistent, but they persist. When patients believe they cannot work or take care of themselves, they are, in a sense, functionally disabled.

Psychotic patients, such as those with schizophrenia and manic-depressive disease, commonly appear to suffer from nonorganic visual disturbances.

They may have delusions regarding loss of the eyes or vision or may be unable to look directly at an object or person or open their eyes. The visual fields in such persons are rarely abnormal.

The fundamental characteristic of functional visual field defects is that they do not ordinarily simulate the defects associated with organic diseases of the visual pathway. Rarely does one see a hemianoptic field defect. If a visual field defect is hemianoptic, it should be viewed with suspicion and considered organic until proven otherwise. Harrington followed up a patient for several years who consistently demonstrated dense bitemporal hemianopsia. Physical evaluation, laboratory studies, roentgenography (albeit with less sophisticated neuroradiologic methods than are available currently), and chiasmal exploration through a frontal craniotomy yielded negative results. Visual acuity remained 20/40 in each eye and there was no optic atrophy. Careful questioning finally elicited the story that a close friend had suffered marked visual loss from a pituitary adenoma. The patient had been relatively undisturbed by her visual field loss, and no amount of suggestion or psychotherapy has affected it through the years.

Another type of functional, or hysterical, hemianopsia is the missing half-field defect reported by Keane. The missing half-field is best observed with confrontation testing, because this method actually encourages the hemianoptic pattern. The usual pattern consists of decreased vision in one eye, an ipsilateral hemianopsia on testing the affected eye, full fields in the other eye, and a complete hemianopsia toward the affected side with both eyes open. The incompatibility of the monocular and binocular fields quickly demonstrates the functional nature of this field loss.

Central and paracentral scotomas and nerve fiber bundle defects are rarely if ever associated with functional loss; when present they should be considered the result of organic disease. On the other hand, the morphologic variation of functional field defects is almost infinite, and in some cases nearly any type of field defect may be demonstrated, depending on the examiner's suggestion.

The visual field defect may change from one type to another on successive examinations or even during the same examination, if the patient is given sufficient leeway to exercise the imagination. Suggestion by the examiner, if strong enough, may cause the patient to demonstrate a scotoma, particularly of the ring type, and we have even been able to elicit an irregular hemianoptic defect by telling the patient that it should be present. A fairly common example of this type of defect is found when a normal blind spot is demonstrated to the patient in the temporal field, and then it is suggested that the same type of scotoma should be present in the same location in the nasal field of the same eye.

Before even beginning to chart the visual fields of a patient suspected of having functional loss, the examiner may obtain certain information from watching the person's reaction to and avoidance of external obstacles. The person with functional loss views the disability with a certain nonchalance not in keeping with his or her tested visual acuity or field loss. This person carefully avoids obstacles placed in the way, never falling over them or getting hurt as does the organically blind individual with grossly restricted fields. In contrast, the malingerer exaggerates the disability and either dashes into objects or stands in a catatonic posture, refusing to move at all. We have often placed a small metal wastebasket between the examining room door and the chair. We then lead the patient from the door to the chair. Organically blind persons generally move cautiously into the room. If they brush against the wastebasket, they will move around it slowly or ask for assistance in negotiating the distance. Typically persons with functional field loss will simply walk around the wastebasket. Malingerers on the other hand, will often walk straight up to the wastebasket and kick it squarely in the center.

When testing with the Goldmann perimeter, a common result is a spiral or fatigue field. If the test object is moved from the periphery toward fixation along successive meridians on the perimeter arc, the stimulus will at first be seen in the normal position; but as each meridian is examined the test object

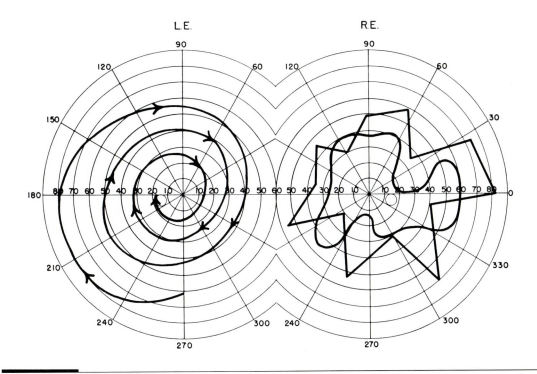

FIGURE 17-1 Two examples of visual field defects associated with hysterical amblyopia. Right eye shows star-shaped interlacing field resulting from alternately testing opposite ends of various meridians. This was form of fatigue field. Left eye shows typical spiral fatigue field often found in hysterical amblyopia and resulting from testing each meridian separately while rotating perimeter arc repeatedly around fixation.

will appear closer and closer to fixation. Thus the chart of the field will assume the appearance of a contracting spiral until finally the stimulus is seen only at fixation. The opposite of this defect, in the form of an expanding spiral, may be elicited by starting the test object close to fixation and moving it outward into the peripheral field along successive meridians (Figure 17-1). Another pattern one may see on the Goldmann perimeter is a star-shaped field with isopters that overlap one another in a braided fashion.

Inversion of the fields is another characteristic psychogenic disturbance. In normal people, if a test object is moved toward fixation from the periphery, the field will be somewhat smaller than if the same test object is moved outward from fixation and the patient is asked to note its disappearance. In the same manner the normal blind spot will often appear to be slightly smaller if the stimulus is moved from the seeing to the blind area than if it is moved from the blind to the seeing area. In a person with functional loss this tendency may be reversed, and a field to an outwardly moving test object is smaller than when the object is brought in from the periphery.

The visual field defects that are the most typical of functional loss are the various forms of concentric contraction, or tubular field (Figure 17-2). This type of field loss is so common in functional defects as to be almost

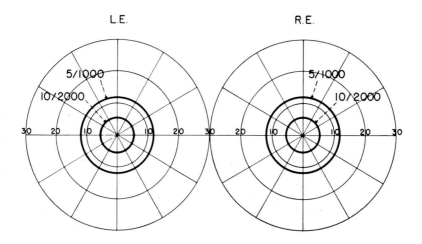

FIGURE 17-2 Tubular, or cylindric, type of concentric contraction of visual field seen in hysteria. Patient was 16-year-old girl whose sister had died shortly before of brain tumor. Vision with Snellen chart was 20/200, although patient could see 1-mm fixation target at 2 meters. Field in each eye was same size in centimeters at both 1 and 2 meters and was charted as though taken directly from tangent screen, with 2000 isopter charted 6 degrees from fixation and 1000 isopter charted 12 degrees from fixation. On tangent screen both fields fell on same circle. To avoid confusion in charting such fields, notation should always be made that radius of field is same in centimeters (not degrees) regardless of distance at which test is performed.

pathognomonic of the condition. Its character is such that it can only be functional or psychogenic in origin.

There is considerable variation in tubular fields. Some are extremely small, whereas others may show only slight reduction in size from the normal isopters. Some have sloping margins, whereas most show extremely steep borders. All instances of true tubular field defects associated with functional loss share one common factor of utmost diagnostic importance: the visual field is cylindric instead of cone shaped. This cannot result from an organic visual field defect.

The result of this cylindric-type field loss is that the visual field measures the same size in millimeters, regardless of the distance of the test object from the patient's eye, assuming that visual stimuli subtending the same visual angle are used at the varying distances. In instances of functional fields with sloping margins, calculating the visual angle subtended by the test objects may be important. Most tubular fields, however, have steep margins so that the size of the test object is inconsequential. In examining such a visual test the tangent screen must be used so that the distance from the examiner to the screen may be varied; an unmarked screen is preferred.

Eliciting such a field is straightforward. The patient is seated before the screen at a distance of 1 meter, and a suitably large fixation target is attached to the center of the screen. One or two meridians are tested rapidly with 5-, 20-, and 50-mm test objects. If the border of the field in these meridians is approximately the same for all three stimuli (i.e., the margin is steep), the largest test object is chosen for the remainder of the test.

One continues to test 8 to 12 meridians at a 1-meter distance, carefully and conspicuously noting the points at which the patient was first able to detect the test object. Our tangent screens are felt covered, and we use small black pins to do this. It is advisable to be ostentatious about this demarcation so that the patient is made aware of the limits of the field. The field is usually circular and may be contracted to a radius of 10, 15, or 20 cm from fixation. The patient is now moved up to a distance of 500 mm from the screen or back to 2 meters (i.e., the distance is halved or doubled).

If the field margins are not steep, the size of the test object should be halved for the 500-mm distance or doubled for the 2-meter distance. If the margins are steep, however, it does not matter which size test object is used.

With the patient in the new position, the examination is repeated using the same meridians and the same speed of test object movement. One should take care to approach the previous marking slowly to give the patient time to respond to the object's appearance.

In functional field contraction, the patient will see the test object at exactly the same spot on the tangent screen at 0.5 meter or 2 meters as at 1 meter. In other words, the field will measure the same diameter in millimeters for both distances.

In charting such a field one should note that the test was performed at varying distances and the field measured the same size in millimeters, not degrees, for the different distances. In general, the functional field may remain surprisingly constant in size, shape, and margin steepness from one examination to the next. The fields of malingering patients, however can change dramatically over short periods of time.

An interesting variant of the tubular field may be demonstrated occasionally. If the test object is held well outside the alleged area of intact field and the patient is directed sharply to look at it, he or she often involuntarily shifts fixation accurately from the central target to the peripheral test object. When asked how many objects he or she sees, the patient often responds "two," even when the central fixation target is smaller than the test object.

This involuntary fixation shift can be demonstrated on the Goldmann perimeter as well. If a large target is used in the normal manner of kinetic perimetry, the patient may deny seeing it until it approaches fixation, thus indicating a grossly constricted field. If the same target is rapidly moved from one area of the field to another, however, extinguishing the stimulus each time before it is moved again, the patient invariably shifts his or her gaze to the new area of appearance of the target. Even slight fixation shifts are easily detected through the telescopic sight on the perimeter. Furthermore, if a bright stimulus is exposed suddenly in an area of the field that has previously been demonstrated as blind, and the patient is commanded sharply to "look at the light," he or she usually involuntarily looks in the direction of the stimulus, thus indicating that it is, in fact, within the field of vision.

Thus far our discussion of functional field loss has centered on manual testing techniques. There are several reasons for this. The great benefit of automated perimetry has been its reproducibility and standardization. In perimetry standardization and flexibility are antagonistic to a great degree. Whereas standardization may be useful for serial testing in organic lesions, flexibility is essential in eliciting functional lesions. The tangent screen is the most flexible apparatus for testing the visual field, and thus it is the most useful for eliciting characteristic responses in patients with functional field loss. Only with the tangent screen can one move the patient readily from one testing distance to another. Furthermore, the tangent screen allows the examiner to record the field (e.g., with small chalk marks or black-tipped pens) in a way that allows the patient to see this while the field is being tested. This cannot be done with the Goldmann perimeter or with computerized perimeters.

The power of suggestion on the part of the examiner is extremely important in eliciting characteristic responses from the patient. This is possible with tangent screen or Goldmann perimetry, but is not possible with automated perimetry because the examiner does not control factors such as the stimulus presentation site or direction. Simple techniques such as commanding the patient to look at a light that should be in an anoptic area require that the examiner control the stimulus presentation.

Most computerized perimeters have built-in measures of patient reliability and reproducibility. These measures include an assessment of fixation losses or repetitions, an intratest measurement of short-term fluctuation, and determination of false-positive and false-negative responses. If a patient with tubular or grossly constricted fields is tested via automated perimeter, however, an interesting dilemma occurs. Smith and Baker found that the number of fixation losses, root mean square (RMS) fluctuation values, and false-positive responses for functional loss patients were approximately the same as for patients with similar organic visual loss. This finding seems unexpected, but careful consideration would predict these results. First, there is no reason for the patient to have a high number of fixation losses. Patients with functional loss are often cooperative and interested in their conditions. They tend to be very good candidates for visual field examination. Functional field loss rarely involves a central scotoma, and so patients have no difficulty seeing the fixation target. They are generally willing to submit to the test and to pay attention; as such they generate no greater number of fixation losses than do normal patients or patients with organic disease.

The abnormality in patients with functional loss is the *absence* of vision in areas that appear functionally normal. It is not the presence of hyperacute vision in areas that we know should not be seen. In false-positive responses the patients respond to lights that they really cannot see. This is exactly the opposite of what is expected in patients with functional field loss; they are expected to fail to respond to lights that we feel they can see. Thus the false-positive rate in such patients, as tested on computerized perimeters, would not be expected to be any higher than in normal patients or in those with organic disease.

The RMS fluctuation value, as measured on computerized perimeters that use a full-thresholding strategy, is a measure of the intratest variability of the patient. At first, it would seem that the patient with functional loss would have a difficult time being consistent in his or her responses between the first and second time a given point is tested randomly within a single examination. If this were the case, it would generate a very high RMS fluctuation value (there would be a large difference between the first and second examinations of single points throughout the field). However, if we consider that the patient with functional loss generally has a tubular field, with normal or near-normal vision within a few degrees of fixation and complete blindness peripheral to this, we can understand why the RMS fluctuation value is not much more elevated than values in patients with similar organic disease. First, any points that are tested twice in the blind area will yield the same zero value on both the first and second test, and thus the fluctuation or difference between the first and second test is zero. Second, within the seeing area the patient exhibits normal responses and thus yields fluctuation values of 1 to 3 decibels, the same as any functionally normal patient would in an area of normal vision. The only area where the patient is likely to exhibit a higher than normal fluctuation value is at the edge of the field. Here the patient may not be sure if a projected spot is in the blind area or the seeing area and may, in fact, give widely varying responses between two tests within the same examination. However, the same response occurs when a patient with organic field loss resulting in a steep-margined defect is tested repeatedly. A small fixation shift can make a stimulus that was projected into a seeing area one time fall on a nonseeing area the next time. This high local fluctuation is characteristic of steep-walled organic lesions. Finding such a change in a functional field is therefore of no diagnostic value. Another reason that the RMS fluctuation value in functional field loss tends to be fairly normal is that the number of fluctuation tests that occur on the margin between the seeing and nonseeing areas of the field is relatively small.

Thus the relatively high local fluctuation on the border of the seeing and nonseeing areas does not raise the total fluctuation value dramatically. The RMS fluctuation value in patients with functional tubular fields is higher than it is in patients with totally normal visual field tests, but it is not higher than in patients with constricted fields from organic causes.

The one value that is significantly elevated in patients with functional loss is the false-negative value. False-negative values are generated when a suprathreshold light is flashed into an area where the patient previously demonstrated sufficient visual sensitivity. This again would be expected because patients with functional loss are reporting vision that is poorer than we believe they possess. Such patients would be expected to respond negatively to suprathreshold stimuli at a higher frequency than would normal patients. The problem here is that patients with dramatic field loss from organic lesions also have a higher than normal false-negative response rate. This is for the same reason that patients with dense steep-margined defects have a higher than normal fluctuation rate. A small fixation shift can cause a stimulus that was formerly projected on a seeing area to fall instead on a nonseeing area on retesting. Thus a high false-negative response rate distinguishes patients with functional field loss from normal patients, but it does not distinguish them from patients with organically based constricted fields.

In sum, then, patients with functional visual field loss tested with computerized perimeters have abnormal results, but they are often not abnormal in a manner that allows us to differentiate them from organically constricted fields. The rare patient exhibits a totally bizarre visual field that does not correspond to any currently recognized anatomic pattern. However, fields like this are also seen in patients who are, for whatever reason, unable to cooperate fully with the test. Again, the field is abnormal, but does not allow distinction from organic disease.

Perhaps the most difficult situation occurs with patients who have functional field defects and a true organic lesion. The functional component of that pathologic process only serves to exaggerate this true organic lesion. Trying to separate the functional from the organic loss is challenging at best and in some cases may be impossible.

Malingering or conscious simulation of visual loss and visual field defects is usually for material or monetary gain. Many instances of malingering occur in an attempt to collect compensation for an alleged injury or to establish a permanent disability. Large sums of money are often involved in these cases, and payment may hinge on the differentiation of organic disease from simulation.

Simulated blindness of both eyes and even simulation of severe bilateral visual field defects is relatively rare. The pretense of marked visual loss is too difficult to sustain for more than a short period of time. Close observation of such a person over a few days or even hours will reveal fraudulent behavior.

Unilateral visual field loss, either central or peripheral, is much more easily simulated and can be sustained indefinitely. Because it is unilateral, however, it is readily subject to detection by means of the many different confusion tests, which lead the patient to believe that his or her good eye is being examined when, in fact, the eye with alleged visual loss is undergoing scrutiny. Such tests may be simple or elaborate. They are large in number and great ingenuity has been used in devising them.

The most common visual field defect in ocular malingering is concentric contraction. This may take the form of the tubular or cylindric field as seen in a nonmalingering functional defect, or it may be a simple depression of all the isopters. In the latter type of contraction, the outline of the visual field may be irregular and obviously unrelated to any anatomic or pathologic condition. In simple tubular fields the outline is usually circular and the margins are extremely steep, but unlike the field in the nonmalingering patient with functional loss the defect is likely to vary, especially if plotted on an unmarked tangent screen or perimeter.

When the field is marked on a tangent screen, its outlines should be clearly shown with pins or chalk. Some time later the examination should be interrupted and the patient taken to another room for another test, such as a test for color perception. While the patient is absent, the markings on the original screen are moved, usually closer to fixation. The patient is then returned to face the screen and the visual field is reexamined. In the classic case the new field will conform to the new markings on the screen. Shift of the fixation target between two examinations of the field may deceive the malingerer into locating the second field eccentrically around fixation.

Use of a prism over one eye while testing the binocular field may confuse the patient so that significant alteration in the size of the field is obtained.

Rapid shifting of test objects on the tangent screen carrier wand, with the patient unaware of these changes, may uncover visual acuity inconsistent with that obtained with Snellen letters.

General statements that apply to the simulator of disease or organ malfunction also apply to the simulator of visual field defects. Malingerers vary in shrewdness and in their intent to deceive. Many malingerers are stupid; some feel ashamed and are therefore clumsy in their deceit. Defects in malingering patients can be extremely difficult to differentiate from those in nonmalingering patients; in fact, the patient may become convinced of his or her illness and so merge into the latter condition.

The nonmalingering patient believes in the illness and cooperates in even the most rigorous examination. The malingerer is afraid to be examined and does everything possible to avoid examination and thus discovery; all through the examination the patient may make excuses for not continuing. The ophthalmoscopic light may produce intense photophobia. Refraction causes excessive watering, headache, blurring of vision, and dizziness. If all else fails, the malingerer may resort to abusing the examiner. The malingerer grossly exaggerates the symptoms during questioning and examination and is belligerent about his or her suffering. When alone and unconscious of observation, however, his or her entire attitude may change. When functional loss is cured, the patient is generally pleased and full of praise for the physician. The malingerer is stubborn and when caught in the lie becomes either surly and defiant or confused and ashamed.

Differentiating psychogenic visual loss from simulation is one of the most interesting challenges in perimetry and frequently requires ingenuity, shrewdness, and a keen understanding of people and psychology.

BIBLIOGRAPHY

The literature on the subject of the visual fields is so voluminous that a complete bibliography would occupy as many pages as this entire book.

The following list of references has been selected to include (1) textbooks and review articles that contain extensive bibliographic material and (2) articles that are particularly pertinent to certain phases of the subject. Many of these articles have become classics in the literature of perimetry, and most contain their own large bibliography.

Textbooks and monographs

Anderson DR: Perimetry, with and without automation, St Louis, 1987, The CV Mosby Co.

Bender ME: Disorders in perception, Springfield, Ill, 1952, Charles C Thomas, Publisher.

Bregeat P: Les syndromes opto-chiasmatique, Paris, 1979, Masson et Cie.

Brockhurst RJ, Boruchoff SA, Hutchinson BT, and Lassell S, editors: Controversy in ophthalmology, Philadelphia, 1977, WB Saunders Co.

Cant JS, editor: The optic nerve, St Louis, 1972, The CV Mosby Co.

Char DH: Clinical ocular oncology, New York, 1989, Churchill Livingstone, Inc.

Cogan DG: Neurology of the visual system, Springfield, Ill, 1966, Charles C Thomas, Publisher.

Critchley M: The parietal lobes, London, 1953, Edward Arnold & Co.

Cushing J and Eisenhardt L: Meningiomas, their classification, regional behavior, life history and surgical end results, Springfield, Ill, 1938, Charles C Thomas, Publisher.

Drance S and Anderson D: Automatic perimetry in glaucoma: a practical guide, San Diego, Calif, 1985, Grune & Stratton, Inc.

Dubois-Poulsen A: Le champ visuel, Société Française d'Ophthalmologie, Paris, 1952, Masson et Cie.

Duke-Elder WS: System of ophthalmology, St Louis, 1969, The CV Mosby Co.

Ellenberger C Jr: Perimetry, principles, technique and interpretation, New York, 1980, Raven Press.

Enoch J, Fitzgerald C, and Campos E: Quantitative layer-by-layer perimetry: an extended analysis, San Diego, Calif, 1989, Grune & Stratton, Inc.

Fankhauser F: Octopus visual field atlas, ed 2, Zurich, Switzerland, 1979, Interzeag Ag Schlieven, Publisher.

Fankhauser F and others: Proceedings of the First International Meeting on Automated Perimetry System Octopus, Zurich, Switzerland, 1979, Interzeag Ag Schlieven, Publisher.

Fraunfelder FT: Drug-induced ocular side effects and drug interactions, ed 2, Philadelphia, 1982, Lea & Febiger.

Glaser JS, editor: Neuro-ophthalmology, St Louis, 1975, The CV Mosby Co.

Grant MW: Toxicology of the eye, Springfield, Ill, 1962, Charles C Thomas, Publisher.

Greve EL: Single and multiple stimulus static perimetry in glaucoma: the two phases of perimetry, The Hague, Holland, 1973, Dr W Junk BV, Publishers.

Hayreh SS: Anterior ischemic optic neuropathy, New York, 1975, Springer-Verlag.

Heijl A and Greve E, editors: Sixth International Visual Fields Symposium, 1984, The Hague, Holland, 1985, Junk, Inc.

Heijl A and Greve E, editors: Seventh International Visual Fields Symposium, 1986, The Hague, Holland, 1987, Nijhoff-Junk, Inc.

Henderson WR: The pituitary adenomata, Br J Surg 26:811, 1939.

Huber A: Eye symptoms in brain tumors, St Louis, 1961, The CV Mosby Co.

Hughes B: The visual fields, Springfield, Ill, 1954, Charles C Thomas, Publisher.

Kolker A and Hetherington J: Becker-Shaffer's diagnosis and therapy of the glaucomas, St Louis, 1983, The CV Mosby Co.

Kooi KA and Marshall RE: Visual evoked potentials in central disorders of the visual system, New York, 1979, Harper & Row, Publishers, Inc.

Lieberman M and Drake M: A simplified guide to computerized perimetry, Thorofare, NJ, 1987, Slack, Inc.

Miller N: Walsh and Hoyt's clinical neuro-ophthalmology, vols 1-3, Baltimore, 1982, 1985, 1988, Williams & Wilkins.

Ourgaud A-G and Etienne R: L'exploration fonctionelle de l'oeil glaucomateux, Société Française d'Ophthalmologie, Paris, 1961, Masson et Cie.

Polyak SL: The retina, Chicago, 1941, University of Chicago Press.

Polyak SL: The vertebrate visual system, Chicago, 1957, University of Chicago Press.

Reed H and Drance SM: The essentials of perimetry, ed 2, London, 1972, Oxford University Press.

Scott GI: Traquair's clinical perimetry, ed 7, St Louis, 1957, The CV Mosby Co.

Shields MB: Textbook of glaucoma, ed 2, Baltimore, 1987, Williams & Wilkins.

Silverstone D and Hirsch J: Automated visual field testing, East Norwalk, Conn, 1986, Appleton-Century-Crofts.

Straatsma BR, Hall MO, Allen RA, and Crescitelli F: The retina, UCLA Forum in Medical Sciences, no 8, Berkeley, 1969, University of California Press.

Tate GW and Lynn JR: Principles of quantitative perimetry, New York, 1977, Grune & Stratton, Inc.

Teuber HL, Battersby WS, and Bender MD: Visual field defects after penetrating missile wounds of the brain, Cambridge, Mass, 1960, Harvard University Press.

Whalen W and Spaeth G, editors: Computerized visual fields: what they are and how to use them, Thorofare, NJ, 1985, Slack, Inc.

Whitnall SE: Anatomy of the human orbit and accessory organs of vision, ed 2, London, 1932, Oxford University Press.

Articles

Chapter 1

Harrington DO: The art of perimetry, Am J Ophthalmol 80:414, 1975.

Harrington DO, Leinfelder PJ, and Lyle DJ: Symposium: the value of perimetry as a diagnostic aid, Trans Am Acad Ophthalmol Otolaryngol 66:744, 1962.

Chapter 2

Enoch JM and Singar RN: Development of quantitative perimetric tests, Doc Ophthalmol 26:215, 1969.

Esterman B: Grid for scoring visual fields. I. Tangent screen, Arch Ophthalmol 77:780, 1967.

Esterman B: Grid for scoring visual fields. II. Perimeter, Arch Ophthalmol 79:400, 1968.

Fankhauser F and Enoch JM: The effect of blur on perimetric thresholds, Arch Ophthalmol 86:240, 1962.

Forstot SL, Weinstein GW, and Feicock KP: Studies with the Tübinger perimeter of Harms and Aulhorn, Ann Ophthalmol 2:834, 1970.

Goldmann H: Demonstration unseres neuen Projektions-kugelperimeters samt theoretischen und klinischen Bemerkungen über Perimetric, Ophthalmologica 111:187, 1946.

Harrington DO: Self-illuminated stimulus for tangent screen perimetry, Am J Ophthalmol 54:301, 1962.

Harrington DO: Tangent screen stimuli of variable luminance, Arch Ophthalmol 72:23, 1964.

Johnson CA and Keltner JL: Optimal rates of movement for kinetic perimetry, Arch Ophthalmol 105(1):73, 1987.

Keltner JL and Johnson CA: Automated and manual perimetry—a six-year overview. Special emphasis on neuro-ophthalmic problems, Ophthalmology 91(1):68, 1984.

Marlow SB: Fields of vision in chronic glaucoma: a comparison of fields with full and reduced illumination, Arch Ophthalmol 38:43, 1947.

Weekers R and La Vergne G: Applications cliniques de la périmétrie statique, Bull Soc Belg Ophthalmol 119:418, 1958.

Chapter 3

Drake MV: Design parameters of automated perimeters, Trans Pac Coast Otoophthalmol Soc 66:297, 1985.

Fankhauser F: Problems related to the design of automatic perimeters, Doc Ophthalmol 47(1):89, 1979.

Fankhauser F: Background illumination and automated perimetry, Arch Ophthalmol 104:1126, 1986 (letter).

Fankhauser F, Spahr J, and Bebie J: Three years' experience with the Octopus Automatic Perimeter, Doc Ophthalmol Proc Ser 14:7, 1977.

Flammer J: The concept of visual field indices, Graefes Arch Clin Exp Ophthalmol 224:389, 1986.

Flammer J, Drance SM, Fankhauser F, and Augustiny L: Differential light threshold in automated static perimetry: factors influencing short-term fluctuation, Arch Ophthalmol 102:876, 1984.

Flammer J, Drance SM, and Zulauf M: Differential light threshold: short- and long-term fluctuation in patients with glaucoma, normal controls, and patients with suspected glaucoma, Arch Ophthalmol 102:704, 1984.

Frisén L: High-pass resolution targets in peripheral vision, Ophthalmology 94:1104, 1987.

Greve EL: Performance of computer assisted perimeters, Doc Ophthalmol 53:343, 1982.

Heijl A: Computerised perimetry. I, Trans Ophthalmol Soc UK 104:76, 1985.

Heijl A, Lindgren G, and Olsson J: Normal variability of static perimetric threshold values across the central visual field, Arch Ophthalmol 105:1544, 1987.

Heijl A, Lindgren G, and Olsson J: Perimetric threshold variability and age, Arch Ophthalmol 106:450, 1988 (letter).

Hoskins HD, Magee S, Drake MV, and Kidd M: A system for the analysis of automated visual fields using the Humphrey Field Analyser, Doc Ophthalmol 49:145, 1987.

Johnson CA and Keltner JL: Automated suprathreshold static perimetry, Am J Ophthalmol 89:731, 1980.

Keltner JL and Johnson CA: Current status of automated perimetry. Is the ideal automated perimeter available? Arch Ophthalmol 104:347, 1986 (editorial).

Lewis RA, Johnson CA, Keltner JL, and Labermeier PK: Variability of quantitative automated perimetry in normal observers, Ophthalmology 93:878, 1986.

Mills RP, Hopp RH, and Drance SM: Comparison of quantitative testing with the Octopus, Humphrey, and Tübingen perimeters, Am J Ophthalmol 102:496, 1986.

Portney GL and Hanible JE: A comparison of four projection perimeters, Am J Ophthalmol 81:678, 1976.

Chapter 4

Amsler M: Earliest symptoms of disease of the macula, Br J Ophthalmol 37:521, 1953.

Bender MB and Furlow LT: Phenomenon of visual extinction in homonymous fields and the psychologic principles involved, Arch Neurol Psychiatr 53:29, 1945.

Bender MB and Teuber HL: Phenomenon of fluctuation, extinction, and completion in visual perception, Arch Neurol Psychiatr 55:627, 1946.

Flocks M, Rosenthal AR, and Hopkins JL: Mass visual screening via television, Trans Am Acad Ophthalmol 85:114, Nov 1978.

Frisén L: A versatile color confrontation test for the central visual field, Arch Ophthalmol 89:3, Jan 1973.

Harrington DO: Perimetry with ultraviolet (black) radiation and luminescent test objects, a preliminary report, Arch Ophthalmol 49:637, 1953.

Harrington DO and Flocks M: Visual field examination by a new tachystoscopic multiple pattern method, Am J Ophthalmol 37:719, 1954.

Harrington DO and Flocks M: Multiple pattern method of visual field examination, JAMA 157:645, 1955.

Harrington DO and Flocks M: The multiple pattern method of visual field examination, a five-year evaluation, Arch Ophthalmol 61:755, 1959.

Harrington DO and Hoyt WF: Ultraviolet radiation perimetry with monochromatic blue stimuli, Arch Ophthalmol 53:870, 1955.

Irvine SR: Measuring scotomas with the prism displacement test, Am J Ophthalmol 61(II):117, 1966.

Johnson CA, Keltner JL, and Balestrery FG: Static and acuity profile perimetry at various adaptation levels, Doc Ophthalmol 50:371, 1981.

Keltner JL and Johnson CA: Mass visual field screening in a driving population, Ophthalmology 87:785, 1982.

Roberts W: The multiple pattern tachistoscopic visual field screener in glaucoma, Arch Ophthalmol 58:244, 1957.

Robertson L: Use of the Harrington multiple pattern field screener in industry, Trans Am Acad Ophthalmol 60:806, 1956.

Smith JL: Color perimetry, Am J Ophthalmol 54:1085, 1962.

Weinstein GW: Clinical aspects of visually evoked potentials, Trans Am Ophthalmol Soc 75:627, 1977.

Wortis SB, Bender MB, and Teuber HL: The significance of the phenomenon of extinction, J Nerv Ment Dis 107:382, 1948.

Chapter 5

Barber AN, Ronstrom GN, and Muelling RJ Jr: Development of the visual pathway: optic chiasm, Arch Ophthalmol 52:447, 1954.

Ballantyne AJ: The nerve fiber pattern of the human retina, Trans Ophthalmol Soc UK 66:179, 1946.

Brouwer B: Projection of the retina on the cortex in man, localization of function in the cerebral cortex, Assoc Res Nerv Ment Dis Proc 13:529, 1934.

Brouwer B and Zeeman WPC: Experimental anatomical investigations concerning the projection of the retina on the primary optic centers in apes, J Neurol Psychopathol 6:1, 1925.

Brouwer B and Zeeman WPC: The projection of the retina in the primary optic neurone in monkeys, Brain 49:1, 1926.

Chacko LW: Laminar pattern of the lateral geniculate body in the primates, J Neurol Neurosurg Psychiatry 11:211, 1948.

Clark WEL: A morphological study of the lateral geniculate body, Br J Ophthalmol 16:264, 1932.

Clark WEL: The visual centers of the brain and their connections, Physiol Rev 22:205, 1942.

Clark WEL and Penman GG: The projection of the retina in the lateral geniculate body, Proc R Soc Lond 114:291, 1934.

Daniel PM and Whitteridge D: The representation of the visual field on the cerebral cortex in monkeys, J Physiol 159:203, 1961.

Dobelle WH, Turkel J, Henderson DC, and Evans JR: Mapping the representation of the visual field by electrical stimulation of human visual cortex, Am J Ophthalmol 88:727, 1979.

Harrington DO: The optic radiations in the temporal lobe, Trans West Ophthalmol Soc 2:131, 1936-1937.

Harrington DO: Autonomic nervous system in ocular disease, Am J Ophthalmol 29:1405, 1946.

Holmes GA: Contribution to the cortical representation of vision, Brain 54:470, 1931.

Horton JC, Greenwood MM, and Hubel DH: Non-retinotopic arrangement of fibers in the cat optic nerve, Nature 282:720, 1979.

Hoyt WF: Anatomic considerations of arcuate scotomas associated with lesions of the optic nerve and chiasm, a nauta axon degeneration study in the monkey, Bull Hopkins Hosp 3(2):57, 1962.

Hoyt WF: Correlative functional anatomy of the optic chiasm, Clin Neurosurg 17:189, 1969.

Hoyt WF and Luis O: Visual fiber anatomy in the infrageniculate pathways of the primate: uncrossed and crossed retinal quadrant fiber projections studied with nauta silver stain, Arch Ophthalmol 68:94, 1962.

Hoyt WF and Luis O: The primate chiasm: details of visual fiber organization studied by silver impregnation techniques, Arch Ophthalmol 70:69, 1963.

Hoyt WF and Tudor RC: The course of the parapapillary temporal retinal axons through the anterior optic nerve, Arch Ophthalmol 69:503, 1963.

Hubel DH and Wiesel TN: Receptive fields of single neurons in the cat's striate cortex, J Physiol (Lond) 148:574, 1959.

Hubel DH and Wiesel TN: Integrative action in the cat's lateral genicular body, J Physiol (Lond) 155:385, 1961.

Hubel DH and Wiesel TN: Receptive fields, binocular interaction and functional architecture in the cat's cortex, J Physiol (Lond) 26:106, 1962.

Hubel DH and Wiesel TN: Binocular interaction on striate cortex of kittens reared with artificial squint, J Neurophysiol 28:1041, 1965.

Hubel DH and Wiesel TN: Functional architecture of the macaque monkey visual cortex, Proc R Soc Lond (Biol) 198:1, 1977.

Lorente de Nó R: Studies on the structure of the cerebral cortex, Jehrb Psychol Neurol 45:381, 1934; 46:113, 1934.

Meyer A: The connections of the occipital lobes and the present status of the cerebral visual affections, Trans Assoc Am Physicians 22:7, 1907.

Penfield W, Evans JP, and Macmillan JA: Visual pathways in man: with particular reference to macular representation, Arch Neurol Psychiatry 33:816, 1935.

Polyak S: A contribution to the cerebral representation of the retina, J Comp Neurol 57:541, 1933.

Polyak S: Projection of the retina upon the cerebral cortex, based upon experiments with monkeys, Assoc Res Nerv Ment Dis Proc 13:535, 1934.

Putnam TJ: IV. The details of the organization of the geniculo-striate system in man, Arch Neurol Psychiatry 16:683, 1926.

Walls GL: The lateral geniculate nucleus and visual histophysiology, vol 9, no 1, Berkeley and Los Angeles, Calif, 1953, University of California Publications in Physiology, University of California Press.

Wilbrand H and Saenger A: Die Neurologie des Auges, vol 7, Wiesbaden, 1917, JF Bergmann.

Chapter 6

Abbie AA: Blood supply of the visual pathways, Med J Aust 2:199, 1938.

Archer DB, Ernest JT, and Krill A: Retinal, choroidal, and papillary circulations under conditions of induced ocular hypertension, Am J Ophthalmol 73:834, 1972.

Bergland R and Ray BS: Arterial supply of human optic chiasm, J Neurosurg 31:327, 1969.

Blumenthal M, Gitter KA, Best M, and Galin MA: Fluorescein angiography during induced ocular hypertension in man, Am J Ophthalmol 69:39, 1970.

Dawson BH: Blood vessels of human optic chiasm and their relation to those of hypophysis and hypothalamus, Brain 81(2):207, 1958.

François J and Neetens A: Central retinal artery and central optic nerve artery, Br J Ophthalmol 47:21, 1963.

François J and Neetens A: Vascularization of optic pathway. I. Lamina cribrosa and optic nerve, Br J Ophthalmol 38:472, 1954.

François J, Neetens A, and Collette JM: Vascular supply of the optic pathway. II. Further studies by micro-arteriography of the optic nerve, Br J Ophthalmol 39:220, 1955.

François J, Neetens A, and Collette JM: Vascularization of the optic pathway. IV. Optic tract and geniculate body, Br J Ophthalmol 40:341, 1956.

François J, Neetens A, and Collette JM: Vascularization of primary optic pathways, Br J Ophthalmol 42:62, 1958.

Hayreh SS: The central artery of the retina, Br J Ophthalmol 47:651, 1963.

Hayreh SS: Blood supply of optic nerve head and its role in optic atrophy, glaucoma, and edema of optic disk, Br J Ophthalmol 53:721, 1969.

Hayreh SS: Pathogenesis of occlusion of central retinal vessels, Am J Ophthalmol 72:998, 1971.

Hayreh SS: Anatomy and physiology of the optic nerve head. In Symposium: Glaucoma, Trans Am Acad Ophthalmol Otolaryngol 78:240, 1974.

Henkind P and Levitsky M: Angioarchitecture of the optic nerve. I. The papilla; II. Lamina cribrosa, Am J Ophthalmol 68:979, 1969.

Hughes B: Blood supply of optic nerve and chiasm and its clinical significance, Br J Ophthalmol 42:106, 1958.

Phelps GK and Phelps CD: Blood pressure and pressure amaurosis, Invest Ophthalmol 14:237, 1975.

Smith CG and Richardson WFG: The course and distribution of the arteries supplying the visual (striate) cortex, Am J Ophthalmol 61:1391, 1966.

Wollschlaeger PB, Wollschlaeger G, Ide CH, and Hart WM: Arterial blood supply of the human optic chiasm and surrounding structures, Ann Ophthalmol 3:862, 1971.

Chapter 7

Harrington DO: Analysis of some unusual and difficult visual field defects, Trans Ophthalmol Soc UK 92:15, 1973.

Jaffe GJ, Alvarado JA, and Juster RP: Age-related changes of the normal visual field, Arch Ophthalmol 104:1021, 1986.

Keltner JL and Johnson CA: Visual function, driving safety, and the elderly, Ophthalmology 94:1180, 1987.

Keltner JL, Johnson CA, and Balestrery FG: Suprathreshold static perimetry: initial clinical trials with the Fieldmaster Automated Perimeter, Arch Ophthalmol 97:260, 1979.

Sloan LL and Brown DJ: Area and luminance of test objects as variables in projection perimetry, clinical studies, Vision Res 2:527, 1962.

Chapter 8

Bunt A and Minkler DS: Foveal sparing, Arch Ophthalmol 95:1445, 1977.

Gasser P and Flammer J: Optic neuropathy of Graves' disease: a report of a perimetric follow-up, Ophthalmologica 192(1):22, 1986.

Gunderson CH and Hoyt WF: Geniculate hemianopia: incongruous homonymous field defects in two patients with partial lesions of the lateral geniculate nucleus, J Neurol Neurosurg Psychiatry 34:1, 1971.

Knox DL and Cogan DG: Eye pain and hemianopia, Am J Ophthalmol 54:1091, 1962.

Koerner F and Teuber HL: Visual field defects after missile injuries to the geniculo-striate pathway in man, Exp Brain Res 18:88, 1973.

Lansche RK and Rucker CW: Progression of defects in visual fields produced by hyaline bodies in the optic disks, Arch Ophthalmol 58:115, 1957.

O'Connell JEA and DuBoulay EPGH: Binasal hemianopia, J Neurol Neurosurg Psychiatry 36:697, 1973.

Radius RL and Anderson DR: The histology of retinal nerve fiber layer bundles and bundle defects, Arch Ophthalmol 97:948, 1979.

Rönne H: Ueber die Inkongruenz und Asymmetrie im Homonym hemianopischen Gesichtsfeld, Klin Mbl Augenheilk 54:309, 1915.

Rönne H: Zur Theorie und Technik der Bjerrumchen Gesichtsfelduntersuchung, Arch Augenheilk 78:284, 1915.

Rönne H: Ueber die Form der nasalen Gesichtsfeldesdefekte bei Glaucom, Arch Ophthalmol 71:52, 1909.

Rönne H: The different types of defects of the field of vision, JAMA 89:1860, 1927.

Sanders TE, Gay AS, and Newman M: Drusen of optic disk: hemorrhagic complications, Trans Am Ophthalmol Soc 68:186, 1970.

Smith JL: Homonymous hemianopia: a review of one hundred cases, Am J Ophthalmol 54:616, 1962.

Walsh FB: Pathological-clinical correlations. I. Indirect trauma to optic nerves and chiasm. II. Certain cerebral involvements associated with defective blood supply, Invest Ophthalmol 5:433, 1966.

Wolff E: The causation of amblyopia following gastric and other hemorrhages, Trans Ophthalmol Soc UK 55:342, 1935.

Chapter 9

Flammer J and Bebie H: Lens opacity meter: a new instrument to quantify lens opacity, Ophthalmologica 195:69, 1987.

Guthauser V and Flammer J: Quantifying visual field damage caused by cataract, Am J Ophthalmol 106:480, 1988.

Chapter 10

Char DH and others: Diagnostic modalities in choroidal melanoma, Am J Ophthalmol 89:223, 1980.

Cogan DG: Hemianopsia and associated symptoms due to parieto-temporal lobe lesions, Am J Ophthalmol 50:1056, 1960.

Chapter 11

Hamed LA, Schatz NJ, Glaser JS, and Gass JDM: Acute idiopathic blind spot enlargement without optic disc edema, Arch Ophthalmol 106:1030, 1988.

Hochheimer BF, D'Anna SA, and Calkins JL: Retinal damage from light, Am J Ophthalmol 88:1039, 1979.

Hoyt WF: Letter, Arch Ophthalmol 108:1031, 1988.

Chapter 12

Airaksinen PJ, Lakowski R, Drance SM, and Price M: Color vision and retinal nerve fiber layer in early glaucoma, Am J Ophthalmol 101:208, 1986.

Airaksinen PJ and others: Diffuse and localized nerve fiber loss in glaucoma, Am J Ophthalmol 98:566, 1984.

Airaksinen PJ and others: Visual field and retinal nerve fiber layer comparisons in glaucoma, Arch Ophthalmol 103:205, 1985.

Alvarado J and others: Age-related changes in trabecular meshwork cellularity, Invest Ophthalmol Vis Sci 21:714, 1981.

Anderson DR and Hendrickson A: Effect of intraocular pressure on rapid axoplasmic transport in monkey optic nerve, Invest Ophthalmol 13:771, 1974.

Armaly MF: Ocular pressure and visual fields, Arch Ophthalmol 81:25, 1969.

Heuer DK and others: The influence of simulated light scattering on automated perimetric threshold measurements, Arch Ophthalmol 106:1247, 1988.

Spaeth GL: The management of cataract in patients with glaucoma: a comparative study. I, Trans Ophthalmol Soc UK 100:195, 1980.

Flindall RJ and Drance SM: Visual field studies of benign choroidal melanomata, Arch Ophthalmol 81:41, 1969.

Weinreb RN and Perlman JP: The effect of refractive correction on automated perimetric thresholds, Am J Ophthalmol 101:706, 1986.

McDonald HR and Irvine AR: Light-induced maculopathy from the operating microscope in extracapsular cataract extraction and intraocular lens implantation, Ophthalmology 90:945, 1983.

McIntyre DJ: Phototoxicity: the eclipse filter, Ophthalmology 92:364, 1985.

Rinkoff J, Machemer R, Hida T, and Chandler D: Temperature-dependent light damage to the retina, Am J Ophthalmol 102:452, 1986.

Armaly MF: Visual field defects in early open angle glaucoma, Trans Am Ophthalmol Soc 69:147, 1971.

Armaly MF: Selective perimetry for glaucomatous defects in ocular hypertension, Arch Ophthalmol 87:518, 1972.

Armaly MF and Araki M: Optic nerve circulation and ocular pressure, Invest Ophthalmol 14:724, 1975.

Aulhorn E and Harms H: Early visual field defects in glaucoma. In Glaucoma Tutzing Symposium, Proceedings of the Twentieth International Congress of Ophthalmology, Basel, Switzerland, 1967, S Karger.

Begg IS, Drance SM, and Sweeney VP: Ischemic optic neuropathy in chronic simple glaucoma, Br J Ophthalmol 55:73, Feb 1971.

Brais P and Drance SM: The temporal field in chronic simple glaucoma, Arch Ophthalmol 88:518, 1972.

Caprioli J, Sears M, and Spaeth GL: Comparison of visual field defects in normal-tension glaucoma and high-tension glaucoma, Am J Ophthalmol 102:402, 1986.

Caprioli J and Spaeth GL: Static threshold examination of the peripheral nasal visual field in glaucoma, Arch Ophthalmol 103:1150, 1985.

Dollery CT, Henkind P, Kohner EM, and Paterson JW: Effect of raised intraocular pressure on the retinal and choroidal circulation, Invest Ophthalmol 7:191, 1968.

Douglas GR, Drance SM, and Schulzer M: The visual field and nerve head in angle-closure glaucoma, Arch Ophthalmol 93:409, 1975.

Drake MV: Neodymium: YAG laser iridotomy, Surv Ophthalmol 32:171, 1987.

Drance SM: Susceptibility of the eye to raised intraocular pressure, Arch Ophthalmol 68:478, 1962.

Drance SM: The glaucomatous visual field, Br J Ophthalmol 56:186, 1972.

Drance SM: Is ischemia the villain in glaucomatous cupping and atrophy? In Brockhurst RJ, Boruchoff SA, Hutchinson BI, and Lessell S, editors: Controversy in ophthalmology, Philadelphia, 1977, WB Saunders Co.

Drance SM and Begg IS: Sector hemorrhage—a probably acute ischemic disc change in chronic simple glaucoma, Can J Ophthalmol 5:137, 1970.

Drance SM, Schulzer M, Douglas GR, and Wijsman K: Short-term effect of intraocular pressure variation on differential light threshold and colour vision, Can J Ophthalmol 22:221, 1987.

Drance SM, Wheeler C, and Pattullo M: The use of static perimetry in the early detection of glaucoma, Can J Ophthalmol 2:249, 1967.

Drance SM, Wheeler C, and Pattullo M: Uniocular open-angle glaucoma, Am J Ophthalmol 65:891, 1968.

Drance SM and others: Symposium on the effect of glaucoma on visual function, Invest Ophthalmol 8:75, Feb 1969.

Drance SM and others: Diffuse visual field loss in chronic open-angle and low-tension glaucoma, Am J Ophthalmol 104:577, 1987.

Drance SM and others: Response of blood flow to warm and cold in normal and low-tension glaucoma patients, Am J Ophthalmol 105(1):35, 1988.

Ernest JT: Pathogenesis of glaucomatous optic nerve disease, Trans Am Ophthalmol Soc 73:366, 1975.

Flammer J and Drance SM: Correlation between color vision scores and quantitative perimetry in suspected glaucoma, Arch Ophthalmol 102(1):38, 1984.

Flammer J, Drance SM, Augustiny L, and Funkhouser A: Quantification of glaucomatous visual field defects with automated perimetry, Invest Ophthalmol Vis Sci 26(2):176, 1985.

Gasser P, Flammer J, and Mahler F: The use of calcium antagonists in the treatment of ocular circulation symptoms in the framework of a vasospastic syndrome, Schweiz Med Wochenschr 118(6):201, 1988.

Greenidge KC, Spaeth GL, and Traverso CE: Change in appearance of the optic disc associated with lowering of intraocular pressure, Ophthalmology 92:897, 1985.

Harrington DO: Pathogenesis of the glaucomatous visual field defect, Transactions of the Fifth Conference on Glaucoma, New York, 1960, Josiah Macy Jr Foundation.

Harrington DO: The pathogenesis of the glaucoma field, Am J Ophthalmol 47:177, 1959.

Harrington DO: The Bjerrum scotoma, Trans Am Ophthalmol Soc 62:324, 1964.

Harrington DO: Differential diagnosis of the arcuate scotoma, Invest Ophthalmol 8:96, 1969.

Hayreh SS, Revie IHS, and Edwards J: Vasogenic origin of visual field defects and optic nerve changes in glaucoma, Br J Ophthalmol 54:461, 1970.

Hayreh SS and Walker WM: Fluorescent fundus photography in glaucoma, Am J Ophthalmol 63:982, 1967.

Heijl A and Krakau CET: An automatic perimeter for glaucoma visual field screening and control: construction and clinical cases, Albrecht Von Graefes Arch Klin Exp Ophthalmol 197:13, 1975.

Heijl A, Lindgren G, and Olsson J: Computer-assisted recognition of glaucomatous field loss, Arch Ophthalmol 106:721, 1988 (letter).

Heijl A and Lundqvist L: The frequency distribution of earliest glaucomatous visual field defects documented by automatic perimetry, Acta Ophthalmol (Copenh) 62:658, 1984.

Hetherington J Jr: Symposium glaucoma, Trans Am Acad Ophthalmol Otolaryngol 78:239, 1974.

Hoyt WF, Frisén L, and Newman NM: Funduscopy of nerve fiber layer defects in glaucoma, Invest Ophthalmol 12:814, 1973.

Hoyt WF, Schlicke B, Eckelhoff RJ: Funduscopic appearance of a nerve fiber bundle defect, Br J Ophthalmol 56:577, 1972.

Kass MA, Kolker AE, and Becker B: Prognostic factors in glaucomatous visual field loss, Arch Ophthalmol 94:1274, 1976.

Kearns TP and Rucker CW: Arcuate defects in the visual fields, Am J Ophthalmol 45:505, 1958.

King D and others: Comparison of visual field defects in normal-tension glaucoma and high-tension glaucoma, Am J Ophthalmol 101:204, 1986.

Kolker AB, Becker B, and Mills DW: Intraocular pressure and visual fields: effects of corticosteroids, Arch Ophthalmol 72:772, 1964.

LeBlanc RP, Lee A, and Baxter M: Peripheral nasal field defects. In Heijl A and Greve EL, editors: Sixth International Visual Fields Symposium, 1984, The Hague, Holland, 1985, Junk, Inc.

Levene RZ: Low tension glaucoma: a critical review and new material, Surv Ophthalmol 24:621, 1980.

Levy NS: Effects of elevated intraocular pressure on slow axonal protein flow, Invest Ophthalmol 13:691, 1974.

Lewis RA and Johnson CA: Early detection of glaucomatous damage. I. Psychophysical disturbances, Surv Ophthalmol 30(2):111, 1985.

Mikelberg FS and Drance SM: The mode of progression of visual field defects in glaucoma, Am J Ophthalmol 98:443, 1984.

Mills RP and Drance SM: Esterman disability rating in severe glaucoma, Ophthalmology 93:371, 1986.

Minckler DS and Spaeth GL: Optic nerve damage in glaucoma, Surv Ophthalmol 26:128, 1981.

Morin JD: Changes in visual fields in glaucoma: static and kinetic perimetry in 2000 patients, Trans Am Ophthalmol Soc 77:622, 1979.

Pederson JE and Anderson DR: The mode of progressive disc cupping in ocular hypertension and glaucoma, Arch Ophthalmol 98:490, 1980.

Posner A and Schlossman A: Development of changes in the visual fields associated with glaucoma, Arch Ophthalmol 39:623, 1948.

Posner A and Schlossman A: The value of changes in the visual fields in the prognosis in glaucoma, Am J Ophthalmol 33:1391, 1950.

Quigley HA and Addicks EM: Quantitative studies of nerve fiber layer defects, Arch Ophthalmol 100:807, 1982.

Radius RL and Bade B: Pressure-induced optic nerve axonal transport interruption in cat eyes, Arch Ophthalmol 99:2163, 1981.

Rock WJ, Drance SM, and Morgan RW: Modification of Armaly visual field screening technique for glaucoma, Can J Ophthalmol 6:283, 1971.

Schulzer M, Mikelberg FS, and Drance SM: A study of the value of the central and peripheral isoptres in assessing visual field progression in the presence of paracentral scotoma measurements, Br J Ophthalmol 71:422, 1987.

Seamone C and others: The value of indices in the central and peripheral visual fields for the detection of glaucoma, Am J Ophthalmol 106:180, 1988.

Sears ML: Visual field loss in glaucoma, Am J Ophthalmol 88:493, 1979.

Shaffer RN and Hetherington J: The case for conservatism in open angle glaucoma management, Can J Ophthalmol 3:11, 1968.

Spaeth GL: The effect of change in intraocular pressure on the natural history of glaucoma: lowering intraocular pressure in glaucoma can result in improvement of visual fields. III, Trans Ophthalmol Soc UK 104:256, 1985.

Susanna R, Drance SM, and Douglas GR: Disk hemorrhages in patients with elevated intraocular pressure, Arch Ophthalmol 97:284, 1979.

Traquair H: The nerve fiber bundle defect, Trans Ophthalmol Soc UK 64:122, 1944.

Tsamparlakis JC: Effects of transient induced elevation of the intraocular pressure on the visual field, Br J Ophthalmol 48:237, 1964.

Varma R and others: Positional changes in the vasculature of the optic disk in glaucoma, Am J Ophthalmol 104:457, 1987.

Werner E and Drance SM: Early visual field disturbances in glaucoma, Arch Ophthalmol 95:1173, 1978.

Werner EB and others: A comparison of experienced clinical observers and statistical tests in detection of progressive visual field loss in glaucoma using automated perimetry, Arch Ophthalmol 106:619, 1988.

Chapter 13

Benton CD Jr and Calhoun FP Jr: Ocular effects of methyl alcohol poisoning: report of a catastrophe involving 230 persons, Trans Am Acad Ophthalmol Otolaryngol 56:875, 1952.

Carroll FD: The etiology and treatment of tobacco-alcohol amblyopia, Trans Am Ophthalmol Otolaryngol Soc 41:385, 1943.

Cordes FC and Harrington DO: Toxic amblyopia due to tobacco and alcohol: treatment with vasodilators; a report of eight cases, Arch Ophthalmol 13:435, 1935.

DeVita EG, Miao M, and Sadun AA: Optic neuropathy in ethambutol-treated renal tuberculosis, J Clin Neuro Ophthalmol 7:77, 1987.

Foulds WS, Chisholm IA, Bronte-Stewart J, and Reid HCR: Investigation and therapy of the toxic amblyopias, Trans Ophthalmol Soc UK 90:739, 1970.

Harrington DO: Amblyopia due to tobacco, alcohol and nutritional deficiency, Am J Ophthalmol 53:967, 1962.

Hobbs HE, Sorsby A, and Freedman A: Retinopathy following chloroquine therapy, Lancet 2:478, 1959.

Okun E, Gouras P, Bernstein H, and Von Sallman L: Chloroquine retinopathy, Arch Ophthalmol 69:59, 1962.

Ramilo O, Kinane BT, and McCracken GH: Chloramphenicol neurotoxicity, Pediatr Infect Dis J 7:358, 1988.

Samples JR and Younge BR: Tobacco-alcohol amblyopia, J Clin Neuro Ophthalmol 1:213, 1981.

Schatz H and Drake MV: Self-injected retinal emboli, Ophthalmology 86:468, 1979.

Chapter 14

Asselman P, Chadwick DW, and Marsden CD: Visual evoked responses in the diagnosis and management of patients suspected of multiple sclerosis, Brain 98:261, 1975.

Björk A, Laurell CG, and Laurell U: Bilateral optic nerve hypoplasia with normal visual acuity, Am J Ophthalmol 86:524, 1978.

Boldt HA, Armin FH, Tourtellette WW, and DeJong RN: Retrochiasmal visual field defects from multiple sclerosis, Arch Neurol 8:565, 1963.

Brown GC, Shields JA, and Goldberg RE: Congenital pits of the optic nerve head, Ophthalmology 87:51, Jan 1980.

Cordes FC: Hereditary optic atrophy (Leber's disease), Trans Am Ophthalmol Soc 31:289, 1933.

Ellenberger C and Ziegler SB: Visually evoked potentials and quantitative perimetry in multiple sclerosis, Ann Neurol 1:561, 1977.

Frisén L: Clinical features of optic neuritis standard examination techniques. I, Bull Soc Belge Ophthalmol 208:131, 1983.

Frisén L, Holmgaard L, and Rosencrantz M: Sectorial optic atrophy and homonymous horizontal sectoranopia: a lateral choroidal artery syndrome? J Neurol Neurosurg Psychiatry 41:374, 1978.

Hart WM, Burde RM, Klingele TG, and Purlmutter JC: Bilateral optic nerve sheath meningioma, Arch Ophthalmol 98:149, Jan 1980.

Hoyt CS: Autosomal dominant optic atrophy: a spectrum of disability, Ophthalmology 87:245, 1980.

Hoyt WF, Rios-Montenegro EN, Behrens MM, and Eckelhoff RJ: Homonymous hemianoptic hypoplasia: funduscopic features in standard and red-free illumination in three patients with congenital hemiplegia, Br J Ophthalmol 6:537, 1972.

Johnson CA, Keltner JL, and Balestrery FG: Suprathreshold static perimetry in glaucoma and other optic nerve disease, Ophthalmology 86:1278, 1979.

Kjer P: Infantile optic atrophy with dominant inheritance. In Handbook of clinical neurology, vol 13, Amsterdam, 1973, North-Holland Publishing Co.

Kline LB and Glaser JS: Dominant optic atrophy: the clinical profile, Arch Ophthalmol 97:1680, 1979.

Knight CL, Hoyt WF, and Wilson CB: Syndrome of incipient prechiasmal optic nerve compression, Arch Ophthalmol 87:1, Jan 1972.

Lorentzen SE: Drusen of the optic disc: a clinical and genetic study, Acta Ophthalmol (suppl 90), 1966.

Mooney AJ: On the color of the optic disc and its relation to various field defects, Trans Ophthalmol Soc UK 84:227, 1964.

Moore JE and Woods AC: Pathology and pathogenesis of syphilitic primary optic atrophy: critical review, Am J Ophthalmol 23:1, 1940.

Nikoskelainen E: Clinical, prognostic, and etiological studies on optic neuritis, Departments of Ophthalmology, Neurology, and Clinical Chemistry, Turku University Central Hospital, Turku, Finland, Acta Ophthalmologica 53:254, 1975.

Patterson VH and Heron JR: Visual field abnormalities in multiple sclerosis, J Neurol Neurosurg Psychiatry 43:205, 1980.

Quigley HA and Anderson DR: The histologic basis of optic disk pallor in experimental optic atrophy, Am J Ophthalmol 83:709, 1977.

Seeley R and Smith JL: Visual field defects in optic nerve hypoplasia, Am J Ophthalmol 73:882, 1972.

Smith JL, Hoyt WF, and Susac JO: Ocular fundus in acute Leber optic neuropathy, Arch Ophthalmol 90:349, 1946.

Stansburg FC: Neuromyelitis optica (Devic's disease): presentation of five cases with pathologic study and review of the literature, Arch Ophthalmol 42:292, 465, 1946.

Trobe JD and Glaser JS: Quantitative perimetry in compressive optic neuropathy, Arch Ophthalmol 96:1210, 1978.

Vail D: Syphilitic opto-chiasmatic arachnoiditis, Am J Ophthalmol 22:505, 1939.

Wilson WB and Keyser RB: Comparison of the pattern and diffuse-light visual evoked responses in definite multiple sclerosis, Arch Neurol 37:30, Jan 1980.

Chapter 15

Chamlin M, Davidoff LM, and Feiring EH: Ophthalmologic changes produced by pituitary tumors, Am J Ophthalmol 40:353, 1955.

Cushing H: The chiasmal syndrome of primary optic atrophy and bitemporal field defects with a normal sella turcica, Arch Ophthalmol 3:505, 704, 1930.

Cushing H and Walker CB: Distortion of the visual fields in cases of brain tumor, binasal hemianopsia, Arch Ophthalmol 41:559, 1912.

Cushing H and Walker CB: Distortions of the visual fields in cases of brain tumor (chiasma lesions with especial reference to bitemporal hemianopsia), Brain 37:341, 1914-1915.

Glaser JS, Hoyt WF, and Corbett J: Visual morbidity with chiasmal glioma, Arch Ophthalmol 85:3, Jan 1971.

Gregorius FK, Hepler RS, and Stern WE: Loss and recovery of vision with suprasellar meningioma, J Neurosurg 42:69, 1975.

Harrington DO: Localizing value of incongruity in defects in the visual fields, Arch Ophthalmol 21:453, 1939.

Kearns TP, Wagener HP, and Millikan CH: Bilateral homonymous hemianopsia, Arch Ophthalmol 53:560, 1955.

Mooney AJ: Perimetry and angiography in the diagnosis of lesions in the pituitary region, Trans Ophthalmol Soc UK 72:49, 1952.

Spalding JMK: Wounds of the visual pathway, J Neurol Neurosurg Psychiatry 15:99, 169, 1952.

Toland J and Mooney A: On the enlarged sella, Trans Ophthalmol Soc UK 93:717, 1973.

Traquair HM, Dott NJ, and Russell WR: Traumatic lesions of the chiasm, Brain 58:398, 1935.

Wagener HP and Love JG: Fields of vision in cases of tumor of Rathke's pouch, Arch Ophthalmol 29:873, 1943.

Chapter 16

Benton S, Levy I, and Swash M: Vision in the temporal crescent in occipital infarction, Brain 103:83, March 1980.

Boldt HA, Arnim FH, Tourtellette WW, and Dejong RN: Retrochiasmal visual field defects from multiple sclerosis, Arch Neurol 8:565, 1963.

Cushing H: Distortions of the visual fields in cases of brain tumor: the field defects produced by temporal lobe lesions, Brain 44:341, 1922.

Dyken ML and Pokras R: The performance of endovitrectomy for disease of the extracranial arteries of the head, Stroke 15:948, 1984.

Frisen L, Holmgaard L, and Rosenkrantz M: Sectorial optic atrophy and homonymous horizontal sectoranopia: a lateral choroidal artery syndrome? J Neurol Neurosurg Psychiatry 34:1, 1971.

Gunderson CH and Hoyt WF: Genticulate hemianopia: incongrous homonymous field defects in two patients with partial lesions of the lateral genticulate nucleus, J Neurol Neurosurg Psychiatry 34:1, 1971.

Harrington DO: Character of the visual field in lesions of the temporal and occipital lobe, Arch Ophthalmol 66:778, 1961.

Harrington DO: Visual field character in temporal and occipital lobe lesions, Trans Am Ophthalmol Soc 59:333, 1961.

Hollenhorst RW: Carotid and vertebral-basilar arterial stenosis and occlusion, neuro-ophthalmologic considerations, Trans Am Acad Ophthalmol Otolaryngol 66:166, 1962.

Horrax G: Visual hallucinations as a cerebral localizing phenomenon, with special reference to their occurrence in tumors of the temporal lobe, Arch Neurol Psychiatry 10:532, 1923.

Horrax G and Putnam TJ: Distortions of visual fields in cases of brain tumors: the field defects and hallucinations produced by tumors of the occipital lobe, Brain 55:499, 1932.

Hoyt WF and Kommerall G: Ocular fundus in homonymous hemianopsia, Klin Monatsbl Augenheilkd 162:456, 1973.

Huber A: Ocular symptoms of cerebral aneurysms, Ophthalmologica 167:165, 1973.

Jaffe NS and Durkin LS: Geniculocalcarine injuries in war casualties, Arch Ophthalmol 49:591, 1953.

Liversedge A and Smith V: The place of ophthalmodynamometry in the investigation of cerebrovascular disease, Brain 84:274, 1961.

McAuley DL and Ross Russell RW: Correlation of CAT scan and visual field defects in vascular lesions of the posterior visual pathways, J Neurol Neurosurg Psychiatry 42:298, 1979.

McLaurin EB and Harrington DO: Intracranial sarcoidosis with optic tract and temporal lobe involvement, Am J Ophthalmol 86:656, 1978.

Riddoch G: Dissociation of visual perception due to occipital injuries with especial reference to appreciation of movement, Brain 40:15, 1917.

Safran A and Glaser S: Statokinetic dissociation in lesions of anterior visual pathways, Arch Ophthalmol 98:291, 1980.

Saper JR: Migraines. I. Classification and pathogenesis, JAMA 239:2480, 1978.

Saper JR: Migraine. II. Treatment, JAMA 239:2480, 1978.

Smith JL: Homonymous hemianopia: a review of one hundred cases, Am J Ophthalmol 54:616, 1962.

Spalding JMK: Wounds of the visual pathways, J Neurol Neurosurg Psychiatry 15:99, 169, 1952.

Troost BT and Newton TH: Occipital lobe arteriovenous malformations, Arch Ophthalmol 93:250, 1975.

Van Buren JM and Baldwin M: The architecture of the optic radiation in the temporal lobe of man, Brain 81:15, 1958.

Chapter 17

Harrington DO: Ocular manifestations of psychosomatic disorders, JAMA 133:669, 1947.

Keane JR: Hysterical hemianopia: the "missing half" field defect, Arch Ophthalmol 97:865, 1977.

Keltner JL, May WN, Johnson CA, and Post RB: The California syndrome: functional visual complaints with potential economic impact, Ophthalmology 92:427, 1985.

Miller BA: A review of practical tests for ocular malingering and hysteria, Surv Ophthalmol 17:241, 1973.

Smith T and Baker R: Perimetric findings in functional disorders using automated techniques, Ophthalmology 94:1562, 1987.

Yasuna ER: Hysterical amblyopia: its differentiation from malingering, Am J Ophthalmol 29:570, 1946.

Index

A

Abuse, drug, visual problems from, 236-237

Acidosis in methyl alcohol poisoning, 227

Acuity, visual; *see* Visual acuity

Adaptation, dark or light, of eye, effect of, on visual field examination, 99

Adenoma(s)
    chromophobic, of pituitary, visual field defects in, 271
    pituitary
        bitemporal hemianopsia in, 118-119
        chromophobic, visual field defects in, 271
        visual fields in
            defects in, *facing 280, 280, 282-284*, 292-293, *294*
            depression in, *110*

Age, effect of, on visual field size, 101

Age-related macular degeneration, visual field defects in, 154, *155*

Agnosia
    from carbon monoxide poisoning, 235
    visual, in occipital cortical lesions, 357

Altitudinal hemianopsia, 120-121; *see also* Hemianopsia, altitudinal

Amaurosis
    in lead poisoning, 228
    from salicylate poisoning, 234

Amaurosis fugax
    in retinal artery obstruction, 163
    visual field defects in, 163
    workup following, 349

Amblyopia(s)
    ethyl alcohol, 224-226
    hysterical, *365*
        in children, 69
    nutritional, 224

☐ Page numbers in italics indicate illustrations.

Amblyopia(s)—cont'd
    quinine, 232-233
    tobacco, 220-223
    tobacco-nutritional, centrocecal scotoma of, 136
    toxic, 219-238
        with bilateral central scotomas, 219-221
        with peripheral field depression or contraction, 231-238

Amsler grid, 58, *59*
    in demonstration of metamorphopsia, 163

Aneurysm(s)
    of anterior cerebral artery, visual field defects in, 303
    of anterior communicating artery, visual field defects in, 303
    of internal carotid artery
        binasal hemianopsia due to, *facing 280*
        right, binasal hemianopsia from, 120
        visual field defects in, *306, 307*
    of ophthalmic artery, visual field defects in, 267
    of optic tracts, 329
    visual field defects due to, 90, 93

Angiography
    cerebral, cortical blindness from, 122-123
    fluorescein, in study of effects of increased intraocular pressure on vascular bed of eye, 215

Angiomatosis retinae, visual field defects in, 175-176

Angioscotoma(s), 136, 141, 144
    in narrow-angle glaucoma, 181
    in retinal arterial spasm, 163

Angioscotometry, 59

Angiospasm in internal capsule, 335

Angiospastic retinopathy, central, visual field defects in, 163-165

Animals, split-brain, behavior patterns in, 360-361

Visual field(s)—cont'd
  defects of—cont'd
    clues indicating presence of, 5
    detection of, tangent screen in, 24-30; *see also* Tangent screen(s)
    from emboli in cerebral and ocular circulation, 91-92
    functional, 363-372; *see also* Functional visual field defects
    in glaucoma, 179-218; *see also* Glaucoma
    homonymous, from damage to geniculate body laminae, 79
    hysterical, 364-372; *see also* Functional visual field defects
    interpretation of, 105
    from intracerebral hemorrhage, 91
    peripheral, from ethambutol, 231
    produced by chiasmal lesions, 277-290
      interpretation of, 290-310
    for red in tobacco amblyopia, 223
    in retinal diseases, 159-178
    scotomas as, 132-144; *see also* Scotoma(s)
    sector of juxtapapillary choroiditis, 151
    from subdural hematoma, 90
    from vascular lesions, 90-92
  definition of, 1
  depression of, 109-132; *see also* Depression, of visual field
  effect of opacities of media on, 145-150
  examination of, 5-103
    with arc perimeter, chart for recording, *31*
    multiple pattern method of, 59-64
    physiologic factors in, 98-100
    therapeutic, for hysterical amblyopia in children, 69
    as threshold measurement, 7
  fixation shifts in, macular sparing in, 124-125
  in glaucoma pathogenesis of, 214-218
  "missing half", 364
  normal, 93-103, *94*
    size of, factors influencing, 101-102
  projection of, in calcarine fissure, *facing 80*
  recording of, charts for, 30-34; *see also* Chart(s) for recording visual fields
  remnant of, central, in late-stage glaucoma, 203-204
  size of, effect of pupillary size on, 147, *148*

Visual field(s)—cont'd
  stimulation of; *see* Stimulation of visual fields
  from tangent screen examination, chart for recording, *31*
  tubular
    in functional loss, 366-368
    in hysterical amblyopia in children, 69
Visual hallucinations
  from carbon monoxide poisoning, 235
  in lesions of occipital cortex, 353, 357
  in parietooccipital meningioma, 347
Visual pathway
  afferent, relationship of, to cortex, 80
  anatomy of, *facing 80*, 71-83
  postchiasmal, 311-361; *see also* Optic tract
    anatomic divisions of, 311, 328-360
    lateral geniculate body in, 311, 332-333; *see also* Geniculate body, lateral
    lesions of, localization of, 312-314
    occipital striate cortex in, 311, 347-360
    optic radiations in, 311, 333-347; *see also* Optic radiation
    optic tracts in, 311, 328-332
  vascular lesions of, visual field defects from, 90-92
  vascular supply of, 85-92
Visual phenomena associated with lesions of cortex, 353, 357-360
Visual-evoked response (VER), delayed, in retrobulbar neuritis with multiple sclerosis, 258, 260
Vitamin B$_{12}$
  for ethyl alcohol amblyopia, 226
  for tobacco amblyopia, 223
Vitreous, opacities of, effect of, on visual fields, 101, 145-150

X

Xanthopsia
  in digitalis toxicity, 230
  from streptomycin, 230

Z

Zinn-Haller, ring of, vascular interference in, nerve fiber bundle scotomas from, 139